Assessing Organizational Diversity with the Simpson Index

Assessing Organizational Diversity with the Simpson Index

By

Salomón Alcocer Guajardo

Cambridge
Scholars
Publishing

Assessing Organizational Diversity with the Simpson Index

Series: Assessing Diversity in Nonprofit, Private, and Public Organizations

By Salomón Alcocer Guajardo

This book first published 2023

Cambridge Scholars Publishing

Lady Stephenson Library, Newcastle upon Tyne, NE6 2PA, UK

British Library Cataloguing in Publication Data
A catalogue record for this book is available from the British Library

ISBN (10): 1-5275-9264-2
ISBN (13): 978-1-5275-9264-3

This book is dedicated posthumously to Dr. Edward Hugh Simpson (1922 – 2019) for creating the diversity index ($S = 1 - \sum p^2$) that is the focus of this book and for his invaluable contribution to the study of diversity.

CONTENTS

Exhibits ix

New York City (NYC) Departments xvi

Acknowledgements xix

Preface xx

Chapter 1 1
Introduction

Chapter 2 12
Simpson Diversity Index

Chapter 3 20
Measurement of Gender Diversity

Chapter 4 40
Measurement of Ethnic Diversity

Chapter 5 78
Measurement of Age Diversity

Chapter 6 105
Composite Index of Organizational Diversity

Chapter 7 129
Analysis of Diversity with Ordinary Least Squares (OLS) Regression

Chapter 8 167
Analysis of Diversity with Robust Regression

Chapter 9 188
Analysis of Diversity with Tobit Regression

Chapter 10 209
Analysis of Diversity with Quantile Regression

Chapter 11 229
Analysis of Diversity with Ridge Regression

Chapter 12 251
Comparison of Statistical Methods

Chapter 13 265
Path Analysis of Organizational Diversity

Chapter 14 306
Summary

References 311

Glossary 319

Index 327

EXHIBITS

Exhibit 2-1   Interpretation of Simpson index scores   14

Exhibit 2-2   Calculation of the Simpson gender diversity score for the New York City Department of Administration for Children Services (ACS) for fiscal year 2019   15

Exhibit 2-3   Interpretation of standardized Simpson index scores   16

Exhibit 2-4   Calculation of the unbiased Simpson gender diversity score for the New York City ACS for fiscal year 2019   17

Exhibit 3-1   Simpson (S_{GB}) biased gender diversity scores for NYC departments for fiscal year 2019   22

Exhibit 3-2   Descriptive statistics for biased Simpson (S_{GB}) gender diversity scores for NYC departments for fiscal year 2019   25

Exhibit 3-3   Unbiased Simpson (S_{GN}) gender diversity scores for NYC departments for fiscal year 2019   27

Exhibit 3-4   Descriptive statistics for the unbiased Simpson (S_{GN}) gender diversity scores for NYC departments for fiscal year 2019   30

Exhibit 3-5   Comparison of biased (S_{GB}) and unbiased (S_{GN}) Simpson gender diversity scores for NYC departments for fiscal year 2019   32

Exhibit 3-6   Paired z-test for equal means for biased (S_{GB}) and unbiased (S_{GN}) unstandardized Simpson gender diversity scores for NYC departments for fiscal year 2019   36

Exhibit 4-1   Calculation of the biased (S_{EB}) and unbiased   42
               (S_{EN}) Simpson ethnic diversity score for the New
               York City ACS for fiscal year 2019

Exhibit 4-2   Biased Simpson (S_{EB1}) ethnic diversity scores for   44
               NYC departments for fiscal year 2019

Exhibit 4-3   Descriptive statistics for biased Simpson (S_{EB})   50
               ethnic diversity scores for NYC departments for
               fiscal year 2019

Exhibit 4-4   Unbiased Simpson (S_{EN}) ethnic diversity scores   53
               for NYC departments for fiscal year 2019

Exhibit 4-5   Descriptive statistics for unbiased Simpson (S_N)   60
               ethnic diversity scores for NYC departments for
               fiscal year 2019

Exhibit 4-6   Comparison of biased (S_{EB}) and unbiased (S_{EN}) 63
               Simpson ethnicity diversity scores for NYC
               departments for fiscal year 2019

Exhibit 4-7   Paired z-test for equal means for biased (S_{EB}) and 71
               unbiased (S_{EN}) Simpson ethnic diversity scores
               for NYC departments for fiscal year 2019

Exhibit 4-8   Pearson correlation analysis of biased (S_{EB}) and   72
               unbiased (S_{EN}) Simpson ethnic diversity scores
               for NYC departments for fiscal year 2019

Exhibit 4-9   Factor analysis (FA) of biased (S_{EB}) and unbiased   73
               (S_{EN}) Simpson ethnic diversity scores for NYC
               departments for fiscal year 2019

Exhibit 5-1   Calculation of the biased (S_{AB}) and unbiased   80
               (S_{AN}) Simpson age diversity score for the New
               York City ACS and EEPC for fiscal year 2019

Exhibit 5-2   Age distribution for each NYC department for   83
               fiscal year 2019

Exhibit 5-3   Biased (S_{AB}) and unbiased (S_{AN}) Simpson age   90
               diversity scores for NYC departments for fiscal
               year 2019

Exhibit 5-4   Descriptive statistics for biased Simpson (S_{AB})   95
               age diversity scores for NYC departments for
               fiscal year 2019

Exhibit 5-5   Descriptive statistics for unbiased Simpson (S_{AN})   96
               age diversity scores for NYC departments for
               fiscal year 2019

Exhibit 5-6   Comparison of biased (S_{AB}) and unbiased (S_{AN})   99
               Simpson age diversity scores for NYC
               departments for fiscal year 2019

Exhibit 5-7   Paired z-test for equal means for biased (S_{AB}) and   101
               unbiased (S_{AN}) Simpson age diversity scores for
               NYC departments for fiscal year 2019

Exhibit 6-1   Calculation of composite organizational diversity   108
               (OD) scores for ACS for fiscal year 2019

Exhibit 6-2   OD scores based on unstandardized biased   110
               Simpson (S_B) diversity coefficients for NYC
               departments for fiscal year 2019

Exhibit 6-3   OD scores based on unstandardized unbiased   113
               Simpson (S_N) diversity coefficients for NYC
               departments for fiscal year 2019

Exhibit 6-4   Descriptive statistics for biased and unbiased   117
               Simpson OD scores for NYC departments for
               fiscal year 2019

Exhibit 6-5   Comparison of OD scores for NYC departments   120
               for fiscal year 2019

Exhibit 6-6   Paired z-test for equal means for biased and   123
               unbiased unstandardized Simpson OD scores for
               NYC departments for fiscal year 2019

Exhibit 6-7   Pearson correlation analysis of biased and   125
               unbiased OD scores for NYC departments for
               fiscal year 2019

Exhibit 6-8   Factor analysis (FA) of biased and unbiased   126
               Simpson OD scores for NYC departments for
               fiscal year 2019

Exhibit 7-1   Assumption of normality for OLS regression   132

Exhibit 7-2   Distribution of biased (S_{GB}) gender diversity   134
               scores by total employees

Exhibit 7-3   Scatterplot of biased (S_{GB}) gender diversity   137
               scores by total employees

Exhibit 7-4   Pearson correlation matrix for independent   139
               variables

Exhibit 7-5   Theoretical model for age, ethnic, and gender   149
               diversity for NYC departments

Exhibit 7-6   OLS regression analysis for age, ethnic, gender   157
               and organizational diversity for NYC
               departments for fiscal year 2019

Exhibit 8-1   Robust regression process   168

Exhibit 8-2   Robust regression analysis for age, ethnic,   174
               gender, and organizational diversity for NYC
               departments for fiscal year 2019

Exhibit 8-3   Comparison of OLS and robust regression   178
               findings for biased (S_B) scores for age, ethnic,
               gender, and organizational diversity for NYC
               departments for fiscal year 2019

Exhibit 8-4   Comparison of OLS and robust regression   182
               findings for unbiased (S_N) scores for age, ethnic,
               gender, and organizational diversity for NYC
               departments for fiscal year 2019

Exhibit 9-1   Tobit regression analysis for age, ethnic, gender,   195
               and organizational diversity for NYC
               departments for fiscal year 2019

Exhibit 9-2   Comparison of OLS and Tobit regression   200
               findings for biased (S_B) scores for age, ethnic,
               gender, and organizational diversity for NYC
               departments for fiscal year 2019

Exhibit 9-3   Comparison of OLS and Tobit regression   204
               findings for unbiased (S_N) scores for age, ethnic,
               gender, and organizational diversity for NYC
               departments for fiscal year 2019

Exhibit 10-1   Quantile regression analysis for age, ethnic,   215
               gender, and organizational diversity for NYC
               departments for fiscal year 2019

Exhibit 10-2   Comparison of OLS and quantile regression   219
               findings for biased (S_B) scores for age, ethnic,
               gender, and organizational diversity for NYC
               departments for fiscal year 2019

Exhibit 10-3   Comparison of OLS and quantile regression   223
               findings for unbiased (S_N) scores for age, ethnic,
               gender, and organizational diversity for NYC
               departments for fiscal year 2019

Exhibit 11-1   Ridge regression process   231

Exhibit 11-2   Ridge regression analysis for age, ethnic, gender,   237
               and organizational diversity for NYC
               departments for fiscal year 2019

Exhibit 11-3   Comparison of OLS and ridge regression findings   241
               for biased (S_B) scores for age, ethnic, gender, and
               organizational diversity for NYC departments for
               fiscal year 2019

Exhibit 11-4   Comparison of OLS and ridge regression findings   246
                for unbiased (S_N) scores for age, ethnic, gender,
                and organizational diversity for NYC
                departments for fiscal year 2019

Exhibit 12-1   Comparative analysis of findings for age   253
                diversity for NYC departments for fiscal year
                2019

Exhibit 12-2   Comparative analysis of findings for ethnicity   257
                diversity for NYC departments for fiscal year
                2019

Exhibit 12-3   Comparative analysis of findings for gender   260
                diversity for NYC departments for fiscal year
                2019

Exhibit 13-1   Talent acquisition and organizational diversity   267

Exhibit 13-2   Theoretical causal model for age, ethnic, and   270
                gender diversity for NYC departments

Exhibit 13-3   Pearson correlation matrix for independent   275
                variables and diversity scores

Exhibit 13-4   OLS regression findings for age and gender   277
                diversity for NYC departments for fiscal year
                2019

Exhibit 13-5   Robust regression findings for age and gender   280
                diversity for NYC departments for fiscal year
                2019

Exhibit 13-6   Hypothesized causal model for age diversity for   282
                NYC departments

Exhibit 13-7   Hypothesized causal model for gender diversity   283
                for NYC departments

Exhibit 13-8   OLS regression analysis for age diversity with   290
               mediating variables for NYC departments for
               fiscal year 2019

Exhibit 13-9   OLS regression causal model for age diversity for   293
               NYC departments

Exhibit 13-   Robust regression analysis for age diversity with   294
10   mediating variables for NYC departments for
               fiscal year 2019

Exhibit 13-   Robust regression causal model for age diversity   295
11   for NYC departments

Exhibit 13-   OLS regression analysis for gender diversity with   297
12   mediating variables for NYC departments for
               fiscal year 2019

Exhibit 13-   OLS regression causal model for gender diversity   299
13   for NYC departments

Exhibit 13-4   Robust regression analysis for gender diversity   300
               with mediating variables for NYC departments
               for fiscal year 2019

Exhibit 13-   Robust regression causal model for gender   302
15   diversity for NYC departments

NYC DEPARTMENTS

NYC Department	Acronym
Administration for Children's Services	ACS
Board of Corrections	BOC
Board of Election	BOE
Borough President-Bronx	BP-BX
Borough President-Brooklyn	BP-BK
Borough President-Manhattan	BP-MAN
Borough President-Queens	BP-QNS
Borough President-Staten Island	BP-SI
Business Integrity Commission	BIC
Campaign Finance Board	CFB
City Commission on Human Rights	CCHR
Civilian Complaint Review Board	CCRB
Conflicts of Interest Board	COIB
Department for the Aging	DFTA
Department of Buildings	DOB
Department of City Planning	DCP
Department of Citywide Administrative Services	DCAS
Department of Consumer Affairs	DCA
Department of Correction	DOC
Department of Cultural Affairs	DCLA
Department of Design and Construction	DDC
Department of Education	DOE
Department of Environment Protection	DEP
Department of Finance	DOF
Department of Health/Mental Hygiene	DOHMH

Department of Homeless Services	DHS
Department of Info Tech and Telecomm	DOITT
Department of Investigation	DOI
Department of Parks and Recreation	PARKS
Department of Probation	DOP
Department of Records and Information Service	DORIS
Department of Sanitation	DSNY
Department of Small Business Services	SBS
Department of Transportation	DOT
Department of Youth and Community Development	DYCD
District Attorney - Bronx County	DA-BX
District Attorney - Kings County	DA-BK
District Attorney - Manhattan	DA-MAN
District Attorney - Queens County	DA-QNS
District Attorney - Richmond County	DA-SI
District Attorney – Special Narcotics	DA-NARC
Equal Employment Practices Commission	EEPC
Financial Information Services Agency	FISA
Fire Department	FDNY
Housing Preservation and Development	HPD
Human Resources Administration / Social Services	HRA
Independent Budget Office	IBO
Landmarks Preservation Committee	LPC
Law Department	LAW
MAYORALTY	MAYORALTY
Municipal Water Finance Authority	MWFA
New York City Council	COUNCIL
New York City Fire Pension Fund	FDNYPF
New York City Police Pension Fund	NYCPPF
New York City Tax Commission	NYCTAX

NYC Civil Service Commission   NYCCSC
NYC Employees Retirement System   NYCERS
NYC Health + Hospitals   NYCHH
NYC Housing Authority   NYCHA
Office of Administrative Trials and Hearings   OATH
Office of Collective Bargaining   OCB
Office of Emergency Management   NYCEM (OEM)
Office of Payroll Administration   OPA
Office of the Actuary   ACTUARY
Office of the City Clerk   CLERK
Office of the Comptroller   COMPTROLLER
Office of the Public Advocate (PA)   PA
Offices of the Public Administrators   PUBADMIN
Police Department   NYPD
School Construction Authority   SCA
Taxi and Limousine Commission   TLC
Teachers Retirement System   TRS

ACKNOWLEDGEMENTS

I wish to thank the Sophie Edminson, Amanda Millar, Adam Rummens, and the production staff at Cambridge Scholars Publishing for their assistance with making this book a reality. I also wish to thank Steve Santiago for his immense and unwavering encouragement and support. This book would not be possible without them.

PREFACE

The use of diversity indices to study demographic, occupational, and social heterogeneity in nonprofit, private, and public organizations has increased enormously over the past 20 years or so. Many diversity-centered studies utilize indices originally designed to measure biodiversity to assess age, ethnic, gender, and other types of heterogeneity in organizational and workforce settings. Concomitant with the adaption of ecological-based diversity indices such as Simpson's diversity index, the use of diversity indices developed for communications and other fields such as Shannon's H index has become more prevalent. While the adaptation of diversity indices designed to measure heterogeneity in communications, ecology, and other fields to organizational settings helps to assess and understand demographic or social diversity, the application of diversity indices to measure and analyze heterogeneity in organization settings has been given little empirical attention.

Because little empirical research has been devoted to examining the adaptation and application of diversity indices to measure and analyze demographic or social diversity in organizations, this book and its companion books address fundamental analytical and measurement issues and questions that arise when diversity indices are applied to demographic and employment data to obtain measures of heterogeneity. The issues and questions addressed in this book series include the following:

- How is measurement bias addressed by a particular diversity index?
- How is the number of categories used for a demographic or social characteristic taken into account by a particular diversity index?
- What are the statistical properties of a distribution of scores of a particular diversity index when it is applied to demographic and employment data?
- What is the appropriate statistical method that should be used based on the distribution of scores obtained by a particular diversity index?
- What is the maximum value of diversity that is obtainable by a particular diversity index?

Although the issues and questions addressed in this book series are fundamental to carrying out empirical research, they are often ignored or taken for granted by practitioners and researchers alike.

This book series consists of 9 books. They are the following:

- *Assessing Organizational Diversity with the Simpson Index* applies the Simpson diversity index to demographic and employment data reported by New York City (NYC) departments in fiscal year 2019. This book focuses on the application and analysis of Simpson diversity formulas for calculating biased and unbiased measures of demographic heterogeneity.
- *Assessing Organizational Diversity with the Shannon Index* applies the Shannon diversity index to the same demographic and employment data used in the first book. This book focuses exclusively on the application and analysis of Shannon diversity formulas for calculating biased and unbiased measures of demographic heterogeneity.
- *Assessing Organizational Diversity with the Heip Index* applies the Hill, Heip, Hurlbert, and Sheldon diversity indices of evenness to the data used in the first and second books. Practically speaking, the Hill, Heip, Hurlbert, and Sheldon indices are modifications of the Shannon index of diversity. From a statistical standpoint, the Shannon-based indices possess statistical properties that are superior to the Shannon index. Similar to the first and second books, this book focuses on the application and analysis of the indices in regard to measuring of demographic heterogeneity in organizations.
- *Assessing Organizational Diversity with the Smith and Wilson Indices* applies the Smith and Wilson (SW) indices to the same data used in the previous books. This book also uses other Simpson-based diversity indices to complement the SW indices such as the Ray and Singer index of concentration. The SW indices are modifications of the Simpson ($D = 1- \sum p^2$) diversity index and assess diversity. Similar to the previous books, this book applies the Simpson-based indices to the same demographic employment data to measure demographic heterogeneity in organizations.
- *Assessing Organizational Diversity with the McIntosh Index* applies the McIntosh evenness index to the same demographic and employment data used in the previous books. This book focuses exclusively on the analysis of diversity scores obtained by the McIntosh index. Because this index takes into account the number of groups used to categorize a demographic or social characteristic

of interest and the size of the workforce simultaneously, the diversity
scores contain less measurement bias and have a greater degree of
compatibility in comparison to the other diversity index covered in
other books.

- *Assessing Organizational Diversity with the Index of Qualitative
  Variation* (IQV) applies the Mueller and Schuessler IQV to the same
  demographic and employment data used in books 1 - 5. Because the
  IQV is not invariant to ordering sequences, this book focuses on the
  application and analysis of heterogeneity scores obtained from the
  different ordering sequences of the data. Similar to the McIntosh
  evenness index presented in the 5th book, the IQV takes into account
  jointly the size of the workforce and the number of groups used in
  the categorization of the demographic or social characteristic of
  interest.

- *Assessing the Validity of Diversity Indices* compares all of the indices
  used in each book jointly and uses factor analysis to determine
  whether they assess the same or different aspects of demographic or
  social diversity. Pearson pairwise correlation analyses also are
  performed to assess the statistical associations amongst the diversity
  indices. Statistical analyses for equality of means are performed as
  well.

- *Assessing Organizational Diversity with Quantile Regression*
  applies quantile regression analysis to several of the diversity indices
  presented in the book series. This book performs quantile regression
  analyses at the 25th, 50th, 75th, and 90th percentiles for age, ethnic,
  and gender diversity.

- *Assessing Organizational Diversity with Structural Equation
  Modeling* (SEM) focuses exclusively on causal modeling. This book
  focuses on the development and analysis of a structural equation
  model for several diversity index discussed in the series. In so doing,
  the analyses treat age, ethic, and gender diversity as an intervening
  or mediation variables of organizational performance.

For purposes of continuity and compatibility, each diversity index is
subjected to the same statistical analyses. Special interest is placed on the
IQV, McIntosh evenness, Shannon, Simpson, and SW indices in this book
series because they have been used in previous research on demographic or
social diversity in nonprofit, private, or public organizations.

This book series is written for practitioners and researchers in human
resources and other fields that are interested in measuring and analyzing

demographic, occupational, or social heterogeneity in organizations. The purpose of the book series is to addresses measurement and analytical issues that practitioners and researchers alike are likely to face when they apply a particular diversity index to demographic and employment data provided by a nonprofit, private, or public organization. As such, this book series should serve as a reference for selecting the diversity index that is best suited for measuring and analyzing heterogeneity in an organizational setting. This book series also should serve as a reference for selecting the statistical method that is best suited for analyzing the distribution of scores obtained by the diversity index of choice.

CHAPTER 1

INTRODUCTION

Since the early 1970s, diversity (or *integration*) indices have been used to assess the level of demographic or social heterogeneity in nonprofit, private, or public organizations (e.g., Akram, Abrar ul Haq, Natarajan, and Chellakan, 2020; Boehm, Kunze, and Bruch, 2014; Choi, 2010; Gazley, Chang, and Bingham, 2010; Grabosky and Rosenbloom, 1975; Guajardo, 2014; Moon and Christensen, 2020; Nachmias and Rosenbloom, 1973). The application of diversity indices to aggregate demographic employment data has centered on measuring age, ethnic, or gender heterogeneity. In the majority of the previous studies, workforce diversity has served as a dependent variable. More recent studies have treated workforce diversity as an independent variable which influences organizational performance (e.g., Gazley, Chang, and Bingham, 2010; Khan, Khan, and Senturk, 2019; Lee-Kuen, Sok-Gee, and Zainudin, 2017; Pitts, 2005). This book takes the position that workforce diversity such as age, ethnic, and gender heterogeneity is an *intervening variable* that influences organizational performance (e.g., Guajardo, 2014; Pitts, 2006).

Indices of diversity and variation

Several indices of diversity (or variation) have been used to measure demographic or social diversity (or heterogeneity) in organizations. They include the following:

- Index of qualitative variation (IQV) or measure of variation (MV; e.g., Grabosky and Rosenbloom, 1975; Kellough, 1990; Kim, 1993; Mueller, Schuessler, and Costner, 1970; Nachmias and Rosenbloom, 1973; Wilcox, 1967);
- McIntosh evenness index (e.g., Guajardo, 2013 and 2015);
- Shannon (Teachman) index (e.g., Choi, 2010; Choi and Rainey, 2010); and,
- Simpson (Blau or Lieberson) diversity index (e.g., Guajardo, 2014; Pitts, 2005; Starks, 2009).

Each index has a theoretical distribution of scores that ranges from 0 to 1. With the exception of the Shannon index, a score of 0 indicates the absence of diversity (or heterogeneity) and a score of 1 indicates absolute diversity. This book focuses solely on the Simpson diversity index.

Briefly, McIntosh (1967) created the diversity index of evenness to assess the level of similarity amongst a group of species with different characteristics living in the same community. The McIntosh evenness index is represented as follows: $D_E = \dfrac{N - \sqrt{\sum n^2}}{N - \frac{N}{\sqrt{s}}}$, where N represents the total number of individuals, n represents the number of individuals within a particular group, and S represents the number of distinct groups in a community or organization.

D_E has a distribution of scores that ranges from 0 to 1. According to McIntosh (1967), a score of 0 indicates an absence of diversity and a score of 1 indicates absolute diversity. *Assessing Organizational Diversity with the McIntosh Index* focuses exclusively on the application of the index to public organizations.

Mueller and Schuessler developed the IQV to assess demographic heterogeneity (or variation) in a community or social setting (Mueller, Schuessler, and Costner, 1970; Wilcox, 1967). The IQV obtains a measurement of heterogeneity by dividing the total observed difference by the maximum possible differences (Mueller, Schuessler, and Costner, 1970; Wilcox, 1967). Symbolically, the IQV index takes the following form:

$$\text{IQV} = \frac{\text{Total observed differences}}{\text{Maximum Possible Differences}} = \frac{\sum f_i f_j}{\frac{n(n-1)}{2} \times \left(\frac{F}{n}\right)^2}$$

The terms of the formula are defined as follows:

f represents the frequency (or number) of individuals;
n represents the number of social characteristics (i.e., groups); and,
F represents the total number of individuals.

The index has a distribution of scores ranging from 0 to 1. Similar to the Simpson and McIntosh indices, a score of 0 indicates a lack of heterogeneity (i.e., homogeneity) and a score of 1 indicates absolute heterogeneity (Mueller, Schuessler, and Costner, 1970). *Assessing Organizational Diversity with the Index of Qualitative Variation* focuses exclusively on the application of the index to public organizations.

Shannon (1948) created the H index of entropy (or uncertainty) for the communications field to obtain the *probability* of successive messages being independent of each other. Since its creation, the H index has been adapted to assess demographic or social diversity in organizations. The index is presented as follows: H = -$\sum[p_k * \ln(p_k)$], where p is the proportion of individuals in the kth category. Unlike the IQV, McIntosh, and Simpson indices, the Shannon index has a distribution of scores ranging from 0 to $\ln(n)$, where ln represents the natural logarithm of a number and n represents the number of demographic or social categories (e.g., Harrison and Klein, 2007). For instance, the maximum value of H is 1.609 ($H_M = \ln(5) = 1.609$) when ethnicity is categorized into 5 groups. The following formula is used to standardize H index scores: $H_s = \frac{-\sum[pk*\ln(pk)]}{\ln(n)}$. When the standardized form of the H index is used, the distribution of the standardized scores ranges from 0 to 1. The Shannon index is the focus of *Assessing Organizational Diversity with the Shannon Index*.

The Simpson diversity index is used the most frequently to assess demographic or social heterogeneity in organizations. Simpson (1949) created the diversity index to obtain the probability that two individuals chosen at random from the same community would share the same (or different) characteristics. Theoretically, Simpson's index has a distribution of scores ranging from 0 to 1. According to Simpson (1949), a score of 0 indicates the absence of diversity and a score of 1 indicates absolute diversity. In actuality, the maximum value for a particular demographic or social characteristic is determined by the following formula: $S_M = \frac{k-1}{k}$, where k is the number of categories or groups formed for the demographic or social characteristic of interest. For instance, the maximum diversity score is 0.80 ($S_M = \frac{k-1}{k} = \frac{4-1}{5} = 0.80$) when ethnicity is categorized into 5 groups. Simpson's index is represented frequently by the following formula: $S_A = 1-\sum p^2$, where p represents the percent of individuals in a particular category or group. The index also is represented as follows: $S_B = 1 - \frac{\sum n(n-1)}{N(N-1)}$, where n is the number of individuals in a category or group and N is the total number of individuals. Standardized Simpson scores are obtained by applying the following formula: $S_S = \frac{S}{\frac{(k-1)}{k}}$, where S equals S_A or S_B and k represents the number of categories or groups.

Statistical methods

Numerous statistical methods have been used to analyze the relationships amongst a set of organizational factors and Simpson, Shannon, or other scores. The statistical methods used in previous *cross-sectional studies* on demographic or social diversity in organizations include the following:

- Ordinary least squares (OLS) regression (e.g., Choi, 2010; Gazley, Chang, and Bingham, 2010; Kellough, 1990; Kim, 1993; Pitts, 2005);
- Tobit regression (e.g., Guajardo, 2016; Poulos and Doerner, 1996); and,
- Quantile regression (e.g., Guajardo, 2016).

These and other statistical methods are used in this book to illustrate how the distribution of Simpson diversity scores impact the findings when statistical assumptions are violated.

This book takes the position that the selection and use of a particular statistical method should be based on whether the distribution of diversity scores obtained by a particular index satisfies the underlying assumptions of the statistical method that is selected. At times, the selection of a particular method is based on academic tradition. For instance, the majority of the studies that analyze demographic diversity in public organizations use OLS regression to perform the multivariate analyses although the diversity indices presented above obtain scores with restricted quantitative continuous distributions that range from 0 to at least $\ln(n)$. By contrast, Tobit and quantile regression methods are used primarily in economics because these methods are better suited for variables with restricted distributions. Methodologically and statistically, Tobit, quantile, and other similar regression methods are better suited to analyze a distribution of diversity scores with a restricted quantitative continuous range of values. The selection and use of a particular statistical method to analyze the relationship amongst a set of organizational factors and demographic (or social) diversity is important because financial, human resources, and policy decisions are often based on the findings of a study.

Analyzing and measuring diversity in organizations

Despite the voluminous number of articles and books that have addressed organizational or workforce diversity, few studies have focused on the application of diversity indices that are used to measure and analyze demographic or social heterogeneity in organizations (e.g., Biemann and Kearney, 2010; Guajardo, 2013 and 2015; Harrison and Klein, 2007; McDonald and Dimmick, 2003). Fewer studies have focused on assessing the reliability and validity of the heterogeneity scores obtained from applying diversity indices to employment data reported by nonprofit, private, or public organizations (e.g., Guajardo, 1996). As a consequence of the lack of extensive research on the adaptation and utilization of diversity indices designed to measure heterogeneity in communications (e.g., Shannon H index) or ecology (e.g., Simpson diversity index), the properties of the diversity scores obtained by a particular index in regard to normality, skewness, and other distribution characteristics are often taken for granted or glossed over at best.

Because there is a paucity of research on the application of diversity indices to employment data, this book addresses methodological and statistical issues and questions that should be addressed when assessing demographic or social diversity in the workplace. The issues and questions include the following:

- Does the use of a particular diversity index produce a distribution of scores that satisfy the underlying assumptions of the statistical method of choice?
- How does the categorization of the demographic or social characteristics of interest affect the reliability and validity of the diversity scores obtained by the chosen index?
- What are the distribution properties of the diversity scores in regard to the range of scores, to the skewness of the distribution, to the peakedness of the distribution, and to other related issues?
- What is the level of compatibility of the diversity scores amongst the organizations in the study in regard to measuring heterogeneity as accurately as possible when there are categories with missing data?

Addressing these and other measurement issues and questions prior to undertaking a statistical analysis of demographic or social diversity in organizations is critical for obtaining statistical findings that are unbiased, reliable, and stable.

Application of the Simpson Index

This book applies the Simpson index to employment and workforce data reported by NYC departments for fiscal year 2019. NYC departments are selected for this book series to highlight the measurements issues that are likely to be confronted in other employment settings regardless of whether the organizations are nonprofit, private, or public institutions. The Simpson diversity index is presented in Chapter 2. The traditional Simpson index formula ($S = 1 - \sum p^2$) is applied to qualitatively categorized demographic employment data to illustrate how diversity scores are calculated for data presented as frequencies or percentages. In addition, the formula for obtaining unbiased Simpson diversity scores is applied to the same data.

In Chapter 3, the index is applied to demographic data to obtain diversity scores for gender. The application of the Simpson index entails the use of the traditional formula ($S = 1 - \sum p^2$) and the use of the formula for calculating unbiased diversity scores. Standardized scores are obtained for each set of diversity scores as well. In addition to assessing the range of the distribution of the scores and to testing for normality and skewness, the distributions of scores are compared statistically for equality.

Chapter 4 applies the Simpson index to demographic data to obtain diversity scores for ethnicity. Because NYC departments categorize ethnicity in two different ways, four sets of unstandardized Simpson diversity scores are obtained. Biased and unbiased diversity scores are calculated for the binary categorization of ethnicity: White or minority. The second set of biased and unbiased diversity scores are calculated for the 5-group categorization of ethnicity: Asian, Black, Hispanic, Some other race (SOR), and White. Standardized coefficients are calculated for each set of unstandardized scores. The two different ways of categorizing ethnicity allow for assessing changes in the distributions of the scores. They also permit for testing the sets of diversity scores for equality.

In Chapter 5, diversity scores for age are obtained by applying the Simpson index to the demographic data. The issues of measurement compatibility and reliability arise due to calculating diversity scores for NYC departments with workforces where the range of ages is confined to a small number of age group categories. The issue of measurement compatibility and reliability is compounded when the formula for obtaining unbiased Simpson diversity scores is applied to the data. Standardized scores are calculated for each set of diversity coefficients. Statistical analyses for equality are performed in addition to testing for normality and skewness. Because the

Simpson index fails to take into account the number of groups in the calculation of the diversity scores, the level of age diversity is inflated for small and midsize NYC departments.

A composite score of organizational diversity is developed in Chapter 6. This is done for illustrative purposes. Weighted and unweighted composite scores of organizational diversity are presented. The distributions of the unweighted scores are tested for equality, normality, and skewness.

Analysis of demographic diversity

OLS regression is presented in Chapter 7. In so doing, statistical models for age, ethnic, and gender diversity are developed and discussed. The assumptions underlying OLS regression are presented. A Pearson pairwise correlation analysis is undertaken as a preliminary step to assess for collinearity amongst the predictors. Regression diagnostics are performed to assess for multicollinearity. The OLS regression findings are compared to the statistical findings of other regression methods in subsequent chapters.

Chapter 8 focuses on the application of robust regression. The rationale for undertaking the robust regression analysis is to adjust for atypical diversity scores. The statistical models analyzed with OLS regression are tested with robust regression. Lastly, the statistical findings obtained with OLS and robust regression are compared and discussed.

Tobit regression is presented in Chapter 9. As stated above, the maximum value of a Simpson diversity score is determined by the number of categories created for the demographic or social characteristic of interest. As such, the maximum value of a particular distribution of Simpson scores does not reach 1. For each Tobit regression, the lower (or left) limit is set at 0 and the upper (or right) limit is set by $\frac{k-1}{k}$, where k is the number of groups. (In subsequent chapters, the following notation is used $\frac{n-1}{n}$ for convenience.) Tobit regression is used to assess the statistical models tested with OLS regression in Chapter 7. After discussing the Tobit findings, they are compared with the statistical findings obtained with OLS regression. Because the distributions of Simpson scores are restricted to a range between 0 and $\frac{n-1}{n}$, Tobit regression is the preferred statistical method to use.

In Chapter 10, the application of quantile regression is presented. The statistical analyses focus on the median although quantile regression may produce findings for multiple percentiles simultaneously. The rationale for presenting quantile regression is that satisfying the assumption of normality is not necessary. Secondly, unlike OLS regression which is influenced by atypical values, quantile regression is less prone to the influence of atypical values. For comparative purposes, the statistical findings obtained with OLS and quantile regression are discussed. *Assessing Organizational Diversity with Quantile Regression* presents a thorough application of quantile regression to different diversity scores obtained with the same demographic data.

Chapter 11 applies ridge regression to address the issue of collinearity amongst the predictors. In so doing, ridge regression is applied to the biased and unbiased Simpson diversity scores. After applying ridge regression to the data, the levels of collinearity obtained by the method are compared to those obtained by the OLS regression model in Chapter 7. Similar to previous chapters, the OLS and ridge regression findings are compared.

Chapter 12 compares the statistical findings for age, ethnic, and gender diversity that were obtained with OLS, robust, Tobit, quantile, and ridge regression. The comparison begins with discussing the findings for age diversity. Specifically, the statistical findings for the biased and unbiased diversity scores for age are compared for each statistical model. Similar comparisons are made for the findings for ethnic and gender diversity.

Path analysis is presented in Chapter 13. The chapter begins with discussing the role of employee turnover and hiring in regard to changes in the level of demographic or social diversity in organizations. A theoretical causal model illustrating the relationships amongst organizational factors and diversity in terms of age and ethnicity is provided. Testable causal models are developed based on a Pearson pairwise correlation analysis and on the statistical findings obtained by the regression analyses performed in previous chapters. Tobit regression is not used to perform the path analysis because the mediating predictors have quantitative continuous distributions that are unrestricted in terms of their values. *Assessing Organizational Diversity with Structural Equation Modeling* provides an in-depth presentation of path analysis and structural equation modeling (SEM). In *Assessing Organizational Diversity with Structural Equation Modeling*, different diversity indices are analyzed and modeled with the use of the same demographic and employment data that are utilized in each companion book.

Lastly, Chapter 14 summarizes the key points of the book. The summary focuses on measurement and analytical issues. Measurement strengths and weaknesses of the Simpson index are discussed in the context of applying the index to the demographic and employment data reported by NYC departments for fiscal year 2019. The summary of analytical issues centers on the use of statistical methods to analyze demographic or social diversity in organizations.

Statistical jargon is minimal throughout the book. Key words appear in *italics* and are defined in a glossary at the end of each chapter. Examples of the application of the Simpson index are provided were appropriate.

Key Words

Cross-sectional studies refer to research projects that collect and analyze data on subjects for one specific time period. By contrast, longitudinal studies collect and analyze data on subjects for multiple time periods such as days, weeks, months, and years.

Integration refers to the hiring of minorities and women into an organization's workforce.

Intervening variable refers to a measure that is influenced by a set of factors where that measure then influences a particular outcome.

Probability refers to the chance or likelihood that an event will occur.

References

Akram, Farheen, Abrar ul Haq, Muhammad, Natarajan, Vinodh K., and Chellakan, R. Stephen. 2020. "Board heterogeneity and corporate performance: An insight beyond agency issues". *Cogent Business and Management*, Vol. 7: 1809299.

Biemann, Torsten. and Kearney. Eric. 2010. "Size does matter: How varying group sizes in a sample affect the most common measures of group diversity". *Organizational Research Methods*, Vol. 13: 582 – 599.

Boehm, Stephan A., Kunze, Florian, and Bruch, Heike. 2014. "Spotlight on age-diversity climate: The impact of age-inclusive HR practices on firm-level outcomes". *Personnel Psychology*, Vol. 67: 667 – 704.

Choi, Sungjoo, and Rainey, Hal G. 2010. "Managing diversity in US federal agencies: Effects of diversity and diversity management on employee perceptions of organizational performance". *Public Administration Review*, Vol. 70: 109 – 121.

Choi, Sungjoo. 2010. "Diversity in the US federal government: Antecedents and correlates of diversity in federal agencies". *Review of Public Personnel Administration*, Vol. 30: 301 – 321

Gazley, Beth, Chang, Won Kyung, and Bingham, Lisa Blomgren. 2010. "Board diversity, stakeholder representation, and collaborative performance in community mediation centers". *Public Administration Review*, Vol. 70: 610 – 620.

Grabosky, Peter N., and Rosenbloom, David H. 1975. "Racial and ethnic integration in the federal service". *Social Science Quarterly*, Vol. 56: 71 – 84.

Guajardo, Salomón A. 1996. "Representative bureaucracy: An estimation of the reliability and validity of the Nachmias-Rosenbloom MV Index". *Public Administration Review*, Vol. 56: 467-477.

Guajardo, Salomón A. 2013. "Workforce diversity: An application of diversity and integration indices to small agencies". *Public Personnel Management*, Vol. 41: 27 – 40.

Guajardo, Salomón A. 2014. "Workforce diversity: Assessing the impact of minority integration on intra-group interaction". *International Journal of Police Science and Management*, Vol. 16: 205 – 220.

Guajardo, Salomón A. 2015. "Measuring diversity in police agencies". *Journal of Ethnicity in Criminal Justice,* Vol. 13: 1 – 15.

Guajardo, Salomón A. 2016. "Ethnic diversity in policing: An application of quantile regression to the New York City Police Department". *Journal of Ethnicity in Criminal Justice*, Vol. 14: 254 – 289.

Harrison, David A., and Klein, Katherine J. 2007. "What's the difference? Diversity constructs as separation, variety, or disparity in organizations". *Academy of Management Review*, Vol. 32: 1199 – 1228.

Kellough, J. Edward, and Elliott, Euel. 1992. "Demographic and organizational influences on racial/ethnic and gender integration in federal agencies". *Social Science Quarterly,* Vol. 73: 1 – 11.

Kellough, J. Edward. 1990. "Integration in the public workplace: Determinants of minority and female employment in federal agencies". *Public Administration Review*, Vol. 50: 557 – 566.

Khan, Imran, Khan, Ismail, and Senturk, Ismail. 2019. "Board diversity and quality of CSR disclosure: Evidence from Pakistan". *Corporate Governance: The International Journal of Business in Society*, Vol. 19: 1187 – 1203.

Kim, Pan Suk. 1993. "Racial integration in the American federal government: With special reference to Asian-Americans". *Review of Public Personnel Administration*, Vol. 13: 52 – 66.

Lee-Kuen, Irean Yap, Sok-Gee, Chan, and Zainudin, Rozaimah. 2017. "Gender diversity and firms' financial performance in Malaysia". *Asian Academy of Management Journal of Accounting and Finance*, Vol. 13: 41 – 62.

McDonald, Daniel. G., and Dimmick, John. 2003. "The conceptualization and measurement of diversity". *Communication Research*, Vol. 30: 60 – 79.

McIntosh, Robert P. 1967. "An index of diversity and the relation of certain concepts to diversity." *Ecology*, Vol. 48: 392 – 404.

Moon, Kuk-Kyoung, and Christensen, Robert K. 2020. "Realizing the performance benefits of workforce diversity in the US federal government: The moderating role of diversity climate". *Public Personnel Management*, Vol. 49: 141 – 165.

Mueller, John H., Schuessler, Karl F., and Costner, Herbert L. 1970. *Statistical reasoning in sociology*. Second edition. New York, NY: Houghton Mufflin Company.

Nachmias, David, and Rosenbloom, David H. 1973. "Measuring Bureaucratic Representation and Integration". *Public Administration Review*, Vol. 33: 590 – 597.

Pitts, David W. 2005. "Diversity, representation, and performance: Evidence about race and ethnicity in public organizations". *Journal of Public Administration Research and Theory*, Vol 15: 615 – 631.

Pitts, David W. 2006. "Modeling the impact of diversity management". *Review of Public Personnel Administration*, Vol. 26: 245 – 268.

Poulos, Tammy Meredith, and Doerner, William G. 1996. "Women in law enforcement: The distribution of females in Florida policing agencies". *Women and Criminal Justice*, Vol. 8: 19 – 3.

Shannon, Claude Elwood. 1948. "A mathematical theory of communication". *The Bell System Technical Journal*, Vol. 27: 379 – 423.

Simpson, Edward Hugh. 1949. "Measurement of diversity". *Nature*, Vol. 163: 688.

Starks, Glenn. L. 2009. "Minority representation in senior positions in U.S. federal agencies: A paradox of underrepresentation". *Public Personnel Management*, Vol. 38: 79 – 90.

Wilcox, Allen R. (1967). *Indices of qualitative variation*. Oak Ridge, TN: Oak Ridge National Laboratory, U.S. Atomic Energy Commission.

CHAPTER 2

SIMPSON DIVERSITY INDEX

The Simpson (1949) diversity index is used frequently to measure the level of demographic heterogeneity (or variation) in nonprofit, public, and private organizations alike (e.g., Guajardo, 2014 and 2015; Chikoto, Ling, and Neely, 2016). Simpson's index also is used to assess the level of economic and revenue diversity amongst financial, nonprofit, and public organizations (e.g., Chikoto, Ling, and Neely, 2016; Hendrick, 2002; Jordan and Wagner, 2008). When Simpson's index is used in this manner, the index is referred to as the Hirschman-Herfindahl Index (HHI). In addition, the Simpson index is applied to measure group and social heterogeneity (e.g., Blau, 1977). When doing so, researchers refer to Simpson's index as the Blau's index of heterogeneity (e.g., Akram, Haq, Natarajan, and Chellakan, 2020; Oba and Fodio, 2013). The Simpson index is used to assess population diversity as well and is called the Lieberson index (e.g., Guajardo, 2013; Lieberson, 1969; Starks, 2009).

The popularity and extensive use of the Simpson index to measure *organizational diversity* is based on the following:

1. The efficient use of data to calculate a diversity coefficient;
2. The order of the data does not impact the value of the diversity coefficient; and,
3. The straightforward method of calculating a diversity coefficient;

However, as explained below, the Simpson index has a few drawbacks.

This chapter presents an overview of the Simpson diversity index. The calculation of a Simpson score (or coefficient) is presented using actual employment numbers and percentages. This chapter also presents how to standardize a Simpson coefficient to conduct an apples-to-apples comparison across different organizations. Guidelines for interpreting a Simpson coefficient are presented in this chapter as well. Finally, this chapter presents how to calculate an unbiased Simpson coefficient.

Defining diversity

In developing the diversity index, Simpson (1949) defined *diversity* as the probability "that two individuals chosen at random and independently from [a] population will be found to belong to the same group." The probability is obtained by applying the following formula: $1 - \sum p_i^2$, where p_i is the percent of individuals belonging to a particular group or having the same demographic characteristic such a gender or ethnicity.

Theoretically, a Simpson diversity coefficient may range from 0 to 1. However, the *empirical maximum value* (EMV or S_M) is determined by the following formula: EMV $= \frac{n-1}{n}$, where n represents the number of distinct demographic characteristics used to calculate a diversity coefficient. When gender is categorized as men and women, the EMV of the Simpson index is 0.50 (EMV $= \frac{2-1}{2} = 0.50$) because 2 social characteristics are being considered. As the number of demographic characteristics increases, the EMV approaches 1.0, but it does not reach the *theoretical maximum value* (TMA).

As will be discussed in Chapter 7, ordinary least squares (OLS) requires that the dependent variable have continuous quantitative values. The theoretical and empirical distributions of the Simpson index do not satisfy this requirement because the EMV is determined by the number of demographic characteristics used to calculate the diversity coefficients. As the example above shows, an EMV of 0.50 is possible when 2 demographic characteristics are used in the analysis. When ethnicity is categorized into 5 distinct groups, an EMV of 0.80 (EMV $= \frac{5-1}{5} = 0.80$) is possible. Strictly speaking, the Simpson index produces a *limited dependent variable* (LDV) where the values are restricted (or truncated) to a range from 0 to $\frac{n-1}{n}$.

Interpreting the Simpson index

As discussed above, the theoretical range of the Simpson coefficients is from 0 to 1, where 0 represents the absence of heterogeneity and 1 represents absolute heterogeneity. Exhibit 2-1 provides a general guide on how to interpret an actual Simpson coefficient (e.g., Guajardo, 2013 and 2015). As Exhibit 2-1 shows, the interpretation of an actual Simpson score differs from the theoretical value due to the number of demographic or social characteristics used to measure demographic or social diversity.

Exhibit 2-1 Interpretation of Simpson index scores
A. Theoretical Maximum Value

TMV	Interpretation
1.00	Absolute (Perfect) diversity (Heterogeneity)
0.81 − 0.99	A high degree of diversity
0.61 − 0.80	A moderately high degree of diversity
0.41 − 0.60	A moderate degree of diversity
0.01 − 0.40	A low degree of diversity
0.00	Absence of diversity (Homogeneous)

B. Empirical Maximum Values

EMV	Interpretation
0.66	Maximum level of actual diversity attained
0.55 - 0.65	High level of actual diversity attained
0.45 - 0.54	Moderately high level of actual diversity attained
0.35 - 0.44	Somewhat moderately high level of actual diversity attained
0.25 - 0.34	Moderate level of actual diversity attained
0.15 - 0.24	Somewhat low level of actual diversity attained
0.01 - 0.14	Low level of actual diversity attained
0.00	Absence of any actual diversity attained

n = 3

EMV	Interpretation
0.50	Maximum level of actual diversity attained
0.40 - 0.49	High level of actual diversity attained
0.30 - 0.39	Moderately high level of actual diversity attained
0.20 - 0.29	Moderate level of actual diversity attained
0.11 - 0.19	Somewhat low level of actual diversity attained
0.01 - 0.10	Low level of actual diversity attained
0.00	Absence of any actual diversity attained

n = 2

Applying the Simpson index to organizational data

A Simpson coefficient may be obtained by using the actual number (frequency) or percent of individuals in different groups. When percentages are used, the following Simpson index formula is used: $S = 1 - \sum p_i^2$, where p_i represents the percent of individuals in each group. If percentages are not readily available, the following formula is used when the actual number of individuals in different groups is provided: $S = 1 - \frac{\sum f^2}{F^2}$, where f represents the number of individuals in each distinct group and F represents the total number of individuals in the population.

Exhibit 2-2 illustrates how to calculate a Simpson coefficient when actual numbers and percentages are provided. As illustrated in Exhibit 2-2, the same Simpson score of 0.343 is obtained when actual numbers or percentages are used. In the example, ACS attained a low degree of gender diversity based on the TMV for fiscal year 2019 (see Exhibit 2-1). However, based on an EMV of 0.50, ACS attained a moderately high level of gender diversity.

Exhibit 2-2 Calculation of the Simpson gender diversity score for the New York City Department of Administration for Children Services (ACS) for fiscal year 2019

Gender	Frequency (f)	f_i^2	Gender	Percent (p)	p_i^2
Women	5,734	32,876,233	Women	78%	0.608
Men	1,617	2,615,401	Men	22%	0.048
Total ($\sum$)	7,351	35,491,634	Total ($\sum$)	100%	0.657

$$S_f = 1 - \frac{\sum f_i^2}{F^2} \qquad\qquad S_p = 1 - \sum p_i^2$$

$$S_f = 1 - \frac{35,491,634}{54,037,201} \qquad\qquad S_p = 1 - 0.657$$

$$S_f = 1 - 0.657$$

$$S_f = 0.343 \qquad\qquad S_p = 0.343$$

Standardized Simpson diversity coefficient

As discussed above, the EMV of the Simpson index is based on the number of demographic categories specified for a particular population. When gender is categorized as men and women, 2 categories are generated with an EMV of 0.50. If gender is categorized as men, women, and nonbinary (or other), then an EMV of 0.667 is obtained due to categorizing gender into 3 groups (see Exhibit 2-1). In case the number of categories for gender differ across different organizations, the standardization of the Simpson coefficients allows for an apple-to-apples comparison of diversity for gender or any other demographic characteristic of interest across the organizations under analysis (e.g., Biemann and Kearney, 2010).

The formula for standardizing a Simpson coefficient is as follows: $S_s = \frac{1 - \sum p^2}{\frac{(n-1)}{n}}$. In this formula, p_i represents the percent of individuals with a particular demographic characteristic of interest and n represents the number of categories specified for a particular demographic characteristic. When a Simpson coefficient is standardized with the formula above, the ratio "describes the actual level of diversity as a proportion of the maximum level possible with the specified number of [categories]" (Lieberson, 1969, 860). For instance, the standardized Simpson coefficient for ACS is 0.69 (S_{STD} = 0.343 ÷ 0.500 = 0.687) which indicates that the department attained a moderately high proportion of the maximum level of gender diversity that is attainable. Exhibit 2-3 provides guidance on how to interpret a standardized Simpson coefficient.

Exhibit 2-3 Interpretation of standardized Simpson index scores

S_S	Interpretation
1.00	Attained the maximum proportion of the EMV
0.90 - 0.99	Attained an extremely high proportion of the EMV
0.80 - 0.89	Attained a moderately high proportion of the EMV
0.70 - 0.79	Attained a somewhat moderately high proportion of the EMV
0.60 - 0.69	Attained a moderate proportion of the EMV
0.50 - 0.59	Attained a somewhat moderate proportion of the EMV
0.40 - 0.49	Attained a moderately low proportion of the EMV
0.30 - 0.39	Attained a somewhat low proportion of the EMV
0.20 - 0.29	Attained a low proportion of the EMV
0.10 - 0.19	Attained an extremely low proportion of the EMV
0.00 - 0.09	Absence of any actual proportion of the EMV attained

Measurement bias of the Simpson index

Although the Simpson index possesses *measurement efficiency* and *invariance* due to its use and ordering of data to obtain a diversity coefficient, the index produces biased scores when applied to small groups and organizations (e.g., Biemann and Kearney, 2010). Specifically, Biemann and Kearney (2010) note that the Simpson index fails to correct for differences in group size where the scores for groups with fewer members are lower in comparison to groups with larger populations. The *measurement bias* produced by the Simpson index is corrected by applying the following formula: $S_N = 1 - \sum \frac{n(n-1)}{N(N-1)}$. Exhibit 2-4 applies the S_N index to the number of men and women in ACS for fiscal year 2019. As shown in Exhibit 2-4, the diversity coefficients are the same for ACS when the biased and unbiased Simpson index formulas are used.

Exhibit 2-4 Calculation of the unbiased Simpson gender diversity score for the New York City ACS for fiscal year 2019

Gender	Frequency (f)	f_i^2	Gender	Number (n)	n_i $(n_i - 1)$	$\dfrac{n_i}{(n_i - 1)}$ $\dfrac{N}{(N-1)}$
Women	5,734	32,878,756	Women	5,734	32,873,022	0.608
Men	1,617	2,614,689	Men	1,617	2,613,072	0.048
Total ($\sum$)	7,351	35,493,445	Total ($\sum$)	7,351	35,486,094	0.657

$$S_B = 1 - \frac{\sum f_i^2}{F^2} \qquad\qquad S_N = 1 - \sum \frac{n_i(n_i - 1)}{N(N-1)}$$

$$S_B = 1 - \frac{35,493,445}{54,037,201}$$

$$S_B = 1 - 0.657 \qquad\qquad S_N = 1 - 0.657$$

$$S_B = 0.343 \qquad\qquad S_N = 0.343$$

Summary

This chapter presented an overview of the Simpson diversity index. In so doing, this chapter illustrated how diversity coefficients are obtained when demographic data are presented as numbers or percentages. In addition, this chapter illustrated how to calculate an EMV for a Simpson coefficient based on the number of categories used to classify a group of individuals based on a demographic or social characteristic of interest. The use of the EMV to obtain a standardized value of a diversity coefficient also was illustrated. Finally, guidelines on how to interpret Simpson diversity coefficients were provided. The next applies the Simpson diversity index to demographic and employment data collected by NYC for each of its agencies and departments for fiscal year 2019, which is the most recent data readily available for public use.

Key Terms

Diversity refers to the probability that individuals chosen randomly from a particular population will have the same demographic or social characteristics.

Empirical maximum value (EMV) refers to the actual highest diversity coefficient that is attainable by an index based on the number of distinct categories within a particular population.

Limited dependent variable (LDV) refers to the quantitative distribution of scores of a variable that is restricted to a particular range so that values are not numerically continuous.

Measurement efficiency refers to the number of mathematical operations that are needed to obtain a diversity coefficient. Indices that require fewer mathematical operations are more efficient in the use of the data in comparison to those that require numerous sets of calculations to obtain a diversity score.

Measurement invariance refers to the ability of an index to produce the same numerical value regardless of the order in which the data are arranged for analysis.

Organizational diversity refers to the extent to which an agency's or institution's workforce is composed of individuals with different demographic or social characteristics.

Theoretical maximum value (TMV) refers to the purported highest coefficient that is attainable by an index based on the number of distinct categories within a particular population.

References

Akram, Farheen, Abrar ul Haq, Muhammad, Natarajan, Vinodh K., and Chellakan, R. Stephen. 2020. "Board heterogeneity and corporate performance: An insight beyond agency issues". *Cogent Business and Management*, Vol. 7: 1809299.

Biemann, Torsten. and Kearney. Eric. 2010. "Size does matter: How varying group sizes in a sample affect the most common measures of group diversity". *Organizational Research Methods*, Vol. 13: 582 – 599.

Blau, Peter Michael. 1977. *Inequality and heterogeneity*. New York, NY: Free Press.

Chikoto, Grace L., Ling, Qianhua, and Neely, Daniel G. 2016. "The adoption and use of the Hirschman–Herfindahl Index in nonprofit research: Does revenue diversification measurement matter?". *Voluntas: International Journal of Voluntary and Nonprofit Organizations*, Vol. 27: 1425 – 1447.

Guajardo, Salomón A. 2013. "Workforce diversity: An application of diversity and integration indices to small agencies". *Public Personnel Management*, Vol. 41: 27 – 40.

Guajardo, Salomón A. 2014. "Workforce diversity: Assessing the impact of minority integration on intra-group interaction". *International Journal of Police Science and Management*, Vol. 16: 205 – 220.

Guajardo, Salomón A. 2015. "Measuring diversity in police agencies". *Journal of Ethnicity in Criminal Justice,* Vol. 13: 1 – 15.

Hendrick, Rebecca. 2002. "Revenue diversification: Fiscal illusion or flexible financial management". *Public Budgeting and Finance*, Vol. 22: 52 – 72.

Jordan, Meagan M., and Wagner, Gary A. 2008. "Revenue diversification in Arkansas cities: The budgetary and tax effort impacts". *Public Budgeting and Finance*, Vol: 28: 68 – 82.

Lieberson, Stanley. 1969. "Measuring population diversity". *American Sociological Review*, Vol. 34: 850 – 862.

Oba, Victor Chiedu, and Fodio, Musa Inuwa. 2013. "Boards' gender mix as a predictor of financial performance in Nigeria: An empirical study". *International Journal of Economics and Finance*, Vol. 5: 170 – 178.

Simpson, Edward Hugh. 1949. "Measurement of diversity". *Nature*, Vol. 163: 688.

Starks, Glenn. L. 2009. "Minority representation in senior positions in U.S. federal agencies: A paradox of underrepresentation". *Public Personnel Management*, Vol. 38: 79 – 90.

CHAPTER 3

MEASUREMENT OF GENDER DIVERSITY

Numerous studies on organizational diversity have applied the Simpson diversity index to measure *gender diversity* in nonprofit, public, and private organizations (e.g., Campbell and Mínguez-Vera, 2008; Guajardo, 2014. Lee-Kuen, Sok-Gee, and Zainudin, 2017). In so doing, the studies have discussed the level of gender diversity across and within nonprofit, public, and private organizations. However, because most of the studies have appeared in peer-reviewed journals and in professional trade publications, the distribution of Simpson scores is seldom discussed and presented. Similarly, publications on gender diversity seldom discuss thoroughly the statistical properties of Simpson scores in terms of central tendency and *normality*.

In applying the Simpson index to public organizations, this chapter presents a descriptive statistical analysis of biased (S_B) and unbiased (S_N) gender diversity scores calculated for each of the 72 NYC departments based on their demographic employment data for fiscal year 2019. Biased Simpson gender diversity scores are calculated by applying the following formula presented in Chapter 2: $S_B = 1 - \sum p_i^2$. Unbiased Simpson diversity scores are calculated by using the following formula presented in Chapter 2: $S_N = 1 - \sum \frac{n(n-1)}{N(N-1)}$.

Tests for normality are conducted to assess whether the distribution of each set of gender diversity scores is distributed normally. A paired z-test is conducted to determine whether the difference in the biased (S_B) and unbiased (S_N) scores is 0 (H_o: $\mu_{SN} - \mu_{SB} = 0$) at $\alpha = 0.01$.

Application of the Simpson index

As presented in Chapter 1, Simpson coefficients are calculated by using numbers or percentages. Exhibit 3-1 presents the biased Simpson (S_{GB}) coefficients for gender diversity for each of the 72 NYC departments for fiscal year 2019. Seven NYC departments attained an EMV of 0.50, which indicates that these departments had an equal percent of men and women in the workforce in fiscal 2019. Several departments attained gender diversity scores of 0.499, which indicates a very slight difference in the percent of men and women in the workforce. Similar results were obtained for departments with gender diversity scores of 0.498; however, the percent of men was higher than the percent of women in some departments. Based on the employment data for fiscal 2019, DSNY attained the lowest gender diversity score of 0.164.

Exhibit 3-1 also shows that a number of NYC departments attained a high proportion of the EMV. For instance, 66% of the departments reached 80% of the proportion of the EMV of 0.50. The findings show that 7 departments attained 100% of the EMV, while 11 departments attained 99% of the EMV. Another 9 departments attained 98% of the EMV. Exhibit 3-1 also shows that 2 departments attained 39% of the EMV. The *coefficient of variation* (CV) shows that the biased (S_{GB}) and standardized biased (S_{SGB}) gender diversity scores have the same amount of variation in terms of their set of values. This is due to dividing each set of gender diversity scores by the EMV of 0.50 to obtain the standardized gender diversity scores.

Exhibit 3-1 Simpson (S$_{GB}$) biased gender diversity scores for NYC departments for fiscal year 2019

Case Number	Department Acronym	Total Employees	Percent Men	Percent Women	Simpson Coefficient (S$_{GB}$)	Standardized Simpson Coefficient (S$_{SGB}$)
44	DHS	2438	0.50	0.50	0.500	1.000
60	CCRB	203	0.51	0.49	0.500	1.000
52	DCP	334	0.51	0.49	0.500	1.000
35	HPD	2441	0.49	0.51	0.500	1.000
26	CFB	115	0.51	0.49	0.500	1.000
21	NYCTAX	49	0.49	0.51	0.500	1.000
19	BIC	80	0.51	0.49	0.500	1.000
59	DA-NARC	215	0.48	0.52	0.499	0.998
31	PA	52	0.48	0.52	0.499	0.998
28	BP-MAN	94	0.48	0.52	0.499	0.998
24	COUNCIL	867	0.48	0.52	0.499	0.998
22	IBO	36	0.53	0.47	0.498	0.996
13	DOF	2102	0.47	0.53	0.498	0.996
8	NYCPPF	144	0.47	0.53	0.498	0.996
4	BOE	833	0.53	0.47	0.498	0.996
72	NYCEM (OEM)	202	0.54	0.46	0.497	0.994
71	DOI	367	0.46	0.54	0.497	0.994
20	ACTUARY	51	0.55	0.45	0.495	0.990
64	COIB	25	0.44	0.56	0.493	0.986
61	DA-SI	170	0.44	0.56	0.493	0.986
55	DA-BK	1140	0.44	0.56	0.493	0.986
54	DA-MAN	1472	0.44	0.56	0.493	0.986
10	DORIS	73	0.44	0.56	0.493	0.986
69	DOC	12296	0.57	0.43	0.490	0.980

Measurement of Gender Diversity

58	DA-QNS	710	0.43	0.57	0.490	0.980
18	SBS	301	0.43	0.57	0.490	0.980
14	COMPTROLLER	784	0.43	0.57	0.490	0.980
37	DCLA	74	0.42	0.58	0.487	0.974
29	BP-BX	93	0.42	0.58	0.487	0.974
17	DCA	416	0.42	0.58	0.487	0.974
6	TRS	349	0.42	0.58	0.487	0.974
56	DA-BX	1082	0.41	0.59	0.484	0.968
3	MAYORALTY	1271	0.41	0.59	0.484	0.968
62	CCHR	139	0.40	0.60	0.480	0.960
33	NYCHA	10962	0.60	0.40	0.480	0.960
32	PUBADMIN	47	0.40	0.60	0.480	0.960
57	OATH	717	0.39	0.61	0.476	0.952
15	TLC	632	0.61	0.39	0.476	0.952
7	OPA	152	0.39	0.61	0.476	0.952
5	NYCERS	444	0.39	0.61	0.476	0.952
1	DCAS	2468	0.61	0.39	0.476	0.952
30	BP-SI	53	0.38	0.62	0.471	0.942
23	MWFA	13	0.38	0.62	0.471	0.942
2	DOITT	1576	0.62	0.38	0.471	0.942
53	LAW	1903	0.37	0.63	0.466	0.932
51	DDC	1340	0.63	0.37	0.466	0.932
50	DOB	1657	0.64	0.36	0.461	0.922
45	DYCD	574	0.36	0.64	0.461	0.922
25	BP-BK	124	0.36	0.64	0.461	0.922
67	NYPD	55960	0.65	0.35	0.455	0.910
39	SCA	827	0.65	0.35	0.455	0.910
34	PARKS	7267	0.66	0.34	0.449	0.898
16	FISA	436	0.66	0.34	0.449	0.898

66	EEPC	12	0.33	0.67	0.442	0.884
65	NYCCSC	15	0.33	0.67	0.442	0.884
27	BP-QNS	109	0.33	0.67	0.442	0.884
9	CLERK	75	0.32	0.68	0.435	0.870
70	DOP	1166	0.31	0.69	0.428	0.856
40	NYCHH	38731	0.31	0.69	0.428	0.856
11	FDNYPF	36	0.31	0.69	0.428	0.856
63	BOC	30	0.30	0.70	0.420	0.840
43	DOHMH	7150	0.29	0.71	0.412	0.824
41	HRA	13018	0.29	0.71	0.412	0.824
36	LPC	83	0.29	0.71	0.412	0.824
12	OCB	17	0.29	0.71	0.412	0.824
42	ACS	7366	0.28	0.72	0.403	0.806
46	DFTA	326	0.27	0.73	0.394	0.788
49	DOT	5716	0.75	0.25	0.375	0.750
48	DEP	6216	0.75	0.25	0.375	0.750
38	DOE	174105	0.23	0.77	0.354	0.708
68	FDNY	17746	0.89	0.11	0.196	0.392
47	DSNY	10134	0.91	0.09	0.164	0.328
Average		5,558.63	0.47	0.54	0.459	0.918
Standard Deviation		21683.98	0.14	0.14	0.059	0.118
Coefficient of Variation (CV)			0.14		0.128	0.128

Exhibit 3-2 Descriptive statistics for biased Simpson (S_{GB}) gender diversity scores for NYC departments for fiscal year 2019

1. Descriptive statistics for biased Simpson scores

A. Measures of central tendency and variability for biased Simpson scores

Central Tendency			Variability		95% Confidence Interval	
Cases (N)	Median	Mean	Variance	Standard Deviation	Lower Limit	Upper Limit
72	0.478	0.459	0.004	0.059	0.445	0.473

B. Tests for normality, skewness, and kurtosis for biased Simpson scores

1. Shapiro-Wilk W test for normal data

Cases (N)	W-statistic	V-statistic	z-statistic	Probability > z
72	0.629	23.396	6.867	0.0001

2. Skewness/Kurtosis tests for Normality for biased Simpson scores

Skewness	Kurtosis	Probability of Skewness	Probability of Kurtosis	Adjusted χ^2	Probability > χ^2
-3.11	14.706	0.0001	0.0001	51.08	0.0001

2. Descriptive statistics for biased standardized Simpson scores

A. Measures of central tendency and variability for biased standardized Simpson scores

Central Tendency			Variability		95% Confidence Interval	
Cases (N)	Median	Mean	Variance	Standard Deviation	Lower Limit	Upper Limit
72	0.956	0.918	0.014	0.119	0.890	0.946

B. Tests for normality, skewness, and kurtosis for biased standardized Simpson scores

1. Shapiro-Wilk W test for normal data

Cases (N)	W-statistic	V-statistic	z-statistic	Probability > z
72	0.629	23.396	6.867	0.0001

2. Skewness/Kurtosis tests for Normality for biased standardized Simpson scores

Skewness	Kurtosis	Probability of Skewness	Probability of Kurtosis	Adjusted χ^2	Probability > χ^2
-3.11	14.706	0.0001	0.0001	51.08	0.0001

Descriptive statistics for the unstandardized (S_{GB}) and standardized biased (S_{SGB}) Simpson gender diversity coefficients are presented in Exhibit 3-2. The *median* (a *measure of tendency*) for the unstandardized biased diversity scores for NYC departments is 0.478, with a *mean* of 0.459 and a *standard deviation* (a *measure of variability*) of 0.019. The 95% *confidence interval* (CI) for the unstandardized biased diversity scores ranges from 0.445 to 0.473. The findings show that 2 diversity scores exceed 3 standard deviations to the left of the mean and should be treated as *outliners*. Exhibit 3-2 also shows that the distribution of the biased unstandardized (S_{GB}) and standardized (S_{SGB}) gender diversity scores fail to meet the assumption of normality, which is important for performing OLS multivariate regression. Specifically, the distributions of the diversity scores are significantly negatively skewed and heavy tailed. Chapter 8 presents robust regression which adjusts the statistical analysis for distributions containing extreme low or high values.

The unbiased unstandardized (S_{GN}) and standardized (S_{SGN}) Simpson gender diversity scores for each of the 72 NYC departments are presented in Exhibit 3-3. In contrast to the range for the biased (S_{GB}) gender diversity scores which starts at 0.164 and ends at 0.500, the range for the unbiased (S_{GN}) diversity scores starts at 0.476 and ends at 0.519. Four departments have diversity scores that exceed the EMV of 0.50. The remaining departments have diversity scores between 0.475 and 0.496. When examining the findings of the unbiased standardized (S_{SGN}) diversity scores, numerous NYC departments have scores that attained at least 95% of the proportion of the EMV of 0.50. The CV of 0.018 shows that the scores for the unbiased Simpson gender diversity index produces coefficients that are similar and that are centered around the mean.

Measurement of Gender Diversity

Exhibit 3-3 Unbiased Simpson (S_{GN}) gender diversity scores for NYC departments for fiscal year 2019

Case Number	Department Acronym	Total Employees	Number of Men	Number of Women	Unbiased Simpson Coefficient (S_{GN})	Unbiased Standardized Simpson Coefficient (S_{SGN})
66	EEPC	12	7	5	0.519	1.038
23	MWFA	13	8	5	0.515	1.031
65	NYCCSC	15	9	6	0.510	1.020
12	OCB	17	10	7	0.506	1.011
64	COIB	25	15	10	0.496	0.991
63	BOC	30	18	12	0.492	0.984
11	FDNYPF	36	22	14	0.489	0.979
22	IBO	36	22	14	0.489	0.979
32	PUBADMIN	47	29	18	0.486	0.972
21	NYCTAX	49	30	19	0.486	0.971
20	ACTUARY	51	31	20	0.485	0.971
31	PA	52	32	20	0.485	0.970
30	BP-SI	53	32	21	0.485	0.970
10	DORIS	73	45	28	0.482	0.965
37	DCLA	74	45	29	0.482	0.965
9	CLERK	75	46	29	0.482	0.964
19	BIC	80	49	31	0.482	0.964
36	LPC	83	51	32	0.482	0.963
29	BP-BX	93	57	36	0.481	0.962
28	BP-MAN	94	57	37	0.481	0.962
27	BP-QNS	109	66	43	0.480	0.960
26	CFB	115	70	45	0.480	0.960
25	BP-BK	124	76	48	0.480	0.959

62	CCHR	139	85	54	0.479	0.958
8	NYCPPF	144	88	56	0.479	0.958
7	OPA	152	93	59	0.479	0.958
61	DA-SI	170	104	66	0.479	0.957
72	NYCEM (OEM)	202	123	79	0.478	0.956
60	CCRB	203	124	79	0.478	0.956
59	DA-NARC	215	131	84	0.478	0.956
18	SBS	301	184	117	0.477	0.955
46	DFTA	326	199	127	0.477	0.955
52	DCP	334	204	130	0.477	0.954
6	TRS	349	213	136	0.477	0.954
71	DOI	367	224	143	0.477	0.954
17	DCA	416	254	162	0.477	0.954
16	FISA	436	266	170	0.477	0.954
5	NYCERS	444	271	173	0.477	0.954
45	DYCD	574	350	224	0.477	0.953
15	TLC	632	386	246	0.477	0.953
58	DA-QNS	710	433	277	0.476	0.953
57	OATH	717	437	280	0.476	0.953
14	COMPTROLLER	784	478	306	0.476	0.953
39	SCA	827	504	323	0.476	0.953
4	BOE	833	508	325	0.476	0.953
24	COUNCIL	867	529	338	0.476	0.953
56	DA-BX	1082	660	422	0.476	0.952
55	DA-BK	1140	695	445	0.476	0.952
70	DOP	1166	711	455	0.476	0.952
3	MAYORALTY	1271	775	496	0.476	0.952
51	DDC	1340	817	523	0.476	0.952

Measurement of Gender Diversity

54	DA-MAN	1472	898	574	0.476	0.952
2	DOITT	1576	961	615	0.476	0.952
50	DOB	1657	1011	646	0.476	0.952
53	LAW	1903	1161	742	0.476	0.952
13	DOF	2102	1282	820	0.476	0.952
44	DHS	2438	1487	951	0.476	0.952
35	HPD	2441	1489	952	0.476	0.952
1	DCAS	2468	1505	963	0.476	0.952
49	DOT	5716	3487	2229	0.476	0.952
48	DEP	6216	3792	2424	0.476	0.952
43	DOHMH	7150	4362	2789	0.476	0.952
34	PARKS	7267	4433	2834	0.476	0.952
42	ACS	7366	4493	2873	0.476	0.952
47	DSNY	10134	6182	3952	0.476	0.952
33	NYCHA	10962	6687	4275	0.476	0.952
69	DOC	12296	7501	4795	0.476	0.952
41	HRA	13018	7941	5077	0.476	0.952
68	FDNY	17746	10825	6921	0.476	0.952
40	NYCHH	38731	23626	15105	0.476	0.952
67	NYPD	55960	34136	21824	0.476	0.952
38	DOE	174105	106204	67901	0.476	0.952
Average		5,558.63	3,390.76	2,167.86	0.481	0.961
Standard Deviation		21,683.98	13,227.23	8,456.75	0.009	0.018
CV					0.018	0.018

Exhibit 3-4 Descriptive statistics for the unbiased Simpson (S_{GN}) gender diversity scores for NYC departments for fiscal year 2019

1. Descriptive statistics for unbiased Simpson scores

A. Measures of central tendency and variability for unbiased Simpson scores

Cases (N)	Central Tendency		Variability		95% Confidence Interval	
	Median	Mean	Variance	Standard Deviation	Lower Limit	Upper Limit
72	0.477	0.481	0.000	0.009	0.479	0.483

B. Tests for normality, skewness, and kurtosis the unbiased Simpson scores

1. Shapiro-Wilk W test for normal data

Cases (N)	W-statistic	V-statistic	z-statistic	Probability > z
72	0.582	26.32	7.123	0.0001

2. Skewness/Kurtosis tests for Normality for unbiased Simpson scores

Skewness	Kurtosis	Probability of Skewness	Probability of Kurtosis	Adjusted χ^2	Probability > χ^2
2.84	10.93	0.0001	0.0001	44.66	0.0001

2. Descriptive statistics for unbiased standardized Simpson scores

A. Measures of central tendency and variability for unbiased standardized Simpson scores

Cases (N)	Central Tendency		Variability		95% Confidence Interval	
	Median	Mean	Variance	Standard Deviation	Lower Limit	Upper Limit
72	0.954	0.961	0.000	0.018	0.957	0.966

B. Tests for normality, skewness, and kurtosis for unbiased standardized Simpson scores

1. Shapiro-Wilk W test for normal data

Cases (N)	W-statistic	V-statistic	z-statistic	Probability > z
72	0.582	26.32	7.123	0.0001

2. Skewness/Kurtosis tests for Normality for unbiased standardized Simpson scores

Skewness	Kurtosis	Probability of Skewness	Probability of Kurtosis	Adjusted χ^2	Probability > χ^2
2.84	10.93	0.0001	0.0001	44.66	0.0001

Exhibit 3-4 presents the descriptive statistics for the unbiased Simpson (S_{GN}) gender diversity scores and the findings of the tests of normality. The median for the unbiased gender diversity scores is 0.477 with a mean of 0.481 and standard deviation of 0.009. The 95% CI for the unbiased diversity scores has a lower limit of 0.479 and an upper limit of 0.483. In contrast to the distribution of biased (S_{GB}) diversity scores, the distribution of the unbiased Simpson (S_{GN}) gender diversity scores is positively skewed and highly peaked. The tests for normality show that the distribution violates the assumption of normality.

Comparison of biased and unbiased gender diversity scores

The sets of biased (S_{GB}) and unbiased (S_{GN}) gender diversity scores are presented and compared in Exhibit 3-5. The statistical findings show that the formula for the unbiased Simpson (S_{GN}) diversity index tends to lower the gender diversity coefficients of NYC departments with higher *biased measurements*. For instance, the gender diversity scores of NYC departments with biased coefficients of 0.50 are decreased by about 0.02 points when the formula for calculating unbiased diversity scores is used. Conversely, the formula for the unbiased Simpson diversity index tends to increase the diversity coefficients of NYC departments with lower biased S_{GB} measurements. For example, the biased gender diversity coefficient for the DSNY increased from 0.164 to 0.476 when the formula for unbiased Simpson diversity coefficients is applied. Similarly, the gender diversity score for the FDNY increased from 0.196 to 0.476 as a result of applying the formula for calculating unbiased Simpson diversity scores. On average, the gender diversity coefficients increased by 0.02 points when the formula for unbiased Simpson diversity scores was used. As Exhibit 3-5 also shows, the unbiased standardized (S_{SGN}) gender diversity scores are slightly higher than the biased standardized (S_{SGB}) diversity scores.

Exhibit 3-5 Comparison of biased (S_{GB}) and unbiased (S_{GN}) Simpson gender diversity scores for NYC departments for fiscal year 2019

Case Number	Department Acronym	Biased Simpson Coefficient (S_{GB})	Unbiased Simpson Coefficient ((S_{GN})	Difference (S_{GN} - S_{GB})	Standardized Simpson Coefficient (S_{SGB})	Unbiased Standardized Simpson Coefficient (S_{SGN})	Difference (S_{SGN} - S_{SGB})
44	DHS	0.500	0.476	-0.024	1.000	0.952	-0.048
19	BIC	0.500	0.482	-0.018	1.000	0.964	-0.036
21	NYCTAX	0.500	0.486	-0.014	1.000	0.971	-0.028
26	CFB	0.500	0.480	-0.020	1.000	0.960	-0.040
35	HPD	0.500	0.476	-0.024	1.000	0.952	-0.048
52	DCP	0.500	0.477	-0.023	1.000	0.954	-0.045
60	CCRB	0.500	0.478	-0.022	1.000	0.956	-0.043
24	COUNCIL	0.499	0.476	-0.023	0.998	0.953	-0.046
28	BP-MAN	0.499	0.481	-0.018	0.998	0.962	-0.037
31	PA	0.499	0.485	-0.014	0.998	0.970	-0.028
59	DA-NARC	0.499	0.478	-0.021	0.998	0.956	-0.042
4	BOE	0.498	0.476	-0.022	0.996	0.953	-0.044
8	NYCPPF	0.498	0.479	-0.019	0.996	0.958	-0.038
13	DOF	0.498	0.476	-0.022	0.996	0.952	-0.044
22	IBO	0.498	0.489	-0.009	0.996	0.979	-0.018
72	NYCEM (OEM)	0.497	0.478	-0.019	0.994	0.956	-0.037
71	DOI	0.497	0.477	-0.020	0.994	0.954	-0.039
20	ACTUARY	0.495	0.485	-0.010	0.990	0.971	-0.019
10	DORIS	0.493	0.482	-0.010	0.986	0.965	-0.021
54	DA-MAN	0.493	0.476	-0.017	0.986	0.952	-0.033
55	DA-BK	0.493	0.476	-0.017	0.986	0.952	-0.033

Measurement of Gender Diversity

61	DA-SI	0.493	0.479	-0.014	0.986	0.957	-0.028
64	COIB	0.493	0.496	0.003	0.986	0.991	0.006
14	COMPTROLLER	0.490	0.476	-0.014	0.980	0.953	-0.028
18	SBS	0.490	0.477	-0.013	0.980	0.955	-0.026
58	DA-QNS	0.490	0.476	-0.014	0.980	0.953	-0.027
69	DOC	0.490	0.476	-0.014	0.980	0.952	-0.029
6	TRS	0.487	0.477	-0.010	0.974	0.954	-0.020
17	DCA	0.487	0.477	-0.010	0.974	0.954	-0.021
29	BP-BX	0.487	0.481	-0.006	0.974	0.962	-0.012
37	DCLA	0.487	0.482	-0.005	0.974	0.965	-0.010
3	MAYORALTY	0.484	0.476	-0.008	0.968	0.952	-0.015
56	DA-BX	0.484	0.476	-0.008	0.968	0.952	-0.015
32	PUBADMIN	0.480	0.486	0.006	0.960	0.972	0.012
33	NYCHA	0.480	0.476	-0.004	0.960	0.952	-0.008
62	CCHR	0.480	0.479	-0.001	0.960	0.958	-0.002
1	DCAS	0.476	0.476	0.000	0.952	0.952	0.000
5	NYCERS	0.476	0.477	0.001	0.952	0.954	0.002
7	OPA	0.476	0.479	0.003	0.952	0.958	0.006
15	TLC	0.476	0.477	0.001	0.952	0.953	0.002
57	OATH	0.476	0.476	0.001	0.952	0.953	0.001
2	DOITT	0.471	0.476	0.005	0.942	0.952	0.010
23	MWFA	0.471	0.515	0.044	0.942	1.031	0.089
30	BP-SI	0.471	0.485	0.014	0.942	0.970	0.028
51	DDC	0.466	0.476	0.010	0.932	0.952	0.020
53	LAW	0.466	0.476	0.010	0.932	0.952	0.020
25	BP-BK	0.461	0.480	0.019	0.922	0.959	0.038
45	DYCD	0.461	0.477	0.016	0.922	0.953	0.032
50	DOB	0.461	0.476	0.015	0.922	0.952	0.031
39	SCA	0.455	0.476	0.021	0.910	0.953	0.043

Chapter 3

67	NYPD	0.455	0.476	0.021	0.910	0.952	0.042
16	FISA	0.449	0.477	0.028	0.898	0.954	0.056
34	PARKS	0.449	0.476	0.027	0.898	0.952	0.054
27	BP-QNS	0.442	0.480	0.038	0.884	0.960	0.076
65	NYCCSC	0.442	0.510	0.068	0.884	1.020	0.135
66	EEPC	0.442	0.519	0.077	0.884	1.038	0.154
9	CLERK	0.435	0.482	0.047	0.870	0.964	0.094
11	FDNYPF	0.428	0.489	0.062	0.856	0.979	0.123
40	NYCHH	0.428	0.476	0.048	0.856	0.952	0.096
70	DOP	0.428	0.476	0.048	0.856	0.952	0.097
63	BOC	0.420	0.492	0.072	0.840	0.984	0.144
12	OCB	0.412	0.506	0.094	0.824	1.011	0.187
36	LPC	0.412	0.482	0.070	0.824	0.963	0.140
41	HRA	0.412	0.476	0.064	0.824	0.952	0.128
43	DOHMH	0.412	0.476	0.064	0.824	0.952	0.128
42	ACS	0.403	0.476	0.073	0.806	0.952	0.145
46	DFTA	0.394	0.477	0.083	0.788	0.955	0.166
48	DEP	0.375	0.476	0.101	0.750	0.952	0.202
49	DOT	0.375	0.476	0.101	0.750	0.952	0.202
38	DOE	0.354	0.476	0.122	0.708	0.952	0.243
68	FDNY	0.196	0.476	0.280	0.392	0.952	0.560
47	DSNY	0.164	0.476	0.312	0.328	0.952	0.624
Average		0.459	0.481	0.022	0.918	0.961	0.043
Standard Deviation		0.059	0.009	0.059	0.118	0.018	
CV		0.128	0.018		0.128	0.018	

The differences between the biased (S_{GB}) and unbiased (S_{GN}) gender diversity coefficients are tested for statistical significance with a paired z-test for differences because 2 sets of scores were calculated using the same demographic data. Specifically, the paired z-test assesses whether the mean of the S_{GN} scores is statistically equivalent to the mean of the S_{GB} scores at $\alpha = 0.01$ (H_O: $\mu_{SGN} = \mu_{SGB}$ at $\alpha = 0.01$). The rationale for assessing whether the scores generated by the unbiased formula are statistically higher than the biased diversity scores is to determine whether the formulas generate scores that are statistically different and to determine whether the *discriminatory power* of the Simpson index is compromised by using the formula for obtaining unbiased diversity scores. Exhibit 3-6 shows that the unbiased (S_{GN}) Simpson gender diversity scores are statistically equivalent to the biased (S_{GB}) scores at $\alpha = 0.01$ (z-statistic = 0.00, p > 0.01). Stated differently, the formula for calculating unbiased Simpson diversity scores produces scores that are similar to the formula for calculating biased diversity scores. Statistically speaking, the differences in the diversity scores are due to measurement error. The findings also show that the discriminatory power of the Simpson index is not enhanced with the use of the formula for calculating unbiased diversity scores.

Exhibit 3-6 Paired z-test for equal means for biased (S$_{GB}$) and unbiased (S$_{GN}$) unstandardized Simpson gender diversity scores for NYC departments for fiscal year 2019

Cases (N)	H$_o$	Mean Difference	Standard Error	Standard Deviation	95% CI		z-statistic	Probability ($|Z| > |z|$)
					Lower Limit	Upper Limit		
72	$\mu_{SGN} = \mu_{SGB}$	0.000	0.007	0.059	-0.014	0.014	0.000	1.000

Summary

This chapter applied the Simpson diversity index to obtain gender diversity scores for 72 NYC departments based on their demographic employment data for fiscal year 2019. When the standardized biased (S_{SGB}) gender diversity scores were reviewed, the statistical findings indicated that a large percent of NYC departments had gender diversity scores that attained a high proportion of the EMV of 0.50. The analysis of the distributions of the biased unstandardized (S_{GB}) and standardized (S_{SGB}) gender diversity scores showed that the sets of coefficients are negatively skewed, are highly peaked, and are nonnormal. By contrast, the distributions of the unbiased unstandardized (S_{GN}) and standardized (S_{SGN}) gender diversity scores are positively skewed, are highly peaked, and are nonnormal. The findings for the unbiased (S_{GN}) gender diversity scores also indicated that almost each coefficient attained the EMV of 0.50. In comparison to the scores obtained with the use of the biased Simpson (S_B) gender diversity index, the unbiased (S_N) index produced scores that were similar in value.

The drawbacks of using the S_N index in comparison to the use of S_B are the following:

- S_N appears to overcorrect for measurement bias where high scores are lowered slightly and lower scores are increased moderately.
- The discriminatory power of the Simpson index is not enhanced when S_N is used to measure gender diversity;
- The distribution of S_N is compact and centered around the mean; and,
- The range of S_N scores becomes truncated so that there is a measurement floor and ceiling which further restricts the values of the LDV.

When measuring gender diversity for NYC departments, the use of the S_B index produces a distribution of a set of coefficients with more variation and which are similar in value to scores obtained by S_N all things being equal.

Key Terms

Biased measurements refer to coefficients or scores that are either high or low due to the formula that is used to obtain the value.

Coefficient of variation (CV) refers to the measure obtained by dividing the standard deviation (σ) of a set of data by the mean ($\bar{x}$) to get an estimate of the dispersion of data points around the mean. Symbolically, the formula is as follows: $CV = \frac{\sigma}{\mu}$

Confidence interval refers to a range of estimated values with a lower and upper limit that indicates where an average score is likely to fall when multiple samples are obtained.

Descriptive statistics refer to measures that summarize the distribution, central tendency, and variability in a set of data.

Discriminatory power refers to the extent to which a diversity index can detect subtle differences in heterogeneity when compared to another index.

Gender diversity refers to how well an organization's workforce is heterogeneous in terms of the employment of men and women.

Kurtosis refers to the thickness of the tails of a distribution of scores in a set of data.

Mean refers to the average score of a set of data. Mathematically, the average is calculated by adding all of the numbers (x) and then dividing the sum by the number of observations (n). The formula for calculating the average is as follows: $\bar{x} = \frac{\Sigma x}{n}$

Measures of central tendency refer to measures that summarize the typical scores in a set of data.

Measures of distribution refer to measures that summarize the frequency or occurrence of scores in a set a data.

Measures of variability refer to measures that summarize the spread of scores in a set of data.

Median refers to the value that splits a set of data at the 50% point.

Normality refers to whether the scores in a set of data are symmetrically distributed so that they fit under a bell-shaped curve.

Outliners refer to scores that are 3 standard deviations below or above the mean of a set of data.

Skewness refers to whether a distribution of scores leans to the right (positive) or to the left (negative) of the median. In a positively skewed distribution, the mean ($\bar{x}$) is larger than the median (M). Conversely, the mean ($\bar{x}$) is smaller than the median (M) in a negatively skewed distribution.

Standard deviation refers to a measure that indicates the average amount of variability in a set of data. A small standard deviation indicates that the data are centered around the mean, and a large standard deviation indicates that the data are dispersed further away from the mean. Values that are 3 standard deviations below or above the mean are generally treated as outliers.

References

Campbell, Kevin, and Mínguez-Vera, Antonio. 2008. "Gender diversity in the boardroom and firm financial performance". *Journal of Business Ethics*, Vol. 83: 435 – 451.

Guajardo, Salomón A. 2014. "Workforce diversity: Ethnicity and gender diversity and disparity in the New York City Police Department". *Journal of Ethnicity in Criminal justice*, Vol. 12: 93 – 115.

Lee-Kuen, Irean Yap, Sok-Gee, Chan, and Zainudin, Rozaimah. 2017. "Gender diversity and firms' financial performance in Malaysia". *Asian Academy of Management Journal of Accounting and Finance*, Vol. 13: 41 – 62.

CHAPTER 4

MEASUREMENT OF ETHNIC DIVERSITY

Similar to the use of the Simpson index to assess gender diversity in nonprofit, public, and private organizations, the index is used often to examine ethnic (or racial) heterogeneity across and within different types of organizations (e.g., Cheong and Sinnakkannu, 2014; Guajardo, 2013, 2014, and 2015; Leslie, 2017; Starks, 2009). *Ethnic diversity* may be based on the categorization of race (or ethnicity) as White or minority, on the categorization of race as Asian, Black, Hispanic, White, and Pacific Islander / Native American, or on the categorization of race as Asian, Black, Hispanic, White, or other (e.g., Guajardo, 2013). In NYC, race is reported as Asian, Black, Hispanic, White, and some other race (SOR). In most studies, the Simpson diversity index is used to measure ethnic diversity based on the categorization of race into at least 5 categories. The ethnic data for NYC allows for applying the Simpson index to the categorization of race into 2 categories (White and minority) and into 5 categories (Asian, Black, Hispanic, White, and SOR). With few exceptions (e.g., Guajardo, 2013 and 2015), the studies that use the Simpson index do not calculate or compare ethnic diversity scores based on different categorizations of the racial data.

This chapter presents and analyzes biased (S_{EB}) and unbiased (S_{EN}) Simpson ethnic diversity scores based on the 2 categorizations of race reported by NYC departments for fiscal year 2019. The first set of biased (S_{EB1}) and unbiased (S_{EN1}) ethnic diversity scores are based on the classification of race as White and minority and has an EMV of 0.50. The second set of S_{EB2} and S_{EN2} diversity scores are based on the categorization of race into 5 categories and has an EMV of 0.80. As in Chapter 3, biased (S_B) diversity scores are calculated by applying the following formula: $S_B = 1 - \sum p_i^2$. Unbiased (S_N) Simpson diversity scores are calculated by using the following formula: $s_N = 1 - \sum \frac{n(n-1)}{N(N-1)}$.

Similar to Chapter 3, tests for normality are conducted to assess whether the distributions of each set of ethnic diversity scores are distributed normally. Several paired z-tests are conducted to determine whether the difference in the mean of the biased (S_B) and unbiased (S_N) scores is 0 (e.g., H₀: μSEN -

μ_{SEB} = 0) at α = 0.01. In addition, a *pairwise correlation analysis* is performed to assess how closely the sets of diversity coefficients align with each other. A *factor analysis* with oblimin oblique rotation is undertaken to determine whether the structures of the biased and unbiased scores are similar and whether they measure the same dimension of diversity.

Application of the Simpson index

Exhibit 4-1 presents the calculation of biased (S_{EB}) and unbiased (S_{EN}) Simpson ethnic diversity scores for ACS for fiscal year 2019. When ethnicity is categorized as White and minority, ACS has biased (S_{EB1}) and unbiased (S_{EN1}) diversity coefficients of 0.233 (S_{B1} = 0.233; S_{N2} = 0.233), indicating a moderate level of racial diversity. When ethnicity is categorized into 5 racial groups, the biased (S_{EB2}) and unbiased (S_{EN2}) diversity coefficients for ACS increase to 0.563 (S_{B2} = 0.563; S_{N2} = 0.563), indicating a somewhat moderate level of racial diversity. As the number of categories increase, the discriminatory power of the Simpson diversity index increases. However, the measurement efficiency of the Simpson index decreases when unbiased coefficients are calculated because more mathematical operations are required to obtain the diversity scores.

Exhibit 4-1 Calculation of the biased (S_{EB}) and unbiased (S_{EN}) Simpson ethnic diversity score for the New York City ACS for fiscal year 2019

A. Calculation of biased and unbiased Simpson coefficients for 2-group categorization of ethnicity

Race	Frequency (f)	f_i^2	Race	Number (n)	$n_i(n_i-1)$	$\dfrac{n_i(n_i-1)}{N(N-1)}$
White	958	917,764	White	958	916,806	0.017
Minority	6,408	41,062,464	Minority	6,408	41,056,056	0.760
Total (Σ)	7,351	41,980,228	Total (Σ)	7,366	41,972,862	0.777

$$S_{EB1} = 1 - \frac{\sum f_i^2}{F^2} \qquad\qquad S_{EN1} = 1 - \sum \frac{n_i(n_i-1)}{N(N-1)}$$

$$S_{EB1} = 1 - \frac{41,980,228}{54,037,201}$$

$$S_{EB1} = 1 - 0.777 \qquad\qquad S_{EN1} = 1 - 0.777$$

$$S_{EB1} = 0.223 \qquad\qquad S_{EN1} = 0.223$$

B. Calculation of biased and unbiased Simpson coefficients for 5-group categorization of ethnicity

Race	Frequency (f)	f_i^2	Race	Number (n)	$n_i(n_i-1)$	$\dfrac{n_i(n_i-1)}{N(N-1)}$
White	958	917,764	White	958	916,806	0.017
Black	4,567	20,857,489	Black	4,567	20,852,922	0.384
Hispanic	1,326	1,758,276	Hispanic	1,326	1,756,950	0.032
SOR	147	21,609	SOR	147	21,462	0.000
Asian	368	135,424	Asian	368	135,056	0.002
Total (Σ)	7,366	23,690,562	Total (Σ)	7,366	23,683,196	0.437

$$S_{EB2} = 1 - \frac{\sum f_i^2}{F^2} \qquad\qquad S_{EN2} = 1 - \sum \frac{n_i(n_i-1)}{N(N-1)}$$

$$S_{EB2} = 1 - \frac{23,690,562}{54,257,956}$$

$$S_{EB2} = 1 - 0.437 \qquad\qquad S_{EN2} = 1 - 0.437$$

$$S_{EB2} = 0.563 \qquad\qquad S_{EN2} = 0.563$$

In Exhibit 4-2, the biased unstandardized (S_{EB1}) and standardized (S_{EB2}) Simpson ethnic diversity scores for each NYC department for fiscal 2019 are presented. S_{EB1} represents the biased coefficients for ethnicity categorized a White and minority; S_{EB2} represents the biased coefficients for ethnicity categorized into 5 racial groups: Asian, Black, Hispanic, White, and SOR. As Exhibit 4-2 shows, the S_{EB1} scores range from 0.164 to 0.50. Four NYC departments attained the EMV of 0.50. Of the 72 NYC departments, 50 had S_{EB1} scores between 0.403 and 0.499. The remaining 18 departments had S_{eB1} scores ranging from 0.164 to 0.394, with DHS having the lowest S_{EB1} score.

When the S_{EB2} scores are reviewed, Exhibit 4-2 shows that 42 NYC departments attained diversity scores ranging from 0.701 to 0.781, indicating that none of the departments obtained the EMV of 0.80. Another 21 departments had S_{EB2} scores ranging from 0.615 to 0.697. The remaining 9 departments had S_{EB2} scores from 0.389 to 0.595.

The findings for the standardized biased ethnic diversity scores differ moderately as shown in Exhibit 4-2. For the S_{SEB1} diversity scores, 4 NYC departments attained 100% of the EMV of 0.50. Another 34 departments attained 90% to 99% of the EMV. In addition, 15 departments attained 80% to 89% of the EMV. Seven departments attained 70% to 79% of the EMV. Lastly, 11 departments obtained 32% to 69% of the EMV of 0.50.

By contrast, none of the NYC departments attained 100% of the EMV of 0.80. Exhibit 4-2. shows that 27 department attained 90% to 99% of the EMV. Thirty-two departments attained 80% to 89% of the EMV. Another 6 departments obtained 70% to 79% of the EMV. The remaining 7 departments obtained 48% to 69% of the EMV of 0.80.

Exhibit 4-3 summarizes the findings of the descriptive statistical analysis for the biased unstandardized (S_{EB}) and standardized (S_{SEB}) Simpson ethnic diversity scores. The biased diversity scores based on the categorization of race as White or minority (S_{EB1}) has a median of 0.455 and a mean of 0.427 with a standard deviation of .082. The 95% CI ranges from 0.408 to 0.446. In addition, the descriptive statistics show that the distribution of the diversity scores is negatively skewed (Skewness = -1.397) and heavy tailed (Kurtosis = 4.157). The tests for normality indicate that the scores fail to meet the assumption of normality.

Exhibit 4-2 Biased Simpson (S$_{EB1}$) ethnic diversity scores for NYC departments for fiscal year 2019

Case Number	Agency	Total White	Total Minority	Total Employees	Simpson Coefficient (S$_{EB1}$)	Standardized Simpson Coefficient (S$_{SEB1}$)
52	DCP	167	167	334	0.500	1.000
21	NYCTAX	25	24	49	0.500	1.000
20	ACTUARY	26	25	51	0.500	1.000
48	DEP	3046	3170	6216	0.500	1.000
59	DA-NARC	103	112	215	0.499	0.998
64	COIB	12	13	25	0.499	0.998
57	OATH	344	373	717	0.499	0.998
47	DSNY	5270	4864	10134	0.499	0.998
12	OCB	9	8	17	0.498	0.996
53	LAW	894	1009	1903	0.498	0.996
58	DA-QNS	376	334	710	0.498	0.996
19	BIC	36	44	80	0.495	0.990
27	BP-QNS	60	49	109	0.495	0.990
72	NYCEM	111	91	202	0.495	0.990
3	MAYORALTY	559	712	1271	0.493	0.986
24	COUNCIL	381	486	867	0.493	0.986
38	DOE	76606	97499	174105	0.493	0.986
54	DA-MAN	824	648	1472	0.493	0.986
37	DCLA	32	42	74	0.490	0.980
71	DOI	154	213	367	0.487	0.974
26	CFB	48	67	115	0.487	0.974
55	DA-BK	479	661	1140	0.487	0.974
49	DOT	2401	3315	5716	0.487	0.974

Measurement of Ethnic Diversity

11	FDNYPF	15	21	36	0.487	0.974
10	DORIS	30	43	73	0.484	0.968
39	SCA	339	488	827	0.484	0.968
60	CCRB	81	122	203	0.480	0.960
65	NYCCSC	6	9	15	0.480	0.960
8	NYCPPF	55	89	144	0.471	0.942
6	TRS	129	220	349	0.466	0.932
67	NYPD	20705	35255	55960	0.466	0.932
14	COMPTROLLER	282	502	784	0.461	0.922
56	DA-BX	390	692	1082	0.461	0.922
16	FISA	157	279	436	0.461	0.922
32	PUBADMIN	17	30	47	0.461	0.922
2	DOITT	552	1024	1576	0.455	0.910
34	PARKS	2543	4724	7267	0.455	0.910
68	FDNY	11535	6211	17746	0.455	0.910
50	DOB	580	1077	1657	0.455	0.910
28	BP-MAN	32	62	94	0.449	0.898
22	IBO	24	12	36	0.442	0.884
63	BOC	10	20	30	0.442	0.884
5	NYCERS	142	302	444	0.435	0.870
51	DDC	429	911	1340	0.435	0.870
4	BOE	258	575	833	0.428	0.856
23	MWFA	4	9	13	0.428	0.856
25	BP-BK	38	86	124	0.428	0.856
36	LPC	58	25	83	0.420	0.840
17	DCA	121	295	416	0.412	0.824
13	DOF	610	1492	2102	0.412	0.824
18	SBS	87	214	301	0.412	0.824
46	DFTA	91	235	326	0.403	0.806

1	DCAS	691	1777	2468	0.403	0.806
61	DA-SI	122	48	170	0.403	0.806
62	CCHR	38	101	139	0.394	0.788
31	PA	14	38	52	0.394	0.788
7	OPA	40	112	152	0.385	0.770
35	HPD	635	1806	2441	0.385	0.770
43	DOHMH	1716	5434	7150	0.365	0.730
29	BP-BX	22	71	93	0.365	0.730
30	BP-SI	41	12	53	0.354	0.708
15	TLC	139	493	632	0.343	0.686
9	CLERK	16	59	75	0.332	0.664
45	DYCD	103	471	574	0.295	0.590
33	NYCHA	1864	9098	10962	0.282	0.564
66	EEPC	2	10	12	0.282	0.564
40	NYCHH	6197	32534	38731	0.269	0.538
41	HRA	1823	11195	13018	0.241	0.482
70	DOP	152	1014	1166	0.226	0.452
69	DOC	1598	10698	12296	0.226	0.452
42	ACS	958	6408	7366	0.226	0.452
44	DHS	219	2219	2438	0.164	0.328
Average		2,051.02	3,507.60	5,558.63	0.427	0.854
Standard Deviation		9304.65	12606.85	21683.98	0.082	0.164
CV					0.192	0.192

Measurement of Ethnic Diversity

Exhibit 4-2 Continued

Case Number	Agency	Total White	Total Black	Total Hispanic	Total SOR	Total Asian	Total Employees	Simpson Coefficient (S_{EB2})	Standardized Simpson Coefficient (S_{SEB2})
62	CCHR	38	36	28	14	24	139	0.781	0.976
35	HPD	635	732	488	293	293	2441	0.774	0.967
33	NYCHA	1864	2521	2631	3398	548	10962	0.762	0.953
17	DCA	121	100	108	12	75	416	0.757	0.947
15	TLC	139	196	171	25	101	632	0.755	0.944
46	DFTA	91	108	59	13	55	326	0.750	0.937
4	BOE	258	267	133	142	33	833	0.745	0.932
2	DOITT	552	426	236	63	299	1576	0.744	0.931
18	SBS	87	99	57	6	51	301	0.742	0.927
51	DDC	429	308	188	27	389	1340	0.741	0.926
7	OPA	40	52	32	2	27	152	0.740	0.925
14	COMPTROLLER	282	204	110	24	165	784	0.738	0.923
8	NYCPPF	55	32	24	4	29	144	0.737	0.922
1	DCAS	691	839	592	74	271	2468	0.735	0.919
50	DOB	580	514	232	66	265	1657	0.735	0.918
43	DOHMH	1716	2860	1216	929	429	7150	0.733	0.916
23	MWFA	4	0	3	2	4	13	0.732	0.916
60	CCRB	81	49	39	18	16	203	0.732	0.915
6	TRS	129	98	38	14	70	349	0.731	0.914
28	BP-MAN	32	26	24	5	7	94	0.731	0.914
10	DORIS	30	16	13	3	11	73	0.727	0.909
13	DOF	610	799	273	63	357	2102	0.725	0.906
71	DOI	154	84	62	18	48	367	0.722	0.903
26	CFB	48	21	14	6	26	115	0.721	0.902
32	PUBADMIN	17	11	14	3	2	47	0.721	0.901

5	NYCERS	142	155	44	9	93	444	0.721	0.901
34	PARKS	2543	2180	1817	291	436	7267	0.720	0.900
66	EEPC	2	5	1	1	3	12	0.719	0.899
39	SCA	339	165	116	17	190	827	0.719	0.899
45	DYCD	103	247	126	34	63	574	0.719	0.898
31	PA	14	5	9	21	3	52	0.718	0.898
67	NYPD	20705	14550	14550	560	5596	55960	0.718	0.897
56	DA-BX	390	281	314	43	54	1082	0.715	0.893
3	MAYORALTY	559	254	191	51	216	1271	0.713	0.892
9	CLERK	16	13	32	1	13	75	0.713	0.891
63	BOC	10	11	6	1	2	30	0.708	0.886
19	BIC	36	13	17	2	12	80	0.704	0.881
24	COUNCIL	381	182	191	35	78	867	0.704	0.880
55	DA-BK	479	319	217	57	68	1140	0.703	0.879
38	DOE	76606	38303	38303	8705	12187	174105	0.702	0.878
25	BP-BK	38	51	19	14	2	124	0.701	0.876
40	NYCHH	6197	17042	7359	0	8134	38731	0.701	0.876
37	DCLA	32	12	0	20	10	74	0.697	0.871
49	DOT	2401	1715	915	57	629	5716	0.696	0.870
59	DA-NARC	103	41	32	19	19	215	0.695	0.869
29	BP-BX	22	18	42	10	0	93	0.688	0.860
11	FDNYPF	15	8	2	0	11	36	0.682	0.852
64	COIB	12	1	3	3	6	25	0.682	0.852
16	FISA	157	57	35	9	179	436	0.679	0.848
48	DEP	3046	1305	808	124	932	6216	0.676	0.845
53	LAW	894	533	247	57	171	1903	0.675	0.844
52	DCP	167	50	43	10	63	334	0.674	0.842
57	OATH	344	208	93	22	50	717	0.663	0.829
65	NYCCSC	6	6	2	0	1	15	0.658	0.823
58	DA-QNS	376	99	121	57	57	710	0.658	0.822

Measurement of Ethnic Diversity

21	NYCTAX	25	9	5	0	10	49	0.657	0.822
12	OCB	9	3	3	1	1	17	0.648	0.810
27	BP-QNS	60	15	13	10	11	109	0.645	0.807
72	NYCEM	111	32	26	14	18	202	0.642	0.803
47	DSNY	5270	2128	2128	203	405	10134	0.639	0.799
20	ACTUARY	26	5	3	1	16	51	0.630	0.787
54	DA-MAN	824	236	265	29	118	1472	0.622	0.777
41	HRA	1823	7420	2343	260	1172	13018	0.615	0.768
69	DOC	1598	7132	2705	246	615	12296	0.595	0.744
42	ACS	958	4567	1326	147	368	7366	0.563	0.704
44	DHS	219	1560	488	73	98	2438	0.540	0.675
70	DOP	152	746	210	23	35	1166	0.540	0.675
68	FDNY	11535	2307	3017	177	710	17746	0.530	0.663
22	IBO	24	4	3	1	4	36	0.520	0.650
36	LPC	58	7	6	7	5	83	0.487	0.609
61	DA-SI	122	14	20	9	5	170	0.457	0.572
30	BP-SI	41	5	3	4	0	53	0.389	0.486
	Average	2,051.02	1,589.10	1,180.61	231.42	506.48	5,558.63	0.683	0.853
	Standard Deviation	9304.65	5210.03	4824.12	1087.36	1798.49	21683.98	0.076	0.095
	CV							0.111	0.111

Exhibit 4-3 Descriptive statistics for biased Simpson (S$_{EB}$) ethnic diversity scores for NYC departments for fiscal year 2019

1. Descriptive statistics for biased Simpson scores

A. Measures of central tendency and variability for biased Simpson scores

Index	Cases (N)	Central Tendency		Variability		95% Confidence Interval	
		Median	Mean	Variance	Standard Deviation	Lower Limit	Upper Limit
S$_{EB1}$	72	0.455	0.427	0.007	0.082	0.408	0.446
S$_{EB2}$	72	0.706	0.683	0.006	0.076	0.665	0.701

B. Tests for normality, skewness, and kurtosis for biased Simpson scores

1. Shapiro-Wilk W test for normal data

Index	Cases (N)	W-statistic	V-statistic	z-statistic	Probability > z
S$_{EB1}$	72	0.818	11.465	5.313	0.0001
S$_{EB2}$	72	0.817	11.519	5.323	0.0001

2. Skewness/Kurtosis tests for Normality for biased Simpson scores

Index	Skewness	Probability of Skewness	Kurtosis	Probability of Kurtosis	Adjusted χ^2	Probability > χ^2
S$_{EB1}$	-1.397	0.0001	4.157	0.0547	16.63	0.0001
S$_{EB2}$	-1.757	0.0001	6.050	0.0013	25.37	0.0001

2. Descriptive statistics for biased standardized Simpson scores

A. Measures of central tendency and variability for biased standardized Simpson scores

Index	Cases (N)	Central Tendency		Variability		95% Confidence Interval	
		Median	Mean	Variance	Standard Deviation	Lower Limit	Upper Limit
S$_{SEB1}$	72	0.910	0.854	0.027	0.165	0.815	0.893
S$_{SEB2}$	72	0.883	0.853	0.009	0.095	0.831	0.876

Measurement of Ethnic Diversity

B. Tests for normality, skewness, and kurtosis for biased standardized Simpson scores

1. Shapiro-Wilk W test for normal data

Index	Cases (N)	W-statistic	V-statistic	z-statistic	Probability > z
S_{SEB1}	72	0.818	11.465	5.313	0.0001
S_{SEB2}	72	0.817	11.519	5.323	0.0001

2. Skewness/Kurtosis tests for Normality for biased standardized Simpson scores

Index	Skewness	Kurtosis	Probability of Skewness	Probability of Kurtosis	Adjusted χ^2	Probability > $\chi2$
S_{SEB1}	-1.397	4.157	0.0001	0.0547	16.63	0.0001
S_{SEB2}	-1.757	6.050	0.0001	0.0013	25.37	0.0001

In comparison to the S_{EB1} scores, the biased diversity scores based on the categorization of race into 5 groups (S_{EB2}) produces higher coefficients due to having more categories and having individuals spread across the 5 the categories (e.g., Guajardo, 2013). The median for the S_{EB2} scores is 0.7.06 with a mean of 0.683 and standard deviation of 0.076 (see Exhibit 4-3). The 95% CI ranges from 0.655 to 0.701. Similar to the S_{EB1} scores, the S_{EB2} scores are negatively skewed (Skewness = -1.757) and heavy tailed (Kurtosis = 6.050). The S_{EB2} scores also fail to meet the assumption of normality. Although the S_{EB2} scores are higher than the coefficients obtained for S_{EB1}, the distribution of the S_{EB2} scores has less variation (S_{B2} CV = 0.111; S_{B1} CV = 0.192) and is centered more closely around the mean; however, S_{EB2} measures the level of ethnic diversity in NYC departments more completely.

The statistical analysis for the standardized diversity scores shows that the distributions fail to meet the assumption of normality (see Exhibit 4-3). However, the standardized diversity scores (S_{SEB1}) for S_{EB1} attain a greater proportion of the EMV in comparison to the S_{SEB2} scores. The reason for the difference is that the EMV for S_{EB1} is 0.50, which is based on the categorization of race as White and minority, while the EMV for S_{EB2} is 0.80 and is based on the categorization of race into 5 ethnic groups. As Exhibit 4-.3 shows, the S_{SEB1} scores have a median of 0.910, a mean of 0.853, and a standard deviation of 0.165. The 95% CI ranges from 0.815 to 0.893.

Because the diversity scores for S_{EB2} are divided by an EMV of 0.800 and because the distribution of the S_{EB2} scores has less variation in comparison to S_{EB1}, the median and mean for S_{SEB2} are lower in comparison to S_{SEB1}. Specifically, S_{SEB2} has a median of 0.883, a mean of 0.853 with a standard deviation of 0.095 (see Exhibit 4-3), which indicates the standardized ethnic diversity scores are centered more closely around the mean in comparison to the S_{SEB1} scores. The 95% CI for the S_{SEB2} scores ranges from 0.831 to 0.876. Lastly, the distribution for the S_{SEB2} scores is more highly peaked (Kurtosis = 6.050) and negatively skewed (Skewness = -1.757) in comparison to the distribution of the S_{SEB1} scores.

Exhibit 4-4 presents the unbiased unstandardized (S_{EN}) and standardized (S_{SEN}) ethnic diversity scores for each NYC department for fiscal year 2019. The S_{EN1} index produces unbiased scores that exceed the EMV of 0.500. In fact, 13 NYC departments have S_{EN1} scores ranging from 0.500 to 0.541. Forty-three departments have S_{EN1} scores ranging from 0.400 to 0.499. Another 8 departments have diversity scores ranging from 0.340 to 0.399. ᑐHS has the lowest S_{EN1} score of 0.164.

Measurement of Ethnic Diversity

Exhibit 4-4 Unbiased Simpson (S$_{EN}$) ethnic diversity scores for NYC departments for fiscal year 2019

Case Number	Agency	Total White	Total Minority	Total Employees	Simpson Coefficient (S$_{EN1}$)	Standardized Simpson Coefficient (S$_{SEN1}$)
12	OCB	9	8	17	0.541	1.081
65	NYCCSC	6	9	15	0.536	1.071
64	COIB	12	13	25	0.530	1.060
21	NYCTAX	25	24	49	0.515	1.030
20	ACTUARY	26	25	51	0.514	1.029
11	FDNYPF	15	21	36	0.510	1.020
19	BIC	36	44	80	0.505	1.010
59	DA-NARC	103	112	215	0.503	1.006
52	DCP	167	167	334	0.502	1.004
27	BP-QNS	60	49	109	0.501	1.003
37	DCLA	32	42	74	0.501	1.002
57	OATH	344	373	717	0.500	1.001
48	DEP	3046	3170	6216	0.500	1.000
47	DSNY	5270	4864	10134	0.499	0.999
58	DA-QNS	376	334	710	0.499	0.998
53	LAW	894	1009	1903	0.499	0.997
72	NYCEM	111	91	202	0.498	0.997
23	MWFA	4	9	13	0.496	0.992
10	DORIS	30	43	73	0.495	0.990
26	CFB	48	67	115	0.494	0.989
24	COUNCIL	381	486	867	0.494	0.987
3	MAYORALTY	559	712	1271	0.493	0.987
54	DA-MAN	824	648	1472	0.493	0.987

Chapter 4

38	DOE	76606	97499	174105	0.493	0.986
71	DOI	154	213	367	0.489	0.979
55	DA-BK	479	661	1140	0.488	0.976
49	DOT	2401	3315	5716	0.487	0.975
39	SCA	339	488	827	0.485	0.970
60	CCRB	81	122	203	0.484	0.968
32	PUBADMIN	17	30	47	0.479	0.958
8	NYCPPF	55	89	144	0.477	0.954
63	BOC	10	20	30	0.472	0.943
6	TRS	129	220	349	0.469	0.937
67	NYPD	20705	35255	55960	0.466	0.932
16	FISA	157	279	436	0.463	0.926
14	COMPTROLLER	282	502	784	0.462	0.924
56	DA-BX	390	692	1082	0.462	0.923
28	BP-MAN	32	62	94	0.458	0.916
22	IBO	24	12	36	0.458	0.915
2	DOITT	552	1024	1576	0.456	0.911
50	DOB	580	1077	1657	0.456	0.911
34	PARKS	2543	4724	7267	0.455	0.910
68	FDNY	11535	6211	17746	0.455	0.910
5	NYCERS	142	302	444	0.437	0.874
51	DDC	429	911	1340	0.436	0.872
25	BP-BK	38	86	124	0.435	0.870
4	BOE	258	575	833	0.429	0.858
36	LPC	58	25	83	0.426	0.852
18	SBS	87	214	301	0.415	0.830
17	DCA	121	295	416	0.414	0.828
13	DOF	610	1492	2102	0.412	0.824

Measurement of Ethnic Diversity

31	PA	14	38	52	0.412	0.824
61	DA-SI	122	48	170	0.406	0.812
46	DFTA	91	235	326	0.406	0.812
1	DCAS	691	1777	2468	0.404	0.807
62	CCHR	38	101	139	0.401	0.802
7	OPA	40	112	152	0.391	0.782
35	HPD	635	1806	2441	0.385	0.770
29	BP-BX	22	71	93	0.375	0.750
43	DOHMH	1716	5434	7150	0.365	0.730
30	BP-SI	41	12	53	0.362	0.724
66	EEPC	2	10	12	0.360	0.720
15	TLC	139	493	632	0.345	0.689
9	CLERK	16	59	75	0.344	0.689
45	DYCD	103	471	574	0.297	0.594
33	NYCHA	1864	9098	10962	0.282	0.565
40	NYCHH	6197	32534	38731	0.269	0.538
41	HRA	1823	11195	13018	0.241	0.482
70	DOP	152	1014	1166	0.227	0.454
42	ACS	958	6408	7366	0.226	0.453
69	DOC	1598	10698	12296	0.226	0.453
44	DHS	219	2219	2438	0.164	0.328
Average		2,051.02	3,507.60	5,558.63	0.435	0.870
Standard Deviation		9304.65	12606.85	21683.98	0.084	0.167
Coefficient of Variation (CV)					0.192	0.192

Exhibit 4-4 Continued

Case Number	Agency	Total White	Total Black	Total Hispanic	Total SOR	Total Asian	Total Employees	Simpson Coefficient (S_{SEN2})	Standardized Simpson Coefficient (S_{SEN2})
23	MWFA	4	0	3	2	4	13	0.793	0.992
62	CCHR	38	36	28	14	24	139	0.786	0.983
66	EEPC	2	5	1	1	3	12	0.785	0.981
35	HPD	635	732	488	293	293	2441	0.774	0.967
33	NYCHA	1864	2521	2631	3398	548	10962	0.762	0.953
17	DCA	121	100	108	12	75	416	0.759	0.949
15	TLC	139	196	171	25	101	632	0.757	0.946
46	DFTA	91	108	59	13	55	326	0.752	0.940
4	BOE	258	267	133	142	33	833	0.746	0.933
7	OPA	40	52	32	2	27	152	0.745	0.931
2	DOITT	552	426	236	63	299	1576	0.745	0.931
18	SBS	87	99	57	6	51	301	0.744	0.930
8	NYCPPF	55	32	24	4	29	144	0.743	0.928
51	DDC	429	308	188	27	389	1340	0.741	0.926
14	COMPTROLLER	282	204	110	24	165	784	0.739	0.924
28	BP-MAN	32	26	24	5	7	94	0.739	0.924
10	DORIS	30	16	13	3	11	73	0.737	0.921
32	PUBADMIN	17	11	14	3	2	47	0.737	0.921
1	DCAS	691	839	592	74	271	2468	0.736	0.920
60	CCRB	81	49	39	18	16	203	0.735	0.919
50	DOB	580	514	232	66	265	1657	0.735	0.919
43	DOHMH	1716	2860	1216	929	429	7150	0.733	0.916
6	TRS	129	98	38	14	70	349	0.733	0.916
63	BOC	10	11	6	1	2	30	0.733	0.916
31	PA	14	5	9	21	3	52	0.732	0.916

Measurement of Ethnic Diversity

#	Agency								
26	CFB	48	21	14	6	26	115	0.728	0.910
13	DOF	610	799	273	63	357	2102	0.725	0.906
71	DOI	154	84	62	18	48	367	0.724	0.905
9	CLERK	16	13	32	1	13	75	0.722	0.903
5	NYCERS	142	155	44	9	93	444	0.722	0.903
34	PARKS	2543	2180	1817	291	436	7267	0.720	0.900
39	SCA	339	165	116	17	190	827	0.720	0.900
45	DYCD	103	247	126	34	63	574	0.720	0.900
67	NYPD	20705	14550	14550	560	5596	55960	0.718	0.897
56	DA-BX	390	281	314	43	54	1082	0.715	0.894
3	MAYORALTY	559	254	191	51	216	1271	0.714	0.892
19	BIC	36	13	17	2	12	80	0.713	0.892
64	COIB	12	1	3	3	6	25	0.710	0.888
37	DCLA	32	12	0	20	10	74	0.707	0.883
25	BP-BK	38	51	19	14	2	124	0.706	0.883
65	NYCCSC	6	6	2	0	1	15	0.705	0.882
24	COUNCIL	381	182	191	35	78	867	0.705	0.881
55	DA-BK	479	319	217	57	68	1140	0.704	0.880
38	DOE	76606	38303	38303	8705	12187	174105	0.702	0.878
11	FDNYPF	15	8	2	0	11	36	0.701	0.876
40	NYCHH	6197	17042	7359	0	8134	38731	0.701	0.876
59	DA-NARC	103	41	32	19	19	215	0.698	0.873
49	DOT	2401	1715	915	57	629	5716	0.696	0.870
29	BP-BX	22	18	42	10	0	93	0.696	0.870
12	OCB	9	3	3	1	1	17	0.689	0.861
16	FISA	157	57	35	9	179	436	0.680	0.850
48	DEP	3046	1305	808	124	932	6216	0.676	0.845
52	DCP	167	50	43	10	63	334	0.676	0.845
53	LAW	894	533	247	57	171	1903	0.675	0.844
21	NYCTAX	25	9	5	0	10	49	0.671	0.839

57	OATH	344	208	93	22	50	717	0.664	0.830
58	DA-QNS	376	99	121	57	57	710	0.659	0.823
27	BP-QNS	60	15	13	10	11	109	0.651	0.814
72	NYCEM	111	32	26	14	18	202	0.645	0.806
20	ACTUARY	26	5	3	1	16	51	0.642	0.803
47	DSNY	5270	2128	2128	203	405	10134	0.639	0.799
54	DA-MAN	824	236	265	29	118	1472	0.622	0.778
41	HRA	1823	7420	2343	260	1172	13018	0.615	0.768
69	DOC	1598	7132	2705	246	615	12296	0.595	0.744
42	ACS	958	4567	1326	147	368	7366	0.563	0.704
70	DOP	152	746	210	23	35	1166	0.540	0.675
44	DHS	219	1560	488	73	98	2438	0.540	0.675
22	IBO	24	4	3	1	4	36	0.534	0.668
68	FDNY	11535	2307	3017	177	710	17746	0.530	0.663
36	LPC	58	7	6	7	5	83	0.493	0.616
61	DA-SI	122	14	20	9	5	170	0.460	0.575
30	BP-SI	41	5	3	4	0	53	0.396	0.496
	Average	2,051.02	1,589.10	1,180.61	231.42	506.48	5,558.63	0.690	0.862
	Standard Deviation	9,304.65	5,210.03	4,824.12	1,087.36	1,798.49	21,683.98	0.077	0.096
	Coefficient of Variation (CV)			0.112				0.112	0.112

When S_{EN1} scores are standardized (S_{SEN1}), NYC departments with S_{EN1} scores exceeding the EMV of 0.500 attain over 100% of the proportion (see Exhibit 4-4). Departments with S_{EN1} scores ranging between 0.400 to 0.499 attain 90% to 99% of the EMV of 0.500, respectively. Thirteen departments attain at least 80% of the EMV of 0.500. DHS with the lowest S_{EN1} score of 0.164 attains 33% of the EMV.

As Exhibit 4-4 summarizes, 46 departments have unstandardized unbiased S_{EN2} scores ranging from 0.701 to 0.793, which are lower than the EMV of 0.80. Another 17 departments have S_{EN2} scores ranging from 0.600 to 0.699. Nine departments have S_{EN2} scores ranging from 0.396 to 0.599. The Office of the Borough President of Staten Island (BP-SI) has the lowest S_{EN2} score of 0.396.

None of the NYC departments attained an EMV of 0.80 (see Exhibit 4-4). Thirty-three departments have S_{EN2} scores than attain at least 90% of the EMV of 0.80. For instance, MFA with a S_{EN2} score of 0.793 attained 99% of the EMV. Another 27 departments have S_{EN2} scores than attain between 80% to 89% of the EMV of 0.80. The remaining departments have S_{EN2} scores that attain between 49% to 79% of the EMV of 0.80.

The descriptive statistical analysis for the unbiased unstandardized (S_{EN}) and standardized (S_{SEN}) diversity scores for NYC departments for fiscal 2019 is presented in Exhibit 4-5. For the S_{EN1} scores based on the categorization of race as White or minority, the median is 0.462 and the mean is 0.435 with a standard deviation of 0.084. The 95% CI ranges from 0.415 to 0.455. The tests for normality indicate that the distribution of S_{EN1} scores is negatively skewed (Skewness = -1.383) and heavy tailed (Kurtosis = 4.301) and fails to meet the assumption of normality.

When race is categorized into 5 ethnic groups and S_{EN2} scores are calculated, a median score of 0.714 is attained with a mean of 0.690 and standard deviation of 0.078 (see Exhibit 4-5). The 95% CI ranges from 0.671 to 0.708. The distribution of the S_{EN2} scores is negatively skewed (Skewness = -1.711), peaked (Kurtosis = 5.863), and fails to meet the assumption of normality. When compared to the variability of the set of S_{EN1} scores (CV = 0.192), the set of S_{EN2} scores are less dispersed (CV = 0.112) and are centered more tightly around the mean.

Exhibit 4-5 Descriptive statistics for unbiased Simpson (S_N) ethnic diversity scores for NYC departments for fiscal year 2019

1. Descriptive statistics for unbiased Simpson scores

A. Measures of central tendency and variability for unbiased Simpson scores

Index	Cases (N)	Central Tendency		Variability		95% Confidence Interval	
		Median	Mean	Variance	Standard Deviation	Lower Limit	Upper Limit
S_{EN1}	72	0.462	0.435	0.007	0.084	0.415	0.455
S_{EN2}	72	0.714	0.690	0.006	0.078	0.671	0.708

B. Tests for normality, skewness, and kurtosis for unbiased Simpson scores

1. Shapiro-Wilk W test for normal data

Index	Cases (N)	W-statistic	V-statistic	z-statistic	Probability > z
S_{EN1}	72	0.846	9.710	4.951	0.0001
S_{EN2}	72	0.822	11.226	5.267	0.0001

2. Skewness/Kurtosis tests for Normality for unbiased Simpson scores

Index	Skewness	Kurtosis	Probability of Skewness	Probability of Kurtosis	Adjusted χ^2	Probability > χ^2
S_{EN1}	-1.383	4.301	0.0001	0.040	16.83	0.0001
S_{EN2}	-1.711	5.863	0.0001	0.002	24.44	0.0001

2. Descriptive statistics for unbiased standardized Simpson scores

A. Measures of central tendency and variability for unbiased standardized Simpson scores

Index	Cases (N)	Central Tendency		Variability		95% Confidence Interval	
		Median	Mean	Variance	Standard Deviation	Lower Limit	Upper Limit
S_{SEN1}	72	0.924	0.870	0.028	0.168	0.831	0.910
S_{SEN2}	72	0.892	0.862	0.009	0.097	0.839	0.885

Measurement of Ethnic Diversity

B. Tests for normality, skewness, and kurtosis for unbiased standardized Simpson scores

1. Shapiro-Wilk W test for normal data

Index	Cases (N)	W-statistic	V-statistic	z-statistic	Probability > z
S_{SEN1}	72	4.301	0.0001	0.040	16.83
S_{SEN2}	72	5.863	0.0001	0.002	24.44

2. Skewness/Kurtosis tests for Normality for unbiased standardized Simpson scores

Index	Skewness	Kurtosis	Probability of Skewness	Probability of Kurtosis	Adjusted χ^2	Probability > χ^2
S_{SEN1}	-1.383	4.301	0.0001	0.040	16.83	0.0001
S_{SEN2}	-1.711	5.863	0.0001	0.002	24.44	0.0001

The descriptive statistical analysis of the standardized unbiased (S_{SEN1} and S_{SEN2}) ethnic diversity scores also shows that the distributions fail to meet the assumption of normality because of negative skewness and peakedness (see Exhibit 4-5). For the categorization of race as White or minority, S_{SEN1} has a median of 0.924, a mean of 0.870, and a standard deviation of 0.168. The 95% CI ranges from 0.831 to 0.910. Similar to the biased (S_{EB}) ethnic diversity scores presented above, the distribution of scores is negatively skewed (Skewness = -1.383) and peaked (Kurtosis = 4.301). The tests for normality also show that the distributions of the scores fail to meet the assumption of normality.

The standardized unbiased ethnic diversity scores based on the categorization of race into 5 ethnic groups (S_{SEN2}) are lower on average than those calculated for S_{SEN1} because they are divided by an EMV of 0.80; S_{SEN1} scores are divided by an EMV of 0.50. As shown in Exhibit 4-5, S_{SEN2} has a median of 0.892, a mean of 0.862, and a standard deviation of 0.097. The 95% CI ranges from 0.839 to 0.885. Compared to the distribution of S_{SEN1} scores, S_{SEN2} has a greater degree of negative skewness (Skewness = -1.711), compactness (Kurtosis = 5.863), and fails to meet the assumption of normality.

Comparison of biased and unbiased ethnic diversity scores

The number of groups formed to categorize ethnicity (or race) increases or decreases diversity scores obtained by the Simpson index (e.g., Guajardo, 2013). Similarly, the formula used to calculate Simpson diversity scores also increases or decreases the coefficients. As presented in Exhibit 4-2 and 4-4, the Simpson ethnic diversity scores increase when the number of categories increased from 2 to 5 and when the formula to adjust for total group size is used. Exhibit 4-6 presents a pairwise comparison of the biased (S_{EB}) and unbiased (S_{EN}) Simpson ethnic diversity scores obtained for each NYC department for fiscal year 2019.

Measurement of Ethnic Diversity

Exhibit 4-6 Comparison of biased (S_{EB}) and unbiased (S_{EN}) Simpson ethnicity diversity scores for NYC departments for fiscal year 2019

Case Number	Agency	Biased Simpson Coefficient (S_{EB1})	Biased Simpson Coefficient (S_{EB2})	Difference ($S_{EB2} - S_{EB1}$)	Standardized Simpson Coefficient (S_{SEB1})	Standardized Simpson Coefficient (S_{SEB2})	Difference ($S_{SEB2} - S_{SEB1}$)
33	NYCHA	0.282	0.762	0.480	0.564	0.953	0.388
66	EEPC	0.282	0.719	0.437	0.564	0.899	0.335
40	NYCHH	0.269	0.701	0.432	0.538	0.876	0.338
45	DYCD	0.295	0.719	0.423	0.590	0.898	0.308
15	TLC	0.343	0.755	0.412	0.686	0.944	0.258
35	HPD	0.385	0.774	0.389	0.770	0.967	0.197
62	CCHR	0.394	0.781	0.386	0.788	0.976	0.187
9	CLERK	0.332	0.713	0.381	0.664	0.891	0.227
44	DHS	0.164	0.540	0.376	0.328	0.675	0.347
41	HRA	0.241	0.615	0.374	0.482	0.768	0.287
69	DOC	0.226	0.595	0.369	0.452	0.744	0.292
43	DOHMH	0.365	0.733	0.368	0.730	0.916	0.187
7	OPA	0.385	0.740	0.355	0.770	0.925	0.156
46	DFTA	0.403	0.750	0.347	0.806	0.937	0.131
17	DCA	0.412	0.757	0.346	0.824	0.947	0.123
42	ACS	0.226	0.563	0.337	0.452	0.704	0.252
1	DCAS	0.403	0.735	0.332	0.806	0.919	0.113
18	SBS	0.412	0.742	0.330	0.824	0.927	0.103
31	PA	0.394	0.718	0.324	0.788	0.898	0.110
29	BP-BX	0.365	0.688	0.323	0.730	0.860	0.131
4	BOE	0.428	0.745	0.318	0.856	0.932	0.076

70	DOP	0.226	0.540	0.314	0.452	0.675	0.222
13	DOF	0.412	0.725	0.313	0.824	0.906	0.082
51	DDC	0.435	0.741	0.305	0.870	0.926	0.055
23	MWFA	0.428	0.732	0.305	0.856	0.916	0.060
2	DOITT	0.455	0.744	0.289	0.910	0.931	0.020
5	NYCERS	0.435	0.721	0.285	0.870	0.901	0.030
28	BP-MAN	0.449	0.731	0.282	0.898	0.914	0.016
50	DOB	0.455	0.735	0.280	0.910	0.918	0.008
14	COMPTROLLER	0.461	0.738	0.277	0.922	0.923	0.001
25	BP-BK	0.428	0.701	0.273	0.856	0.876	0.020
63	BOC	0.442	0.708	0.266	0.884	0.886	0.001
8	NYCPPF	0.471	0.737	0.266	0.942	0.922	-0.021
6	TRS	0.466	0.731	0.265	0.932	0.914	-0.019
34	PARKS	0.455	0.720	0.265	0.910	0.900	-0.010
32	PUBADMIN	0.461	0.721	0.260	0.922	0.901	-0.020
56	DA-BX	0.461	0.715	0.254	0.922	0.893	-0.028
60	CCRB	0.480	0.732	0.252	0.960	0.915	-0.045
67	NYPD	0.466	0.718	0.252	0.932	0.897	-0.035
10	DORIS	0.484	0.727	0.243	0.968	0.909	-0.059
71	DOI	0.487	0.722	0.235	0.974	0.903	-0.071
39	SCA	0.484	0.719	0.235	0.968	0.899	-0.069
26	CFB	0.487	0.721	0.234	0.974	0.902	-0.073
3	MAYORALTY	0.493	0.713	0.221	0.986	0.892	-0.094
16	FISA	0.461	0.679	0.218	0.922	0.848	-0.073
55	DA-BK	0.487	0.703	0.216	0.974	0.879	-0.096
24	COUNCIL	0.493	0.704	0.211	0.986	0.880	-0.105
19	BIC	0.495	0.704	0.209	0.990	0.881	-0.110
38	DOE	0.493	0.702	0.209	0.986	0.878	-0.108

Measurement of Ethnic Diversity

49	DOT	0.487	0.696	0.209	0.974	0.870	-0.105
37	DCLA	0.490	0.697	0.207	0.980	0.871	-0.109
59	DA-NARC	0.499	0.695	0.196	0.998	0.869	-0.130
11	FDNYPF	0.487	0.682	0.194	0.974	0.852	-0.122
64	COIB	0.499	0.682	0.182	0.998	0.852	-0.146
65	NYCCSC	0.480	0.658	0.178	0.960	0.823	-0.137
53	LAW	0.498	0.675	0.177	0.996	0.844	-0.153
48	DEP	0.500	0.676	0.176	1.000	0.845	-0.155
52	DCP	0.500	0.674	0.174	1.000	0.842	-0.158
57	OATH	0.499	0.663	0.164	0.998	0.829	-0.170
58	DA-QNS	0.498	0.658	0.160	0.996	0.822	-0.174
21	NYCTAX	0.500	0.657	0.158	1.000	0.822	-0.178
27	BP-QNS	0.495	0.645	0.150	0.990	0.807	-0.183
12	OCB	0.498	0.648	0.150	0.996	0.810	-0.186
72	NYCEM	0.495	0.642	0.147	0.990	0.803	-0.188
47	DSNY	0.499	0.639	0.140	0.998	0.799	-0.199
20	ACTUARY	0.500	0.630	0.130	1.000	0.787	-0.212
54	DA-MAN	0.493	0.622	0.129	0.986	0.777	-0.209
22	IBO	0.442	0.520	0.077	0.884	0.650	-0.235
68	FDNY	0.455	0.530	0.075	0.910	0.663	-0.248
36	LPC	0.420	0.487	0.067	0.840	0.609	-0.231
61	DA-SI	0.403	0.457	0.054	0.806	0.572	-0.235
30	BP-SI	0.354	0.389	0.035	0.708	0.486	-0.222
Average		0.427	0.683	0.256	0.854	0.853	-0.001
Standard Deviation		0.082	0.076	0.098	0.164	0.095	0.170
CV		0.192	0.111		0.192	0.111	

Exhibit 4-6 Continued

Case Number	Agency	Unbiased Simpson Coefficient (S_{N1})	Unbiased Simpson Coefficient (S_{N2})	Difference ($S_{N2} - S_{N1}$)	Standardized Simpson Coefficient (S_{SN1})	Standardized Simpson Coefficient (S_{SN2})	Difference ($S_{SN2} - S_{SN1}$)
23	MWFA	0.496	0.793	0.297	0.992	0.992	-0.001
62	CCHR	0.401	0.786	0.385	0.802	0.983	0.181
66	EEPC	0.360	0.785	0.425	0.720	0.981	0.261
35	HPD	0.385	0.774	0.389	0.770	0.967	0.197
33	NYCHA	0.282	0.762	0.480	0.565	0.953	0.388
17	DCA	0.414	0.759	0.345	0.828	0.949	0.121
15	TLC	0.345	0.757	0.412	0.689	0.946	0.256
46	DFTA	0.406	0.752	0.346	0.812	0.940	0.128
4	BOE	0.429	0.746	0.317	0.858	0.933	0.075
7	OPA	0.391	0.745	0.354	0.782	0.931	0.150
2	DOITT	0.456	0.745	0.289	0.911	0.931	0.020
18	SBS	0.415	0.744	0.329	0.830	0.930	0.100
8	NYCPPF	0.477	0.743	0.265	0.954	0.928	-0.026
51	DDC	0.436	0.741	0.305	0.872	0.926	0.055
14	COMPTROLLER	0.462	0.739	0.277	0.924	0.924	0.000
28	BP-MAN	0.458	0.739	0.281	0.916	0.924	0.007
10	DORIS	0.495	0.737	0.242	0.990	0.921	-0.069
32	PUBADMIN	0.479	0.737	0.257	0.958	0.921	-0.038
1	DCAS	0.404	0.736	0.332	0.807	0.920	0.112
60	CCRB	0.484	0.735	0.251	0.968	0.919	-0.049
50	DOB	0.456	0.735	0.280	0.911	0.919	0.008
43	DOHMH	0.365	0.733	0.368	0.730	0.916	0.187
6	TRS	0.469	0.733	0.264	0.937	0.916	-0.021

Measurement of Ethnic Diversity

63	BOC	0.472	0.733	0.261	0.943	0.916	-0.027
31	PA	0.412	0.732	0.321	0.824	0.916	0.092
26	CFB	0.494	0.728	0.233	0.989	0.910	-0.079
13	DOF	0.412	0.725	0.313	0.824	0.906	0.082
71	DOI	0.489	0.724	0.235	0.979	0.905	-0.073
9	CLERK	0.344	0.722	0.378	0.689	0.903	0.214
5	NYCERS	0.437	0.722	0.285	0.874	0.903	0.028
34	PARKS	0.455	0.720	0.265	0.910	0.900	-0.010
39	SCA	0.485	0.720	0.235	0.970	0.900	-0.070
45	DYCD	0.297	0.720	0.423	0.594	0.900	0.306
67	NYPD	0.466	0.718	0.252	0.932	0.897	-0.035
56	DA-BX	0.462	0.715	0.254	0.923	0.894	-0.029
3	MAYORALTY	0.493	0.714	0.221	0.987	0.892	-0.094
19	BIC	0.505	0.713	0.208	1.010	0.892	-0.118
64	COIB	0.530	0.710	0.180	1.060	0.888	-0.173
37	DCLA	0.501	0.707	0.205	1.002	0.883	-0.119
25	BP-BK	0.435	0.706	0.271	0.870	0.883	0.013
65	NYCCSC	0.536	0.705	0.170	1.071	0.882	-0.190
24	COUNCIL	0.494	0.705	0.211	0.987	0.881	-0.106
55	DA-BK	0.488	0.704	0.216	0.976	0.880	-0.096
38	DOE	0.493	0.702	0.209	0.986	0.878	-0.108
11	FDNYPF	0.510	0.701	0.191	1.020	0.876	-0.144
40	NYCHH	0.269	0.701	0.432	0.538	0.876	0.338
59	DA-NARC	0.503	0.698	0.195	1.006	0.873	-0.133
49	DOT	0.487	0.696	0.209	0.975	0.870	-0.105
29	BP-BX	0.375	0.696	0.321	0.750	0.870	0.120
12	OCB	0.541	0.689	0.148	1.081	0.861	-0.221
16	FISA	0.463	0.680	0.217	0.926	0.850	-0.075
48	DEP	0.500	0.676	0.176	1.000	0.845	-0.155

52	DCP	0.502	0.676	0.173	1.004	0.845	-0.160
53	LAW	0.499	0.675	0.177	0.997	0.844	-0.153
21	NYCTAX	0.515	0.671	0.156	1.030	0.839	-0.191
57	OATH	0.500	0.664	0.163	1.001	0.830	-0.171
58	DA-QNS	0.499	0.659	0.160	0.998	0.823	-0.175
27	BP-QNS	0.501	0.651	0.150	1.003	0.814	-0.189
72	NYCEM	0.498	0.645	0.147	0.997	0.806	-0.190
20	ACTUARY	0.514	0.642	0.128	1.029	0.803	-0.226
47	DSNY	0.499	0.639	0.140	0.999	0.799	-0.199
54	DA-MAN	0.493	0.622	0.129	0.987	0.778	-0.209
41	HRA	0.241	0.615	0.374	0.482	0.768	0.287
69	DOC	0.226	0.595	0.369	0.453	0.744	0.292
42	ACS	0.226	0.563	0.337	0.453	0.704	0.252
70	DOP	0.227	0.540	0.313	0.454	0.675	0.221
44	DHS	0.164	0.540	0.376	0.328	0.675	0.347
22	IBO	0.458	0.534	0.077	0.915	0.668	-0.247
68	FDNY	0.455	0.530	0.075	0.910	0.663	-0.248
36	LPC	0.426	0.493	0.067	0.852	0.616	-0.236
61	DA-SI	0.406	0.460	0.054	0.812	0.575	-0.237
30	BP-SI	0.362	0.396	0.035	0.724	0.496	-0.228
Average		0.435	0.690	0.255	0.87	0.86	-0.008
Standard Deviation		0.084	0.077	0.098	0.17	0.096	0.170
CV		0.192	0.112		0.192	0.112	

As Exhibit 4-6 shows, the Simpson ethnic diversity scores increase significantly when ethnicity (or race) is categorized into 5 groups (S_{EB2}) instead of 2 (S_{EB1}). For instance, The S_{EB1} score for NYCHA is 0.282 with a S_{EB2} score of 0.762, representing an increase of 0.48 points. EEPC has a S_{EB1} score of 0.282 and a S_{EB2} score of 0.719, a difference of 0.437 points. However, when the standardized unbiased (S_{SEB1} and S_{SEB2}) ethnic diversity scores are compared, the scores either increase or decrease due to the increase in the number of ethnic groups and due to dividing the S_{SEB2} scores by the EMV of 0.80. For instance, NYCHA has a S_{SEB1} score of 0.564 and a S_{SEB2} score of 0.973, a difference of 0.388 points. By contrast, FDNY has a S_{SEB1} score of 0.910 and a S_{SEB2} score of 0.663, a difference of -0.248 points.

The unbiased (S_{EN}) ethnic diversity scores also increase when ethnicity or race is categorized into 5 groups (S_{EN2}) instead of 2 (S_{EN1}). For instance, NYCHA has a S_{EN1} score of 0.282 and a S_{EN2} score of 0.762, an increase of 0.480 points; NYCHH has a S_{EN1} score of 0.269 and a S_{EN2} score of 0.701, an increase of 0.432 points (see Exhibit 4-6). In addition, the ethnic diversity score of the NYC department with the lowest S_{EN1} score of 0.164 increases to a S_{EN2} score of 0.540 when race was categorized into 5 groups. Although the expansion of the ethnic (or racial) data from 2 to 5 categories increased the diversity scores, the distribution of S_{EN2} scores becomes more compact in comparison to the distribution of the S_{EN1} scores, which suggests an over correction of measurement bias.

When the standardized unbiased (S_{SEN1} and S_{SEN2}) ethnic diversity scores are compared, the scores either increased or decreased due to the increase in the number of ethnic groups and due to dividing the S_{SEN2} scores by the EMV of 0.80. For instance, OCB has a S_{SEN1} score of 1.081 and a S_{SEB2} score of 0.861, a difference of -0.221 points (see Exhibit 4-6). Similarly, NYCCSC has a S_{SEN1} score of 1.071 and a S_{SEB2} score of 0.882, a difference of -0.190 points. By contrast, DHS has a S_{SEB1} score of 0.328 and a S_{SEB2} score of 0.675, a difference of 0.347 points.

The findings of the 6 paired z-tests for equality of means (H_O: $\mu_1 = \mu_2$) are presented in Exhibit 4-7. The *planned pairwise comparisons* are the following:

1. The mean of S_{EB2} equals the mean of S_{EB1} (H_{O1}: $\mu_{SEB2} = \mu_{SEB1}$) at $\alpha = .01$;
2. The mean of S_{SEB2} equals the mean of S_{SEB1} (H_{O2}: $\mu_{SSEB2} = \mu_{SSEB1}$) at $\alpha = .01$;

3. The mean of S_{EN2} equals the mean of S_{EN1} (H_{O3}: $\mu_{SEN2} = \mu_{SEN1}$) at α = .01;

4. The mean of S_{SEN2} equals the mean of S_{SEN1} (H_{O4}: $\mu_{SSEN2} = \mu_{SSEN1}$) at α = .01;

5. The mean of S_{EN2} equals the mean of S_{EB2} (H_{O5}: $\mu_{SEN2} = \mu_{SEB2}$) at α = .01;

6. The mean of S_{SEN2} equals the mean of S_{SEB1} (H_{O6}: $\mu_{SSEN2} = \mu_{SSEB1}$) at α = .01;

The reason for conducting the planned comparisons is to assess whether the unbiased ethnic diversity scores (S_{EN1} and S_{EN2}) are statistically higher in comparison to their respective biased scores (S_{EB1} and S_{EB2}).

As Exhibit 4.7 shows, S_{EB2} produces biased ethnic diversity scores that are statistically higher in comparison to those produced by S_{EB1} at α = 0.01 (z-statistic = 22.131, p < 0.001), which is due to increasing the number of ethnic or racial groups from 2 to 5. However, the standardized scores for S_{SEB2} and S_{EB2} are statistically equal at α = 0.01 (z-statistic = -0.0397, p = 0.968), which indicates that both sets of biased scores attain the same proportion of their respective EMV. When the means of the unbiased (S_{EN1}) and biased (S_{EB1}) score are compared, the statistical findings show that the scores of S_{EN1} are statistically higher than those produced by S_{EB1} at α = 0.01 (z-statistic = 4.535, p < 0.001), which indicates that S_{EN1} corrects for measurement bias associated with total employment of each NYC department. Similar results are obtained for the comparison of standardized scores for S_{SEN1} and S_{SEB1} at α = 0.01 (z-statistic = 4.535, p < 0.001); however, S_{SEN1} attains a higher proportion of the EMV in comparison to S_{SEB1}. The finding for the planned comparison for S_{EN2} and S_{EB2} shows that the scores of S_{EN2} are statistically higher than those produced by S_{EB2} at α = 0.01 (z-statistic = 4.540, p < 0.001), which indicates that S_{EN2} corrects for measurement bias associated with total employment of each NYC department when ethnicity is categorized into 5 groups. Lastly, the findings show that the standardized scores for S_{SEN2} are statistically higher than the S_{SEB2} scores at α = 0.01 (z-statistic = 95.119, p < 0.001), which indicates S_{SEN2} attains a higher proportion of the EMV in comparison to S_{SEB2}.

Exhibit 4-7 Paired z-test for equal means for biased (S$_{EB}$) and unbiased (S$_{EN}$) Simpson ethnic diversity scores for NYC departments for fiscal year 2019

Planned Comparisons	Cases (N)	H$_o$	Mean Difference	Standard Error	Standard Deviation	95% CI		z-statistic	Probability ($|Z| > |z|$)
						Lower Limit	Upper Limit		
1	72	$\mu_{EB2} = \mu_{EB1}$	0.256	0.012	0.098	0.233	0.278	22.131	0.0001
2	72	$\mu_{SEB2} = \mu_{SEB1}$	-0.001	0.020	0.170	-0.040	0.038	-0.0397	0.9683
3	72	$\mu_{EN1} = \mu_{EB1}$	0.008	0.002	0.015	0.005	0.011	4.535	0.0001
4	72	$\mu_{SEN1} = \mu_{SEB1}$	0.016	0.004	0.030	0.009	0.023	4.535	0.0001
5	72	$\mu_{EN2} = \mu_{EB2}$	0.007	0.002	0.013	0.004	0.010	4.540	0.0001
6	72	$\mu_{SEN2} = \mu_{SEB2}$	0.179	0.002	0.016	0.176	0.183	95.119	0.0001

Correlation and factor analysis of biased and unbiased ethnic diversity scores

Although the sets of ethnic diversity scores of S_{EB} and S_{EN} differ statistically, the pairwise z-tests do not reveal how closely the coefficients are correlated with each other. A *Pearson correlation analysis* is undertaken to assess whether the sets are diversity coefficients are associated statistically with each other and whether the association is positive since the S_{EN} scores are higher than the S_{EB} scores. Each *pairwise correlation* is tested for statistical significance at $\alpha = 0.01$ (H_O: $r_{xy} = 0$ at $\alpha = 0.01$). Exhibit 4-8 summarizes the statistical findings of the pairwise *correlational analysis* performed on the biased (S_{EB}) and unbiased (S_{EN}) Simpson ethnic diversity scores.

Exhibit 4-8 Pearson correlation analysis of biased (S_{EB}) and unbiased (S_{EN}) Simpson ethnic diversity scores for NYC departments for fiscal year 2019

	Biased Simpson Scores		Unbiased Simpson Scores	
	S_{EB1}	S_{EB2}	S_{EN1}	S_{EN2}
S_{EB1}	1.000			
S_{EB2}	0.224	1.000		
S_{EN1}	0.984 *	0.224	1.000	
S_{EN2}	0.228	0.986 *	0.257	1.000

N= 72
* P < 0.01

The correlational analysis shows that the scores for S_{EB1} and S_{EB2} are not associated statistically with each other at $\alpha = 0.01$ ($r = 0.224$, $p > 0.05$), indicating the absence of a significant statistical relationship amongst the 2 sets of scores (see Exhibit 4-8). The reason for the lack of a significant relationship amongst S_{EB1} and S_{eB2} is that scores for S_{EB1} are based on the categorization of ethnicity (or race) into White and minority while the scores for S_{EB2} are based on the categorization of ethnicity into 5 groups. The pairwise Pearson correlation for S_{EB1} and S_{EN1} is statistically significant at $\alpha = 0.01$ ($r = 0.984$, $p < 0.01$), showing that the sets of scores are similar and vary in the same direction. The significant relationship amongst the S_{EB1} and S_{EN1} is due to the scores being calculated on the ethnic data categorized into White and minority. Exhibit 4-8 also shows an insignificant statistical relationship amongst the scores for S_{EB1} and S_{EN1} at $\alpha = 0.01$ ($r = 0.228$, $p > 0.05$), which is due to the diversity coefficients being calculated on 2 different categorizations of the ethnic data. A significant statistical relationship exists amongst the S_{EB2} and S_{EN2} scores at $\alpha = 0.01$ ($r = 0.986$, $p < 0.01$), indicating that the scores are related positively.

The correlation analysis suggests that the S_{EB} and S_{EN} scores have different underlying structures that assess different dimensions of ethnic diversity. A factor analysis (FA) is used to determine whether the 2 different ways NYC departments report the ethnic composition of their workforce effects the structure of the scores generated by the S_{EB} and S_{EN} formulas (see Exhibit 4-9). Specifically, a FA analysis with principal component analysis (PCA) extraction is used for the index validation process because an a priori theory (or model) regarding the Simpson index is lacking (see Williams, Onsman, and Brown, 2010). The use of PCA extraction also helps to establish a preliminary FA solution (see Pett, Lackey, and Sullivan, 2003). Because the Pearson correlation analysis above shows that the S_{EB} and S_{EN} scores are correlated statistically, direct *oblimin oblique* rotation is used to obtain a pattern matrix containing the factors and their item loadings and a factor correlation matrix containing the correlations coefficients amongst the factors (see Yong and Pearce, 2013).

Exhibit 4-9 Factor analysis (FA) of biased (S_{EB}) and unbiased (S_{EN}) Simpson ethnic diversity scores for NYC departments for fiscal year 2019

A. Unrotated principal-component factors (N = 72)

Factor	Eigenvalue	Difference	Proportion	Cumulative
Factor 1	2.452	0.934	0.61	0.61
Factor 2	1.518	1.489	0.38	0.99
Factor 3	0.030	0.030	0.01	1.00
Factor 4	0.000		0.00	1.00

B. Unrotated factor loading and uniqueness variance

Variable	Factor 1	Factor 2	Uniqueness
S_{EB1}	0.777	0.623	0.008
S_{EB2}	0.778	-0.623	0.007
S_{EN1}	0.787	0.611	0.008
S_{EN2}	0.789	-0.608	0.007

B. Oblique oblimin rotated factor loading and uniqueness variance

Variable	Factor 1	Factor 2	Uniqueness
S_{EB2}	0.999	-0.010	0.007
S_{EN2}	0.994	0.010	0.007
S_{EN1}	0.008	0.994	0.008
S_{EB1}	-0.008	0.998	0.008

The findings of the FA analyses for the S_{EB} and S_{EN} ethnic diversity scores of each NYC department for fiscal 2019 are summarized in Exhibit 4-9. The FA analysis with PCA extraction and oblimin oblique rotation extracted 2 factors which account for 99% of the variance. Factor 1 has an *eigenvalue* of 2.452 and accounts for 61% of the variance. The second factor has an eigenvalue of 1.518 and accounts for 38% of the variance.

The pattern matrix obtained by the oblimin oblique rotation grouped the S_{EB} and S_{EN} scores into 1 of 2 factors (see Exhibit 4-9). Factor 1 is composed of S_{EB2} and S_{EN2}. For factor 1, S_{B2} has a factor loading of 0.999, and S_{EN2} has a factor loading of 0.994. Factor 2 is composed of S_{EN2} and S_{SB1}. For factor 2, S_{EN1} has a factor loading of 0.994, and S_{EB1} has a factor loading of 0.998. Because the diversity scores for S_{EB2} and S_{EN2} are based on the categorization of ethnicity or race into 5 groups, the coefficients have similar structures and values that assess the same dimension of ethnic diversity. Similarly, the structure and values of the S_{EN1} and S_{EB1} are similar and assess the same dimension of ethnic diversity when the ethnic data are categorized into White and minority. Stated differently, when ethnic data for persons of color are aggregated into 1 category, the structure of the Simpson index is changed so that the scores do not capture the scope of diversity that exists within and across NYC departments. In sum, the FA analysis shows that the categorization of ethnicity (or race) into 2 or 5 categories changes the underlying structure of the Simpson diversity scores.

Summary

This chapter applied the Simpson diversity index to assess the ethnic diversity of 72 NYC departments based on their demographic employment data for fiscal year 2019. Four sets of ethnic diversity scores were calculated: 2 sets for the categorization of ethnicity (or race) into 2 groups, and 2 sets for the categorization of ethnicity (or race) into 5 groups. Standardized scores also were calculated for each set of biased and unbiased Simpson diversity scores.

Descriptive statistical analyses were performed on each set of Simpson diversity scores. The findings show that the diversity scores are negatively skewed, heavy tailed, and fail to satisfy the assumption of normality, The statistical analyses also show that the unbiased diversity scores are significantly higher than the biased scores. When comparing the distributions of the biased and unbiased diversity scores, the distributions of the unbiased scores are centered more closely around the mean in comparison to the distributions of the biased scores regardless of the number of ethnic groups that are formed.

In addition to conducting the descriptive statistical analysis, correlational and FA analyses were conducted to validate the statistical associations amongst the sets of diversity scores. The Pearson correlational analysis revealed that the sets of diversity scores based on the categorization of ethnicity into 2 groups were positively correlated with each other. Similarly, the scores based on the categorization of ethnicity into 5 groups were related statistically. The FA analysis produced 2 factors. Factor 1 was composed of the diversity scores generated by the ethnicity data categorized into 5 groups; Factor 2 was composed of scores based on the categorization of ethnicity or race into 2 groups. The correlation and FA analyses revealed that the number of categories that are constructed to measure ethnic diversity changes the structure of the scores so that different dimensions of diversity are assessed.

The comparison of the unbiased (S_N) and biased (S_B) Simpson diversity scores reaffirmed the drawbacks of using the S_N index. The drawbacks are the following:

- When demographic data are categorized into a few categories, S_N overcorrects for measurement bias and produces scores that exceed the EMV.
- When demographic data are categorized into a few categories, S_N produces scores that exceed the maximum proportion allowed by the EMV.
- The discriminatory power of S_N is compromised as the number of categories are increased to measure diversity;
- The distribution of S_N is compact and centered around the mean; and,
- The range of S_N scores becomes truncated so that there is a measurement floor and ceiling which further restricts the values of the LDV.

In comparison to the ethnic diversity scores generated by S_N, the S_B index produces a distribution of a set of coefficients with more variation all things being equal.

Key Terms

Correlational analysis refers to the statistical technique of matching the values of two or more sets of measures to assess how closely their values are similar to each other.

Eigenvalue refers to the factor by which an eigenvector is scaled or stretched.

Ethnic diversity refers to how well an organization's workforce is heterogeneous in terms of the employment of men and women from different ethnic and racial groups.

Factor analysis refers to the statistical technique used to assess whether a set of correlated measures are structurally similar in that they provide redundant numerical information in regard to what they are purportedly measuring.

Oblimin oblique rotation refers to the statistical technique for performing oblique rotations to transform vectors in a factor or principal component analysis into a simpler structure so that measures that assess the same construct are grouped together.

Pairwise correlation analysis refers to the statistical technique of matching the values of two sets of measures at a time to determine how closely the values are similar to each other.

Pearson correlation analysis refers to the statistical technique of matching the values of two or more sets of scores that are measured quantitatively.

Planned pairwise comparisons refer to statistical tests that compare two sets of scores for statistical significance prior to undertaking the analysis.

References

Cheong, Calvin W. H., and Sinnakkannu, Jothee. 2014. "Ethnic diversity and firm financial performance: Evidence from Malaysia". *Journal of Asia-Pacific Business*, Vol. 15: 73 – 100.

Guajardo, Salomón A. 2013. "Workforce diversity: An application of diversity and integration indices to small agencies". *Public Personnel Management*, Vol. 41: 27 – 40.

Guajardo, Salomón A. 2014. "Workforce diversity: Assessing the impact of minority integration on intra-group interaction". *International Journal of Police Science and Management*, Vol. 16: 205 – 220.

Guajardo, Salomón A. 2015. "Measuring diversity in police agencies". *Journal of Ethnicity in Criminal Justice,* Vol. 13: 1 – 15.

Leslie, Lisa M. 2017. "A status-based multilevel model of ethnic diversity and work unit performance". *Journal of Management*, Vol. 43: 426 – 454.

Pett, Marjorie A., Lackey, Nancy R., and Sullivan, John J. 2003. *Making sense of factor analysis: The use of factor analysis for instrument development in health care research.* Thousand Oaks, California: Sage Publications Inc.

Starks, Glenn. L. 2009. "Minority representation in senior positions in U.S. federal agencies: A paradox of underrepresentation". *Public Personnel Management*, Vol. 38: 79 – 90.

Williams, Brett, Onsman, Andrys, and Brown, Ted. 2010, "Exploratory factor analysis: A five-step guide for novices". *Journal of Emergency Primary Health Care (JEPHC)*, Vol. 8: 1 – 13.

Yong, An Gie, and Pearce, Sean. 2013. "A beginner's guide to factor analysis: Focusing on exploratory factor analysis". *Tutorials in Quantitative Methods for Psychology*, Vol. 9: 79 – 94.

CHAPTER 5

MEASUREMENT OF AGE DIVERSITY

Numerous studies have used the Simpson diversity index to assess *age diversity* in private firms and its impact on organizational performance (e.g., De Meulenaere, Boone, and Buyl, 2016; Ellwart, Bündgens, and Rack, 2014; Ferrero-Ferrero, Fernández-Izquierdo, and Muñoz-Torres, 2015; Khan, Khan, and Senturk, 2019; Li, Gong, Burmeister, Wang, Alterman, and Robinson, 2021). Age diversity and its impact on nonprofit organizations has been examined by researchers as well (e.g., Buse, Bernstein, and Bilimoria, 2016). Studies also have applied the Simpson index to small groups to assess the impact of age diversity on team performance (e.g., Kearney, Gebert, and Voelpel, 2009; Timmerman, 2000). Despite the plethora of studies that have applied to Simpson diversity index to age-related demographic data, few studies have applied the index to similar data collected by public sector organizations (e.g., Moon and Christensen, 2020).

This chapter focuses on the measurement of age diversity in NYC departments for fiscal year 2019. Special emphasis is placed on the calculation of unbiased (S_{AN}) diversity coefficients and their corresponding standardized (S_{SAN}) scores based on the number of employees in each age group category. This discussion centers on how the unbiased (S_{AN}) diversity coefficients overestimate the level of age diversity across NYC departments when the workforce is composed of employees with ages concentrated within a few age group categories. Similar to Chapter 3 and 4, this chapter provides a descriptive statistical analysis on the biased (S_{AB}) and unbiased (S_{AN}) unstandardized and standardized scores. This chapter also assesses whether the S_{AN} coefficients are statistically higher in comparison to the S_{AB} coefficients (H_O: $\mu_{SAN} = \mu_{SAB}$) at $\alpha = 0.01$.

Application of the Simpson index

Exhibit 5-1 presents the Simpson age diversity scores for ACS and EEPC for fiscal year 2019. For fiscal 2019, the biased (S_{AB}) diversity score for ACS was 0.887 and a similar unbiased (S_{AN}) diversity score of 0.887, indicating a moderately high level of age diversity. By contrast, EECP had a biased (S_{AB}) diversity score of 0.750 and an higher unbiased (S_{AN}) diversity score of 0.818, indicating that the level of age diversity in the organization was moderately high to high. However, the age diversity scores of NYC departments are incompatible. The level of age diversity attained by EECP is based on data of 5 age group categories, and the diversity scores for ACS are based data of 10 age group categories. At a glance, one may infer that ACS and EEPC have workforces that are similar in terms of the number of employees in each age group category based solely on the diversity scores.

The standardized diversity scores for EECP are misleading as well. As Exhibit 5-1 shows, the EMV_1 for ACS is 0.909 ($EMV_1 = \frac{n-1}{n} = \frac{9}{10} = 0.909$); the EMV_2 for EECP is 0.800 ($EMV_2 = \frac{n-1}{n} = \frac{4}{5} = 0.800$). When the S_{AB1} score for ACS is divided by the EMV_1 of 0.909, the department has a standardized biased score of 0.985 ($S_{SAB1} = S_{AB1}/EMV_1 = 0.887 \div 0.909 = 0.985$), indicating that its age diversity coefficient attains 96% of the EMV_1. The same value is obtained when the standardized score is calculated for the unbiased S_{AN1} score. By contrast, EECP has a standardized (S_{SAB2}) biased score of 0.938 ($S_{SAB2} = 0.750 \div 0.800 = 0.938$), indicating that its age diversity coefficient attains 94% of the EMV_2. When EECP's unbiased (S_{AN2}) score is divided by the EMV of 0.800, a standardized S_{SAN2} score of 1.023 ($S_{SAN2} = S_{AN2}/EMV_2 = 0818 \div 0.800 = 1.023$) is calculated, indicating that standardized score attains over 100% of the EMV_2.

Exhibit 5-1 Calculation of the biased (S_{AB}) and unbiased (S_{AN}) Simpson age diversity score for the New York City ACS and EEPC for fiscal year 2019

A. Calculation of biased and unbiased Simpson age diversity for ACS

Age Group	Frequency (f)	f^2
Under 20	0	0
20 - 24	147	21,609
25 - 29	737	543,169
30 - 34	958	917,764
35 - 39	958	917,764
40 - 44	958	917,764
45 - 49	810	656,100
50 - 54	884	781,456
5 5 - 59	958	917,764
60 - 64	589	346,921
Over 65	368	135,424
Total (Σ)	7,367	6,155,735
EMV$_1$	0.900	

$$S_{AB1} = 1 - \frac{\sum f^2}{F^2}$$

$$S_{AB1} = 1 - \frac{6,155,735}{54,272,689}$$

$$S_{AB1} = 1 - \ 0.113$$

$$S_{AB1} = 0.887$$

$$S_{AB1} = 0.985$$

Age Group	Number (n)	$n_i(n_i - 1)$	$\dfrac{n_i(n_i - 1)}{N(N-1)}$
Under 20	0	0	0.000
20 - 24	147	21,462	0.000
25 - 29	737	542,432	0.010
30 - 34	958	916,806	0.017
35 - 39	958	916,806	0.017
40 - 44	958	916,806	0.017
45 - 49	810	655,290	0.012
50 - 54	884	780,572	0.014
5 5 - 59	958	916,806	0.017
60 - 64	589	346,332	0.006
Over 65	368	135,056	0.002
Total (Σ)	7,367	6,148,368	0.113
EMV$_1$	0.900		

$$S_{AN1} = 1 - \sum \frac{n_i(n_i - 1)}{N(N-1)}$$

$$S_{AN1} = 1 - \ 0.113$$

$$S_{AN1} = 0.887$$

$$S_{AN1} = 0.985$$

Measurement of Age Diversity

B. Calculation of biased and unbiased Simpson age diversity for EEPC

Age Group	Frequency (f)	f_i^2
Under 20	0	0
20 - 24	0	0
25 - 29	0	0
30 - 34	4	16
35 - 39	3	9
40 - 44	3	9
45 - 49	1	1
50 - 54	0	0
5 5 - 59	0	0
60 - 64	1	1
Over 65	0	0
Total ($\sum$)	12	36
EMV_2	0.800	

$$S_{AB2} = 1 - \frac{\sum f_i^2}{F^2}$$

$$S_{AB2} = 1 - \frac{36}{144}$$

$$S_{AB2} = 1 - 0.250$$

$$S_{AB2} = 0.750$$

$$S_{sAB2} = 0.938$$

Age Group	Number (n)	$n_i (n_i - 1)$	$\dfrac{n_i (n_i - 1)}{N(N-1)}$
Under 20	0	0	0.000
20 - 24	0	0	0.000
25 - 29	0	0	0.000
30 - 34	4	12	0.091
35 - 39	3	6	0.045
40 - 44	3	6	0.045
45 - 49	1	0	0.000
50 - 54	0	0	0.000
5 5 - 59	0	0	0.000
60 - 64	1	0	0.000
Over 65	0	0	0.000
Total ($\sum$)	12	24	0.182
EMV_2	0.800		

$$S_{AN2} = 1 - \sum \frac{n_i (n_i - 1)}{N(N-1)}$$

$$S_{AN2} = 1 - 0.182$$

$$S_{AN2} = 0.818$$

$$S_{sAN2} = 1.023$$

The use of the formula for obtaining unbiased (S_{AN}) Simpson diversity scores presents several analytical and practical issues. They are the following:

- Measurement efficiency of the Simpson index decreases when the formula is applied to data categorized into many groups;
- The formula fails to adjust for differences in the number of groups with missing employment data;
- The formula overcorrects for the size of the workforce; and,
- The formula produces standardized scores that exceed the EMV.

Overview of age-related data for NYC departments for fiscal year 2019

Exhibit 5-2 presents the reported age-related data of each NYC department for fiscal year 2019. As highlighted in Exhibit 5-1, the age of employees is categorized into 1 of 11 groups. For instance, employees under the age of 21 are grouped in the first category, while employees between the ages of 21 to 24 are grouped in the second category. Employees with ages 65 and older are grouped into the last category.

Based on the 11 categories used by NYC to report the number of employees in each age group category, each department should have an EMV of 0.909 (EMV $= \frac{n-1}{n} = \frac{11-1}{11} = 0.909$). However, as Exhibit 5-2 summarizes, only 3 departments reported employees in each of the 11 categories. Fifty-four departments have employees grouped in 10 of the 11 categories and have an EMV of 0.900. An EMV of 0.889 is calculated for departments with employees grouped in 9 of the 11 categories. Of the 72 NYC departments, 1 has employees grouped in 5 of the 11 categories and has an EMV of 0.800.

Because NYC departments have workforces composed of employees of different age ranges that are grouped into a different number of age group categories, the *measurement compatibility* and *measurement validity* of the Simpson age diversity coefficients are compromised if the EMV score based on the 11 age group categories is used to calculate standardized diversity scores. In addition, the issues of measurement compatibility and validity are compounded further when standardized scores for each department are calculated based on the actual number of age group categories that contain data. As illustrated in Exhibit 5-2, the standardized age diversity scores for ACS and EEPC are based on different EMV coefficients that are calculated on differences in the number age group categories that contain data.

Measurement of Age Diversity

Exhibit 5-2 Age distribution for each NYC department for fiscal year 2019

Case Number	Agency	Employees Under 20	Employees 20 - 24	Employees 25 - 29	Employees 30 - 34	Employees 35 - 39	Employees 40 - 44
1	DCAS	0	49	173	247	321	271
2	DOITT	0	0	79	173	205	268
3	MAYORALTY	0	64	241	267	203	127
4	BOE	8	42	75	75	58	75
5	NYCERS	0	9	13	31	49	58
6	TRS	0	0	0	17	31	35
7	OPA	0	2	5	9	12	21
8	NYCPPF	0	6	16	19	14	12
9	CLERK	0	1	4	7	10	10
10	DORIS	0	3	6	13	9	6
11	FDNYPF	0	0	0	4	3	5
12	OCB	0	0	0	4	2	1
13	DOF	0	21	126	210	189	168
14	COMPTROLLER	0	16	78	102	94	86
15	TLC	0	19	95	120	95	76
16	FISA	0	0	4	17	48	48
17	DCA	0	12	54	83	71	54
18	SBS	0	6	42	63	45	30
19	BIC	0	10	14	12	5	4
20	ACTUARY	0	0	4	6	6	5
21	NYCTAX	0	0	3	2	2	1
22	IBO	0	1	2	6	9	4
23	MWFA	0	0	1	3	3	1
24	COUNCIL	17	104	173	139	104	61
25	BP-BK	0	2	10	15	11	15

26	CFB	0	5	22	23	18	12
27	BP-QNS	0	5	8	11	9	3
28	BP-MAN	0	2	16	13	14	9
29	BP-BX	1	3	12	6	14	6
30	BP-SI	0	1	5	4	1	6
31	PA	1	11	13	11	7	1
32	PUBADMIN	0	2	2	5	6	2
33	NYCHA	0	219	767	987	1096	1315
34	PARKS	581	945	945	727	727	654
35	HPD	0	24	171	269	244	269
36	LPC	0	4	7	18	13	7
37	DCLA	0	0	2	10	16	11
38	DOE	0	5223	19152	22634	22634	20893
39	SCA	0	8	50	50	74	99
40	NYCHH	0	387	3098	4260	4260	4648
41	HRA	0	0	260	911	1302	1432
42	ACS	0	147	737	958	958	958
43	DOHMH	0	72	644	930	930	858
44	DHS	0	49	244	317	366	317
45	DYCD	6	34	34	69	98	63
46	DFTA	0	0	13	20	20	29
47	DSNY	0	101	608	1317	1723	1824
48	DEP	0	186	435	622	684	746
49	DOT	0	114	457	629	686	629
50	DOB	0	17	99	166	215	249
51	DDC	0	27	147	161	147	121
52	DCP	0	10	57	77	43	33
53	LAW	0	38	266	324	304	228

Measurement of Age Diversity

54	DA-MAN	0	191	265	221	191	118
55	DA-BK	0	46	217	205	137	91
56	DA-BX	0	65	303	216	119	76
57	OATH	0	22	43	43	57	72
58	DA-QNS	0	43	114	114	64	50
59	DA-NARC	0	4	30	37	32	15
60	CCRB	0	26	51	47	22	16
61	DA-SI	0	9	26	32	31	12
62	CCHR	0	4	25	35	19	17
63	BOC	0	0	9	4	7	4
64	COIB	0	1	4	4	4	4
65	NYCCSC	0	0	0	1	2	0
66	EEPC	0	0	0	4	3	3
67	NYPD	0	2798	7834	9513	10073	8394
68	FDNY	0	710	2484	3017	3017	2839
69	DOC	0	369	1721	2336	2213	1721
70	DOP	0	35	117	140	93	82
71	DOI	0	18	66	73	48	33
72	NYCEM	0	6	46	44	28	28
Total		615	12,348	42,845	53,257	54,370	50,437

86

Chapter 5

Exhibit 5-2 Continued

Case Number	Agency	Employees 45 - 49	Employees 50 - 54	Employees 55 - 59	Employees 60 - 64	Employees Over 65	Total Employees
1	DCAS	296	321	395	271	123	2,468
2	DOITT	236	205	189	142	79	1,576
3	MAYORALTY	102	89	76	64	38	1,271
4	BOE	67	100	117	100	117	833
5	NYCERS	75	58	67	44	40	444
6	TRS	49	70	66	49	31	349
7	OPA	18	24	33	17	11	152
8	NYCPPF	12	19	24	14	9	144
9	CLERK	12	9	10	7	7	75
10	DORIS	9	6	6	8	8	73
11	FDNYPF	6	5	5	5	3	36
12	OCB	5	2	2	0	1	17
13	DOF	189	294	420	315	168	2,102
14	COMPTROLLER	86	86	102	86	47	784
15	TLC	63	70	57	32	6	632
16	FISA	78	65	70	70	35	436
17	DCA	37	37	33	17	17	416
18	SBS	30	21	36	18	9	301
19	BIC	13	10	8	3	0	80
20	ACTUARY	4	3	6	6	10	51
21	NYCTAX	3	6	8	14	10	49
22	IBO	3	3	0	6	2	36
23	MWFA	0	4	1	0	0	13
24	COUNCIL	52	52	61	43	61	867

Measurement of Age Diversity

25	BP-BK	11	20	16	11	12	124
26	CFB	8	9	8	8	2	115
27	BP-QNS	11	17	12	13	20	109
28	BP-MAN	8	2	13	6	10	94
29	BP-BX	9	12	12	7	11	93
30	BP-SI	4	8	9	8	7	53
31	PA	0	3	1	1	3	52
32	PUBADMIN	4	4	9	9	4	47
33	NYCHA	1535	1864	1754	987	438	10,962
34	PARKS	654	727	654	436	218	7,267
35	HPD	269	269	366	342	220	2,441
36	LPC	10	5	7	5	7	83
37	DCLA	13	3	10	3	4	74
38	DOE	20893	19152	17411	12187	13928	174,105
39	SCA	99	124	141	108	74	827
40	NYCHH	4648	5035	5810	4648	1937	38,731
41	HRA	1562	2083	2604	1823	1041	13,018
42	ACS	810	884	958	589	368	7366
43	DOHMH	787	858	930	715	429	7,150
44	DHS	268	293	293	195	98	2,438
45	DYCD	63	63	52	52	40	574
46	DFTA	39	52	59	49	46	326
47	DSNY	1621	1317	912	507	203	10,134
48	DEP	746	932	932	622	311	6,216
49	DOT	629	800	857	572	343	5,716
50	DOB	215	199	232	166	99	1,657
51	DDC	121	134	201	147	134	1,340
52	DCP	17	20	27	30	20	334
53	LAW	190	171	152	133	95	1,903

Chapter 5

54	DA-MAN	103	118	118	74	74	1,472
55	DA-BK	103	114	103	80	46	1,140
56	DA-BX	76	76	87	43	22	1,082
57	OATH	79	65	79	93	165	717
58	DA-QNS	50	85	71	57	64	710
59	DA-NARC	13	19	28	22	15	215
60	CCRB	6	12	10	4	8	203
61	DA-SI	14	26	10	9	3	170
62	CCHR	13	6	8	7	6	139
63	BOC	1	2	1	1	1	30
64	COIB	3	1	1	3	0	25
65	NYCCSC	1	3	1	3	4	15
66	EEPC	1	0	0	1	0	12
67	NYPD	6715	5036	3358	1679	560	55,960
68	FDNY	2307	1597	1065	532	177	17,746
69	DOC	1476	1107	738	246	369	12,296
70	DOP	117	233	187	117	47	1,166
71	DOI	29	29	33	22	15	367
72	NYCEM	20	8	8	6	6	202
Total		47,816	45,156	42,136	28,706	22,536	400,221

Specifically, the EMV for ACS is based on age data reported for 10 categories, and the EMV for EEPC is based on data reported for 5 categories. The standardized diversity coefficients for ACS and EEPC do not have the same meaning or interpretation because the scores are incompatible.

Biased and unbiased age diversity scores

Exhibit 5-3 summarizes the biased (S_{AB}) and unbiased (S_{AN}) unstandardized and standardized age diversity scores for each NYC department for fiscal year 2019. Parks has a biased (S_{AB}) diversity score of 0.901, which is based on data reported for each of the 11 age group categories. DDC has a biased (S_{AB}) diversity score of 0.890, while Council has a score of 0.881; however, the S_{AB} score for Council is based on having data for each of the 11 age group categories, while the S_{AB} score for DDC is based on data for 10 of 11 age group categories. Based solely on the S_{AB} scores, it appears that DDC is more diverse in term of the age composition of its workforce in comparison to Council. A similar inference can be made about the biased diversity score for the Comptroller office ($S_{AB} = 0.889$) when compared to the score for Council ($S_{AB} = 0.881$). At a glance, the S_{AB} scores for NYCCSC and NYCTAX of 0.821 suggest that they attained the same level of age diversity because their employees are spread similarly across the various age group categories. Although NYCCSC and NYCTAX have the same S_{AN} score, NYCCSC has employees spread evenly across 7 age group categories; by contrast, NYCTAX has a workforce spread across 9 age group categories with most of its employees clustered around the older age groups.

When the formula for obtaining unbiased (S_{AN}) scores is applied to the data, the overcorrection for workforce size compounds the issue of measurement incompatibility and heightens the questionability of measurement validity (see Exhibit 5-3). For instance, NYCCSC has a S_{AN} score of 0.879 based on a workforce of 15 employees spread across 5 of the 11 age group categories in comparison to NYCHA with a S_{AN} score of 0.878 that is based on a workforce of 10,962 employees spread across 10 age group categories. To illustrate the point further, COIB has a S_{AN} score of 0.900 based on a workforce of 25 employees spread across 9 age group categories in comparison to PARKS with a S_{AN} score of 0.900 that is based on a workforce of 7,267 employees spread across each age group category. On the surface, the assessment of the S_{AN} diversity coefficients suggest that the level of age diversity attained by each NYC department is compatible and that the coefficients are based on each department having employees in each age group category.

Exhibit 5-3 Biased (S$_{AB}$) and unbiased (S$_{AN}$) Simpson age diversity scores for NYC departments for fiscal year 2019

Case Number	Agency	Total Employees	Number of Age Groups	EMV For Number of Age Groups	S$_{AB}$	S$_{AN}$	S$_{SAB1}$ (EMV = 0.909)	S$_{SAB2}$	S$_{SAN1}$ (EMV = 0.909)	S$_{SAN2}$
34	PARKS	7,267	11	0.909	0.901	0.901	0.991	0.991	0.991	0.991
45	DYCD	574	11	0.909	0.892	0.894	0.981	0.981	0.983	0.983
24	COUNCIL	867	11	0.909	0.881	0.882	0.969	0.969	0.970	0.970
4	BOE	833	10	0.900	0.894	0.895	0.983	0.993	0.984	0.994
38	DOE	174,105	10	0.900	0.891	0.891	0.980	0.990	0.980	0.990
51	DDC	1,340	10	0.900	0.890	0.891	0.979	0.989	0.980	0.990
14	COMPTROLLER	784	10	0.900	0.889	0.891	0.978	0.988	0.980	0.989
58	DA-QNS	710	10	0.900	0.888	0.890	0.977	0.987	0.979	0.989
29	BP-BX	93	10	0.900	0.888	0.897	0.977	0.986	0.987	0.997
25	BP-BK	124	10	0.900	0.888	0.895	0.976	0.986	0.984	0.994
10	DORIS	73	10	0.900	0.887	0.900	0.976	0.986	0.990	1.000
8	NYCPPF	144	10	0.900	0.887	0.893	0.976	0.986	0.983	0.993
49	DOT	5,716	10	0.900	0.887	0.887	0.975	0.985	0.976	0.986
42	ACS	7366	10	0.900	0.887	0.887	0.975	0.985	0.975	0.985
43	DOHMH	7,150	10	0.900	0.887	0.887	0.975	0.985	0.975	0.985
35	HPD	2,441	10	0.900	0.886	0.887	0.975	0.985	0.975	0.985
48	DEP	6,216	10	0.900	0.886	0.886	0.974	0.984	0.975	0.984
44	DHS	2,438	10	0.900	0.884	0.885	0.973	0.983	0.973	0.983
40	NYCHH	38,731	10	0.900	0.884	0.884	0.973	0.982	0.973	0.982
9	CLERK	75	10	0.900	0.882	0.894	0.971	0.980	0.984	0.994
50	DOB	1,657	10	0.900	0.882	0.883	0.971	0.980	0.971	0.981
54	DA-MAN	1,472	10	0.900	0.882	0.883	0.970	0.980	0.971	0.981
27	BP-QNS	109	10	0.900	0.881	0.889	0.969	0.979	0.978	0.988

Measurement of Age Diversity

59	DA-NARC	215	10	0.900	0.880	0.884	0.968	0.978	0.973	0.983
39	SCA	827	10	0.900	0.879	0.880	0.967	0.977	0.969	0.978
53	LAW	1,903	10	0.900	0.879	0.880	0.967	0.977	0.968	0.977
5	NYCERS	444	10	0.900	0.878	0.880	0.966	0.976	0.968	0.978
33	NYCHA	10,962	10	0.900	0.878	0.878	0.966	0.976	0.966	0.976
55	DA-BK	1,140	10	0.900	0.876	0.877	0.964	0.974	0.965	0.975
70	DOP	1,166	10	0.900	0.876	0.877	0.964	0.974	0.965	0.974
30	BP-SI	53	10	0.900	0.875	0.892	0.963	0.973	0.981	0.991
2	DOITT	1,576	10	0.900	0.875	0.876	0.963	0.972	0.963	0.973
13	DOF	2,102	10	0.900	0.875	0.876	0.963	0.972	0.963	0.973
28	BP-MAN	94	10	0.900	0.875	0.884	0.962	0.972	0.973	0.982
36	LPC	83	10	0.900	0.875	0.885	0.962	0.972	0.974	0.984
71	DOI	367	10	0.900	0.874	0.876	0.961	0.971	0.964	0.974
57	OATH	717	10	0.900	0.873	0.875	0.961	0.970	0.962	0.972
32	PUBADMIN	47	10	0.900	0.871	0.890	0.959	0.968	0.979	0.989
15	TLC	632	10	0.900	0.871	0.872	0.958	0.968	0.959	0.969
17	DCA	416	10	0.900	0.871	0.873	0.958	0.967	0.960	0.970
18	SBS	301	10	0.900	0.870	0.872	0.957	0.966	0.960	0.969
19	BIC	80	10	0.900	0.868	0.879	0.955	0.964	0.967	0.977
67	NYPD	55,960	10	0.900	0.867	0.867	0.954	0.963	0.954	0.963
41	HRA	13,018	10	0.900	0.867	0.867	0.953	0.963	0.953	0.963
61	DA-SI	170	10	0.900	0.866	0.871	0.953	0.962	0.958	0.968
52	DCP	334	10	0.900	0.866	0.869	0.953	0.962	0.956	0.965
68	FDNY	17,746	10	0.900	0.866	0.866	0.952	0.962	0.952	0.962
26	CFB	115	10	0.900	0.865	0.873	0.952	0.961	0.960	0.970
47	DSNY	10,134	10	0.900	0.865	0.865	0.951	0.961	0.951	0.961
7	OPA	152	10	0.900	0.864	0.870	0.950	0.960	0.957	0.966
69	DOC	12,296	10	0.900	0.864	0.864	0.950	0.960	0.950	0.960
3	MAYORALTY	1,271	10	0.900	0.863	0.864	0.950	0.959	0.950	0.960
62	CCHR	139	10	0.900	0.853	0.859	0.938	0.948	0.945	0.954

72	NYCEM	202	10	0.900	0.844	0.848	0.928	0.937	0.933	0.942
56	DA-BX	1,082	10	0.900	0.843	0.844	0.927	0.936	0.928	0.937
60	CCRB	203	10	0.900	0.840	0.844	0.924	0.934	0.929	0.938
31	PA	52	10	0.900	0.824	0.840	0.906	0.915	0.924	0.933
1	DCAS	2,468	9	0.889	0.884	0.885	0.973	0.995	0.973	0.995
20	ACTUARY	51	9	0.889	0.876	0.894	0.964	0.986	0.983	1.005
46	DFTA	326	9	0.889	0.869	0.871	0.955	0.977	0.958	0.980
64	COIB	25	9	0.889	0.864	0.900	0.950	0.972	0.990	1.013
16	FISA	436	9	0.889	0.862	0.864	0.948	0.969	0.950	0.972
37	DCLA	74	9	0.889	0.850	0.861	0.935	0.956	0.948	0.969
22	IBO	36	9	0.889	0.848	0.872	0.933	0.954	0.959	0.981
21	NYCTAX	49	9	0.889	0.821	0.838	0.903	0.924	0.922	0.943
63	BOC	30	9	0.889	0.813	0.841	0.895	0.915	0.925	0.946
11	FDNYPF	36	8	0.875	0.868	0.893	0.955	0.992	0.982	1.020
6	TRS	349	8	0.875	0.856	0.858	0.942	0.978	0.944	0.981
65	NYCCSC	15	7	0.857	0.821	0.879	0.903	0.958	0.967	1.026
12	OCB	17	7	0.857	0.809	0.860	0.890	0.944	0.946	1.003
23	MWFA	13	6	0.833	0.785	0.850	0.864	0.942	0.935	1.021
66	EEPC	12	5	0.800	0.753	0.822	0.829	0.942	0.904	1.027
Average		5,559			0.868	0.876	0.954	0.969	0.964	0.979
Standard Deviation		21683.98			0.025	0.017	0.028	0.018	0.018	0.019
CV					0.029	0.019	0.029	0.018	0.019	0.020

Standardized biased (S_{SAB}) and unbiased (S_{SAN}) scores are calculated for each NYC department using an EMV of 0.909 (EMV $= \frac{n-1}{n} = \frac{10}{11} = 0.909$) and an EMV based on the actual number of age group categories that contain employee data in each NYC department (see Exhibit 5-3). For illustrative purposes, the use of the EMV of 0.909 is based on the assumption that each department has employees in each age group category. In addition, the standardized scores based on the EMV of 0.909 serves to illustrate that the validity of the standardized scores is questionable as *measurement reliability* is maintained. The standardized scores also help to show that the diversity scores are incompatible.

When the EMV score of 0.909 is used to obtain standardized (S_{SAB1}) coefficients for each NYC department based on biased (S_{AB}) diversity scores, the proportion attained by each department in terms of the EMV of 0.909 is underreported (see Exhibit 5-3). For instance, the S_{SAB1} score of 0.983 for BOE underreports the actual proportion attained by the department in terms of the EMV because the EMV score of 0.909 is based on departments with data in each age group category. In the case of BOE, the department has data in 10 of the 11 age group categories. When the standardized (S_{SAB2}) score is calculated with the EMV score of 0.900 (EMV $= \frac{n-1}{n} = \frac{9}{10} = 0.900$) which adjusts for the actual number of age group categories with data, the coefficient increases to 0.993. However, in doing so, the S_{SAB2} score for BOE loses its measurement compatibility with the standardized scores of departments with different number of age group categories that contain data. On a positive note, the measurement validity of using the EMV of 0.900 for BOE and its peers with 10 age group categories with data increases because the standardized scores are based on the actual number of age group categories populated with data.

Briefly, the calculation of unbiased (S_{SAN2}) standardized scores for the unbiased (S_{AN}) diversity coefficients compounds the measurement issues discussed above (see Exhibit 5-3). For example, Parks has a S_{SAN2} score of 0.991 that is based on having data for each age group category, while COIB has a S_{SAN2} score of 1.013 that is based on having data for 9 age group categories. On the surface, the S_{SAN2} score for COIB suggests that it surpassed the same EMV score used to calculate the standardized score for Parks. The formula used to calculate unbiased (S_{AN2}) diversity scores overcorrects for group size and does not adjust for the actual number of age group categories that contain data.

Descriptive statistical analysis of age diversity scores

The descriptive statistical analysis of the biased (S_{AB}) age diversity scores for NYC departments for fiscal year 2019 shows that the sets of coefficients fail to satisfy the assumption of normality (see Exhibit 5-4). The S_{AB} distribution has a median of 0.875, a mean of 0.868, a standard deviation of 0.026, and a 95% CI ranging from 0.861 to 0.874. The analysis also shows that the distribution is negatively skewed (Skewness = -2.152) and heavy tailed (Kurtosis = 8.542). Similarly, the distribution of standardized (S_{SAB2}) scores with the adjustment for workforce size is negatively skewed (Skewness = -1.168), peaked (Kurtosis = 4.133), and fails to meet the assumption of normality. The distribution of S_{SAB2} scores has a median of 0.972, a mean of 0.969, a standard deviation of 0.018, and a 95% CI ranging from 0.965 to 0.974.

Similar findings are obtained for the unbiased (S_{AN}) age diversity scores for NYC departments for fiscal year 2019. Specifically, Exhibit 5-5 shows that the sets of unbiased (S_{AN}) diversity coefficients fail to meet the assumption of normality. The distribution of S_{AN1} scores has a median of 0.879, a mean of 0.876 with a standard deviation of 0.876, and a 95% CI ranging from 0.872 to 0.880. In addition, the distribution of S_{AN1} scores is negatively skewed (Skewness = -0.966), peaked (Kurtosis = 3.712), and fails to meet the assumption of normality. By contrast, the standardized (S_{SAN2}) scores with the adjustment for workforce size are distributed normally (Skewness = 0.040; Kurtosis = 3.599) and meet the assumption of normality. The distribution of S_{SAN2} scores has a median of 0.981, a mean of 0.979, a standard deviation of 0.019, and a 95% CI ranging from 0.975 to 0.984.

Exhibit 5-4 Descriptive statistics for biased Simpson (S_{AB}) age diversity scores for NYC departments for fiscal year 2019

1. Descriptive statistics for biased Simpson scores

A. Measures of central tendency and variability for biased Simpson scores

Index	Cases (N)	Central Tendency		Variability		95% Confidence Interval	
		Median	Mean	Variance	Standard Deviation	Lower Limit	Upper Limit
S_{AB}	72	0.875	0.868	0.001	0.026	0.861	0.874

B. Tests for normality, skewness, and kurtosis for biased Simpson scores

1. Shapiro-Wilk W test for normal data

Index	Cases (N)	W-statistic	V-statistic	z-statistic	Probability > z
S_{AB}	72	0.785	13.519	5.672	0.0001

2. Skewness/Kurtosis tests for Normality for biased Simpson scores

Index	Skewness	Kurtosis	Probability of Skewness	Probability of Kurtosis	Adjusted χ^2	Probability > $\chi2$
S_{AB}	-2.152	8.542	0.0001	0.0001	34.31	0.0001

2. Descriptive statistics for biased standardized Simpson scores

A. Measures of central tendency and variability for biased standardized Simpson scores

Index	Cases (N)	Central Tendency		Variability		95% Confidence Interval	
		Median	Mean	Variance	Standard Deviation	Lower Limit	Upper Limit
S_{SAB1}	72	0.962	0.954	0.001	0.028	0.948	0.961
S_{SAB2}	72	0.972	0.969	0.000	0.018	0.965	0.974

B. Tests for normality, skewness, and kurtosis for biased standardized Simpson scores

1. Shapiro-Wilk W test for normal data

Index	Cases (N)	W-statistic	V-statistic	z-statistic	Probability > z
S_{SAB1}	72	0.785	13.519	5.672	0.0001
S_{SAB2}	72	0.904	6.052	3.922	0.0001

2. Skewness/Kurtosis tests for Normality for biased standardized Simpson scores

Index	Skewness	Kurtosis	Probability of Skewness	Probability of Kurtosis	Adjusted χ^2	Probability > $\chi2$
S_{SAB1}	-2.152	8.542	0.0001	0.0001	34.31	0.0001
S_{SAB2}	-1.168	4.133	0.0002	0.0577	13.79	0.001

Exhibit 5-5 Descriptive statistics for unbiased Simpson (S_{AN}) age diversity scores for NYC departments for fiscal year 2019

1. Descriptive statistics for unbiased Simpson scores

A. Measures of central tendency and variability for unbiased Simpson scores

	Central Tendency		Variability		95% Confidence Interval	
Index	Cases (N)	Median	Mean	Variance	Standard Deviation	Lower Limit	Upper Limit
S_{AN}	72	0.879	0.876	0.000	0.876	0.872	0.880

B. Tests for normality, skewness, and kurtosis for unbiased Simpson scores

1. Shapiro-Wilk W test for normal data

Index	Cases (N)	W-statistic	V-statistic	z-statistic	Probability > z
S_{AN}	72	0.93341	4.194	3.122	0.0009

Measurement of Age Diversity

2. Skewness/Kurtosis tests for Normality for unbiased Simpson scores

Index	Skewness	Kurtosis	Probability of Skewness	Probability of Kurtosis	Adjusted χ^2	Probability > χ^2
S_{AN}	-0.966	3.712	0.001	0.149	10.29	0.0058

2. Descriptive statistics for unbiased standardized Simpson scores

A. Measures of central tendency and variability for unbiased standardized Simpson scores

		Central Tendency		Variability		95% Confidence Interval	
Index	Cases (N)	Median	Mean	Variance	Standard Deviation	Lower Limit	Upper Limit
S_{SAN1}	72	0.967	0.964	0.000	0.018	0.959	0.968
S_{SAN2}	72	0.981	0.979	0.000	0.019	0.975	0.984

B. Tests for normality, skewness, and kurtosis for unbiased standardized Simpson scores

1. Shapiro-Wilk W test for normal data

Index	Cases (N)	W-statistic	V-statistic	z-statistic	Probability > z
S_{SAN1}	72	0.933	4.194	3.122	0.0009
S_{SAN2}	72	0.971	1.853	1.343	0.0896

2. Skewness/Kurtosis tests for Normality for unbiased standardized Simpson scores

Index	Skewness	Kurtosis	Probability of Skewness	Probability of Kurtosis	Adjusted χ^2	Probability > χ^2
S_{SAN1}	-0.966	3.712	0.001	0.149	10.290	0.0058
S_{SAN2}	0.040	3.599	0.879	0.193	1.780	0.4110

Comparison of biased and unbiased age diversity scores

The biased (S_{AB}) and unbiased (S_{AN}) age diversity scores are compared in Exhibit 5-6. When adjusting for workforce size, the S_{AN} diversity coefficients are larger in comparison to the S_{AB} scores. As discussed above and in previous chapters, the formula used to obtain the S_N scores overcorrects for workforce size where NYC departments with small staffs have similar or larger diversity scores in comparison to departments with larger staffs. When standardized unbiased (S_{SAN2}) and biased (S_{SAB2}) scores are calculated based on the actual number of age group categories with employee data, the differences amongst the standardized unbiased S_{SAN2} scores are larger than the standardized biased S_{SAB2} scores. The findings also show that the S_{SAB2} scores are clustered more closely around the mean in comparison to the S_{SAN2} scores, which is due to several S_{SAN2} scores exceeding the EMV score for the number of age group categories containing employee data.

Five paired z-tests are conducted to determine whether the scores of the sets of age diversity scores are statistically equal. Identical to the planned comparisons performed in previous chapters, the reason for conducting the statistical analyses is to assess whether the unbiased age diversity scores (S_{SAN1} and S_{SAN2}) are statistically higher in comparison to their respective biased scores (S_{AB1} and S_{aB2}). The 5 planned pairwise comparisons are the following:

1. The mean of S_{AN} equals the mean of S_{aB} (H_{O1}: $\mu_{AN} = \mu_{AB}$) at $\alpha = .01$;
2. The mean of S_{SAB2} equals the mean of S_{SAB1} (H_{O2}: $\mu_{SAB2} = \mu_{SAB1}$) at $\alpha = .01$;
3. The mean of S_{AN2} equals the mean of S_{AN1} (H_{O3}: $\mu_{AN2} = \mu_{AN1}$) at $\alpha = .01$;
4. The mean of S_{SAN1} equals the mean of S_{SAB1} (H_{O4}: $\mu_{SAN1} = \mu_{SAB1}$) at $\alpha = .01$; and,
5. The mean of S_{SAN2} equals the mean of S_{SAB2} (H_{O5}: $\mu_{SAN2} = \mu_{SAB2}$) at $\alpha = .01$.

The statistical findings of the paired z-tests for equality of means (H_O: $\mu_1 = \mu_2$) are presented in Exhibit 5-7.

Measurement of Age Diversity

Exhibit 5-6 Comparison of biased (S_AB) and unbiased (S_AN) Simpson age diversity scores for NYC departments for fiscal year 2019

Case Number	Agency	Number of Age Groups	S_{AB}	S_{AN}	Difference ($S_{AN} - S_{AB}$)	S_{SAN1}	S_{SAB1}	Difference ($S_{SAN1} - S_{SAB1}$)	S_{SAN2}	S_{SAB2}	Difference ($S_{SAN2} - S_{SAB2}$)
34	PARKS	11	0.901	0.901	0.000	0.991	0.991	0.000	0.991	0.991	0.000
45	DYCD	11	0.892	0.894	0.002	0.983	0.981	0.002	0.983	0.981	0.002
27	BP-QNS	11	0.881	0.889	0.008	0.978	0.969	0.009	0.988	0.979	0.009
64	COIB	10	0.864	0.900	0.036	0.990	0.950	0.040	1.013	0.972	0.041
10	DORIS	10	0.887	0.900	0.012	0.990	0.976	0.014	1.000	0.986	0.014
29	BP-BX	10	0.888	0.897	0.010	0.987	0.977	0.011	0.997	0.986	0.011
4	BOE	10	0.894	0.895	0.001	0.984	0.983	0.001	0.994	0.993	0.001
25	BP-BK	10	0.888	0.895	0.007	0.984	0.976	0.008	0.994	0.986	0.008
9	CLERK	10	0.882	0.894	0.012	0.984	0.971	0.013	0.994	0.980	0.013
8	NYCPPF	10	0.887	0.893	0.006	0.983	0.976	0.007	0.993	0.986	0.007
30	BP-SI	10	0.875	0.892	0.017	0.981	0.963	0.019	0.991	0.973	0.019
38	DOE	10	0.891	0.891	0.000	0.980	0.980	0.000	0.990	0.990	0.000
51	DDC	10	0.890	0.891	0.001	0.980	0.979	0.001	0.990	0.989	0.001
14	COMPTROLLER	10	0.889	0.891	0.001	0.980	0.978	0.001	0.989	0.988	0.001
32	PUBADMIN	10	0.871	0.890	0.019	0.979	0.959	0.021	0.989	0.968	0.021
58	DA-QNS	10	0.888	0.890	0.001	0.979	0.977	0.001	0.989	0.987	0.001
49	DOT	10	0.887	0.887	0.000	0.976	0.975	0.000	0.986	0.985	0.000
35	HPD	10	0.886	0.887	0.000	0.975	0.975	0.000	0.985	0.985	0.000
43	DOHMH	10	0.887	0.887	0.000	0.975	0.975	0.000	0.985	0.985	0.000
42	ACS	10	0.887	0.887	0.000	0.975	0.975	0.000	0.985	0.985	0.000
48	DEP	10	0.886	0.886	0.000	0.975	0.974	0.000	0.984	0.984	0.000
36	LPC	10	0.875	0.885	0.011	0.974	0.962	0.012	0.984	0.972	0.012
44	DHS	10	0.884	0.885	0.000	0.973	0.973	0.000	0.983	0.983	0.000
59	DA-NARC	10	0.880	0.884	0.004	0.973	0.968	0.005	0.983	0.978	0.005
40	NYCHH	10	0.884	0.884	0.000	0.973	0.973	0.000	0.982	0.982	0.000
28	BP-MAN	10	0.875	0.884	0.009	0.973	0.962	0.010	0.982	0.972	0.010
50	DOB	10	0.882	0.883	0.001	0.971	0.971	0.001	0.981	0.980	0.001
54	DA-MAN	10	0.882	0.883	0.001	0.971	0.970	0.001	0.981	0.980	0.001
24	COUNCIL	10	0.881	0.882	0.001	0.970	0.969	0.001	0.970	0.969	0.001
39	SCA	10	0.879	0.880	0.001	0.969	0.967	0.001	0.978	0.977	0.001

5	NYCERS	10	0.878	0.880	0.002	0.968	0.966	0.002	0.978	0.976	0.002
53	LAW	10	0.879	0.880	0.000	0.968	0.967	0.001	0.977	0.977	0.001
19	BIC	10	0.868	0.879	0.011	0.967	0.955	0.012	0.977	0.964	0.012
33	NYCHA	10	0.878	0.878	0.000	0.966	0.966	0.000	0.976	0.976	0.000
55	DA-BK	10	0.876	0.877	0.001	0.965	0.964	0.001	0.975	0.974	0.001
70	DOP	10	0.876	0.877	0.001	0.965	0.964	0.001	0.974	0.974	0.001
71	DOI	10	0.874	0.876	0.002	0.964	0.961	0.003	0.974	0.971	0.003
2	DOITT	10	0.875	0.876	0.001	0.963	0.963	0.001	0.973	0.972	0.001
13	DOF	10	0.875	0.876	0.000	0.963	0.963	0.000	0.973	0.972	0.000
57	OATH	10	0.873	0.875	0.001	0.962	0.961	0.001	0.972	0.970	0.001
26	CFB	10	0.865	0.873	0.008	0.960	0.952	0.008	0.970	0.961	0.008
17	DCA	10	0.871	0.873	0.002	0.960	0.958	0.002	0.970	0.967	0.002
18	SBS	10	0.870	0.872	0.003	0.960	0.957	0.003	0.969	0.966	0.003
15	TLC	10	0.871	0.872	0.001	0.959	0.958	0.002	0.969	0.968	0.002
61	DA-SI	10	0.866	0.871	0.005	0.958	0.953	0.006	0.968	0.962	0.006
52	DCP	10	0.866	0.869	0.003	0.956	0.953	0.003	0.965	0.962	0.003
67	NYPD	10	0.867	0.867	0.000	0.954	0.954	0.000	0.963	0.963	0.000
41	HRA	10	0.867	0.867	0.000	0.953	0.953	0.000	0.963	0.963	0.000
68	FDNY	10	0.866	0.866	0.000	0.952	0.952	0.000	0.962	0.962	0.000
47	DSNY	10	0.865	0.865	0.000	0.951	0.951	0.000	0.961	0.961	0.000
3	MAYORALTY	10	0.863	0.864	0.001	0.950	0.950	0.001	0.960	0.959	0.001
69	DOC	10	0.864	0.864	0.000	0.950	0.950	0.000	0.960	0.960	0.000
62	CCHR	10	0.853	0.859	0.006	0.945	0.938	0.007	0.954	0.948	0.007
72	NYCEM	10	0.844	0.848	0.004	0.933	0.928	0.005	0.942	0.937	0.005
60	CCRB	10	0.840	0.844	0.004	0.929	0.924	0.005	0.938	0.934	0.005
56	DA-BX	10	0.843	0.844	0.001	0.928	0.927	0.001	0.937	0.936	0.001
31	PA	10	0.824	0.840	0.016	0.924	0.906	0.018	0.933	0.915	0.018
20	ACTUARY	9	0.876	0.894	0.018	0.983	0.964	0.019	1.005	0.986	0.020
1	DCAS	9	0.884	0.885	0.000	0.973	0.973	0.000	0.995	0.995	0.000
22	IBO	9	0.848	0.872	0.024	0.959	0.933	0.027	0.981	0.954	0.027
46	DFTA	9	0.869	0.871	0.003	0.958	0.955	0.003	0.980	0.977	0.003
7	OPA	9	0.864	0.870	0.006	0.957	0.950	0.006	0.966	0.960	0.006
16	FISA	9	0.862	0.864	0.002	0.950	0.948	0.002	0.972	0.969	0.002
37	DCLA	9	0.850	0.861	0.012	0.948	0.935	0.013	0.969	0.956	0.013
63	BOC	9	0.813	0.841	0.028	0.925	0.895	0.031	0.946	0.915	0.032
21	NYCTAX	9	0.821	0.838	0.017	0.922	0.903	0.019	0.943	0.924	0.019

Measurement of Age Diversity

		N									
11	FDNYPF	8	0.868	0.893	0.025	0.982	0.955	0.027	1.020	0.992	0.028
6	TRS	8	0.856	0.858	0.002	0.944	0.942	0.003	0.981	0.978	0.003
65	NYCCSC	7	0.821	0.879	0.059	0.967	0.903	0.064	1.026	0.958	0.068
12	OCB	7	0.809	0.860	0.051	0.946	0.890	0.056	1.003	0.944	0.059
23	MWFA	6	0.785	0.850	0.065	0.935	0.864	0.072	1.021	0.942	0.079
66	EEPC	5	0.753	0.822	0.068	0.904	0.829	0.075	1.027	0.942	0.086
Average			0.868	0.876	0.009	0.964	0.954	0.009	0.979	0.969	0.010
Standard Deviation			0.025	0.017	0.015	0.018	0.028	0.016	0.019	0.018	0.018
CV			0.029	0.019		0.029	0.020		0.018		

Exhibit 5-7 Paired z-test for equal means for biased (S_{AB}) and unbiased (S_{AN}) Simpson age diversity scores for NYC departments for fiscal year 2019

Planned Comparisons	Cases (N)	H_o	Mean Difference	Standard Error	Standard Deviation	95% Confidence Interval		z-statistic	Probability ($|Z| > |z|$)
						Lower Limit	Upper Limit		
1	72	$\mu_{AN} = \mu_{AB}$	0.009	0.002	0.015	0.005	0.012	4.865	0.0001
2	72	$\mu_{SAB2} = \mu_{SAB1}$	0.015	0.002	0.017	0.011	0.019	7.614	0.0001
3	72	$\mu_{AN2} = \mu_{AN1}$	0.016	0.002	0.018	0.011	0.020	7.208	0.0001
4	72	$\mu_{SAN1} = \mu_{SAB1}$	0.009	0.002	0.016	0.006	0.013	4.865	0.0001
5	72	$\mu_{SAN2} = \mu_{SAB2}$	0.010	0.002	0.018	0.006	0.014	4.703	0.0001

As Exhibit 5-7 shows, S_{AN} produces unbiased age diversity scores that are statistically higher in comparison to those produced by S_{AB} at $\alpha = 0.01$ (z-statistic = 4.865, p < 0.001), which is due to adjusting for the size of the workforce. The standardized scores for S_{SAB2} are statistically higher in comparison to S_{SAB1} at $\alpha = 0.01$ (z-statistic = 7.614, p < 0.001), which is due to using the actual number of age group categories with employee data to calculate the EMV for each department. Similarly, the findings show that the standardized (S_{SAN2}) scores for S_{AN2} are statistically higher than those produced by S_{SAN1} at $\alpha = 0.01$ (z-statistic = 7.208, p < 0.001), which is due to calculating the standardized scores with the EMV obtained for the actual number of age group categories containing employment data for each department. The 5th planned comparison for S_{SAN2} and S_{SAB2} shows that the scores of S_{SN2} are statistically higher than those produced by S_{SAB2} at $\alpha = 0.01$ (z-statistic = 4.703, p < 0.001), which is due to S_{AN2} overcorrecting for measurement bias associated with total employment of each NYC department and due to using the actual number of age group categories containing employment data to calculate the EMV for each department.

Summary

This chapter applied the Simpson diversity index to age-related data reported by each NYC department for fiscal year 2019. The analysis of the age diversity scores shows that the biased (S_{AB}) scores for each department are incompatible because not all departments have data for each age group category. The analysis of the biased (S_{AB}) scores also shows that departments with small workforces have diversity scores equal to or higher in comparison to departments with larger workforces. The incompatibility in the diversity scores is due the Simpson index not adjusting for the actual number of age group categories with missing data. When the formula for calculating unbiased (S_{AN}) age diversity coefficients is applied to the data, the issues of measurement incompatibility and measurement validity are compounded due to the overcorrection for total workforce size and due to not adjusting for the number of age group categories with missing employee data. Although the application of the Simpson diversity index formulas to the age-related employee data do not impact the measurement reliability of the diversity scores, the compatibility and validity of the diversity scores is questionable because not all departments have data for each age group category.

The drawbacks of using the Simpson index formulas to obtain biased (S_{AB}) and unbiased (S_{AN}) age diversity scores are compounded when not all age group categories contain employee data. The drawbacks are the following:

- Measurement compatibility amongst the diversity scores is diminished when the number of age group categories with data differ across departments;
- Measurement validity of diversity coefficients is questionable when departments with small workforces and with a small number of age group categories with employee data have higher scores in comparison to departments with larger staff spread across more age group categories;
- Standardized (S_{SAN}) unbiased diversity scores calculated for S_{AN} exceed the EMV of some departments when the actual number of age group categories with employee data are used to obtain the appropriate EMV; and.
- The distribution of the biased (S_{AB}) and unbiased (S_{AN}) age diversity scores fail to meet the assumption of normality because the coefficients are negatively skewed and heavy tailed.

In comparison to the age diversity scores generated by S_{AN}, the S_{AB} index produces a distribution of a set of coefficients with more variation all things being equal.

Key Terms

Age diversity refers to how well an organization's workforce is heterogeneous in terms of the employment of men and women of different ages.

Measurement compatibility refers to whether two or more scores obtained in the same manner have the same meaning or interpretation when the scores are calculated on data with different characteristics.

Measurement reliability refers to whether a method used to calculate a set of scores produces consistent results over multiple applications of the method.

Measurement validity refers to whether similar inferences can be made on a set of scores that are calculated from data with different characteristics.

References

Buse, Kathleen, Bernstein, Ruth Sessler, and Bilimoria, Diana. 2016. "The influence of board diversity, board diversity policies and practices, and board inclusion behaviors on nonprofit governance practices". *Journal of Business Ethics*, Vol. 133: 179 – 191.

De Meulenaere, Kim, Boone, Christophe, and Buyl, Tine. 2016. "Unraveling the impact of workforce age diversity on labor productivity: The moderating role of firm size and job security". *Journal of Organizational Behavior*, Vol. 37: 193 – 212.

Ellwart, Thomas, Bündgens, Silke, and Rack, Oliver. 2013. "Managing knowledge exchange and identification in age diverse teams". *Journal of Managerial Psychology*, Vol. 28: 950 – 972.

Ferrero-Ferrero, Idoya, Fernández-Izquierdo, M. Ángeles, and Muñoz-Torres, M. Jesús. 2015. "Age diversity: An empirical study in the board of directors". *Cybernetics and Systems*, Vol. 46: 249 – 270.

Kearney, Eric, Gebert, Diether, and Voelpel, Sven C. 2009. "When and how diversity benefits teams: The importance of team members' need for cognition". *Academy of Management Journal*, Vol. 52: 581 – 598.

Khan, Imran, Khan, Ismail, and Senturk, Ismail. 2019. "Board diversity and quality of CSR disclosure: Evidence from Pakistan". *Corporate Governance: The International Journal of Business in Society*, Vol. 19: 1187 – 1203.

Li, Yixuan, Gong, Yaping, Burmeister, Anne, Wang, Mo, Alterman, Valeria, Alonso, Alexander, and Robinson, Samuel. 2021. "Leveraging age diversity for organizational performance: An intellectual capital perspective". *Journal of Applied Psychology*, Vol. 106: 71 – 91.

Moon, Kuk-Kyoung, and Christensen, Robert K. 2020. "Realizing the performance benefits of workforce diversity in the US federal government: The moderating role of diversity climate". *Public Personnel Management*, Vol. 49: 141 – 165.

Timmerman, Thomas A. 2000. "Racial diversity, age diversity, interdependence, and team performance". *Small Group Research*, Vol. 31: 592 – 606.

CHAPTER 6

COMPOSITE INDEX OF ORGANIZATIONAL DIVERSITY

The analysis of demographic and *occupational diversity* (OD) in organizations is analyzed separate of each other although they occur and are affected simultaneously as employees enter and leave the workforce. In an attempt to arrive at a *composite diversity index* of *organizational diversity*, researchers have combined two or more sets of measures to construct a single indicator to describe the overall level of diversity of an organization or work team (e.g., Chatman and Flynn, 2001; Kolo, 2012; Michie and Oughton, 2013; Randel and Jaussi, 2003). The construction of a composite index based on several diversity indices has been criticized by researchers, however (e.g., Harrison and Klein, 2007). The criticism leveled against the construction of a composite index of diversity is three-fold (e.g., Harrison and Klein, 2007): 1) demographic-based diversity scores are incompatible; 2) demographic-based diversity scores are statistically uncorrelated; and 3) there is a lack of *convergent validity* amongst demographic-based diversity scores. Despite the criticism made against the construction and use of a composite index of organizational diversity, this book takes the position that a composite index of diversity provides a crude estimate of overall organizational diversity given that nonprofit, private, and public organizations do not report employment data in tables that summarize concomitantly the different demographic, occupational, and social characteristics of employees. Stated differently, if demographic, occupational, and social characteristics of employees are reported in a singular format which facilitates the calculation of a diversity score which accounts for all of the characteristics of interest, there would be no need to construct an imperfect composite index of OD out of several seemingly incompatible and uncorrelated sets of diversity scores.

This chapter presents and analyzes several composite indices of OD for NYC departments for fiscal year 2019. The first set of composite indices are based on unstandardized (S_{BOD}) and standardized (S_{SBOD}) biased diversity scores for age, ethnicity, and gender. The second set of composite scores are calculated from unstandardized (S_{NOD}) and standardized (S_{SNOD}) unbiased diversity scores for age, ethnicity, and gender. Similar to the statistical analyses presented and discussed in previous chapters, tests for normality are conducted to assess whether the distribution of each set of OD scores is distributed normally. Several paired z-tests are conducted to determine whether differences in the average of the OD scores is 0 (e.g., H_o: $\mu_{BOD} - \mu_{NOD} = 0$) at $\alpha = 0.01$. In addition, a pairwise Pearson correlation analysis is performed to assess how closely the sets of OD coefficients align with each other. A factor analysis (FA) with oblimin oblique rotation is undertaken to determine whether the structure of the OD scores is similar.

Constructing a composite index of OD

Although the construction and use of a composite index of diversity is imperfect and questionable, this chapter presents the construction and analysis of a composite index of diversity obtained by averaging the age, ethnic, and gender diversity scores discussed in the previous chapters. Specifically, two methods for constructing a composite diversity score of organizational diversity are presented. The first method averages the biased (S_B) diversity scores for age, ethnicity, and gender by summing the three sets of diversity coefficients and dividing by 3. The formula for constructing the composite index is the following:

$$S_{BOD} = \frac{S_{GB} + S_{EB} + S_{AB}}{n} = S_{SBOD} = \frac{\sum UIS}{n}$$

The formula also is applied to the unbiased (S_N) diversity coefficients to compute a composite index.

The second method uses the standardized (S_S) scores of each set of S_B diversity coefficients to construct a weighted composite index of organizational diversity. The formula is the following:

$$S_{SBOD} = \frac{1/3 * S_{SGB} + S_{SEB} + 2/3 * S_{SAB}}{n} = S_{SBOD} = \frac{\sum SISW}{n}$$

In the formula above, the standardized (S_S) score of each set of diversity scores is used because the scores are on the same scale ranging from 0 to 1. A weight of 1/3 is assigned to the standardized (S_{SGB}) scores for gender diversity to reduce their contribution to the construction of the composite index. With respect to the standardized (S_{SAB}) scores for age diversity, a weight of 2/3 is assigned to give the coefficients the least amount of significance to the construction of the composite index. The reason for reducing the contribution of the S_{SAB} scores to the composite index is twofold: 1) the standardized scores of some NYC departments are inflated because they have fewer age group categories containing employee data and because they have lower EMV values which overstate the standardized scores, and 2) age diversity may not be as important as increasing ethnic and gender diversity for many NYC departments. The same formula is applied to the unbiased standardized (S_{SN}) scores for age, ethnic, and gender diversity. As illustrated Exhibit 6-1, the sum of the weighs is 1.

When the unweighted formula for computing a composite OD score for ACS for fiscal year 2019 is applied to the unstandardized biased (S_B) diversity scores, the department has an average OD score of 0.618 (see Exhibit 6-1). However, the OD score is based on diversity scores with different EMV values. For instance, the EMV for gender is 0.50. When ethnicity is categorized into 5 group, the EMV is 0.80. For ACS, the EMV for age diversity is 0.90, which differs from other NYC departments as discussed in Chapter 5.

When the weighted formula is applied to the standardized biased (S_{SB}) diversity scores, ACS has a composite OD index of 0.543, which is due to reducing the influence of the standardized diversity scores for gender and age (see Exhibit 6-1). As Exhibit 6-1 shows, applying a weight of 1/3 to the standardized score for gender decreases the value from 0.806 to 0.269. Applying a weigh of 2/3 to the standardized diversity score for age reduces the value from 0.985 to 0.657. Although the OD score based on the standardized diversity coefficients is lower than the OD score calculated from unstandardized coefficients, the weighted OD score is computed from diversity scores with a same range of 0 to 1.

Exhibit 6-1 Calculation of composite organizational diversity (OD) scores for ACS for fiscal year 2019

Unstandardized S_B Index (UI)	UI Score (UIS)	Standardized S_B Index (SI)	SI Score (SIS)	Weight (W)	SISW
S_{GB}	0.403	S_{SGB}	0.806	0.333	0.269
S_{EB}	0.563	S_{SEB}	0.704		0.704
S_{AB}	0.887	S_{SAG}	0.985	0.667	0.657
Total ($\sum$) n = 3	1.8532	Total ($\sum$) n = 3	2.495761	1.000	1.630

$$S_{BOD} = \frac{S_{GB} + S_{EB} + S_{AB}}{n}$$

$$S_{BOD} = \frac{\sum UIS}{n}$$

$$S_{BOD} = \frac{1.8532}{3}$$

$$S_{BOD} = 0.618$$

$$S_{SBOD} = \frac{1/3 * S_{SGB} + S_{SEB} + 2/3 * S_{SAB}}{n}$$

$$S_{SBOD} = \frac{\sum SISW}{n}$$

$$S_{SBOD} = \frac{1.630}{3}$$

$$S_{SBOD} = 0.543$$

Unstandardized S_N Index (NI)	NI Score (NIS)	Standardized S_N Index (NSI)	NSI Score (NSIS)	Weight (W)	NSISW
S_{GN}	0.476	S_{SGN}	0.952	0.333	0.317
S_{EN}	0.563	S_{SEN}	0.704		0.704
S_{AN}	0.887	S_{SAN}	0.985	0.667	0.657
Total ($\sum$) n = 3	1.926	Total ($\sum$) n = 3	2.641	1.000	1.678

$$S_{NOD} = \frac{\sum NIS}{n}$$

$$S_{NOD} = \frac{1.926}{3}$$

$$S_{NOD} = 0.642$$

$$S_{SNOD} = \frac{\sum NSISW}{n}$$

$$S_{SNOD} = \frac{1.678}{3}$$

$$S_{SNOD} = 0.559$$

Exhibit 6-1 also shows the OD scores for the unbiased (S_N) unstandardized and standardized age, ethnic, and gender diversity scores. An OD score of 0.642 is obtained for ACS when the age, ethnic, and gender diversity scores are summed and averaged. Because the S_N diversity scores adjust for the size of the ACS workforce, the coefficients for age, ethnic, and gender diversity are larger in comparison to the scores of the biased S_B measurements. Consequently, the OD coefficient for the unbiased (S_N) diversity scores is larger in comparison to the OD score for the biased (S_B) scores. Similarly, when the weights are applied to the unbiased (S_{SN}) standardized diversity coefficients for age, ethnicity, and gender, ACS has an OD coefficient of 0.559 which is larger in comparison to the OD coefficient of 0.543 for the biased (S_{SB}) diversity scores.

The OD scores for each NYC department for fiscal year 2019 are presented in Exhibit 6-2. As Exhibit 6-2 shows, the OD scores based on the unstandardized biased (S_B) are presented first. The OD scores based the standardized unbiased (S_B) are presented in the last column.

The statistical findings show that HDP has the highest unweighted OD score of 0.720, which is the average of a gender diversity coefficient of 0.500, an ethnic diversity score of 0.774, and an age diversity score of 0.886 (see Exhibit 6-2). However, when the OD formula with weights is applied to the department's standardized S_B diversity coefficients, an OD score of 0.652 is obtained. Exhibit 6-2 also shows that FDNY has the lowest unweighted OD score of 0.531 and the lowest weighted OD score of 0.478, which is due to having low gender diversity ($S_{GB} = 0.196$), somewhat moderate ethnic diversity ($S_{EB} = 0.530$), and moderately high age diversity ($S_{AB} = 0.866$).

Chapter 6

Exhibit 6-2 OD scores based on unstandardized biased Simpson (S_B) diversity coefficients for NYC departments for fiscal year 2019

Case Number	Department Acronym	Unstandardized S_B scores				Standardized S_B Scores			
		S_{GB}	S_{EB}	S_{AB}	S_{BOD}	S_{SGB}	S_{SEB}	S_{SAB}	S_{SBOD}
35	HPD	0.500	0.774	0.886	0.720	1.000	0.967	0.985	0.652
4	BOE	0.498	0.745	0.894	0.712	0.996	0.932	0.993	0.642
8	NYCPPF	0.498	0.737	0.887	0.708	0.996	0.922	0.986	0.637
33	NYCHA	0.480	0.762	0.878	0.707	0.960	0.953	0.976	0.641
14	COMPTROLLER	0.490	0.738	0.889	0.706	0.980	0.923	0.988	0.636
17	DCA	0.487	0.757	0.871	0.705	0.974	0.947	0.967	0.639
62	CCHR	0.480	0.781	0.853	0.704	0.960	0.976	0.948	0.642
10	DORIS	0.493	0.727	0.887	0.702	0.986	0.909	0.986	0.632
28	BP-MAN	0.499	0.731	0.875	0.702	0.998	0.914	0.972	0.632
15	TLC	0.476	0.755	0.871	0.701	0.952	0.944	0.968	0.635
18	SBS	0.490	0.742	0.870	0.700	0.980	0.927	0.966	0.633
13	DOF	0.498	0.725	0.875	0.699	0.996	0.906	0.972	0.629
51	DDC	0.466	0.741	0.890	0.699	0.932	0.926	0.989	0.632
1	DCAS	0.476	0.735	0.884	0.698	0.952	0.919	0.995	0.633
71	DOI	0.497	0.722	0.874	0.698	0.994	0.903	0.971	0.627
2	DOITT	0.471	0.744	0.875	0.697	0.942	0.931	0.972	0.631
26	CFB	0.500	0.721	0.865	0.695	1.000	0.902	0.961	0.625
24	COUNCIL	0.499	0.704	0.881	0.695	0.998	0.880	0.969	0.620
7	OPA	0.476	0.740	0.864	0.693	0.952	0.925	0.960	0.627
50	DOB	0.461	0.735	0.882	0.693	0.922	0.918	0.980	0.626
5	NYCERS	0.476	0.721	0.878	0.692	0.952	0.901	0.976	0.623
6	TRS	0.487	0.731	0.856	0.691	0.974	0.914	0.978	0.630

Composite Index of Organizational Diversity

59	DA-NARC	0.499	0.695	0.880	0.691	0.998	0.869	0.978	0.618
32	PUBADMIN	0.480	0.721	0.871	0.691	0.960	0.901	0.968	0.622
19	BIC	0.500	0.704	0.868	0.691	1.000	0.881	0.964	0.619
55	DA-BK	0.493	0.703	0.876	0.691	0.986	0.879	0.974	0.619
60	CCRB	0.500	0.732	0.840	0.691	1.000	0.915	0.934	0.623
45	DYCD	0.461	0.719	0.892	0.690	0.922	0.898	0.981	0.620
34	PARKS	0.449	0.720	0.901	0.690	0.898	0.900	0.991	0.620
29	BP-BX	0.487	0.688	0.888	0.688	0.974	0.860	0.986	0.614
3	MAYORALTY	0.484	0.713	0.863	0.687	0.968	0.892	0.959	0.618
39	SCA	0.455	0.719	0.879	0.684	0.910	0.899	0.977	0.618
25	BP-BK	0.461	0.701	0.888	0.683	0.922	0.876	0.986	0.614
31	PA	0.499	0.718	0.824	0.680	0.998	0.898	0.915	0.614
56	DA-BX	0.484	0.715	0.843	0.680	0.968	0.893	0.936	0.613
67	NYPD	0.455	0.718	0.867	0.680	0.910	0.897	0.963	0.614
52	DCP	0.500	0.674	0.866	0.680	1.000	0.842	0.962	0.606
64	COIB	0.493	0.682	0.864	0.679	0.986	0.852	0.972	0.610
58	DA-QNS	0.490	0.658	0.888	0.679	0.980	0.822	0.987	0.602
37	DCLA	0.487	0.697	0.850	0.678	0.974	0.871	0.956	0.611
43	DOHMH	0.412	0.733	0.887	0.677	0.824	0.916	0.985	0.616
9	CLERK	0.435	0.713	0.882	0.677	0.870	0.891	0.980	0.612
53	LAW	0.466	0.675	0.879	0.673	0.932	0.844	0.977	0.602
40	NYCHH	0.428	0.701	0.884	0.671	0.856	0.876	0.982	0.605
46	DFTA	0.394	0.750	0.869	0.671	0.788	0.937	0.977	0.617
57	OATH	0.476	0.663	0.873	0.671	0.952	0.829	0.970	0.598
20	ACTUARY	0.495	0.630	0.876	0.667	0.990	0.787	0.986	0.591
54	DA-MAN	0.493	0.622	0.882	0.666	0.986	0.777	0.980	0.586
16	FISA	0.449	0.679	0.862	0.663	0.898	0.848	0.969	0.598
23	MWFA	0.471	0.732	0.785	0.663	0.942	0.916	0.942	0.619
72	NYCEM (OEM)	0.497	0.642	0.844	0.661	0.994	0.803	0.937	0.586

21	NYCTAX	0.500	0.657	0.821	0.659	1.000	0.822	0.924	0.590
11	FDNYPF	0.428	0.682	0.868	0.659	0.856	0.852	0.992	0.599
27	BP-QNS	0.442	0.645	0.881	0.656	0.884	0.807	0.979	0.585
49	DOT	0.375	0.696	0.887	0.653	0.750	0.870	0.985	0.592
69	DOC	0.490	0.595	0.864	0.650	0.980	0.744	0.960	0.570
38	DOE	0.354	0.702	0.891	0.649	0.708	0.878	0.990	0.591
63	BOC	0.420	0.708	0.813	0.647	0.840	0.886	0.915	0.592
48	DEP	0.375	0.676	0.886	0.646	0.750	0.845	0.984	0.584
44	DHS	0.500	0.540	0.884	0.641	1.000	0.675	0.983	0.554
65	NYCCSC	0.442	0.658	0.821	0.640	0.884	0.823	0.958	0.585
66	EEPC	0.442	0.719	0.753	0.638	0.884	0.899	0.942	0.607
41	HRA	0.412	0.615	0.867	0.631	0.824	0.768	0.963	0.562
12	OCB	0.412	0.648	0.809	0.623	0.824	0.810	0.944	0.571
22	IBO	0.498	0.520	0.848	0.622	0.996	0.650	0.954	0.539
42	ACS	0.403	0.563	0.887	0.618	0.806	0.704	0.985	0.543
70	DOP	0.428	0.540	0.876	0.615	0.856	0.675	0.974	0.536
61	DA-SI	0.493	0.457	0.866	0.605	0.986	0.572	0.962	0.514
36	LPC	0.412	0.487	0.875	0.591	0.824	0.609	0.972	0.510
30	BP-SI	0.471	0.389	0.875	0.579	0.942	0.486	0.973	0.483
47	DSNY	0.164	0.639	0.865	0.556	0.328	0.799	0.961	0.516
68	FDNY	0.196	0.530	0.866	0.531	0.392	0.663	0.962	0.478
	Average	0.459	0.683	0.868	0.670	0.918	0.853	0.969	0.602
	Standard Deviation	0.059	0.076	0.025	0.036	0.118	0.095	0.018	0.037
	Coefficient of Variation (CV)	0.128	0.111	0.029	0.054	0.128	0.111	0.018	0.062

Exhibit 6-3 OD scores based on unstandardized unbiased Simpson (S_N) diversity coefficients for NYC departments for fiscal year 2019

Case Number	Department Acronym	Unstandardized S_N scores				Standardized S_N Scores			
		S_{GN}	S_{EN}	S_{AN}	S_{NOD}	S_{SGN}	S_{SEN}	S_{SAN}	S_{SNOD}
23	MWFA	0.515	0.793	0.850	0.720	1.031	0.992	0.942	0.654
35	HPD	0.476	0.774	0.887	0.712	0.952	0.967	0.985	0.647
66	EEPC	0.519	0.785	0.822	0.709	1.038	0.981	0.942	0.652
62	CCHR	0.479	0.786	0.859	0.708	0.958	0.983	0.948	0.645
10	DORIS	0.482	0.737	0.900	0.706	0.965	0.921	0.986	0.633
4	BOE	0.476	0.746	0.895	0.706	0.953	0.933	0.993	0.638
33	NYCHA	0.476	0.762	0.878	0.705	0.952	0.953	0.976	0.640
8	NYCPPF	0.479	0.743	0.893	0.705	0.958	0.928	0.986	0.635
32	PUBADMIN	0.486	0.737	0.890	0.704	0.972	0.921	0.968	0.630
17	DCA	0.477	0.759	0.873	0.703	0.954	0.949	0.967	0.637
51	DDC	0.476	0.741	0.891	0.703	0.952	0.926	0.989	0.634
14	COMPTROLLER	0.476	0.739	0.891	0.702	0.953	0.924	0.988	0.633
64	COIB	0.496	0.710	0.900	0.702	0.991	0.888	0.972	0.622
15	TLC	0.477	0.757	0.872	0.702	0.953	0.946	0.968	0.636
28	BP-MAN	0.481	0.739	0.884	0.701	0.962	0.924	0.972	0.631
46	DFTA	0.477	0.752	0.871	0.700	0.955	0.940	0.977	0.637
9	CLERK	0.482	0.722	0.894	0.700	0.964	0.903	0.980	0.626
34	PARKS	0.476	0.720	0.901	0.699	0.952	0.900	0.991	0.626
2	DOITT	0.476	0.745	0.876	0.699	0.952	0.931	0.972	0.632
1	DCAS	0.476	0.736	0.885	0.699	0.952	0.920	0.995	0.633
43	DOHMH	0.476	0.733	0.887	0.699	0.952	0.916	0.985	0.630
65	NYCCSC	0.510	0.705	0.879	0.698	1.020	0.882	0.958	0.620

Chapter 6

50	DOB	0.476	0.735	0.883	0.698	0.952	0.919	0.980	0.630
18	SBS	0.477	0.744	0.872	0.698	0.955	0.930	0.966	0.631
7	OPA	0.479	0.745	0.870	0.698	0.958	0.931	0.960	0.630
45	DYCD	0.477	0.720	0.894	0.697	0.953	0.900	0.981	0.624
11	FDNYPF	0.489	0.701	0.893	0.694	0.979	0.876	0.992	0.621
25	BP-BK	0.480	0.706	0.895	0.694	0.959	0.883	0.986	0.620
26	CFB	0.480	0.728	0.873	0.693	0.960	0.910	0.961	0.624
5	NYCERS	0.477	0.722	0.880	0.693	0.960	0.903	0.976	0.624
71	DOI	0.477	0.724	0.876	0.693	0.954	0.905	0.971	0.624
13	DOF	0.476	0.725	0.876	0.692	0.954	0.906	0.972	0.624
39	SCA	0.476	0.720	0.880	0.692	0.952	0.900	0.977	0.623
19	BIC	0.482	0.713	0.879	0.691	0.953	0.892	0.964	0.619
29	BP-BX	0.481	0.696	0.897	0.691	0.964	0.870	0.986	0.616
38	DOE	0.476	0.702	0.891	0.690	0.962	0.878	0.990	0.618
6	TRS	0.477	0.733	0.858	0.690	0.952	0.916	0.978	0.629
63	BOC	0.492	0.733	0.841	0.689	0.954	0.916	0.915	0.618
24	COUNCIL	0.476	0.705	0.882	0.688	0.984	0.881	0.969	0.615
40	NYCHH	0.476	0.701	0.884	0.687	0.953	0.876	0.982	0.616
67	NYPD	0.476	0.718	0.867	0.687	0.952	0.897	0.963	0.619
59	DA-NARC	0.478	0.698	0.884	0.687	0.956	0.873	0.978	0.614
49	DOT	0.476	0.696	0.887	0.686	0.952	0.870	0.985	0.615
60	CCRB	0.478	0.735	0.844	0.686	0.956	0.919	0.934	0.620
31	PA	0.485	0.732	0.840	0.686	0.970	0.916	0.915	0.616
55	DA-BK	0.476	0.704	0.877	0.686	0.952	0.880	0.974	0.615
3	MAYORALTY	0.476	0.714	0.864	0.685	0.952	0.892	0.959	0.616
12	OCB	0.506	0.689	0.860	0.685	1.011	0.861	0.944	0.609
37	DCLA	0.482	0.707	0.861	0.683	0.965	0.883	0.956	0.614
48	DEP	0.476	0.676	0.886	0.679	0.952	0.845	0.984	0.606

Composite Index of Organizational Diversity

56	DA-BX	0.476	0.715	0.844	0.678	0.952	0.894	0.936	0.612
53	LAW	0.476	0.675	0.880	0.677	0.952	0.844	0.977	0.604
58	DA-QNS	0.476	0.659	0.890	0.675	0.953	0.823	0.987	0.600
52	DCP	0.477	0.676	0.869	0.674	0.954	0.845	0.962	0.601
20	ACTUARY	0.485	0.642	0.894	0.674	0.971	0.803	0.986	0.595
16	FISA	0.477	0.680	0.864	0.674	0.954	0.850	0.969	0.605
27	BP-QNS	0.480	0.651	0.889	0.674	0.960	0.814	0.979	0.596
57	OATH	0.476	0.664	0.875	0.672	0.953	0.830	0.970	0.598
21	NYCTAX	0.486	0.671	0.838	0.665	0.971	0.839	0.924	0.593
54	DA-MAN	0.476	0.622	0.883	0.660	0.952	0.778	0.980	0.583
47	DSNY	0.476	0.639	0.865	0.660	0.952	0.799	0.961	0.586
72	NYCEM (OEM)	0.478	0.645	0.848	0.657	0.956	0.806	0.937	0.583
41	HRA	0.476	0.615	0.867	0.652	0.952	0.768	0.963	0.576
69	DOC	0.476	0.595	0.864	0.645	0.952	0.744	0.960	0.567
42	ACS	0.476	0.563	0.887	0.642	0.952	0.704	0.985	0.559
44	DHS	0.476	0.540	0.885	0.634	0.952	0.675	0.983	0.549
22	IBO	0.489	0.534	0.872	0.632	0.979	0.668	0.954	0.543
70	DOP	0.476	0.540	0.877	0.631	0.952	0.675	0.974	0.547
68	FDNY	0.476	0.530	0.866	0.624	0.952	0.663	0.962	0.540
36	LPC	0.482	0.493	0.885	0.620	0.963	0.616	0.972	0.528
61	DA-SI	0.479	0.460	0.871	0.603	0.957	0.575	0.962	0.512
30	BP-SI	0.485	0.396	0.892	0.591	0.970	0.496	0.973	0.489
Average		0.481	0.690	0.876	0.682	0.961	0.862	0.969	0.610
Standard Deviation		0.009	0.077	0.017	0.026	0.018	0.096	0.018	0.032
Coefficient of Variation (CV)		0.018	0.112	0.019	0.038	0.018	0.112	0.018	0.053

Different statistical findings are obtained for the OD scores that are calculated using the unbiased (S_N) unstandardized and standardized diversity coefficients (see Exhibit 6-3). The findings show that MWFA has the highest weighted OD score of 0. 0.720, which is the average of an unbiased gender diversity coefficient of 0.515, an ethnic diversity score of 0.793, and an age diversity score of 0.850. By contrast, MWFA has an OD score of 0.663 when the biased (S_B) diversity scores for age, ethnicity, and gender are totaled and averaged. The reason for the difference in the OD scores is that the formula for calculating unbiased (S_N) diversity scores overcorrects for the size of MWFA's workforce and yields higher diversity coefficients. Exhibit 6-3 also shows that HDP has a lower unbiased (S_{NOD}) OD diversity score of 0.712 in comparison to its biased (S_{BOD}) OD diversity score of 0.720. The difference in HDP's S_{BOD} and S_{NOB} OD scores is due a decrease in the gender diversity coefficient when the formula for calculating unbiased (S_N) scores is applied to its gender-based data. Lastly, Exhibit 6-3 shows that BP-SI has the lowest unweighted OD score of 0. 0.591 and the lowest weighted OD score of 0.489, which is due to having a low unbiased ethnic diversity score of 0.396.

Descriptive statistical analysis of OD scores

The descriptive statistical analysis indicates that the OD scores are negatively skewed, heavy tailed, and fail to meet the assumption of normality (see Exhibit 6-4). For instance, the distribution of S_{BOD} scores has a negative skewness coefficient of 1.595 and a kurtosis of 5.774. The findings also show that the distribution of the S_{BOD} scores has a median of 0.680, a mean of 0.670, a standard deviation of 0.037, and a 95% CI ranging from 0.661 to 0.678. With respect to the distribution of S_{SBOD} scores that are based on the standardized biased (S_B) diversity scores for age, ethnicity, and gender, the analysis indicates that the distribution is negatively skewed (Skewness = -1.568), peaked (Kurtosis = 5.127), and fails to meet the assumption of normality. Because weights are assigned to the standardized biased diversity coefficients, the distribution of the S_{SBOD} scores has a median of 0.614, mean of 0.602, standard deviation of 0.037, and a 95% CI ranging from 0.593 to 0.611. Similar findings are obtained for the OD scores based on the unbiased (S_N) diversity scores.

Exhibit 6-4 Descriptive statistics for biased and unbiased Simpson OD scores for NYC departments for fiscal year 2019

1. Descriptive statistics for biased Simpson scores

A. Measures of central tendency and variability for biased Simpson scores

Index	Cases (N)	Central Tendency		Variability		95% Confidence Interval	
		Median	Mean	Variance	Standard Deviation	Lower Limit	Upper Limit
S_{BOD}	72	0.680	0.670	0.001	0.037	0.661	0.678
S_{SBOD}	72	0.614	0.602	0.001	0.037	0.593	0.611

B. Tests for normality, skewness, and kurtosis for biased Simpson scores

1. Shapiro-Wilk W test for normal data

Index	Cases (N)	W-statistic	V-statistic	z-statistic	Probability > z
S_{BOD}	72	0.857	8.998	4.785	0.0001
S_{SBOD}	72	0.838	10.233	5.066	0.0001

2. Skewness/Kurtosis tests for Normality for biased Simpson scores

Index	Skewness	Kurtosis	Probability of Skewness	Probability of Kurtosis	Adjusted χ^2	Probability > χ^2
S_{BOD}	-1.595	5.774	0.0001	0.0022	22.88	0.0001
S_{SBOD}	-1.568	5.127	0.0001	0.0072	21.09	0.0001

2. Descriptive statistics for unbiased standardized Simpson scores

A. Measures of central tendency and variability for unbiased standardized Simpson scores

Index	Cases (N)	Central Tendency		Variability		95% Confidence Interval	
		Median	Mean	Variance	Standard Deviation	Lower Limit	Upper Limit
S_{NOD}	72	0.690	0.682	0.001	0.026	0.676	0.688
S_{SNOD}	72	0.619	0.610	0.001	0.033	0.602	0.617

Chapter 6

B. Tests for normality, skewness, and kurtosis for unbiased standardized Simpson scores

1. Shapiro-Wilk W test for normal data

Index	Cases (N)	W-statistic	V-statistic	z-statistic	Probability > z
S_{NOD}	72	0.840	10.091	5.035	0.0001
S_{SNOD}	72	0.831	10.665	5.156	0.0001

2. Skewness/Kurtosis tests for Normality for unbiased standardized Simpson scores

Index	Skewness	Kurtosis	Probability of Skewness	Probability of Kurtosis	Adjusted χ^2	Probability > χ^2
S_{NOD}	-1.544	5.041	0.0001	0.0086	20.59	0.0001
S_{SNOD}	-1.655	5.614	0.0001	0.0029	23.23	0.0001

Comparison of biased and unbiased of OD scores

Exhibit 6-5 compares the sets of OD scores of each NYC department for fiscal year 2019. The findings show that the OD score for DSNY that is based on the unbiased (S_N) diversity coefficient is larger in comparison to the OD score based on the biased (S_B) coefficient by 0.104 points ($S_{NOD} - S_{BOD} = 0.660 - 0.556 = 0.104$). A difference of 0.208 is obtained when the standardized OD scores are compared ($S_{SNOD} - S_{SBOD} = 0.620 - 0.411 = 0.104$). In addition, the findings show that DHS has a larger OD score based on unstandardized biased (S_{BOD}) diversity scores in comparison to the OD score based on unstandardized unbiased (S_{NOD}) diversity sores. Specifically, DHS's S_{NOD} coefficient is 0.008 points smaller in comparison to the S_{BOD} coefficient ($S_{NOD} - S_{BOD} = 0.634 - 0.641 = -0.008$).

Similar to previous chapters, paired z-tests are conducted to determine whether the sets of OD scores are statistically equal. Specifically, 4 planned pairwise comparisons are undertaken. The reason for conducting the paired z-tests is to assess whether the unbiased OD (S_{NOD} and S_{SNOD}) scores are statistically higher in comparison to their respective biased scores (S_{BOD} and S_{SBOD}). The 4 planned pairwise comparisons are the following:

1. The mean of S_{BOD} equals the mean of S_{NOD} (H_{O1}: $\mu_{BOD} = \mu_{NOB}$) at $\alpha = .01$;
2. The mean of S_{SBOD} equals the mean of S_{SNOD} (H_{O2}: $\mu_{SBOD} = \mu_{SNOD}$) at $\alpha = .01$;
3. The mean of S_{SNOD} equals the mean of S_{NOD} (H_{O3}: $\mu_{SNOD} = \mu_{NOD}$) at $\alpha = .01$; and,
4. The mean of S_{SBOD} equals the mean of S_{SNOD} (H_{O4}: $\mu_{SBOD} = \mu_{SNOD}$) at $\alpha = .01$.

The statistical findings of the paired z-tests for equality of means (H_O: $\mu_1 = \mu_2$) are presented in Exhibit 6-6.

Exhibit 6-5 Comparison of OD scores for NYC departments for fiscal year 2019

Case Number	Department Acronym	S_{BOD}	S_{NOD}	Difference ($S_{NOD} - S_{BOD}$)	S_{SBOD}	S_{SNOD}	Difference ($S_{SNOD} - S_{SBOD}$)
47	DSNY	0.556	0.660	0.104	0.411	0.620	0.208
68	FDNY	0.531	0.624	0.093	0.418	0.605	0.187
66	EEPC	0.638	0.709	0.070	0.604	0.664	0.060
12	OCB	0.623	0.685	0.062	0.574	0.642	0.068
65	NYCCSC	0.640	0.698	0.058	0.599	0.651	0.052
23	MWFA	0.663	0.720	0.057	0.625	0.663	0.038
63	BOC	0.647	0.689	0.042	0.582	0.633	0.052
38	DOE	0.649	0.690	0.041	0.554	0.635	0.081
11	FDNYPF	0.659	0.694	0.035	0.600	0.644	0.044
49	DOT	0.653	0.686	0.034	0.566	0.633	0.067
48	DEP	0.646	0.679	0.034	0.563	0.630	0.067
46	DFTA	0.671	0.700	0.029	0.584	0.640	0.056
36	LPC	0.591	0.620	0.029	0.558	0.605	0.047
42	ACS	0.618	0.642	0.024	0.566	0.614	0.048
9	CLERK	0.677	0.700	0.023	0.607	0.640	0.033
64	COIB	0.679	0.702	0.022	0.639	0.645	0.006
43	DOHMH	0.677	0.699	0.021	0.595	0.638	0.043
41	HRA	0.631	0.652	0.021	0.574	0.617	0.043
27	BP-QNS	0.656	0.674	0.017	0.602	0.628	0.026
70	DOP	0.615	0.631	0.017	0.577	0.609	0.032
40	NYCHH	0.671	0.687	0.016	0.601	0.633	0.032
32	PUBADMIN	0.691	0.704	0.014	0.635	0.642	0.006
30	BP-SI	0.579	0.591	0.013	0.584	0.595	0.010
25	BP-BK	0.683	0.694	0.011	0.624	0.637	0.013

Composite Index of Organizational Diversity

16	FISA	0.663	0.674	0.011	0.609	0.628	0.019
22	IBO	0.622	0.632	0.010	0.616	0.612	-0.004
34	PARKS	0.690	0.699	0.009	0.619	0.637	0.018
39	SCA	0.684	0.692	0.008	0.620	0.635	0.014
67	NYPD	0.680	0.687	0.007	0.617	0.631	0.014
20	ACTUARY	0.667	0.674	0.007	0.636	0.632	-0.005
45	DYCD	0.690	0.697	0.006	0.625	0.636	0.011
21	NYCTAX	0.659	0.665	0.006	0.630	0.622	-0.007
37	DCLA	0.678	0.683	0.005	0.634	0.632	-0.002
50	DOB	0.693	0.698	0.005	0.627	0.637	0.010
31	PA	0.680	0.686	0.005	0.636	0.629	-0.007
7	OPA	0.693	0.698	0.005	0.633	0.636	0.003
10	DORIS	0.702	0.706	0.004	0.649	0.643	-0.006
51	DDC	0.699	0.703	0.004	0.633	0.640	0.007
62	CCHR	0.704	0.708	0.004	0.639	0.639	0.000
29	BP-BX	0.688	0.691	0.004	0.640	0.636	-0.003
53	LAW	0.673	0.677	0.004	0.622	0.628	0.007
2	DOITT	0.697	0.699	0.002	0.634	0.637	0.003
5	NYCERS	0.692	0.693	0.002	0.634	0.635	0.001
15	TLC	0.701	0.702	0.001	0.637	0.638	0.001
57	OATH	0.671	0.672	0.001	0.625	0.625	0.001
19	BIC	0.691	0.691	0.001	0.645	0.635	-0.011
1	DCAS	0.698	0.699	0.000	0.640	0.641	0.000
28	BP-MAN	0.702	0.701	0.000	0.650	0.639	-0.011
33	NYCHA	0.707	0.705	-0.001	0.643	0.640	-0.003
6	TRS	0.691	0.690	-0.002	0.644	0.637	-0.006
26	CFB	0.695	0.693	-0.002	0.647	0.635	-0.012
56	DA-BX	0.680	0.678	-0.002	0.630	0.625	-0.005
17	DCA	0.705	0.703	-0.002	0.645	0.638	-0.007

61	DA-SI	0.605	0.603	-0.002	0.606	0.597	-0.009
3	MAYORALTY	0.687	0.685	-0.002	0.635	0.630	-0.005
18	SBS	0.700	0.698	-0.002	0.645	0.636	-0.008
8	NYCPPF	0.708	0.705	-0.003	0.654	0.642	-0.012
72	NYCEM (OEM)	0.661	0.657	-0.004	0.629	0.617	-0.012
58	DA-QNS	0.679	0.675	-0.004	0.638	0.628	-0.009
14	COMPTROLLER	0.706	0.702	-0.004	0.649	0.640	-0.009
59	DA-NARC	0.691	0.687	-0.005	0.647	0.633	-0.014
60	CCRB	0.691	0.686	-0.005	0.642	0.628	-0.014
69	DOC	0.650	0.645	-0.005	0.623	0.613	-0.010
55	DA-BK	0.691	0.686	-0.005	0.643	0.632	-0.011
71	DOI	0.698	0.693	-0.005	0.647	0.634	-0.013
54	DA-MAN	0.666	0.660	-0.005	0.633	0.622	-0.011
52	DCP	0.680	0.674	-0.006	0.641	0.626	-0.015
4	BOE	0.712	0.706	-0.007	0.656	0.642	-0.014
24	COUNCIL	0.695	0.688	-0.007	0.646	0.631	-0.015
13	DOF	0.699	0.692	-0.007	0.649	0.634	-0.015
35	HPD	0.720	0.712	-0.008	0.660	0.644	-0.016
44	DHS	0.641	0.634	-0.008	0.627	0.611	-0.016
Average		0.670	0.682	0.012	0.616	0.632	0.015
Standard Deviation		0.036	0.026	0.023	0.043	0.013	0.040
Coefficient of Variation (CV)		0.054	0.038		0.070	0.020	

Exhibit 6-6 Paired z-test for equal means for biased and unbiased unstandardized Simpson OD scores for NYC departments for fiscal year 2019

Cases (N)	H_o	Mean Difference	Standard Error	Standard Deviation	95% CI		z-statistic	Probability $(|Z| > |z|)$
					Lower Limit	Upper Limit		
72	$\mu_{SBOD} = \mu_{BOD}$	-0.068	0.001	0.010	-0.070	-0.066	-57.17	0.0001
72	$\mu_{SNOD} = \mu_{SBOD}$	0.012	0.003	0.023	0.007	0.018	4.59	0.0001
72	$\mu_{SNOD} = \mu_{NOD}$	-0.073	0.001	0.007	-0.074	-0.071	-83.36	0.0001
72	$\mu_{SNOD} = \mu_{SBOD}$	0.008	0.002	0.015	0.004	0.011	4.39	0.0001

As Exhibit 6-6 shows, the OD scores based on the standardized biased (S_{SBOD}) are statistically lower in comparison to OD scores obtained for the unstandardized biased (S_{SBOD}) scores at $\alpha = 0.01$ (z-statistic = -57.17, p < 0.001), which is due to the use of weights. Similarly, the findings show that the OD scores for the standardized unbiased (S_{SNOD}) diversity scores are statistically lower than the OD scores obtained for the unstandardized unbiased (S_{NOD}) diversity scores at $\alpha = 0.01$ (z-statistic = -83.36, p < 0.001), which is due to the use of weights. The findings also show that the OD scores based on the standardized unbiased (S_{SNOD}) diversity scores are statistically higher in comparison to OD scores for the standardized biased (S_{SBOD}) diversity scores at $\alpha = 0.01$ (z-statistic = 4.59, p < 0.001), which is due to adjusting for the size of the workforce or the number of group categories containing employee data. Lastly, the findings show that the OD scores calculated from the standardized unbiased (S_{SNOD}) diversity scores are statistically higher in comparison to the OD scores based on the standardized biased (S_{SBOD}) diversity scores at $\alpha = 0.01$ (z-statistic = 4.39, p < 0.001). Despite applying weights to both sets of OD scores, the reason for the significant statistical finding is that the S_{SNOD} scores adjust for the size of the workforce or for the number of group categories containing employee data.

Correlation and factor analysis of biased and unbiased OD scores

Similar to the Pearson correlation analysis undertaken to assess the relationship amongst the sets of ethnic diversity coefficients presented in Chapter 4, a correlation analysis is performed to assess whether the sets of OD scores are associated statistically with each other and whether the association is positive or negative. The reason for undertaking the correlation analysis is that pairwise z-tests do not reveal how closely the coefficients are correlated with each other despite the sets of OD scores differing statistically. Consistent with the correlation analysis conducted in Chapter 4, each pairwise correlation is tested for statistical significance at $\alpha = 0.01$ (H_O: $r_{xy} = 0$ at $\alpha = 0.01$). Exhibit 6-7 summarizes the findings of the pairwise correlational analysis performed on the sets of OD scores.

The correlational analysis shows that the sets of OD coefficients are correlated statistically with each other at $\alpha = 0.01$ (see Exhibit 6-7). For example, the pairwise Pearson correlation for OD scores based on the S_{BOD} and S_{SBOD} diversity coefficients is significant statistically at $\alpha = 0.01$ (r = 0.963, p < 0.01), showing that the sets of OD scores vary in the same direction

Exhibit 6-7 Pearson correlation analysis of biased and unbiased OD scores for NYC departments for fiscal year 2019

	Biased Simpson Scores			Unbiased Simpson Scores			
	S_{BOD}		S_{SBOD}		S_{NOD}		S_{SNOD}
S_{BOD}	1.000						
S_{SBOD}	0.963	*	1.000				
S_{NOD}	0.783	*	0.910	*	1.000		
S_{SNOD}	0.782	*	0.918	*	0.993	*	1.000

N= 72
* P < 0.01

despite the use of weights to calculate the OD scores for the S_{SBOD} diversity coefficients. The correlation amongst the OD scores obtained from the unstandardized (S_{BOD}) and standardized (S_{NOD}) diversity coefficients is significant statistically at $\alpha = 0.01$ ($r = 0.783$, $p < 0.01$), indicating that the scores vary in the same direction. A similar positive statistical relationship exists amongst the OD scores calculated from the standardized unbiased (S_{SNOD}) and unstandardized biased (S_{BOD}) diversity scores at $\alpha = 0.01$ ($r = 0. 0.782$, $p < 0.01$). Exhibit 6-7 also shows a positive statistical relationship amongst the OD scores for S_{SBOD} and S_{NOD} at $\alpha = 0.01$ ($r = 0.910$, $p < 0.01$). Similarly, a positive statistical relationship is found amongst the OD scores for S_{SBOD} and S_{SNOD} $\alpha = 0.01$ ($r = 0.918$, $p < 0.01$). A significant positive statistical relationship exists amongst the OD scores for S_{NOD} and S_{SNOD} scores at $\alpha = 0.01$ ($r = 0.993$, $p < 0.01$), indicating that the OD scores are related positively.

The correlation analysis suggests that the OD scores have similar underlying structures that assess the same dimension of OD. FA is used to determine whether the 4 sets of OD scores have similar structures that measure the same construct (see Exhibit 6-8). Identical to the FA performed on the different sets of ethnic diversity scores in Chapter 4, a FA analysis with principal component analysis (PCA) extraction is used for the index validation process because an a priori theory (or model) regarding the construction of a composite OD score is lacking. The use of PCA extraction also helps to establish a preliminary FA solution (see Pett, Lackey, and Sullivan, 2003). Direct oblimin oblique rotation is used to obtain a pattern matrix containing the factors and their item loadings and a factor correlation matrix containing the correlations coefficients amongst the factors because the Pearson correlation analysis above shows that the sets of OD scores are correlated statistically (see Yong and Pearce, 2013).

Exhibit 6-8 Factor analysis (FA) of biased and unbiased Simpson OD scores for NYC departments for fiscal year 2019

A. Unrotated principal-component factors (N = 72)

Factor	Eigenvalue	Difference	Proportion	Cumulative
Factor 1	3.676	3.364	0.919	0.919
Factor 2	0.313	0.302	0.078	0.997
Factor 3	0.011	0.011	0.003	1.000
Factor 4	0.000		0.000	1.000

B. Unrotated factor loading and uniqueness variance

Variable	Factor 1	Uniqueness
S_{BOD}	0.919	0.156
S_{SBOD}	0.988	0.023
S_{NOD}	0.962	0.074
S_{SNOD}	0.964	0.070

C. Oblique oblimin rotated factor loading and uniqueness variance

Variable	Factor 1	Uniqueness
S_{BOD}	0.919	0.156
S_{SBOD}	0.988	0.023
S_{NOD}	0.962	0.074
S_{SNOD}	0.964	0.070

The findings of the FA analyses for the OD scores of each NYC department for fiscal 2019 are summarized in Exhibit 6-8. The FA analysis with PCA extraction and oblimin oblique rotation extracted 1 factor which accounts for 92% of the variance. Factor 1 has an eigenvalue of 3.676 and accounts for 92% of the variance. The pattern matrix obtained from the oblimin oblique rotation grouped the OD scores into 1 factor (see Exhibit 6-8). Factor 1 is composed of the four sets of OD scores. As Exhibit 6-8 summarizes, S_{BOD} has a factor loading of 0.919. S_{SBOD} has a factor loading of 0.998. In addition, S_{NOD} has a factor loading of 0.962, and S_{SNOD} has a factor loading of 0.964. In sum, the FA analysis shows that the sets of OD scores measure the same construct.

Summary

Although the construction and use of a composite index of diversity for an organization is questionable because it is the product of combining several sets of seemingly incompatible and uncorrelated diversity scores, the ability to capture different types of diversity that occur concomitantly in organizations as employees enter and leave the workforce in one index is difficult to accomplish due to organizations reporting employee demographic data in separate formats. Despite concerns and questions about the construct and measurement validity of constructing a composite index to assess organizational diversity, researchers will continue to construct and use composite indices of diversity to estimate an organization's overall demographic, occupational, or social heterogeneity. In light of the criticism leveled against combining several diversity coefficients to construct a composite index, this chapter presented the construction and analyses of OD scores based on unstandardized and standardized coefficients of age, ethnicity, and gender diversity based on demographic data reported by each NYC department for fiscal year 2019. In so doing, weighted and unweighted methods of constructing a composite index were illustrated.

While the sets of OD scores presented in this chapter are correlated statistically and assess the same construct of OD, the sets of OD scores fail the meet the assumption of normality due to excessive skewness and kurtosis. The OD scores also have a range from 0 to 1, making the composite index a LDV. For illustrative purposes, the OD scores will be used as *dependent variables* in *multivariate analyses* undertaken in subsequent chapters,

Key Terms

Composite diversity index refers to a summary score that is calculated by combining age, ethnic, gender, or other demographic- or social-based diversity measures.

Convergent validity refers to whether two or more sets of scores that measure the same construct are correlated statistically with each other.

Dependent variables refer to a set or sets of measures that have values that are influenced positively or negatively as the values of other sets of measures increase or decrease.

Multivariate analysis refers to the statistical assessment of how a set of two or more measures influence the values of one or more dependent variables.

Occupational diversity refers to how well an organization's workforce is heterogenous in terms of the number of employees in different classes and types of job classifications and titles.

Organizational diversity refers to how well an organization's workforce is heterogeneous in terms of the employment of men and women of different demographic, economic, and social backgrounds.

References

Chatman, Jennifer. A., and Flynn, Francis J. 2001. "The influence of demographic heterogeneity on the emergence and consequences of cooperative norms in work teams". *Academy of Management Journal*, Vol. 44: 956 – 974.

Harrison, David A., and Klein, Katherine J. 2007. "What's the difference? Diversity constructs as separation, variety, or disparity in organizations". *Academy of Management Review*, Vol. 32: 1199 – 1228.

Kolo, Philipp. 2012. *Measuring a new aspect of ethnicity: The appropriate diversity index* (No. 221). Göttingen, Lower Saxony, Germany: Ibero-America Institute for Economic Research (IAI), University of Göttingen.

Michie, Jonathan, and Oughton, Christine. 2013. *Measuring diversity in financial services markets: A diversity index*. London, England: Centre for Financial and Management Studies, University of London.

Pett, Marjorie A., Lackey, Nancy R., and Sullivan, John J. 2003. *Making sense of factor analysis: The use of factor analysis for instrument development in health care research*. Thousand Oaks, California: Sage Publications Inc.

Randel, Amy E., and Jaussi, Kimberly S. 2003. "Functional background identity, diversity, and individual performance in cross-functional teams". *Academy of Management Journal*, Vol. 46: 763 – 774.

Yong, An Gie, and Pearce, Sean. 2013. "A beginner's guide to factor analysis: Focusing on exploratory factor analysis". *Tutorials in Quantitative Methods for Psychology*, Vol. 9: 79 – 94.

CHAPTER 7

ANALYSIS OF DIVERSITY WITH ORDINARY LEAST SQUARES (OLS) REGRESSION

Although the Simpson diversity index has an EMV ranging from 0 to $\frac{n-1}{n}$ that does not reach 1, numerous studies have used OLS regression to test whether a group of *independent variables* (or predictors) is related statistically with age, ethnic, gender, or other demographic-based diversity scores that serve as dependent variables (e.g., Akram, Haq, Natarajan, and Chellakan. 2020; Cheong, and Sinnakkannu, 2014; De Meulenaere, Boone, and Buyl, 2016; Ferrero-Ferrero, Fernández-Izquierdo, and Muñoz-Torres, 2015; Guajardo, 2014; Leslie, 2017). With few exceptions (e.g., Ferrero-Ferrero, Fernández-Izquierdo, and Muñoz-Torres, 2015; Leslie, 2017; Li, Gong, Burmeister, Wang, Alterman, Alonso, and Robinson, 2021; Moon and Christensen, 2020; Oba and Fodio, 2013), the majority of the studies do not provide information in regard to the independent variables and measures of diversity satisfying statistical assumptions concerning *multicollinearity*, normality, outliers, *truncation*, or other factors which may produce unreliable statistical findings when OLS regression is used to regress the independent variables on one or more measures of diversity. Methodologically and statistically, the independent variables and measures of diversity should satisfy the underlying assumptions of OLS regression prior to performing the statistical analysis so that the findings are reliable and represent the statistical relationships amongst the independent variables and the measures of diversity as accurately as possible.

This chapter applies OLS regression to the age, ethnic, gender, and OD diversity scores calculated for NYC departments for fiscal year 2019. The purpose for doing is twofold: 1) to illustrate how the results of the OLS regression change when a set of independent variables are regressed on biased (S_B) and unbiased (S_N) diversity scores, and 2) to compare the various OLS regression models with each other to highlight how the *intercept* (α) and *regression coefficients* (β) of each model change due to how the diversity scores are calculated and transformed. This chapter also discusses the underlying assumptions of OLS regression and how the age, ethnic, and gender diversity scores calculated for NYC departments violate several of the underlying assumptions. The theoretical statistical model guiding the OLS regression analyses is also discussed. In subsequent chapters, alternative regression methods are presented, and the statistical findings are compared to those obtained with the OLS regression.

Underlying assumptions of OLS regression

OLS regression has several underlying assumptions placed on the independent and dependent variables that should be met prior to undertaking the analysis (e.g., Lind, Marchal, and Wathen, 2018). The underlying assumptions of OLS regression are the following:

1. The dependent variable is quantitative continuous;
2. The relationship amongst the dependent and independent variables is linear so changes in the values of the independent variables produces changes in the values of the dependent variable;
3. The values of the dependent variable are normally distributed;
4. The values of the independent and dependent variables are not interconnected and are not calculated in part or in whole on the same data sources;
5. There are no outliers so that the independent and dependent variables do not have extreme low or high values;
6. There are no significant high collinear statistical relationships amongst the set of independent variables; and,
7. There is truncation so that the values of the independent or dependent variables do not have a minimum or maximum limit.

When the OLS regression assumptions are violated, the regression coefficients are biased, unreliable, and invalid despite the robustness of the method (e.g., Alma, 2011; Bingen, Siau, and Rousseeuw, 1986; Rousseeuw, Van Aelst, Van Driessen, and Agulló, 2004).

Although the distributions of the Simpson diversity scores for age, ethnicity, and gender are quantitative, the distributions of each set of diversity scores are truncated at a minimum value of 0 and a maximum value determined by $\frac{n-1}{n}$ (i.e., EMV $= \frac{n-1}{n}$) which does not exceed the value of 1. With the range of 0 to $\frac{n-1}{n}$, the diversity scores can take any decimal value. For instance, when gender is categorized dichotomously as men and women, the distribution of the gender diversity measures ranges from 0 to 0.50 (EMV =

$\frac{n-1}{n} = \frac{2-1}{2} = 0.50$). When ethnicity is categorized into 5 ethnic groups, the distribution of the ethnic diversity scores ranges from 0 to 0.80 (EMV $= \frac{n-1}{n} = \frac{4-1}{5} = 0.80$). With respect to the distribution of the age diversity scores, the range spans from 0 to an EMV of 0.80 to 0.91, depending on the number of age group categories that contain employee data. Because the distributions of the diversity scores have a set lower limit of 0 and a maximum upper limit of $\frac{n-1}{n}$, the scores are truncated and restricted from taking a value above 1.

One method which may be used to overcome the issue of having a maximum value determined by $\frac{n-1}{n}$ is to use the *reciprocal value* (RV $= \frac{1}{S}$) of a Simpson diversity score. However, the distribution of the reciprocal values will be truncated at the bottom so that the lowest value does not fall below the RV of $\frac{n-1}{n}$. For instance, a gender diversity score of 0.134 will have a RV of 7.46 (RV $= \frac{1}{S} = \frac{1}{0.134} = 7.463$); conversely, the EMV of 0.50 for gender diversity will have a RV of 2 (RV $= \frac{1}{0.50} = 2$), which truncates the distribution of scores at the bottom. When ethnic diversity scores are based on categorizing ethnic or racial data into 5 groups, the distribution of reciprocal values for ethnic diversity will have a lower limit of 1.25. The issue of converting the scores for age diversity to reciprocal values to overcome the maximum value of 1 becomes more complicated because there are multiple EMV values. Specifically, the distribution for the age diversity scores has several lower limits. NYC departments with employment data in each of the 11 age group categories have a lower limit of 1.10, while departments with employment data in 10 age group categories have a lower limit of 1.11. Those with employment data in 5 age group categories have a lower limit of 1.25. If one assumes that each department has employees in each of the 11 age group categories, the lower limit of the distribution of reciprocal values for the age diversity scores is 1.10. In short, while the upper limit of the distribution for the reciprocal values is unrestricted, the lowest possible value is determined the reciprocal of $\frac{n-1}{n}$.

As discussed in previous chapters, the distribution of the age, ethnic, and gender diversity scores are skewed, peaked, and nonnormal. Exhibit 7-1 highlights the statistical findings of the test for normality. The distributions of biased (S_{GB}) and unbiased (S_{BN}) diversity coefficients for gender are negatively or positively skewed, heavy tailed, and nonnormal. Similarly, the

Exhibit 7-1 Assumption of normality for OLS regression

Index	Cases (N)	Central Tendency		Variability		Normality	
		Median	Mean	Variance	Standard Deviation	Skewness	Kurtosis
S_{GB}	72	0.478	0.459	0.004	0.059	-3.11	14.706
S_{GN}	72	0.477	0.481	0.000	0.009	2.84	10.93
S_{EB1}	72	0.455	0.427	0.007	0.082	-1.397	4.157
S_{EB2}	72	0.706	0.683	0.006	0.076	-1.757	6.050
S_{EN1}	72	0.462	0.435	0.007	0.084	-1.383	4.301
S_{EN2}	72	0.714	0.690	0.006	0.078	-1.711	5.863
S_{AB}	72	0.875	0.868	0.001	0.026	-2.152	8.542
S_{AN}	72	0.879	0.876	0.000	0.876	-0.966	3.712
S_{BOD}	72	0.680	0.670	0.001	0.037	-1.595	5.774
S_{NOD}	72	0.690	0.682	0.001	0.026	-1.544	5.041

biased (S_{EB}) and unbiased (S_{EN}) diversity coefficients for ethnicity are negatively skewed, heavy tailed, and nonnormal whether classified as White or minority or whether categorized into 5 racial groups. Exhibit 7-1 shows similar findings for age and organizational diversity.

In terms of the presence of extreme values, each of the distributions for age, ethnic, and gender diversity has either low or high scores. For instance, the formula for obtaining unbiased (S_{GN}) diversity scores for gender produces measurements that exceeded the EMV value 0.50. By contrast, the formula for obtaining biased (S_{GB}) diversity scores for gender produces extreme low measurements. A few extreme low scores are present for the biased (S_{EB}) and unbased (S_{EN}) diversity scores for ethnicity. Extreme scores are present in the distribution of biased (S_{AB}) and unbiased (S_{AN}) age diversity scores. Two factors contribute to inflating the age diversity coefficients. First, the age diversity scores for some departments are based on workforces that are concentrated heavily on several age group categories so that the employees are not spread evening across each of the age group categories. Second, the formula for obtaining unbiased (S_{AN}) age diversity scores overcorrects for the size of the workforce and does not adjust for the number of age group categories containing employment data. The presence of extreme low scores tends to lower the value of the y-axis intercept and the regression coefficients, while extreme high scores tend to increase the value of the y-axis intercept and the regression coefficients (see Exhibit 7-3).

Exhibit 7-2 and 7-3 indicate that there is a lack of linearity amongst the size of the departments in terms of employees and gender diversity. In fact, the biased (S_{GB}) gender diversity scores do not appear to increase as the size of total workforce increases. In addition, Exhibit 7-3 highlights the presence of several atypical gender diversity scores. The graphs also illustrate how the slopes of the regression lines change when atypical values are present and absent from the set of gender diversity scores. Similar relationships exist among other independent variables and the diversity scores for age, ethnicity, and gender.

Exhibit 7-2 Distribution of biased (S$_{GB}$) gender diversity scores by total employees

Case Number	Agency	Total Employees	S$_{GB}$	Case Number	Agency	Total Employees	S$_{GB}$
44	DHS	2,438	0.500	44	DHS	2,438	0.500
35	HPD	2,441	0.500	19	BIC	80	0.500
52	DCP	334	0.500	21	NYCTAX	49	0.500
60	CCRB	203	0.500	26	CFB	115	0.500
26	CFB	115	0.500	35	HPD	2,441	0.500
19	BIC	80	0.500	52	DCP	334	0.500
21	NYCTAX	49	0.500	60	CCRB	203	0.500
24	COUNCIL	867	0.499	24	COUNCIL	867	0.499
59	DA-NARC	215	0.499	28	BP-MAN	94	0.499
28	BP-MAN	94	0.499	31	PA	52	0.499
31	PA	52	0.499	59	DA-NARC	215	0.499
13	DOF	2,102	0.498	4	BOE	833	0.498
4	BOE	833	0.498	8	NYCPPF	144	0.498
8	NYCPPF	144	0.498	13	DOF	2,102	0.498
22	IBO	36	0.498	22	IBO	36	0.498
72	NYCEM	202	0.497	72	NYCEM	202	0.497
71	DOI	367	0.497	71	DOI	367	0.497
20	ACTUARY	51	0.495	20	ACTUARY	51	0.495
54	DA-MAN	1,472	0.493	10	DORIS	73	0.493
55	DA-BK	1,140	0.493	54	DA-MAN	1,472	0.493
61	DA-SI	170	0.493	55	DA-BK	1,140	0.493
10	DORIS	73	0.493	61	DA-SI	170	0.493
64	COIB	25	0.493	64	COIB	25	0.493
69	DOC	12,296	0.490	14	COMPTROLLER	784	0.490

Analysis of Diversity with Ordinary Least Squares (OLS) Regression

14	COMPTROLLER	784	0.490	18	SBS	301	0.490
58	DA-QNS	710	0.490	58	DA-QNS	710	0.490
18	SBS	301	0.490	69	DOC	12,296	0.490
17	DCA	416	0.487	6	TRS	349	0.487
6	TRS	349	0.487	17	DCA	416	0.487
29	BP-BX	93	0.487	29	BP-BX	93	0.487
37	DCLA	74	0.487	37	DCLA	74	0.487
3	MAYORALTY	1,271	0.484	3	MAYORALTY	1,271	0.484
56	DA-BX	1,082	0.484	56	DA-BX	1,082	0.484
33	NYCHA	10,962	0.480	32	PUBADMIN	47	0.480
62	CCHR	139	0.480	33	NYCHA	10,962	0.480
32	PUBADMIN	47	0.480	62	CCHR	139	0.480
1	DCAS	2,468	0.476	1	DCAS	2,468	0.476
57	OATH	717	0.476	5	NYCERS	444	0.476
15	TLC	632	0.476	7	OPA	152	0.476
5	NYCERS	444	0.476	15	TLC	632	0.476
7	OPA	152	0.476	57	OATH	717	0.476
2	DOITT	1,576	0.471	2	DOITT	1,576	0.471
30	BP-SI	53	0.471	23	MWFA	13	0.471
23	MWFA	13	0.471	30	BP-SI	53	0.471
53	LAW	1,903	0.466	51	DDC	1,340	0.466
51	DDC	1,340	0.466	53	LAW	1,903	0.466
50	DOB	1,657	0.461	25	BP-BK	124	0.461
45	DYCD	574	0.461	45	DYCD	574	0.461
25	BP-BK	124	0.461	50	DOB	1,657	0.461
67	NYPD	55,960	0.455	39	SCA	827	0.455
39	SCA	827	0.455	67	NYPD	55,960	0.455
34	PARKS	7,267	0.449	16	FISA	436	0.449
16	FISA	436	0.449	34	PARKS	7,267	0.449

Chapter 7

27	BP-QNS	109	0.442	27	BP-QNS	109	0.442
65	NYCCSC	15	0.442	65	NYCCSC	15	0.442
66	EEPC	12	0.442	66	EEPC	12	0.442
9	CLERK	75	0.435	9	CLERK	75	0.435
40	NYCHH	38,731	0.428	11	FDNYPF	36	0.428
70	DOP	1,166	0.428	40	NYCHH	38,731	0.428
11	FDNYPF	36	0.428	70	DOP	1,166	0.428
63	BOC	30	0.420	63	BOC	30	0.420
41	HRA	13,018	0.412	12	OCB	17	0.412
43	DOHMH	7,150	0.412	36	LPC	83	0.412
36	LPC	83	0.412	41	HRA	13,018	0.412
12	OCB	17	0.412	43	DOHMH	7,150	0.412
42	ACS	7366	0.403	42	ACS	7366	0.403
46	DFTA	326	0.394	46	DFTA	326	0.394
48	DEP	6,216	0.375	48	DEP	6,216	0.375
49	DOT	5,716	0.375	49	DOT	5,716	0.375
38	DOE	174,105	0.354				
68	FDNY	17,746	0.196				
47	DSNY	10,134	0.164				

Exhibit 7-3 Scatterplot of biased (S_GB) gender diversity scores by total employees

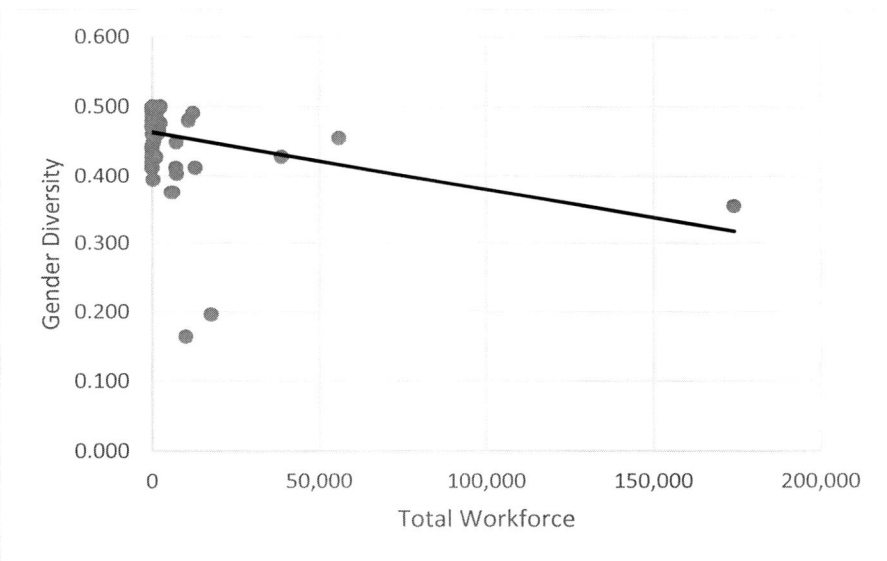

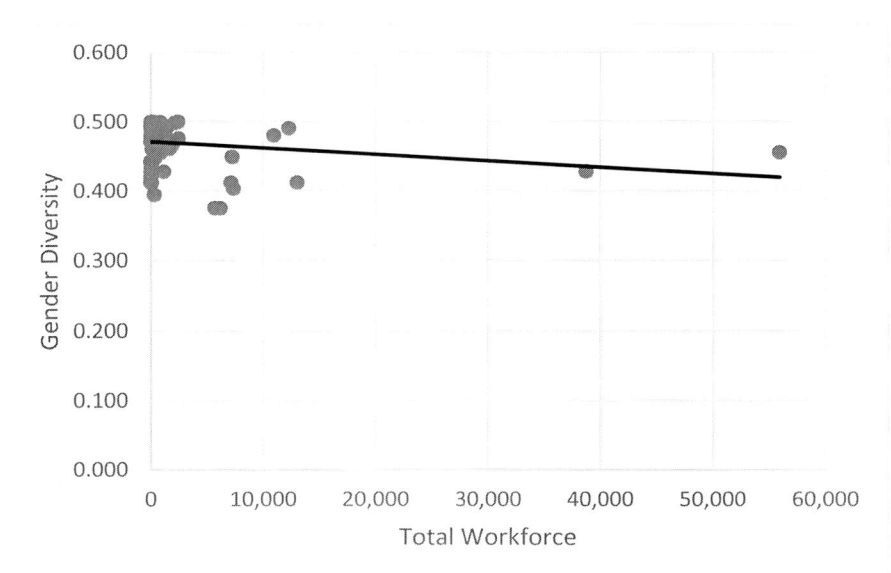

Statistically, strong positive or negative relationships of 0.70 or higher suggest the presence of multicollinearity (see Daoud, 2017; Shrestha, 2020; Yoo, Mayberry, Bae, Singh, He, and Lillard, 2014). Moderate positive or negative statistical relationships amongst independent variable ranging from 0.35 to 0.70 also suggest the existence of collinearity. The statistical findings of the collinearity amongst the independent variables are presented in Exhibit 7-4. As Exhibit 7-4 shows, the statistical relationships amongst several of the independent variables are significant and suggests the presence of multicollinearity. For instance, the statistical association amongst median year of service (Myos) and workforces composed predominantly of employees over the age of 40 (O40cluster) is moderately high at 0.703 ($r = 0.703$, $p < 0.001$). Similarly, the association amongst workforces composed predominantly of women (Wcluster) and workforces with high women employment turnover (Wscluster) is somewhat high at 0.650 ($r = 0.650$, $p < 0.001$). The relationship amongst Wcluster and workforces with predominantly new women hires (Whcluster) also is somewhat high at 0.519 ($r = 0.519$, $p < 0.001$). A moderately high positive relationship of 0.710 ($r = 0.710$, $p < 0.001$) exists amongst workforces composed predominantly of ethnic minority employees (Mcluster) and workforces with high minority employee turnover (Mscluster). Further, a strong high positive relationship of 0.850 ($r = 0.850$, $p < 0.001$) exists amongst Mcluster and workforces with predominantly new minority hires (Mhcluster). As discussed below, additional tests for multicollinearity are performed to determine whether the inclusion of independent variables that are related statistically to other predicators have a deleterious impact on the regression results.

Analysis of Diversity with Ordinary Least Squares (OLS) Regression

Exhibit 7-4 Pearson correlation matrix for independent variables

	SEA	Employees	Myos	Mftsal	Pctunion	Wcluster	Mincluster	O40cluster	Wscluster	Mscluster	Whcluster	Mhcluster
SEA	1.00											
Employees	-0.021	1.00										
Myos	-0.138	0.144	1.00									
Mftsal	0.196	-0.029	0.168	1.00								
Pctunion	-0.316 **	0.250 *	0.281 *	-0.398 ***	1.00							
Wcluster	-0.069	0.287 *	0.077	-0.172	-0.029	1.00						
Mcluster	-0.381 **	0.019	0.085	-0.363 **	0.346 **	0.209	1.00					
O40cluster	-0.239 *	-0.054	0.703 ***	0.205	0.143	0.147	0.036	1.00				
Wscluster	-0.104	0.217	-0.131	-0.295 *	0.005	0.650 ***	0.142	-0.053	1.00			
Mscluster	-0.318 **	-0.013	0.022	-0.493 ***	0.266 *	0.118	0.710 ***	0.012	0.102	1.00		
Whcluster	-0.199	0.078	0.075	-0.152	0.063	0.519 ***	0.047	0.200	0.513 ***	0.017	1.00	
Mhcluster	-0.433 ***	0.006	0.146	-0.270 *	0.331 **	0.118	0.850 ***	0.072	0.084	0.653 ***	0.005	1.00

* $p < 0.05$; $p < 0.01$; $p < 0.001$

Lastly, the diversity coefficients for age, ethnicity, and gender calculated for each NYC department for fiscal year 2019 are independent of each other. Each department's set of diversity coefficients are calculated from demographic and employment data pertaining solely to their workforces. Stated differently, not one of the sets of diversity scores obtained for each department is calculated in part or in whole on demographic data reported by another department. As such, each department's set of diversity scores are separate and uncorrelated to the set of diversity scores of another department. For instance, the gender diversity score obtained for ACS is calculated exclusively from the number of men and women in the department's workforce. In addition, the gender diversity score obtained for DOC is calculated exclusively from demographic data reported by the department. Similarly, the sets of diversity coefficients for age and ethnicity for each department are independent of each other. The organizational diversity (OD) coefficient (OD $= \frac{SGB + SEB + SAB}{3}$) of each department is independent of each other as well.

Each set of diversity coefficients for age, ethnicity, and gender are independent within each department. The diversity coefficient for gender is calculated solely from data pertaining to men and women within each department. In addition, the diversity coefficient for ethnicity is calculated exclusively from data pertaining to the number of ethnic groups within each department. Similarly, the diversity coefficient for age is obtained solely from data pertaining to the number of employees in each age group category within each department. However, each department's OD coefficient is correlated with the diversity scores for age, ethnicity, and gender of department because the OD diversity score is the average of summing each set of diversity scores.

Predictors of age, ethnic, and gender diversity

Research examining demographic and social diversity in nonprofit, public, and private sector organizations use a number of *predictors* to estimate changes in the level of age, ethnic, and gender heterogeneity. The predictors include the following:

- Age measured as years of age of employees in an organization (e.g., Boehm, Kunze, and Bruch, 2014; Klein, Conn, Smith, and Sorra, 2001; De Meulenaere, Boone, and Buyl, 2016; Li, Gong, Burmeister, Wang, Alterman, Alonso, and Robinson, 2021; Randel and Jaussi, 2003; Timmerman, 2000);

- Budget measured as the total budget allocation of the organization (e.g., Gazley, Chang, and Bingham, 2010; Guajardo, 2015);
- Employee or employment tenure measured as years of service in an organization (e.g., Alexander, Nuchols, Bloom, and Lee, 1995; Boehm, Kunze, and Bruch, 2014; Choi and Rainey, 2010; De Meulenaere, Boone, and Buyl, 2016; Kearney, Gebert, and Voelpel, 2009; Khan, Khan, and Senturk, 2019; Klein, Conn, Smith, and Sorra, 2001; Leslie, 2017; Randel and Jaussi, 2003);
- New hires measured as the number of candidates that entered into the organization (e.g., Cornwell and Kellough, 1994; Kellough, 1990; Kellough, and Elliott, 1992);
- Organizational size measured as the total number of employees (e.g., Alexander, Nuchols, Bloom, and Lee, 1995; Akram, Haq, Natarajan, and Chellakan. 2020; Boehm, Kunze, and Bruch, 2014; Cheong, and Sinnakkannu, 2014; Choi, 2010; Choi and Rainey, 2010; Cornwell and Kellough, 1994; De Meulenaere, Boone, and Buyl, 2016; Ferrero-Ferrero, Fernández-Izquierdo, and Muñoz-Torres, 2015; Guajardo, 2014 and 2015; Kearney, Gebert, and Voelpel, 2009; Kellough, and Elliott, 1992; Khan, Khan, and Senturk, 2019; Kim, 1993; Leslie, 2017; Li, Gong, Burmeister, Wang, Alterman, Alonso, and Robinson, 2021; Moon and Christensen, 2020; Oba and Fodio, 2013; Randel and Jaussi, 2003);
- Pay measured as annual income (e.g., Alexander, Nuchols, Bloom, and Lee, 1995; Klein, Conn, Smith, and Sorra, 2001).
- Percent women measured as the proportion of women in the total workforce (e.g., Campbell and Mínguez-Vera, 2008: Leslie, 2017; Oba and Fodio, 2013);
- Turnover measured as the intension to terminate employment or attrition rate (e.g., Boehm, Kunze, and Bruch, 2014; Li, Gong, Burmeister, Wang, Alterman, Alonso, and Robinson, 2021; Moon and Christensen, 2020);
- Type of organization measured as a dichotomous variable to differentiate between 2 different kinds of institutions (e.g., Alexander, Nuchols, Bloom, and Lee, 1995; Boehm, Kunze, and Bruch, 2014; Gazley, Chang, and Bingham, 2010; Guajardo, 2014; Randel and Jaussi, 2003); and,
- Unionization measured as the percentage of the workforce in a collective bargaining unit (e.g., Boehm, Kunze, and Bruch, 2014; Cornwell and Kellough, 1994; Guajardo, 2015; Kellough, and Elliott, 1992; Li, Gong, Burmeister, Wang, Alterman, Alonso, and Robinson, 2021; Riccucci, 1986).

The extant research shows inconsistent statistical findings amongst the independent variables and ethnic and gender diversity in nonprofit, public, and private organizations.

When age is correlated with demographic-based diversity, research findings show inconsistent statistical relationships amongst age and diversity. In some studies, age is correlated positively with age diversity (e.g., Boehm, Kunze, and Bruch, 2014; De Meulenaere, Boone, and Buyl, 2016; Li, Gong, Burmeister, Wang, Alterman, Alonso, and Robinson, 2021; Timmerman, 2000). However, research also shows that age is related negatively with age diversity (e.g., Li, Gong, Burmeister, Wang, Alterman, Alonso, and Robinson, 2021). Age also is correlated positively with gender diversity (e.g., Li, Gong, Burmeister, Wang, Alterman, Alonso, and Robinson, 2021). On the other hand, age is found to be unrelated statistically with team heterogeneity (e.g., Randel and Jaussi, 2003). With respect to the statistical relationship amongst age and ethnic diversity, Timmerman (2000) suggests that age and racial diversity are unrelated statistically. Generally speaking, the hypotheses tested by previous research in regard to age, ethnic, and gender diversity are the following:

H_{O1}: The level of age diversity increases with the age of the workforce;
H_{O2}: The level of ethnic diversity increases with the age of the workforce; and,
H_{O3}: The level of gender diversity increases with the age of the workforce.

The size of an organization's budget may be related statistically with demographic-based diversity. For example, Gazley, Chang, and Bingham (2010) indicate that an insignificant statistical relationship exists amongst an organization's budget and racial diversity. Guajardo (2015) posits that an organization's financial resources are necessary to recruit and hire new employees. As new employees are hired into an organization, the level of age, ethnic, and gender diversity increases or decreases concomitantly due to the demographic and social characteristics of the new hires. Similarly, the overall level of organizational diversity increases or decreases with the changes in the level of demographic- and social-based diversity. The hypotheses tested in previous studies with respect to budget size and demographic-based diversity are the following:

H_{O4}: The level of age diversity increases with the size of the budget;
H_{O5}: The level of ethnic diversity increases with the size of the budget; and,
H_{O6}: The level of gender diversity increases with the size of the budget.

Employment tenue is related statistically with demographic-based diversity. A positive relationship exists amongst employment tenure and age diversity (e.g., Boehm, Kunze, and Bruch, 2014). However, when examining the statistical relationship amongst tenure and age diversity in US federal agencies, a negative relationship was found amongst the variables (e.g., Choi and Rainey, 2010). An insignificant statistical finding exists amongst tenure and gender diversity (e.g., Kearney, Gebert, and Voelpel, 2009; Klein, Conn, Smith, and Sorra, 2001). When tenure and gender diversity were examined in US federal agencies, a positive statistical relationship was found amongst the variables (e.g., Choi and Rainey, 2010). Choi and Rainey (2010) also found a significant negative relationship amongst tenure and race diversity in US federal agencies. Lastly, an insignificant statistical relationship was found amongst tenure and organizational diversity (e.g., Randel and Jaussi, 2003). The hypotheses tested in previous research with respect to tenure and demographic-based diversity are the following:

H_{O7}: The level of age diversity increases with employment tenure;
H_{O8}: The level of ethnic diversity increases with employment tenure; and,
H_{O9}: The level of gender diversity increases with employment tenure.

The number of new hires changes the level of age, ethnic, gender and other types of demographic- and social-based diversity simultaneously in an organization. For instance, in US federal agencies, the number of new hires increases the share of jobs held by some ethnic groups across job titles (e.g., Cornwell and Kellough, 1994; Kellough and Elliott, 1992). The number of new hires also increases the share of jobs held by women across job titles (e.g., Cornwell and Kellough, 1994; Kellough and Elliott, 1992). When the rate of new hires was regressed on ethnic diversity in US federal agencies, an insignificant statistical relationship exists (e.g., Kellough, 1990). The hypotheses tested in regard to the statistical relationship amongst the number of new hires and demographic-based diversity are the following:

H_{O10}: The level of age diversity increases with the number of new hires;
H_{O11}: The level of ethnic diversity increases with the number of new hires; and,
H_{O12}: The level of gender diversity increases with the number of new hires.

The statistical relationship amongst organizational size and demographic-based diversity is examined extensively in previous research. For instance, a positive relationship exists amongst the size of the staff of registered nurses and demographic diversity (e.g., Alexander, Nuchols, Bloom, and Lee, 1995). Similarly, a positive relationship exists amongst the organizational size of financial firms and demographic diversity (e.g., Cheong, and Sinnakkannu, 2014). When examining the relationship of the size of US federal agencies and demographic-based diversity, negative statistical relationships are present. Specifically, the size of US federal agencies is related negatively with age, ethnic, and gender diversity (e.g., Choi and Rainey, 2010). However, Boehm, Kunze, and Bruch (2014) show that organizational size is unrelated to age diversity. The hypotheses tested in previous research with respect to the statistical relationship amongst organizational size and demographic-based diversity are the following:

H_{O13}: The level of age diversity increases with organizational size;
H_{O14}: The level of ethnic diversity increases with organizational size; and,
H_{O15}: The level of gender diversity increases with organizational size.

Research on demographic-based diversity also assesses the statistical relationship amongst pay and heterogeneity in the workforce. For example, a positive relationship exists amongst pay and gender diversity (e.g., Klein, Conn, Smith, and Sorra, 2001). However, an insignificant statistical relationship exists amongst the pay of registered nurses and demographic diversity (e.g., Alexander, Nuchols, Bloom, and Lee, 1995). The hypotheses tested with respect to the statistical relationship amongst pay and demographic-based diversity are the following:

H_{O16}: The level of age diversity increases with compensation;
H_{O17}: The level of ethnic diversity increases with compensation; and,
H_{O18}: The level of gender diversity increases with compensation.

The gender composition of the workforce also is used to assess demographic diversity in organizations. Specifically, the percent of women in the workforce is tested for statistical significance with different types of demographic diversity. An insignificant statistical relationship exists amongst the percent of women in the workforce and age diversity (e.g., Leslie, 2017). However, the percent of women in the workforce is related positively with the average ethnic status of the workforce (e.g., Leslie, 2017). The percent of women in the workforce also is related positively with gender diversity (e.g., Oba and Fodio, 2013), which is not surprising since the proportion of women in the workforce is used to calculate the Simpson diversity score for gender.

In some instances, gender diversity is used as a predictor of demographic diversity (e.g., Choi, 2014). When assessing the statistical relationship amongst gender and ethnic diversity in US federal agencies, Choi (2014) indicates that gender diversity is related positively with ethnic diversity. Conversely, ethnic diversity is related positively with gender diversity (e.g., Choi, 2014). The hypotheses tested with respect to the statistical relationship amongst the percent of women in the workforce and demographic-based diversity are the following:

H_{O19}: The level of age diversity increases with the proportion of women in the workforce;
H_{O20}: The level of ethnic diversity increases with the proportion of women in the workforce; and,
H_{O21}: The level of gender diversity increases with the proportion of women in the workforce.

Employee turnover leads to new hires and subsequently changes the level of demographic-based diversity in organizations (e.g., Guajardo, 2015; Lewis, 1991). A negative statistical relationship exists amongst turnover and age diversity (e.g., Li, Gong, Burmeister, Wang, Alterman, Alonso, and Robinson, 2021). However, an insignificant statistical relationship exists amongst turnover and gender diversity (e.g., Li, Gong, Burmeister, Wang, Alterman, Alonso, and Robinson, 2021). When assessing the relationship amongst collective turnover intension of workgroups and demographic diversity, an insignificant statistical relationship exists amongst turnover and age diversity (e.g., Boehm, Kunze, and Bruch, 2014). The hypotheses tested by previous research with respect to the statistical relationship amongst turnover and demographic-based diversity are the following:

H_{O22}: The level of age diversity increases with turnover;
H_{O23}: The level of ethnic diversity increases with turnover; and,
H_{O24}: The level of gender diversity increases with turnover.

Research on demographic-based diversity shows that the level of age, ethnic, or gender heterogeneity differs across different types of organizations. For instance, non-service firms have higher levels of age diversity in comparison to service-based firms (e.g., Boehm, Kunze, and Bruch, 2014). Consulting firms have higher levels of organizational diversity than non-consulting firms (e.g., Randel and Jaussi, 2003). By contrast, when assessing whether the type of hospital is a significant predictor of demographic diversity amongst nurses, governmental and nongovernmental hospitals are similar with respect to the level of demographic diversity amongst nurses (e.g., Alexander, Nuchols, Bloom, and Lee, 1995). A similar statistical relationship is found for non- and for-profit hospitals and demographic diversity (e.g., Alexander, Nuchols, Bloom, and Lee, 1995).

When assessing the level of racial diversity between private and nonprofit organizations, an insignificant statistical relationship exists (e.g., Gazley, Chang, and Bingham, 2010). The hypotheses tested by previous research with respect to the statistical relationship amongst type of organization and demographic-based diversity are the following:

H_{O25}: The level of age diversity increases with a change in the type of organization;
H_{O26}: The level of ethnic diversity increases with a change in the type of organization; and,
H_{O27}: The level of gender diversity increases with a change in the type of organization.

Lastly, the percent of an organization's workforce in a collective bargaining unit is hypothesized to increase demographic-based diversity. The statistical findings are inconsistent in previous studies. For instance, union strength does not increase the share of women and minorities in US federal jobs (e.g., Cornwell and Kellough, 1994). On the other hand, union strength increases minority and women representation in US federal employment (e.g., Kellough and Elliott, 1992). When assessing the relationship amongst union strength and ethnic diversity in US federal agencies, an insignificant statistical relationship exists (e.g., Kellough, 1990). A similar insignificant statistical finding is found for union density and gender diversity (e.g., Li, Gong, Burmeister, Wang, Alterman, Alonso, and Robinson, 2021). By contrast, union density is related positively with age diversity (e.g., Li, Gong, Burmeister, Wang, Alterman, Alonso, and Robinson, 2021). However, Boehm, Kunze, and Bruch (2014) show that an insignificant statistical relationship exists amongst unionization and age diversity. The hypotheses tested by previous research with respect to the statistical relationship amongst unionization and demographic-based diversity are the following:

H_{O28}: The level of age diversity increases with the percent of employees in a collective bargaining unit;
H_{O29}: The level of ethnic diversity increases with the percent of employees in a collective bargaining unit; and,
H_{O30}: The level of gender diversity increases with the percent of employees in a collective bargaining unit.

Theoretical statistical model of age, ethnic, and gender diversity

Based on the independent variables presented above, the generic theoretical statistical model guiding the regression analyses in this and subsequent chapters for NYC departments for fiscal year 2019 is the following:

$$\hat{S} = \alpha + \beta_1\text{Elected} + \beta_2\text{SEA} + \beta_3\text{Employees} + \beta_4\text{Myos} + \beta_5\text{Mftsal} + \beta_6\text{Pctunion} + \beta_7\text{Wcluster} + \beta_8\text{Mcluster} + \beta_9\text{ O40cluster} + \beta_{10}\text{Wscluster} + \beta_{11}\text{Mscluster} + \beta_{12}\text{Whcluster} + \beta_{13}\text{Mhcluster} + \varepsilon_{ij}.$$

The terms of the regression equation are the following:

$\hat{S}$ refers to the Simpson diversity scores calculated separately for age, ethnicity, gender, and organizational diversity for fiscal year 2019;

α refers to the y-axis intercept for the regression line;

B_n refers to the regression coefficient associated with each independent variable in the equation that is significant statistically at $p < 0.05$;

Elected refers to whether the department is an elected office (1) or another type of organization (0);

SEA refers to the percent of the adopted operating budget that is allocated to salary expenses in fiscal year 2019;

Employees refers to the total number of employees on the payroll in each department in fiscal year 2019;

Myos refers to the median number of years of service of each department's workforce in fiscal year 2019;

Mftsal refers to the median full-time salary of each department's workforce in fiscal year 2019;

Pctunion refers to the percent of the workforce in each department that has membership in a collective bargaining unit in fiscal year 2019;

Wcluster (women employee cluster) refers to the relative clustering score obtained by dividing the percent of women employees by the percent of men employees in each department to assess the magnitude of women-dominated employment in fiscal year 2019;

Mcluster (minority employee cluster) refers to the relative clustering score obtained by dividing the percent of minority employees by the percent of White employees in each department to assess the magnitude of minority-dominated employment in fiscal year 2019;

O40cluster (employees over the age of 40 cluster) refers to the relative clustering score obtained by dividing the percent of employees under the age of 40 by the percent of employees over the age of 40 in each department to assess the magnitude of employment of older persons in fiscal year 2019;

Wscluster (women employee separation cluster) refers to the relative clustering score obtained by dividing the percent of women employees that terminated their employment by the percent of men employees that terminated their employment in each department to assess the magnitude of women-dominated termination in fiscal year 2019;

Mscluster (minority employee separation cluster) refers to the relative clustering score obtained by dividing the percent of minority employees that terminated their employment by the percent of White employees that terminated their employment in each department to assess the magnitude of minority-dominated termination in fiscal year 2019;

Whcluster (women employee hired cluster) refers to the relative clustering score obtained by dividing the percent of women hired by the percent of men hired in each department to assess the magnitude of women-dominated hiring in fiscal year 2019;

Mhcluster (minority employee hired cluster) refers to the relative clustering score obtained by dividing the percent of minorities hired by the percent of men hired in each department to assess the magnitude of minority-dominated hiring in fiscal year 2019; and,

ε_{ij} refers to measurement error in the statistical model.

Exhibit 7-5 provides a graphical representation of the theoretical model and of the hypothesized statistical relationships amongst the independent variables and the Simpson diversity scores for age, ethnic, gender, and organizational diversity.

Exhibit 7-5 Theoretical model for age, ethnic, and gender diversity for NYC departments

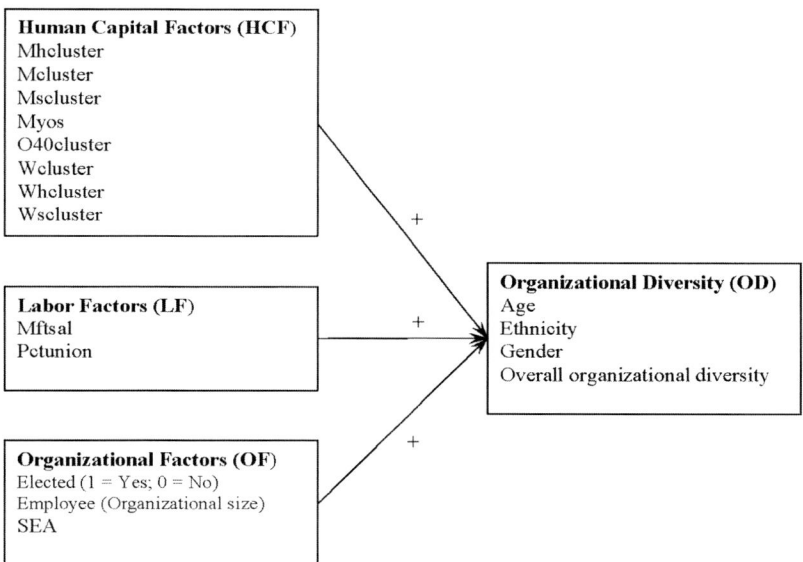

Rationale for independent variables

As discussed above, the type of organization has an impact on whether its workforce will have an high or low level of age, ethnic, or gender diversity. In general, NYC departments fall into 1 of 3 categories: authorities, elected offices, or executive offices. NYC departments that are headed by an elected official such as City Council (Council), Office of the Comptroller (Comptroller) and Office the Mayor (Mayorality) are coded as 1. Executive departments that have directors that report to the mayor are coded as 0. Similarly, departments such as the NYC Housing Authority (NYCHA), Municipal Water Finance Authority (MWFA), and School Construction Authority (SCA) are coded a 0 because they are governed by boards and operate independently. As Exhibit 7-5 illustrates, departments with elected officials have higher levels of age, ethnic, and gender diversity in comparison to other NYC departments.

Operating budgets are used often to assess an organization's capacity to hire employees or to fill position vacancies that occur due to retirements or terminations. However, the use of an organization's total operating budget does not accurately represent its capacity to fill position vacancies or to hire new employees. For example, DOE has an operating budgeting of approximately $25 billion and allocates 62% to salary expenses. NYCHH has an operating budget of about $10 billion and allocates 26% to salary expenses. By contrast, NYPD has an operating budget of about $5 billion and allocates 90% to salary expenses. Although DOE has a larger operating budget in comparison to the NYPD, DOE has a lower fiscal capacity to hire new employees and to fill positions vacancies due to its lower proportional budget allocation for salary expenses. In this and subsequent chapters, the percent of operating expenses allocated to salaries (SEA) is used instead of each department's total operating budget. Each department's SEA measure is calculated by the following formula:

$$SEA = \frac{Total\ Salary\ Allocation}{Total\ Operating\ Budget}$$

Age, ethnic, and gender diversity are hypothesized to be related positively with SEA. Statistically, a unit increase in SEA produces an increase in age, ethnic, and gender diversity as measured by the Simpson diversity index (see Exhibit 7-5).

The total number of employees in an organization's workforce serves as a measure of size and of an organization's human resources capacity to hire new staff or to fill position vacancies as they occur. Theoretically, organizations with larger workforces have greater opportunities to fill new positions or to fill position vacancies that occur due to *involuntary* or *voluntary terminations* in comparison to smaller organizations. Because larger organizations should have a larger number of position vacancies in comparison to smaller organizations, larger organizations should have the ability to hire applicants from different demographic groups at higher numbers in comparison to smaller organizations. By hiring employees from different demographic groups at higher numbers, larger organizations should have higher levels of age, ethnic, and gender diversity in comparison to smaller organizations. In this and subsequent chapters, a unit increase in the total number employees produces an increase in age, ethnic, and gender diversity (see Exhibit 7-5).

Employment tenure is measured by median years of service (Myos). Organizations with higher Myos have more stable workforces in comparison to organizations with lower Myos. Because organizations with higher Myos have more stable workforces, they have lower rates of involuntary and voluntary terminations. In turn, their levels of age, ethnic, and gender diversity are equal to or greater in comparison to organizations with lower Myos. A unit increase in Myos produces an increase in age, ethnic, and gender diversity (see Exhibit 7-5).

Compensation is associated with demographic diversity. In this and subsequent chapters, median full-time salary (Mftsal) serves as a proxy for annual salary and as a proxy for an organization's compensation structure. Organizations with higher salary structures should attract qualified applicants from different demographic groups in greater numbers in comparison to organizations with lower salary structures. Stated differently, organizations with the ability to offer higher salaries have a comparative advantage over organizations that offer lower salaries with respect to hiring qualified applicants from different demographic groups. As Exhibit 7-5 shows, a unit increase in Mftsal produces an increase in age, ethnic, and gender diversity.

Unions play an important role in the hiring process and in maintaining or increasing collective bargaining strength in the workforce. Prior research shows that unions also influence demographic diversity positively in organizations. In NYC departments, the percent of the workforce in a collective bargaining unit (Pctunion) ranges from 0% to 99%. Departments with higher Pctunion should have greater union representation in the hiring process where collective bargaining representatives influence the rate to which qualified applicants from different demographic groups are hired. A unit increase in Pctunion produces an increase in age, ethnic, and gender diversity (see Exhibit 7-5).

Workforces composed predominantly of women should have higher levels of demographic diversity. In previous research, the percent of women in the workforce serves as a measure of assess the influence of women to hire women and minorities into the organization. This measure, however, does not assess fully the magnitude to which women are the predominant employees in an organization. Gender diversity scores are used as an indirect measure of the ability of women to increase age and ethnic diversity. The use of gender diversity scores presumes that organizations with similar levels of heterogeneity have compatible workforces with respect to the composition of men and women. For instance, NYCTAX and CCRB both have a Simpson gender diversity score of 0.500; however, NYCTAX has more males in the workforce in comparison to CCRB. A similar situation exists for DCAS and NYCERS where both departments have a Simpson gender diversity score of 0.476. While DCAS has more women in the workforce, NYCERS has more men in the workforce. This study uses a measure relative *clustering* to assess the magnitude to which women dominate (Wcluster) the workforce of NYC departments (see Massey and Denton, 1988). For each NYC department, Wcluster is calculated by the following formula:

$$\text{Wcluster} = \frac{Percent\ of\ women}{Percent\ of\ men} - 1$$

A value of 0 indicates that a department's workforce is composed equally of men and women. When a positive score is obtained, a department's workforce is composed predominately of women; conversely, a negative score indicates a workforce is composed predominantly of men. For instance, DHS has a Wcluster score of 0.00 which indicates the department has the same number of men and women in the workforce. DOE has a Wcluster score of 2.35, indicating its workforce is composed predominantly of women. By contrast, DSNY has a Wcluster score of -0.91, indicating its workforce is composed primarily of men. A unit increase in Wcluster produces an increase in the age, ethnic, and gender diversity (see Exhibit 7-5).

A relative cluster score to assess the magnitude to which each department's workforce is composed predominantly of persons of color (Mcluster) is calculated as well. The formula for calculating each department's Mcluster score for fiscal year 2019 is the following:

$$\text{Mcluster} = \frac{Percent\ of\ minorities}{Percent\ of\ Whites} - 1$$

A Mcluster score of 0 indicates a department's workforce is composed equally of White and minority employees. Positive Mcluster scores indicate a workforce is composed predominantly of persons of color; negative scores indicate a workforce is composed primarily of White employees. DCP, for example, has a Mcluster score of 0.0, indicating its workforce is composed equally of Whites and persons of color. However, DHS has a Mcluster score of 9.11, indicating its workforce is composed overwhelming of persons of color. Briefly, the rationale for using a relative clustering score based on ethnicity is that the use of percent minority or the use of ethnic diversity scores do not accurately assess the magnitude to which departments differ in terms of the ethnic composition of their workforces. As Exhibit 7-5 shows, a unit increase in Mcluster produces an increase in age, ethnic, and gender diversity.

Similar to the relative clustering scores calculated for ethnicity and gender, a relative clustering score for age is calculated. The formula is the following:

$$O40cluster = \frac{Percent\ of\ employees\ under\ the\ age\ of\ 40}{Percent\ of\ employees\ over\ the\ age\ of\ 40} - 1$$

In addition to O40cluster serving as a proxy for age, the measure provides a better assessment of the magnitude to which NYC departments are composed of employees under or over the age of 40. Stated differently, O40cluster measures whether NYC departments differ with respect to the composition of the workforces in terms of age. An O40cluster score of 0.00 indicates an equal number of employees under and over the age of 40 in a department's workforce. A positive score indicates the workforce is composed predominantly of employees under the age of 40. Negative scores indicate the workforce is composed mainly of employees over the age of 40. For instance, NYCERS has an 040cluster score of 0.00, indicating that its workforce is composed equally of employees under and over the age of 40; BOC has an 040cluster score of 2.00, indicating that its workforce is composed overwhelmingly of employees under the age of 40. For O40cluster, a unit increase in the relative clustering score produces an increase in age, ethnic, and gender diversity (see Exhibit 7-5).

Workforce turnover provides organizations with an opportunity to increase the demographic diversity of their workforces. Prior studies, however, have not assessed whether the turnover rate amongst men and women is similar in organizations or whether differences in the rates of turnover are related statistically with age, ethnic, and gender diversity. A relative clustering score for women separations (Wscluster) is calculated to assess whether NYC departments differ with respect to the number of women involuntarily or voluntarily terminating their employment in comparison to men. The formula for calculating Wscluster is the following:

$$Wscluster = \frac{Percent\ of\ women\ separations}{Percent\ of\ men\ separations} - 1$$

A positive score indicates that more women terminated their employment in comparison to men in fiscal year 2019; conversely, when a negative score is obtained, it indicates more men terminated their employment in comparison to women. For instance, the data show that BOC had a Wscluster score of 2.00, indicating that more women terminated their employment with the department in comparison to men. During the same fiscal year, DSNY had a Wscluster score of -0.84, indicating that slightly more men terminated their employment with the department in comparison to women. A Wscluster score of 0.000 shows that the same number of men and women terminated their employment. A unit increase in Wscluster produces an increase in age, ethnic, and gender diversity (see Exhibit 7-5).

A relative clustering score is calculated for minority and White separations (Mscluster) for fiscal year 2019. The rationale for doing so is to assess whether the termination of minority employees produced an increase in age, ethnic, and gender diversity in NYC departments in fiscal year 2019. The formula for calculating the Mscluster score is the following:

$$\text{Mscluster} = \frac{Percent\ of\ minority\ separations}{Percent\ of\ White\ separations} - 1$$

A Mscluster score of 0.00 indicates the same number of minorities and Whites terminated their employment in fiscal year 2019. A positive Mscluster score indicates that more minority employees terminated their employment with a department in comparison to Whites; a negative Mscluster score indicates that more Whites terminated their employment in comparison to minority employees. For fiscal year 2019, PA has a Mscluster score of 5.69, showing that more minority employees terminated their employment with the department in comparison to Whites. By contrast, BIC has a Mscluster score of -0.09, indicating that slightly more Whites terminated their employment in comparison to minority employees. The hypothesis for this predicator is that a unit increase in Mscluster produces an increase in age, ethnic, and gender diversity (see Exhibit 7-5).

The number of new hires has an impact on the demographic composition of an organization's workforce. As stated previously, the level of age, ethnic, and gender diversity changes concurrently in a department when new hires enter its workforce. Prior studies, however, have not assessed whether the hiring of new employees composed primary of men or women is related statistically with age, ethnic, and gender diversity. In addition, prior studies have not assessed whether differences in the hiring rate between men and women increases the demographic diversity in the workforce. A relative clustering score for the number of new hires that are women (Whcluster) is calculated to assess whether the gender composition of the total number of new hires is related statistically with age, ethnic, and gender diversity. The formula for calculating the Whcluster score for each NYC department for fiscal year 2019 is the following:

$$\text{Whcluster} = \frac{Percent\ of\ new\ women\ employees}{Percent\ of\ new\ men\ employees} - 1$$

A Whcluster score of 0.00 shows that the total number of new hires is compose equally of men and women. A positive Whcluster score indicates that the total number new hires is composed predominantly of women, while a negative score indicates that more men are hired in comparison to women.

For fiscal year 2019, DFTA has a Whcluster score of 12.29, indicating that the number of new hires was overwhelmingly women. DEP, however, has a Whcluster score of -0.68, indicating that slightly more men were hired into the workforce. In this and subsequent chapters, a unit increase in Whcluster produces an increase in age, ethnic, and gender diversity (see Exhibit 7-5).

Lastly, a similar relative cluster score is calculated for the number of persons of color (Mhcluster) that were hired by NYC departments in fiscal year 2019. The reason for calculating a Mhcluster score is that previous research does not address whether differences in the hiring rate of minorities and Whites is related statistically with demographic diversity. Put differently, previous research does not address adequately whether minority hiring produces significant changes in the level of age, ethnic and gender diversity. The formula for calculating the Mhcluster score is the following:

$$\text{Mhcluster} = \frac{Percent\ of\ new\ employees\ of\ color}{Percent\ of\ employees\ that\ are\ White} - 1$$

A Mhcluster score of 0.00 indicates that the number of new hires is composed equally of persons of color and Whites. A positive Mhcluster score shows that more persons of color are hired in comparison to Whites. Conversely, a negative score indicates that more Whites are hired in comparison to persons of color. For fiscal year 2019, DOP has a Mscluster score of 10.5, indicating that the department overwhelmingly hired more persons of color in comparison to Whites. On the other hand, FDNY has a Mscluster score of -0.113, indicating that the department hired slightly more Whites than persons of color in fiscal year 2019. A unit increase in Mhcluster produces an increase in age, ethnic, and gender diversity (see Exhibit 7-5).

Dependent variables

In previous chapters, the Simpson diversity index was used to calculate heterogeneity scores for age, ethnicity, and gender for 72 NYC departments based on demographic employment data for fiscal year 2019. Specifically, biased (S_B) and unbiased (S_N) diversity coefficients were discussed. In Chapter 6, a set of composite OD scores were calculated based on the S_B and S_N diversity coefficients for age, ethnicity, and gender. In this and subsequent chapters, the S_B and S_N diversity coefficients for age, ethnicity, gender, and OD serve as the dependent variables in the OLS regression analyses below.

OLS regression analysis

Exhibit 7-6 summarizes the *simultaneous OLS regression* analyses for age, ethnic, gender, and organizational diversity. Panel A provides the findings of the biased (S_B) measures of diversity. The findings for the unbiased (S_N) measures of diversity are presented in Panel B. For each equation, the regression coefficients (β) are tested for statistical significance at $\alpha = 0.05$. *Variance inflation factor* (VIF) scores are used to assess multicollinearity amongst the predictors. The formula for obtaining VIF scores is the following: $\text{VIF} = \frac{1}{1-R^2}$, where R^2 represents the *coefficient of determination*. VIF scores below 1.0 indicate the absence of collinearity. Low levels of collinearity exist amongst the predictors when VIF scores range from 1 to 4. Moderate levels of collinearity exist when VIF scores range from 5 to 10, indicating that predictors are correlated and are providing redundant information. When VIF scores exceed 10, multicollinearity levels are exceedingly high amongst predictors, findings are unreliable and unstable, and the R^2 value is large due redundancy amongst the predicators.

In Panel A, the statistical findings for the biased (S_{GB}) gender diversity scores show that none of the predictors are related statistically with the dependent variable. For instance, the level of gender diversity in departments with elected officials (1) and without elected officials (0) are statistically the same ($\beta_1 = 0.01$, $p > 0.05$). The percent of the operating budget allocated to salary expenses (SEA) does not increase or decrease gender diversity ($\beta_2 = -0.0001$, $p > 0.05$). In addition, the total size of the workforce (Employees) does not contribute to higher or lower levels of gender diversity ($\beta_3 = -0.0000005$, $p > 0.05$). High turnover amongst women ($\beta_{10} = 0.012$, $p > 0.05$) and minorities ($\beta_{11} = 0.002$, $p > 0.05$) does not change the level of gender diversity. Similar insignificant statistical findings are present when the number of women ($\beta_{12} = -0.00$, $p > 0.05$) hired outpaces the number of men that are hired and when the number of persons of color ($\beta_{13} = -0.001$, $p > 0.05$) hired outpaces the number of men hired. Although a R^2 value of 0.26 is reported, the value is statistically equal to 0.00 because none of the predicators produce an increase or decrease in the level of gender diversity.

Exhibit 7-6 OLS regression analysis for age, ethnic, gender and organizational diversity for NYC departments for fiscal year 2019

A. OLS regression for biased (S_B) diversity scores

Predictors	Gender Diversity (S_{GB}) β Coefficient	t-statistic	Ethnic Diversity (S_{EB}) β Coefficient	t-statistic	Age Diversity (S_{AB}) β Coefficient	t-statistic	Organizational Diversity (S_{OO}) β Coefficient	t-statistic	VIF
Elected	0.0100222 (0.0211684)	0.47	-0.0346973 (0.0288702)	-1.20	0.02796320 (0.0073853)	3.79 ***	0.0010960 (0.0137855)	0.08	1.67
SEA	-0.0001446 (0.0311158)	0.00	-0.0548222 (0.0424367)	-1.29	-0.02284840 (0.0108558)	-2.10 *	-0.0259384 (0.0202635)	-1.28	1.58
Employees	-0.0000005 (0.0000004)	-1.37	0.0000004 (0.0000005)	0.76	0.00000021 (0.0000001)	1.67	0.0000000 (0.0000002)	0.13	1.37
Myos	-0.0031933 (0.0023399)	-1.36	-0.0023674 (0.0031912)	-0.74	-0.00072870 (0.0008163)	-0.89	-0.0020965 (0.0015238)	-1.38	2.44
Mftsal	-0.0000006 (0.0000006)	-0.90	-0.0000011 (0.0000008)	-1.25	-0.0000033 (0.0000002)	-1.53	-0.0000007 (0.0000004)	-1.61	2.03
Petunion	-0.0618134 (0.0351700)	-1.76	-0.0380349 (0.0479660)	-0.79	0.04206870 (0.0122703)	3.43 **	-0.0192598 (0.0229037)	-0.84	2.11
Wcluster	-0.0087890 (0.0152766)	-0.58	-0.0167990 (0.0208348)	-0.81	-0.00711590 (0.0053298)	-1.35	-0.0109213 (0.0099486)	-1.10	2.34
Mcluster	0.0042241 (0.0081005)	0.52	0.0094895 (0.0110477)	0.86	-0.00814650 (0.0028261)	-2.88 **	0.0018557 (0.0052753)	0.35	4.63
O40cluster	0.0091009 (0.0076699)	1.19	0.0066266 (0.0104604)	0.63	0.00292210 (0.0026759)	1.09	0.0062165 (0.0049948)	1.24	2.49
Wscluster	0.0122934 (0.0139977)	0.88	-0.0101793 (0.0190906)	-0.53	-0.00337570 (0.0048836)	-0.69	-0.0004205 (0.0091157)	-0.05	2.21
Mscluster	0.0017878 (0.0070739)	0.25	0.0014905 (0.0096476)	0.15	0.00060320 (0.0024680)	0.24	0.0012938 (0.0046067)	0.28	2.53
Whcluster	-0.0052104 (0.0053404)	-0.98	0.0011866 (0.0072834)	0.16	0.00105660 (0.0018632)	0.57	-0.0009891 (0.0034778)	-0.28	1.65
Mhcluster	-0.0010515 (0.0050718)	-0.21	-0.0121854 (0.0069171)	-1.76	0.00471180 (0.0017695)	2.66 *	-0.0028417 (0.0033029)	-0.86	4.09
Intercept	0.5560840 (0.0633018)	8.78 ***	0.8507759 (0.0863331)	9.85 ***	0.87749200 (0.0220850)	39.73 ***	0.7614507 (0.0412239)	18.47 ***	
$F_{13,58}$	1.56		0.89		4.76 ***		0.96		2.40
R^2	0.26		0.17		0.52		0.18		
Adjusted R^2	0.09		-0.02		0.41		-0.01		
N	72		72		72		72		

B. OLS regression for unbiased (S_X) diversity scores

Predictors	Gender Diversity (S_{GX})		Ethnic Diversity (S_{EX})		Age Diversity (S_{AX})		Organizational Diversity (S_{BOD})		
	β Coefficient	t-statistic	β Coefficient	t-statistic	β Coefficient	t-statistic	β Coefficient	t-statistic	VIF
Elected	-0.0090903 (0.0025607)	-3.50 **	-0.0482130 (0.0292796)	-1.65	0.0125348 (0.0057782)	2.17 *	-0.0149228 (0.0099208)	-1.50	1.67
SEA	0.0070863 (0.0038229)	1.85	-0.0455908 (0.0430385)	-1.06	-0.0104432 (0.0084934)	-1.23	-0.0163159 (0.0145828)	-1.12	1.58
Employees	-0.0000001 (0.0000000)	-2.02	0.0000002 (0.0000005)	0.49	0.0000001 (0.0000001)	0.56	0.0000001 (0.0000002)	0.41	1.37
Myos	0.0001202 (0.0002875)	0.42	-0.0021419 (0.0032365)	-0.66	-0.0005328 (0.0006387)	-0.83	-0.0008515 (0.0010966)	-0.78	2.44
Mfisal	0.0000000 (0.0000001)	0.55	-0.0000010 (0.0000009)	-1.17	-0.0000003 (0.0000002)	-1.57	-0.0000004 (0.0000003)	-1.41	2.03
Pctunion	-0.0127857 (0.0043210)	-2.96 **	-0.0573847 (0.0486462)	-1.18	0.0207722 (0.0096001)	2.16 *	-0.0164661 (0.0164828)	-1.00	2.11
Wcluster	0.0060758 (0.0018769)	3.24 **	-0.0080546 (0.0211302)	-0.38	0.0030452 (0.0041700)	0.73	0.0003555 (0.0071596)	0.05	2.34
Mcluster	0.0017751 (0.0009952)	1.78	0.0125151 (0.0112044)	1.12	-0.0055869 (0.0022111)	-2.53 *	0.0029011 (0.0037964)	0.76	4.63
O4Ocluster	-0.0006505 (0.0009423)	-0.69	0.0054227 (0.0106087)	0.51	0.0019535 (0.0020936)	0.93	0.0022419 (0.0035946)	0.62	2.49
Wscluster	-0.0002454 (0.0017198)	-0.14	-0.0108045 (0.0193613)	-0.56	-0.0035016 (0.0038209)	-0.92	-0.0048505 (0.0065602)	-0.74	2.21
Mscluster	-0.0006858 (0.0008691)	-0.79	0.0005037 (0.0097844)	0.05	-0.0003891 (0.0019309)	-0.20	-0.0001904 (0.0033153)	-0.06	2.53
Whcluster	-0.0008539 (0.0006561)	-1.30	-0.0000665 (0.0073867)	-0.01	-0.0004047 (0.0014577)	-0.28	-0.0004417 (0.0025028)	-0.18	1.65
Mhcluster	-0.0011117 (0.0006231)	-1.78	-0.0140542 (0.0070152)	-2.00	0.0029747 (0.0013844)	2.15 *	-0.0040637 (0.0023770)	-1.71	4.09
Intercept	0.4827186 (0.0077772)	62.07 ***	0.8625738 (0.0875573)	9.85 ***	0.8894504 (0.0172790)	51.48 ***	0.7449143 (0.0296671)	25.11 ***	
$F_{13,58}$	4.54 ***		0.92		1.91 *		0.87		
R^2	0.50		0.17		0.30		0.16		
Adjusted R^2	0.39		-0.02		0.14		-0.02		2.40
N	72		72		72		72		

Standard errors are in parentheses. * $p < 0.05$; ** $p < 0.01$; *** $p < 0.001$

The statistical findings for the unbiased (S_{GN}) gender diversity scores show that several predictors produce a change in the level of heterogeneity (see Panel B). For instance, NYC departments with elected officials have lower levels of gender diversity in comparison to departments without an elected official ($\beta_1 = -0.009$, $p < 0.01$). Specifically, the change from a department headed by a nonelected official to one headed by an elected official decreases the level of gender diversity by about 0.01 points. The level of gender diversity also decreases as the percent of the workforce that is unionized (Pctunion) increases ($\beta_5 = -0.013$, $p < 0.01$), where a percent increase in unionization reduces the level of heterogeneity of gender by about 0.01 points. However, gender diversity increases as the number of women employees (Wcluster) in the workforce increases ($\beta_7 = 0.006$, $p < 0.01$). The other predictors produce insignificant statistical findings where a unit increase does not change the level of gender diversity either positively or negatively. For example, SEA does not produce a positive or negative change in gender diversity ($\beta_1 = 0.007$, $p > 0.05$). The predictors in the model account for 50% ($R^2 = 0.50$) of the explained variance.

The statistical findings for the S_{GN} model are suspect. First, as discussed in Chapter 3, the formula for calculating the S_{GN} scores overcorrects for the size of the workforce and increases the diversity scores. In fact, several of the S_{GN} scores are outliers due to their value exceeding the EMV of 0.50. Second, collinearity is present amongst the predictors. For instance, Mcluster has a VIF score of 4.63, indicating a somewhat moderate level of collinearity. Similarly, Mhcluster has a VIF score of 4.09. The levels of collinearity for the other predicators range from 1.37 to 2.53, indicating the independent variables are correlated to some extent.

The OLS regression models produce insignificant statistical findings for ethnic diversity (see Exhibit 7-6). In Panel A, the findings for S_{EB} show that none of the predictors produce changes in the level of ethnic heterogeneity in NYC departments. For instance, departments headed by elected and nonelected officials have similar levels for ethnic diversity ($\beta_1 = -0.035$, $p > 0.05$). Departments with low and high levels of SEA have similar levels of ethnic diversity ($\beta_2 = -0.055$, $p > 0.05$). In addition, departments with small, moderate, and large workforces have similar levels of ethnic diversity ($\beta_3 = 0.0000004$, $p > 0.05$). The level of unionization also does not produce changes in the level of ethnic diversity ($\beta_6 = -0.038$, $p > 0.05$). Similar insignificant statistical findings exist for the other predictors in the model.

Despite the increase in the ethnic diversity scores due to using the formula for calculating unbiased (S_{EN}) coefficients, insignificant statistical relationships exist among the predictors and the dependent variable (see Panel B). NYC departments headed by elected and nonelected officials have similar levels of ethnic diversity (β_1 = -0.048, p > 0.05). The departments also have similar levels of ethnic diversity regardless of the level of SEA (β_2 = -0.045, p > 0.05). They also have similar levels of ethnic diversity despite differences in the size of their workforces (β_3 = 0.0000002, p > 0.05). In addition, the levels of ethnic diversity are similar amongst the departments despite differences in Pctunion (β_6 = -0.057, p > 0.05). The departments also have similar levels of ethnic diversity whether they have workforces composed primarily of persons of color or of Whites (β_8 = 0.013, p > 0.05).

The statistical findings of the OLS regression model for age diversity show that several of the predictors produce changes in the value of the dependent variable (see Exhibit 7-6). In Panel A, the S_{AB} scores are influenced by 5 predicators. For instance, NYC departments headed by elected officials have higher levels of age diversity in comparison to departments headed by nonelected officials (β_1 = 0.023, p < 0.001), where changing from a nonelected office to an elected office increases the level of age heterogeneity by about 0.02 points. A negative statistical relationship exists amongst age diversity and SEA, where a unit increase in SEA decreases age heterogeneity by about 0.02 points (β_2 = -0.023, p < 0.05). However, age diversity increases by about 0.04 points with a percent increase in unionization (β_6 = 0.042, p < 0.01). On the other hand, age diversity decreases by about 0.01 points with an increase in the number of persons of color (Mcluster) in the workforce (β_8 = -0.008, p < 0.01). By contrast, age diversity increases when the number of persons of color hired (Mhcluster) outpaces the number of Whites hired into the workforce (β_{13} = 0.005, p < 0.05). Insignificant statistical findings are obtained for the other independent variables where the level of age diversity does not change with a unit change in the value of each predictor. As Panel A shows, the model explains 52% (R^2 = 0.52) of the variance.

Slightly different findings are obtained for the S_{AN} scores (Panel B). In contrast to the model for S_{AB} scores discussed above, this model explains 30% (R^2 = 0.30) of the variance and fewer predicators produce a change in the level of age diversity. Departments headed by an elected official have higher levels of age diversity in comparison to other departments (β_1 = 0.013, p < 0.05) where a change from a department with a nonelected official to one headed by an elected official increases the level of age diversity by about 0.01 points. Further, age diversity increases by about 0.02 points with a unit increase in Pctunion (β_6 = 0.021, p < 0.05). However, age diversity decreases by about 0.01 points with a unit increase is Mcluster (β_8 = -0.005, p < 0.05). On the other hand, age diversity increases by less than 0.01 points with a unit increase is Mhcluster (β_{13} = 0.003, p < 0.05). In this model, a unit increase in SEA does not produce a unit increase in age diversity (β_2 = -0.01, p > 0.05). Similar insignificant statistical findings are found for the other predictors in the model.

The statistical findings for age diversity are questionable for several reasons. First, the S_{AB} and S_{AN} scores are incompatible. As discussed in Chapter 5, the departments differ with respect to the number of age group categories that contain employment data. Three of the departments have data for each of the 11 age group categories and have an EMV of 0.909. Most the NYC departments have data for 10 of the 11 age group categories and have an EMV of 0.900. Few of the departments have data for 5 age group categories and have an EMV of 0.800. The measurement incompatibility is compounded when the S_{AN} coefficients are calculated because the scores for departments with small workforces are inflated. In other words, the application of the formula for calculating the S_{AN} scores produces atypically large diversity scores where outliers are present in the OLS regression model. Third, the VIF scores for the predictors indicate the presence of low to moderate levels of collinearity amongst the predictors. As such, the findings are unreliable and unstable.

Summary

This chapter discussed OLS multivariate regression and the statistical assumptions which should be satisfied by the dependent variable for the findings to be reliable and stable. In so doing, this chapter discussed how the diversity scores for age, ethnicity, and gender calculated from the employment data reported by NYC departments for fiscal year 2019 do not satisfy the statistical assumptions of OLS regression. This chapter also discussed the issue of multicollinearity amongst the predictors. A Pearson correlation analysis was undertaken to illustrate the statistical associations amongst the predictors. The analysis indicated that several of the predictors have high positive correlation coefficients where they vary in the same direction. Chapter 11 addresses the issue of multicollinearity more thoroughly by performing ridge regression. *Assessing Organizational Diversity with Structural Equation Modeling* provides a further discussion of how to address multicollinearity amongst predictors by undertaking partial least square regression.

OLS multivariate regression was used to assess whether any of the predictors produced a change in the levels age, ethnic, and gender diversity amongst NYC departments. The model for the S_{GB} scores yielded insignificant statistical findings where none of the predictors produced a change in the level of gender diversity. However, the findings of the OLS regression model for S_{GN} scores indicated that several of the predictors changed the level of gender diversity. However, the findings are suspect because collinearity amongst the predictors is present and because atypically high scores are produced by the formula to adjust for size of the workforce. The OLS models for ethnic diversity produced insignificant statistical findings for the S_{EB} and S_{EN} scores. Lastly, the OLS models for age diversity indicated that several of the predictors changed the level of heterogeneity for age in NYC departments. Similar to the significant statistical findings for gender diversity, the findings for age diversity are suspect and confounded by measurement incompatibility, atypical high scores, outliers, and issues of collinearity amongst the predictors.

Briefly, the next chapter discusses and undertakes the analysis of outliers in the distributions of the age, ethnic, and gender diversity scores by performing robust regression. Chapter 8, however, does not address the issue of truncation where the range of the distributions of the diversity scores are restricted by different EMV values (see Chapter 9). Chapter 8 also does not address the issue of collinearity amongst the independent variables (see Chapter 11).

Key Terms

Clustering refers to the level of concentration of members of a particular demographic groups in an organization's workforce.

Coefficient of determination is a statistic which indicates the amount of variance this is explained by a set of predictors. In simultaneous OLS regression, adjusted R^2 and R^2 summarize the amount of variance that is explained by the model.

Independent variables refer to a set of measures that are hypothesized to influence either positively or negatively the values of a dependent variable.

Intercept refers to the point where the regression line passes through the y-axis.

Involuntary terminations refer to separations where employees are fired or where employees are removed from positions due to actions that are beyond their control to end their employment with the organization such as suffering a fatality while on duty.

Multicollinearity refers to the extent to which independent variables are associated statistically with each other so that their relationships provide redundant information into the regression equation and produce statistically biased and unreliable results.

Predictors refer to independent variables used to estimate value changes in the dependent variable.

Reciprocal value refers to the measure obtained by dividing a number into 1: $RV = \frac{1}{x}$.

Regression coefficients refer to the units of change that occur in the dependent variable with each unit change that occurs in the independent variable. Each independent variable has a regression coefficient associated with it.

Simultaneous OLS regression refers to entering each of the independent variables specified in the statistical model concurrently so that the relationships of the predictors on the dependent variable are summarized in 1 equation. By contrast, forward selection OLS regression enters each independent variable individually into the analysis and at each step the equation summarizes the independent variables with significant statistical relationships with the dependent variable. At the end of the analysis, a summary equation is produced which contains only the independent variables with significant statistical regression coefficients.

Truncation refers to measurement distributions that have either a minimum or maximum value so that a continuous variable can only have scores within a particular range of scores.

Variance inflation factor (VIF) is a statistic that assesses the level of collinearity amongst two or more independent variables in the regression equation. VIF scores are calculated by using the following formula: $VIF = \frac{1}{1 - R^2}$.

Voluntary terminations refer to separations where employees end their employment with an organization by retiring or by resigning to vacate a position.

References

Akram, Farheen, Abrar ul Haq, Muhammad, Natarajan, Vinodh K., and Chellakan, R. Stephen. 2020. "Board heterogeneity and corporate performance: An insight beyond agency issues". *Cogent Business and Management*, Vol. 7: 1809299.

Alexander, Jeffrey, Nuchols, Beverly, Bloom, Joan, and Lee, Shoou-Yih. 1995. "Organizational demography and turnover: An examination of multiform and nonlinear heterogeneity". *Human Relations*, Vol. 48: 1455 – 1480.

Alma, Özlem Gürünlü. 2011. "Comparison of robust regression methods in linear regression". *International Journal of Contemporary Mathematical Sciences*, Vol. 6: 409 – 421.

Bingen, Franz, Siau, Carlos, and Rousseeuw, Peter. 1986. "Applying robust regression techniques to institutional data". *Research in Higher Education*, Vol. 25: 277 – 297.

Boehm, Stephan A., Kunze, Florian, and Bruch, Heike. 2014. "Spotlight on age-diversity climate: The impact of age-inclusive HR practices on firm-level outcomes". *Personnel Psychology*, Vol. 67: 667 – 704.

Campbell, Kevin, and Mínguez-Vera, Antonio. 2008. "Gender diversity in the boardroom and firm financial performance". *Journal of Business Ethics*, Vol. 83: 435 – 451.

Cheong, Calvin W. H., and Sinnakkannu, Jothee. 2014. "Ethnic diversity and firm financial performance: Evidence from Malaysia". *Journal of Asia-Pacific Business*, Vol. 15: 73 – 100.

Choi, Sungjoo, and Rainey, Hal G. 2010. "Managing diversity in US federal agencies: Effects of diversity and diversity management on employee perceptions of organizational performance". *Public Administration Review*, Vol. 70: 109 – 121.

Choi, Sungjoo. 2010. "Diversity in the US federal government: Antecedents and correlates of diversity in federal agencies". *Review of Public Personnel Administration*, Vol. 30: 301 – 321

Cornwell, Christopher, and Kellough, J. Edward. 1994. "Women and minorities in federal government agencies: Examining new evidence from panel data". *Public Administration Review*, Vol. 54: 265 – 270.

Daoud, Jamal I. (2017). "Multicollinearity and regression analysis". *Journal of Physics: Conference Series*, Vol. 949: 012009.

De Meulenaere, Kim, Boone, Christophe, and Buyl, Tine. 2016. "Unraveling the impact of workforce age diversity on labor productivity: The moderating role of firm size and job security". *Journal of Organizational Behavior*, Vol. 37: 193 – 212.

Ferrero-Ferrero, Idoya, Fernández-Izquierdo, M. Ángeles, and Muñoz-Torres, M. Jesús. 2015. "Age diversity: An empirical study in the board of directors". *Cybernetics and Systems*, Vol. 46: 249 – 270.

Gazley, Beth, Chang, Won Kyung, and Bingham, Lisa Blomgren. 2010. "Board diversity, stakeholder representation, and collaborative performance in community mediation centers". *Public Administration Review*, Vol. 70: 610 – 620.

Guajardo, Salomón A. 2014. "Workforce diversity: Assessing the impact of minority integration on intra-group interaction". *International Journal of Police Science and Management*, Vol. 16: 205 – 220.

Guajardo, Salomón A. 2015. "Assessing organizational efficiency and workforce diversity: An application of data envelopment analysis to New York City agencies". *Public Personnel Management*, Vol. 44: 239 – 265.

Kearney, Eric, Gebert, Diether, and Voelpel, Sven C. 2009. "When and how diversity benefits teams: The importance of team members' need for cognition". *Academy of Management journal*, Vol. 52: 581 – 598.

Kellough, J. Edward, and Elliott, Euel. 1992. "Demographic and organizational influences on racial/ethnic and gender integration in federal agencies". *Social Science Quarterly,* Vol. 73: 1 – 11.

Khan, Imran, Khan, Ismail, and Senturk, Ismail. 2019. "Board diversity and quality of CSR disclosure: Evidence from Pakistan". *Corporate Governance: The International Journal of Business in Society*, Vol. 19: 1187 – 1203.

Kim, Pan Suk. 1993. "Racial integration in the American federal government: With special reference to Asian-Americans". *Review of Public Personnel Administration*, Vol. 13: 52 – 66.

Klein, Katherine. J., Conn, Amy Buhl, Smith, D. Brent, and Sorra, Joann Speer. 2001. "Is everyone in agreement? An exploration of within-group agreement in employee perceptions of the work environment". *Journal of Applied Psychology*, Vol. 86: 3 – 16.

Leslie, Lisa M. 2017. "A status-based multilevel model of ethnic diversity and work unit performance". *Journal of Management*, Vol. 43: 426 – 454.

Lewis, Gregory B. 1991. "Turnover and the quiet crisis in the federal civil service". *Public Administration Review*, Vol. 51: 145 – 155.

Li, Yixuan, Gong, Yaping, Burmeister, Anne, Wang, Mo, Alterman, Valeria, Alonso, Alexander, and Robinson, Samuel. 2021. "Leveraging age diversity for organizational performance: An intellectual capital perspective". *Journal of Applied Psychology*, Vol. 106: 71 – 91.

Lind, Douglas A., Marchal, William G., and Wathen, Samuel A. 2017. *Statistical techniques in business and economics.* Seventeenth edition. New York, NY: McGraw-Hill Education.

Massey, Douglas S., and Denton, Nancy A. 1988. "The dimensions of residential segregation". *Social Forces*, Vol. 67: 281 – 315.

Moon, Kuk-Kyoung, and Christensen, Robert K. 2020. "Realizing the performance benefits of workforce diversity in the US federal government: The moderating role of diversity climate". *Public Personnel Management*, Vol. 49: 141 – 165.

Oba, Victor Chiedu, and Fodio, Musa Inuwa. 2013. "Boards' gender mix as a predictor of financial performance in Nigeria: An empirical study". *International Journal of Economics and Finance*, Vol. 5: 170 – 178.

Randel, Amy E., and Jaussi, Kimberly S. 2003. "Functional background identity, diversity, and individual performance in cross-functional teams". *Academy of Management Journal*, Vol. 46: 763 – 774.

Riccucci, Norma M. 1986. "Female and minority employment in city government: The role of unions". *Policy Studies Journal*, Vol. 15: 3 – 15.

Rousseeuw, Peter J, Van Aelst, Stefan., Van Driessen, Katrien., and Agulló, Jose. 2004. "Robust multivariate regression". *Technometrics*, Vol. 46: 293 – 305.

Shrestha, Noora. 2020. "Detecting multicollinearity in regression analysis". *American Journal of Applied Mathematics and Statistics*, Vol. 8: 39 – 42.

Timmerman, Thomas A. 2000. "Racial diversity, age diversity, interdependence, and team performance". *Small Group Research*, Vol. 31: 592 – 606.

Yoo, Wonsuk, Mayberry, Robert, Bae, Sejong, Singh, Karan, He, Qinghua Peter, and Lillard Jr, James W. 2014. "A study of effects of multicollinearity in the multivariable analysis". *International Journal of Applied Science and Technology,* Vol. 4: 9 –19.

CHAPTER 8

ANALYSIS OF DIVERSITY WITH ROBUST REGRESSION

Atypical small or large measurements produce unreliable and unstable estimates when the underlying assumptions of OLS regression are violated (e.g., Alma, 2011; Preisser, and Qaqish, 1999; Szpiro and Lumley, 2010; Verardi, and Dehon, 2010; Western, 1995). In fact, the presence of a single atypical measurement may produce an erroneous regression coefficient (e.g., Bingen, Siau, and Rousseeuw, 1986; Verardi and Croux, 2009). As discussed in previous chapters, several NYC departments have either low or high diversity scores for age, ethnicity, or gender due to applying the formula for calculating unbiased (S_N) heterogeneity coefficients or due to a lack of data for several of the demographic categories. Although the discussion of atypical measurements has focused primarily on the diversity scores, atypical measurements are present amongst the set of independent variables such as the size of the organization, the percent of the operating budget allocated to salary expenses, and the percent of the workforce with collective bargaining membership. Because OLS regression estimates are influenced by atypical measurements amongst the dependent and independent variables, *robust regression* is applied to the statistical models presented and analyzed in Chapter 7.

This chapter presents an overview of robust regression and then applies the method to the diversity coefficients for age, ethnicity, and gender that are calculated from the employment data reported by NYC departments for fiscal year 2019. The underlying assumptions of robust regression are reviewed briefly since they are similar to the underlying assumptions of OLS regression. After discussing the assumptions, robust regression analyses are undertaken and discussed. Lastly, the statistical findings of the OLS and robust regression analyses are compared.

Overview of robust regression

Robust regression is designed to produce a statistical equation that adjusts for the presence of atypical measurements in a dataset so that the regression coefficients are unbiased, reliable, and stable (e.g., Filzmoser and Todorov, 2011). Specifically, robust regression reduces the influence of the atypical measurements through *downweighing* the variables with large errors (or *residuals*). Exhibit 8-1 highlights the steps taken to perform a robust regression analysis.

Exhibit 8-1 Robust regression process

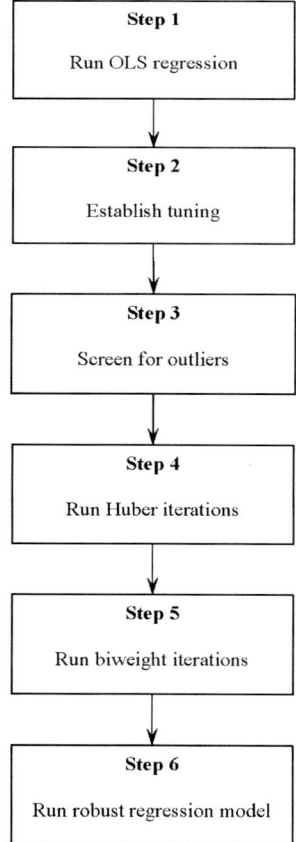

As Exhibit 8-1 illustrates, the first step is to conduct an OLS regression for the dependent variable of interest. This step was undertaken in the previous chapter where OLS regression analyses were performed for the biased (S_B) and unbiased (S_N) diversity coefficients for age, ethnicity, and gender. The analyses were performed despite violating several of the underlying assumptions of OLS regression such as linearity, normality, and no truncation either at the lower or upper end of the distribution. The discussion on the assumption of no atypical scores (or outliers) focused primarily on the diversity scores which serve as the dependent variables in the OLS regression analyses presented in Chapter 7. Although the discussion on the assumption of no atypical measurements (or outlies) was not geared toward the independent variables, the distributions of the quantitative continuous independent variables have atypical values which also affect the regression coefficients.

Step 2 requires the establishment of the *tuning* criterion (see Exhibit 8-1). For instance, a tuning constant of 6 may be applied to the data. In such a case, the constant of 6 means 6 times the median absolute deviation from the median residual. A low tuning criterion would downweigh the atypical values quickly but may produce unstable regression coefficients. An high tuning criterion would lessen the downweigh so that regression coefficients are similar to those of OLS regression. In this chapter, the tuning constant is set at 7.

The screening (or detection) of atypical values occurs in Step 3 (see Exhibit 8-1). Generally speaking, values that exceed ± 3 standard deviations from the mean are considered atypical measures. In case of the diversity scores for age, ethnicity, and gender, atypical scores are those that exceed the EMV for a particular categorization of a demographic characteristic. For instance, when the Simpson diversity index is applied to the categorization of gender as men and women, the EMV is 0.50 (EMV $= \frac{n-1}{n} = \frac{2-1}{2} = \frac{1}{2} = 0.50$) and scores above the EMV are atypical. Atypical Simpson scores also occur when diversity coefficients are extremely low or high. For instance, DSNY has a gender diversity coefficient of 0.164 for fiscal year 2019, while most of the scores range from 0.354 to 0.500. Two simple ways to check for the presence of atypical values are 1) to graph the data and determine whether there are scores that are outside of the general distribution or 2) to assess whether extremely low or high scores are ± 3 standard deviations from the mean.

Step 4 entails assigning Huber weights to the cases (see Exhibit 8-1). When Huber weights are assigned, cases with small residuals are given a weight of 1. By contrast, cases with large residuals are given weights less than one to decrease their influence. The assignment of Huber weights stops when the maximum change in weights drops below a particular tolerance level. Mathematically, the weights are calculated from absolute residuals, meaning the value of the residual is used regardless of whether it is positive or negative. For example, the absolute value of a residual of $|-4|$ is 4, and the absolute value of a residual of $|4|$ is 4.

In step 5, biweights are assigned to the cases after Huber weights are assigned (see Exhibit 8-1). The rationale for assigning biweights is that Huber weights are hampered by extreme atypical values. In addition, the Huber weights facilitate the process of assigning biweights to the cases that have difficulty converging or that have multiple solutions. The process of assigning biweights to cases stops when data convergence is attained.

The final step of the process entails running the robust regression analysis (see Exhibit 8-1). This chapter tests the same regression models examined with OLS regression in Chapter 7. In contrast to the OLS regression analyses undertaken in Chapter 7 which did not adjust for atypical values, the robust regression analyses performed below downweigh the influence of atypical diversity values. However, the robust regression models do not adjust for violations of linearity, normality, multicollinearity, and other underlying assumptions (see Hamilton, 1991).

Underlying assumptions of robust regression

Similar to OLS regression, robust regression requires satisfying a number of underlying assumptions in regard to the independent and dependent variables prior to undertaking the analysis. With the exception of the presence of atypical values, the underlying assumptions of robust regression are the following:

1. The dependent variable is quantitative continuous;
2. The relationship between the dependent and independent variables is linear so changes in the values of the independent variables produces changes in the values of the dependent variable;
3. The values of the dependent variable are normally distributed;
4. The values of the independent and dependent variables are not interconnected and are not calculated in part or in whole on the same data sources;
5. There are no significant high collinear statistical relationships amongst the set of independent variables; and,

6. There is truncation so that the values of the independent or dependent variables do not have a minimum or maximum limit.

Like OLS regression, robust regression produces regression coefficients that are biased, unreliable, and unstable when statistical assumptions are not adequately satisfied.

Robust regression models

Robust regression analyses are undertaken for the biased (S_B) and unbiased (S_N) diversity scores for age, ethnicity, gender, and organizational heterogeneity. The same independent variables that were used to conduct the OLS regression in Chapter 7 are used to perform the robust regression analyses below. The generic theoretical statistical model guiding the robust regression analysis is the following:

$\hat{S} = \alpha + \beta_1\text{Elected} + \beta_2\text{SEA} + \beta_3\text{Employees} + \beta_4\text{Myos} + \beta_5\text{Mftsal} + \beta_6\text{Pctunion} + \beta_7\text{Wcluster} + \beta_8\text{Mcluster} + \beta_9\text{ O40cluster} + \beta_{10}\text{Wscluster} + \beta_{11}\text{Mscluster} + \beta_{12}\text{Whcluster} + \beta_{13}\text{Mhcluster} + \varepsilon_{ij}.$

The terms of the regression equation are the following:

$\hat{S}$ refers to the Simpson diversity scores calculated separately for age, ethnicity, gender, and organizational diversity for fiscal year 2019;

α refers to the y-axis intercept for the regression line;

B_n refers to the regression coefficient associated with each independent variable in the equation that is significant statistically at $p < 0.05$;

Elected refers to whether the department is an elected office (1) or another type of organization (0);

SEA refers to the percent of the adopted operating budget that is allocated to salary expenses in fiscal year 2019;

Employees refers to the total number of employees on the payroll in each department in fiscal year 2019;

Myos refers to the median number of years of service of each department's workforce in fiscal year 2019;

Mftsal refers to the median full-time salary of each department's workforce in fiscal year 2019;

Pctunion refers to the percent of the workforce in each department that has membership in a collective bargaining unit in fiscal year 2019;

Wcluster refers to the relative clustering score obtained by dividing the percent of women employees by the percent of men employees in each department to assess the magnitude of women-dominated employment in fiscal year 2019;

Mcluster refers to the relative clustering score obtained by dividing the percent of minority employees by the percent of White employees in each department to assess the magnitude of minority-dominated employment in fiscal year 2019;

O40cluster refers to the relative clustering score obtained by dividing the percent of employees under the age of 40 by the percent of employees over the age of 40 in each department to assess the magnitude of employment of older persons in fiscal year 2019;

Wscluster refers to the relative clustering score obtained by dividing the percent of women employees that terminated their employment by the percent of men employees that terminated their employment in each department to assess the magnitude of women-dominated termination in fiscal year 2019;

Mscluster refers to the relative clustering score obtained by dividing the percent of minority employees that terminated their employment by the percent of White employees that terminated their employment in each department to assess the magnitude of minority-dominated termination in fiscal year 2019;

Whcluster refers to the relative clustering score obtained by dividing the percent of women hired by the percent of men hired in each department to assess the magnitude of women-dominated hiring in fiscal year 2019;

Mhcluster refers to the relative clustering score obtained by dividing the percent of minorities hired by the percent of men hired in each department to assess the magnitude of minority-dominated hiring in fiscal year 2019; and,

ε_{ij} refers to measurement error in the statistical model.

Similar to Chapter 7, each regression coefficient (β) is tested for statistical significance at $\alpha = 0.05$. In Chapter 7, Exhibit 7-5 illustrates the hypothesized statistical relationships amongst the predicators and the diversity scores for age, ethnicity, gender, and organizational heterogeneity.

Robust regression analysis

Exhibit 8-2 summarizes the robust regression findings for the biased (S_B) and unbiased (S_N) diversity scores for NYC departments for fiscal year 2019. The statistical findings for the biased (S_B) diversity scores for gender (S_{GB}) show that 2 independent variables are significant statistical predictors of the level of gender heterogeneity in NYC departments. For instance, departments headed by an elected official have an higher level of gender diversity in comparison to departments headed by nonelected officials ($\beta_1 = 0.006$, $p < 0.05$). Specifically, the change from a department with a nonelected official to one headed by an elected official increases the level of gender diversity by about 0.006 points. However, departments with workforces composed primarily of women decreases the level of gender diversity by about 0.06 points ($\beta_7 = -0.057$, $p < 0.05$). The percent of the budget allocated to salary expenses (SEA) does not increase or decrease the level of gender diversity in NYC departments ($\beta_2 = -0.003$, $p > 0.05$). Similarly, the size of the department (Employees) has no influence on the level of gender diversity ($\beta_3 = -0.0000001$, $p > 0.05$). Insignificant statistical findings are present for the remaining predictors. The model accounts for 62% ($R^2 = 0.62$) of the explained variance.

When robust regression analyses are performed on the unbiased (S_N) diversity scores for gender, different statistical findings are obtained (see Exhibit 8-2). The findings indicate that the level of gender diversity in NYC departments is influenced by the size of the workforce (Employees) and by the number of persons of color (Mscluster) terminating their employment that exceeds the number of whites doing the same. With respect to Employees, a unit increase in the size of a department decreases gender diversity; however, the change is less than 0.01 points ($\beta_3 = -0.0000001$, $p < 0.05$). With respect to Mscluster, a unit increase in the number of persons of color ending their employment increases gender diversity by less than 0.01 points ($\beta_{11} = 0.001$, $p < 0.01$). The level of gender diversity is the same for the departments regardless of the type of official heading the workforce ($\beta_1 = -0.002$, $p > 0.05$). Similar insignificant statistical relationships exist for SEA (β_2 0.002, $p > 0.05$) and the remaining independent variables in the model. This model explains 20% ($R^2 = 0.20$) of the variance.

Exhibit 8-2 Robust regression analysis for age, ethnic, gender, and organizational diversity for NYC departments for fiscal year 2019

A. Robust regression for biased (S_B) diversity scores

Predictors	Gender Diversity (S_{GB})		Ethnic Diversity (S_{EB})		Age Diversity (S_{AB})		Organizational Diversity (S_{OB})	
	β Coefficient	t-statistic	β Coefficient	t-statistic	β Coefficient	t-statistic	β Coefficient	t-statistic
Elected	0.0059029 (0.00286070)	2.06 *	-0.0094976 (0.01965210)	-0.48	0.0267727 (0.00565020)	4.74 ***	0.0111066 (0.00754860)	1.47
SEA	-0.0027584 (0.00420490)	-0.66	-0.0189735 (0.02922560)	-0.65	-0.0195238 (0.00840270)	-2.32 **	-0.0193493 (0.01109570)	-1.74
Employees	-0.0000001 (0.00000005)	-1.19	0.0000002 (0.00000033)	0.70	0.0000001 (0.00000010)	1.48	0.0000000 (0.00000013)	0.19
Myos	-0.0003185 (0.00031620)	-1.01	-0.0041546 (0.00220670)	-1.88	-0.0005524 (0.00063450)	-0.87	-0.0008442 (0.00083440)	-1.01
Mfiscal	-0.0000001 (0.00000008)	-1.21	-0.0000011 (0.00000058)	-1.84	-0.0000004 (0.00000017)	-2.34 *	-0.0000006 (0.00000022)	-2.64 *
Pctunion	0.0004566 (0.00475280)	0.10	-0.0057253 (0.03284050)	-0.17	0.0336151 (0.00944210)	3.56 **	0.0127930 (0.01254150)	1.02
Wcluster	-0.0565638 (0.00206450)	-27.4 ***	-0.0123534 (0.01537250)	-0.80	-0.0022155 (0.00441980)	-0.50	-0.0180500 (0.00544760)	-3.31 **
Mcluster	-0.0008274 (0.00109470)	-0.76	0.0007930 (0.00758600)	0.10	-0.0024224 (0.00218110)	-1.11	-0.0034275 (0.00288860)	-1.19
O40cluster	0.0012646 (0.00103650)	1.22	0.0098268 (0.00712250)	1.38	0.0003157 (0.00204780)	0.15	0.0019944 (0.00273500)	0.73
Wscluster	-0.0021786 (0.00189160)	-1.15	-0.0087620 (0.01372240)	-0.64	-0.0072143 (0.00394540)	-1.83	-0.0050902 (0.00499150)	-1.02
Mscluster	-0.0001767 (0.00095600)	-0.18	-0.0035680 (0.00660160)	-0.54	0.0004856 (0.00189810)	0.26	-0.0007037 (0.00252250)	-0.28
Whcluster	-0.0008221 (0.00072170)	-1.14	0.0034325 (0.01323810)	0.26	0.0041461 (0.00380610)	1.09	0.0012186 (0.00190440)	0.64
Mhcluster	0.0001115 (0.00068540)	0.16	-0.0090088 (0.00475420)	-1.89	0.0014934 (0.00136690)	1.09	-0.0020190 (0.00180860)	-1.12
Intercept	0.5130728 (0.00855450)	59.98 ***	0.8379511 (0.05896250)	14.21 ***	0.8868285 (0.01695250)	52.31 ***	0.7423977 (0.02257320)	32.89 ***
$F_{13,58}$	149.81 ***		1.91		5.91 ***		4.91 ***	
R^2	0.62		0.16		0.19		0.33	
AICR	155.15		104.55		133.93		112.23	
BICR	200.12		144.67		168.89		154.12	
Deviance	0.01		0.17		0.01		0.03	
N	72		72		72		72	

Analysis of Diversity with Robust Regression

B. Robust regression for unbiased (S_N) diversity scores

Predictors	Gender Diversity (S_GN)		Ethnic Diversity (S_EN)		Age Diversity (S_AN)		Organizational Diversity (S_OON)	
	β Coefficient	t-statistic	β Coefficient	t-statistic	β Coefficient	t-statistic	β Coefficient	t-statistic
Elected	-0.0017363 (0.0010450)	-1.66	-0.0281521 (0.0190953)	-1.47	0.0141544 (0.0056955)	2.49 *	-0.0095716 (0.0069724)	-1.37
SEA	0.0019828 (0.0015361)	1.29	0.0007349 (0.0283975)	0.03	-0.0035481 (0.0083719)	-0.42	-0.0049234 (0.0103690)	-0.47
Employees	0.0000000 (0.0000000)	-2.06 *	0.0000001 (0.0000003)	0.29	0.0000000 (0.0000001)	0.49	0.0000000 (0.0000001)	0.30
Myos	0.0002270 (0.0001155)	1.96	-0.0033892 (0.0021442)	-1.58	-0.0007293 (0.0006296)	-1.16	-0.0012935 (0.0007829)	-1.65
Mfiscal	0.0000000 (0.0000000)	-0.82	-0.0000010 (0.0000006)	-1.81	-0.0000003 (0.0000002)	-1.95	-0.0000005 (0.0000002)	-2.34 *
Petunion	-0.0029348 (0.0017363)	-1.69	-0.0247552 (0.0319100)	-0.78	0.0180636 (0.0094628)	1.91	-0.0096455 (0.0116515)	-0.83
Wcluster	0.0006207 (0.0007542)	0.82	-0.0054382 (0.0149369)	-0.36	0.0045524 (0.0041103)	1.11	0.0023595 (0.0054540)	0.43
Mcluster	-0.0007481 (0.0003999)	-1.87	0.0082375 (0.0073710)	1.12	-0.0041274 (0.0021795)	-1.89	0.0002823 (0.0026914)	0.10
O40cluster	-0.0000789 (0.0003786)	-0.21	0.0075631 (0.0069207)	1.09	0.0018670 (0.0020636)	0.90	0.0026837 (0.0025270)	1.06
Wscluster	0.0011797 (0.0006910)	1.71	-0.0068724 (0.0133336)	-0.52	-0.0040953 (0.0037662)	-1.09	-0.0052590 (0.0048686)	-1.08
Mscluster	0.0010303 (0.0003492)	2.95 **	-0.0045363 (0.0064146)	-0.71	0.0004643 (0.0019033)	0.24	-0.0023147 (0.0023422)	-0.99
Whcluster	-0.0003292 (0.0002636)	-1.25	0.0012684 (0.0128630)	0.10	-0.0004949 (0.0014369)	-0.34	-0.0003905 (0.0046967)	-0.08
Mhcluster	-0.0002446 (0.0002504)	-0.98	-0.0160518 (0.0046195)	-3.47 **	0.0020906 (0.0013646)	1.53	-0.0037324 (0.0016868)	-2.21 *
Intercept	0.4793348 (0.0031251)	153.38 ***	0.8419254 (0.0572919)	14.70 ***	0.8927956 (0.0170318)	52.42 ***	0.7495324 (0.0209194)	35.83 ***
$F_{13,58}$		2.58 **		3.10 **		1.93 *		2.55
R^2		0.20		0.14		0.21		0.16
AICR		117.72		113.06		119.58		118.03
BICR		160.19		153.26		154.36		156.49
Deviance		0.00		0.16		0.01		0.02
N		72		72		72		72

Standard errors are in parentheses. * $p < 0.05$; ** $p < 0.01$; *** $p < 0.001$

The statistical model for the biased ethnic diversity scores (S_{EB}) is insignificant statistically where none of the predictors increase or decrease the level of ethnic heterogeneity in NYC departments (see Exhibit 8-2). For example, the level of ethnic diversity is the same for each department regardless of the type of official heading the workforce (β_1 = -0.009, p > 0.05). An insignificant statistical relationship exists for SEA and the level of ethnic diversity in the departments (β_2 = -0.019, p > 0.05). In addition, the size of the workforce (Employees) does not increase or decrease the level of ethnic diversity (β_3 = 0.0000002, p > 0.05).

Exhibit 8-2 shows slightly different statistical findings for the unbiased (S_{EN}) ethnic diversity scores. The robust regression model indicates that the level of ethnic diversity decreases by about 0.02 points with a unit increase in Mhcluster (β_{13} = -0.016, p < 0.01). Insignificant statistical relationships are found for the remaining predictors. For instance, the level of ethnic diversity is the same regardless of the type of person heading the NYC departments (β_1 = -0.028, p > 0.05). The percent of the budget allocated to salary expenses does not increase or decrease the level of ethnic diversity (β_2 = 0.0007, p > 0.05). In addition, the size of the workforce does not change the level of ethnic diversity (β_3 = 0.0000001, p > 0.05). Turnover also does not increase or decrease the level of ethnic diversity (β_{10} = 0.0000001, p > 0.05; β_{11} = 0.0000001, p > 0.05). The model explains 14% (R^2 = 0.14) of the variance.

With respect to the statistical findings for the biased (S_{AB}) diversity scores for age, Exhibit 8-2 shows that the level of age diversity amongst NYC departments is influenced by several predictors. For instance, the change from a department headed by a nonelected official to one headed by an elected official increases the level of age diversity by about 0.03 points (β_1 = 0.027, p < 0.001). The level of age diversity increases by about 0.03 points with a unit increase in Pctunion (β_6 = 0.034, p < 0.01). However, age diversity decreases by about 0.02 points with a unit increase in SEA (β_2 = -0.0195, p < 0.01). Age diversity also decreases as the level of median full-time salary (Mftsal) increases, but the decrease is less than 0.01 points (β_5 = -0.0000004, p < 0.05). On the other hand, the size of the workforce (Employees) does not change the level of age diversity amongst NYC departments (β_3 = 0.0000001, p > 0.05). In addition, age diversity is not influenced by turnover (β_{10} = -0.007, p > 0.05; β_{11} = 0.0005, p > 0.05) or by the number of new hires (β_{12} = 0.004, p > 0.05; β_{13} = 0.001, p > 0.05). This model accounts for 19% (R^2 = 0.19) of the variance.

Lastly, the statistical model for the unbiased (S_{AN}) diversity scores for age shows that the level of heterogeneity is influenced by the type of person heading the department (see Exhibit 8-2). The change from a NYC department headed by a nonelected official to one headed by an elected official decreases the level of age diversity by about 0.01 points ($\beta_1 = -0.014$, $p < 0.05$). None of the other predictors influence a change in the level of age diversity amongst the departments. For example, an insignificant statistical relationship exists amongst SEA and the level of age diversity ($\beta_2 = -0.004$, $p > 0.05$). A similar insignificant statistical relationship exists amonst Employees and the level of age diversity ($\beta_3 = 0.0000000$, $p > 0.05$). Pctunion also has no influence on the level of age diversity in NYC departments ($\beta_6 = 0.018$, $p > 0.05$). The remaining independent variables have insignificant statistical relationships with age diversity as well. This model explains 21% ($R^2 = 0.21$) of the variance.

Comparison of OLS and robust regression

The statistical findings obtained with robust regression differ from those generated by the OLS regression analyses presented in Chapter 7 (see Exhibit 8-3 and Exhibit 8-4). Exhibit 8.3 presents the OLS and robust regression findings for the biased (S_B) diversity scores for age, ethnicity, gender, and organizational heterogeneity. With respect to the biased (S_{GB}) gender diversity scores, the OLS regression analysis shows insignificant statistical findings for each of the predictors. By contrast, the robust regression analysis produces significant and insignificant statistical findings, and the model accounts for 62% ($R^2 = 0.62$) of the variance. For instance, the OLS regression yields an insignificant statistical relationship amongst Elected and the level of gender diversity ($\beta_{A1} = 0.01$, $p > 0.05$). By contrast, robust regression finds a significant statistical finding amongst Elected and the level of gender diversity ($\beta_{B1} = 0.006$, $p < 0.05$). OLS regression also produces an insignificant statistical finding for Wcluster and the level of gender diversity ($\beta_{A7} = 0.009$, $p > 0.05$); however, robust regression produces a significant statistical relationship amongst Wcluster and the level of gender diversity ($\beta_{B7} = -0.056$, $p < 0.05$). Both OLS and robust regression yield similar insignificant statistical findings for the other predictors. While the OLS regression model fails to find significant statistical findings, the robust regression model is significant statistically and has explanatory power.

Exhibit 8-3 Comparison of OLS and robust regression findings for biased (S_B) scores for age, ethnic, gender, and organizational diversity for NYC departments for fiscal year 2019

A. OLS regression for biased (S_B) diversity scores

Predictors	Gender Diversity (S_{GB})		Ethnic Diversity (S_{EB})		Age Diversity (S_{AB})		Organizational Diversity (S_{BOD})		VIF
	β Coefficient	t-statistic	β Coefficient	t-statistic	β Coefficient	t-statistic	β Coefficient	t-statistic	
Elected	0.0100222 (0.0211684)	0.47	-0.0346973 (0.0288702)	-1.20	0.02796320 (0.0073853)	3.79 ***	0.0010960 (0.0137855)	0.08	1.67
SEA	-0.0001446 (0.0311158)	0.00	-0.0548222 (0.0424367)	-1.29	-0.02284840 (0.0108558)	-2.10 *	-0.0259384 (0.0202635)	-1.28	1.58
Employees	-0.0000005 (0.0000004)	-1.37	0.0000004 (0.0000005)	0.76	0.0000021 (0.0000001)	1.67	0.0000000 (0.0000002)	0.13	1.37
Myos	-0.0031933 (0.0023399)	-1.36	-0.0023674 (0.0031912)	-0.74	-0.00072870 (0.0008163)	-0.89	-0.0020965 (0.0015238)	-1.38	2.44
Mftsal	-0.0000006 (0.0000006)	-0.90	-0.0000011 (0.0000008)	-1.25	-0.0000033 (0.0000002)	-1.53	-0.0000007 (0.0000004)	-1.61	2.03
Pctunion	-0.0618134 (0.0351700)	-1.76	-0.0380349 (0.0479660)	-0.79	0.04206870 (0.0122703)	3.43 **	-0.0192598 (0.029037)	-0.84	2.11
Wcluster	-0.0087890 (0.0152766)	-0.58	-0.0167990 (0.0208348)	-0.81	-0.00717590 (0.0053298)	-1.35	-0.0109213 (0.0099486)	-1.10	2.34
Mcluster	0.0042241 (0.0081005)	0.52	0.0094895 (0.0110477)	0.86	-0.00814650 (0.0028261)	-2.88 **	0.0018557 (0.0052753)	0.35	4.63
O40cluster	0.0091009 (0.0076699)	1.19	0.0066266 (0.0104604)	0.63	0.00292210 (0.0026759)	1.09	0.0062165 (0.0049948)	1.24	2.49
Wscluster	0.0122934 (0.0139977)	0.88	-0.0101793 (0.0190906)	-0.53	-0.00337570 (0.0048836)	-0.69	-0.0004205 (0.0091157)	-0.05	2.21
Mscluster	0.0017878 (0.0070739)	0.25	0.0014905 (0.0096476)	0.15	0.00060320 (0.0024680)	0.24	0.0012938 (0.0046067)	0.28	2.53
Whcluster	-0.0052104 (0.0053404)	-0.98	0.0011866 (0.0072834)	0.16	0.00105660 (0.0018632)	0.57	-0.0009891 (0.0034778)	-0.28	1.65
Mhcluster	-0.0010515 (0.0050718)	-0.21	-0.0121854 (0.0069171)	-1.76	0.00471180 (0.0017695)	2.66 *	-0.0028417 (0.0033029)	-0.86	4.09
Intercept	0.5560840 (0.0633018)	8.78 ***	0.8507759 (0.0863331)	9.85 ***	0.87749200 (0.0220850)	39.73 ***	0.7614507 (0.0412239)	18.47 ***	
$F_{13,58}$	1.56		0.89		4.76		0.96		2.40
R^2	0.26		0.17		0.52		0.18		
Adjusted R^2	0.09		-0.02		0.41		-0.01		
N	72		72		72		72		

Analysis of Diversity with Robust Regression

B. Robust regression for biased (S_0) diversity scores

Predictors	Gender Diversity (S_{G0})		Ethnic Diversity (S_{R0})		Age Diversity (S_{A0})		Organizational Diversity (S_{O0})	
	β Coefficient	t-statistic	β Coefficient	t-statistic	β Coefficient	t-statistic	β Coefficient	t-statistic
Elected	0.0059029 (0.00286070)	2.06 *	-0.0094976 (0.01965210)	-0.48	0.0267727 (0.00565020)	4.74 ***	0.0111066 (0.00754860)	1.47
SEA	-0.0027584 (0.00420490)	-0.66	-0.0189735 (0.02922560)	-0.65	-0.0195238 (0.00840270)	-2.32 **	-0.0193493 (0.01109570)	-1.74
Employees	-0.0000001 (0.00000005)	-1.19	0.0000002 (0.00000033)	0.70	0.0000001 (0.00000010)	1.48	0.0000000 (0.00000013)	0.19
Myos	-0.0003185 (0.00031620)	-1.01	-0.0041546 (0.00220670)	-1.88	-0.0005524 (0.00063450)	-0.87	-0.0008442 (0.00083440)	-1.01
Mftsal	-0.0000001 (0.00000008)	-1.21	-0.0000001 (0.00000058)	-1.84	-0.0000004 (0.00000017)	-2.34 *	-0.0000006 (0.00000022)	-2.64 *
Petunion	0.0004566 (0.00475280)	0.10	-0.0057253 (0.03284050)	-0.17	0.0336151 (0.00944210)	3.56 **	0.0127930 (0.01254150)	1.02
Wcluster	-0.0565638 (0.00206450)	-27.4 ***	-0.0123534 (0.01537250)	-0.80	-0.0022155 (0.00441980)	-0.50	-0.0180500 (0.00544760)	-3.31 **
Mcluster	-0.0008274 (0.00109470)	-0.76	0.0007930 (0.00758600)	0.10	-0.0024224 (0.00218110)	-1.11	-0.0034275 (0.00288860)	-1.19
O40cluster	0.0012646 (0.00103650)	1.22	0.0098268 (0.00712250)	1.38	0.0003157 (0.00204780)	0.15	0.0019944 (0.00273500)	0.73
Wscluster	-0.0021786 (0.00189160)	-1.15	-0.0087620 (0.01372240)	-0.64	-0.0072143 (0.00394540)	-1.83	-0.0050902 (0.00499150)	-1.02
Mscluster	-0.0001767 (0.00095600)	-0.18	-0.0035680 (0.00660160)	-0.54	0.0004856 (0.00189810)	0.26	-0.0007037 (0.00252250)	-0.28
Whcluster	-0.0008221 (0.00072170)	-1.14	0.0034325 (0.01323810)	0.26	0.0041461 (0.00380610)	1.09	0.0012186 (0.00190440)	0.64
Mhcluster	0.0001115 (0.00068540)	0.16	-0.0090088 (0.00475420)	-1.89	0.0014934 (0.00136690)	1.09	-0.0020190 (0.00180860)	-1.12
Intercept	0.5130728 (0.00855450)	59.98 ***	0.8379511 (0.05896250)	14.21 ***	0.8868285 (0.01695250)	52.31 ***	0.7423977 (0.02257320)	32.89 ***
$F_{13,58}$	149.81 ***		1.91		5.91 ***		4.91 ***	
R^2	0.62		0.16		0.19		0.33	
AICR	155.15		104.55		133.93		112.23	
BICR	200.12		144.67		168.89		154.12	
Deviance	0.01		0.17		0.01		0.03	
N	72		72		72		72	

Standard errors are in parentheses. * $p < 0.05$; ** $p < 0.01$; *** $p < 0.001$

Exhibit 8-3 also shows that the OLS and robust regression analyses fail to detect significant statistical findings for the biased (S_{EB}) diversity scores for ethnic heterogeneity. For instance, the OLS and robust regression models indicate that NYC departments headed by elected and nonelected officials have the same level of the ethnic diversity ($\beta_{A1} = 0.035$, p > 0.05; $\beta_{B1} = -0.009$, p > 0.05). Similar insignificant statistical findings exist amongst SEA and the level of ethnic diversity ($\beta_{A2} = -0.0548222$, p > 0.05; $\beta_{B2} = -0.0189735$, p > 0.05). The size of the workforce (Employees) also fails to influence the level of ethnic diversity in NYC departments ($\beta_{A3} = 0.0000004$, p > 0.05; $\beta_{B3} = 0.0000002$, p > 0.05). Unionization also does not influence the level of ethnic diversity in NYC departments ($\beta_{A6} = -0.038$, p > 0.05; $\beta_{B6} = -0.006$, p > 0.05).

As Exhibit 8-3 highlights, the OLS and robust regression analyses differ with respect to the statistical findings obtained for the biased (S_{AB}) diversity scores for age diversity. For instance, the findings of the OLS regression model indicate that age diversity is influenced by whether the head of a department is elected or not ($\beta_{A1} = 0.023$, p < 0.001); similarly, the findings for robust regression show that age diversity is influenced by whether the head of a department is elected or not ($\beta_{B2} = 0.027$, p < 0.05). With respect to SEA, the OLS regression model shows that age diversity decreases by about 0.02 points with a unit increase in SEA ($\beta_{A2} = -0.023$, p < 0.05). The robust regression model finds a similar rate of decrease in age diversity as SEA increases ($\beta_{B2} = -0.019$, p < 0.01). In addition, the findings of the OLS and robust regression models are similar with respect to the rate of increase in age diversity per a unit increase in Pctunion ($\beta_{A6} = 0.042$, p < 0.01; $\beta_{B6} = 0.034$, p < 0.01). However, the OLS and robust regression models differ with respect to the influence of Mftsal and Mhcluster. Specifically, the findings of the OLS regression model indicate an insignificant statistical relationship amongst Mftsal and the level of age diversity ($\beta_{A5} = -0.0000003$, p > 0.05); the findings of the robust regression model yield a significant statistical relationship amongst Mftsal and age diversity, where the level of age diversity decreases by less than 0.01 points per a unit increase in Mftsal ($\beta_{B5} = -0.0000004$, p < 0.05). While the OLS regression model finds a positive significant relationship amongst Mhcluster and age diversity ($\beta_{A13} = 0.005$, p < 0.05), robust regression finds an insignificant statistical relationship amongst Mhcluster and age diversity ($\beta_{B13} = 0.001$, p > 0.05). Lastly, the OLS regression model explains 52% ($R^2 = 0.52$) of the variance, but the robust regression model explains 19% ($R^2 = 0.19$) of the variance.

The statistical findings of the OLS and robust regression analyses also differ with respect to the relationships amongst the predictors and the unbiased (S_N) diversity scores for age, ethnicity, gender, and organizational heterogeneity (see Exhibit 8-4). For example, the findings of the OLS regression model indicate that the level of gender diversity is lower in NYC departments headed by an elected official in comparison to departments that are not (β_{A1} = -0.009, $p < 0.001$), but the robust regression model shows an insignificant statistical relationship amongst the variables (β_{B1} = -0.002, $p > 0.05$). The findings of the OLS regression model show an insignificant statistical relationship amongst Employees and the level of gender diversity (β_{A3} = -0.0000001, $p > 0.05$), but the findings of the robust regression model reveal a significant negative relationship amongst Employees and the level of gender diversity (β_{B3} = -0.0000001, $p < 0.05$). While the OLS regression analysis yields a significant negative relationship amongst Pctunion and the level of gender diversity (β_{A6} = -0.013, $p < 0.01$), the robust regression model fails to detect a significant relationship amongst the variables (β_{B6} = -0.003, $p > 0.05$). With respect to Wcluster, the OLS regression model detects a significant positive relationship amongst the predictor and the level of gender diversity (β_{A7} = 0.006, $p < 0.01$), but the robust regression model fails to detect a similar statistical relationship amongst the variables (β_{B7} = 0.0006, $p > 0.05$). The OLS and robust regression analyses also differ with respect to the statistical significance of Mscluster. While the findings of the OLS regression model reveal an insignificant statistical relationship amongst Mscluster and the level of gender diversity (β_{A11} = -0.0007, $p > 0.05$), the robust regression model detects a positive statistical relationship amongst the variables (β_{B11} = 0.001, $p < 0.01$). The findings also show that the OLS regression model explains 50% (R^2 = 0.50) of the variance, and the robust regression model explains 20% (R^2 = 0.20) of the variance.

Exhibit 8-4 Comparison of OLS and robust regression findings for unbiased (S_N) scores for age, ethnic, gender, and organizational diversity for NYC departments for fiscal year 2019

A. OLS regression for unbiased (S_N) diversity scores

Predictors	Gender Diversity (S_{GN}) β Coefficient	t-statistic	Ethnic Diversity (S_{EN}) β Coefficient	t-statistic	Age Diversity (S_{AN}) β Coefficient	t-statistic	Organizational Diversity (S_{NOD}) β Coefficient	t-statistic	VIF
Elected	-0.0090903	-3.50 **	-0.0482130	-1.65	0.0125348	2.17 *	-0.0149228	-1.50	1.67
	(0.0026007)		(0.0292796)		(0.0057782)		(0.0099208)		
SEA	0.0070863	1.85	-0.0455908	-1.06	-0.0104432	-1.23	-0.0163159	-1.12	1.58
	(0.0038229)		(0.0430385)		(0.0084934)		(0.0145828)		
Employees	-0.0000001	-2.02	0.0000002	0.49	0.0000001	0.56	0.0000001	0.41	1.37
	(0.0000000)		(0.0000005)		(0.0000001)		(0.0000002)		
Myos	0.0001202	0.42	-0.0021419	-0.66	-0.0005328	-0.83	-0.0008515	-0.78	2.44
	(0.0002875)		(0.0032365)		(0.0006387)		(0.0010966)		
Mfisal	0.0000000	0.55	-0.0000010	-1.17	-0.0000003	-1.57	-0.0000004	-1.41	2.03
	(0.0000001)		(0.0000009)		(0.0000002)		(0.0000003)		
Pctunion	-0.0127857	-2.96 **	-0.0573847	-1.18	0.0207722	2.16 *	-0.0164661	-1.00	2.11
	(0.0043210)		(0.0486462)		(0.0096001)		(0.0164828)		
Wcluster	0.0060758	3.24 **	-0.0080546	-0.38	0.0030452	0.73	0.0003555	0.05	2.34
	(0.0018769)		(0.0211302)		(0.0041700)		(0.0071596)		
Mcluster	0.0017751	1.78	0.0125151	1.12	-0.0055869	-2.53 *	0.029011	0.76	4.63
	(0.0009952)		(0.0112044)		(0.0022111)		(0.0037964)		
O40cluster	-0.0006505	-0.69	0.0054227	0.51	0.0019535	0.93	0.0022419	0.62	2.49
	(0.0009423)		(0.0106087)		(0.0020936)		(0.0035946)		
Wscluster	-0.0002454	-0.14	-0.0108045	-0.56	-0.0035016	-0.92	-0.0048505	-0.74	2.21
	(0.0017198)		(0.0193613)		(0.0038209)		(0.0065602)		
Mscluster	-0.0006858	-0.79	0.0005037	0.05	-0.0003891	-0.20	-0.0001904	-0.06	2.53
	(0.0008691)		(0.0097844)		(0.0019309)		(0.0033153)		
Whcluster	-0.0008539	-1.30	-0.0000665	-0.01	-0.0004047	-0.28	-0.0004417	-0.18	1.65
	(0.0006561)		(0.0073867)		(0.0014577)		(0.0025028)		
Mhcluster	-0.0011117	-1.78	-0.0140542	-2.00	0.0029747	2.15 *	-0.0040637	-1.71	4.09
	(0.0006231)		(0.0070152)		(0.0013844)		(0.0023770)		
Intercept	0.4827186	62.07 ***	0.8625738	9.85 ***	0.8894504	51.48 ***	0.7449143	25.11 ***	
	(0.0077772)		(0.0875573)		(0.0172790)		(0.0296671)		
$F_{13,58}$	4.54 ***		0.92		1.91 *		0.87		2.40
R^2	0.50		0.17		0.30		0.16		
Adjusted R^2	0.39		-0.02		0.14		-0.02		
N	72		72		72		72		

Analysis of Diversity with Robust Regression

B. Robust regression for unbiased (Ss) diversity scores

Predictors	Gender Diversity (S_GN) β Coefficient	t-statistic	Ethnic Diversity (S_EN) β Coefficient	t-statistic	Age Diversity (S_AN) β Coefficient	t-statistic	Organizational Diversity (S_OD) β Coefficient	t-statistic
Elected	-0.0017363 (0.0010450)	-1.66	-0.0281521 (0.0190953)	-1.47	0.0141544 (0.0056955)	2.49 *	-0.0095716 (0.0069724)	-1.37
SEA	0.0019828 (0.0015361)	1.29	0.0007349 (0.0283975)	0.03	-0.0035481 (0.0083719)	-0.42	-0.0049234 (0.0103690)	-0.47
Employees	0.0000000 (0.0000000)	-2.06 *	0.0000001 (0.0000003)	0.29	0.0000000 (0.0000001)	0.49	0.0000000 (0.0000001)	0.30
Myos	0.0002270 (0.0001155)	1.96	-0.0033892 (0.0021442)	-1.58	-0.0007293 (0.0006296)	-1.16	-0.0012935 (0.0078829)	-1.65
Mfisal	0.0000000 (0.0000000)	-0.82	-0.0000010 (0.0000006)	-1.81	-0.0000003 (0.0000002)	-1.95	-0.0000005 (0.0000002)	-2.34 *
Petunion	-0.0029348 (0.0017363)	-1.69	-0.0247552 (0.0319100)	-0.78	0.0180636 (0.0094628)	1.91	-0.0096455 (0.0116515)	-0.83
Wcluster	0.0006207 (0.0007542)	0.82	-0.0054382 (0.0149369)	-0.36	0.0045524 (0.0041103)	1.11	0.0023595 (0.0054540)	0.43
Mcluster	-0.0007481 (0.0003999)	-1.87	0.0082375 (0.0073710)	1.12	-0.0041274 (0.0021795)	-1.89	0.0002823 (0.0026914)	0.10
O40cluster	-0.0000789 (0.0003786)	-0.21	0.0075631 (0.0069207)	1.09	0.0018670 (0.0020636)	0.90	0.0026837 (0.0025270)	1.06
Wscluster	0.0011797 (0.0006910)	1.71	-0.0068724 (0.0133336)	-0.52	-0.0040953 (0.0037662)	-1.09	-0.0052590 (0.0048686)	-1.08
Mscluster	0.0010303 (0.0003492)	2.95 **	-0.0045363 (0.0064146)	-0.71	0.0004643 (0.0019033)	0.24	-0.0023147 (0.0023422)	-0.99
Whcluster	-0.0003292 (0.0002636)	-1.25	0.0012684 (0.0128630)	0.10	-0.0004949 (0.0014369)	-0.34	-0.0003905 (0.0046967)	-0.08
Mhcluster	-0.0002446 (0.0002504)	-0.98	-0.0160518 (0.0046195)	-3.47 **	0.0020906 (0.0013646)	1.53	-0.0037324 (0.0016868)	-2.21 *
Intercept	0.4793348 (0.0031251)	153.38 ***	0.8419254 (0.0572919)	14.70 ***	0.8927956 (0.0170318)	52.42 ***	0.7495324 (0.0209194)	35.83 ***
$F_{13,58}$	2.58 **		3.10 **		1.93 *		2.55	
R^2	0.20		0.14		0.21		0.16	
AICR	117.72		113.06		119.58		118.03	
BICR	160.19		153.26		154.36		156.49	
Deviance	0.00		0.16		0.01		0.02	
N	72		72		72		72	

Standard errors are in parentheses. * p < 0.05; ** p < 0.01; *** p < 0.001

With respect to the statistical findings for the unbiased (S_{EN}) ethnic diversity scores, Exhibit 8-4 shows that the OLS and robust regression models produce similar results. The OLS and robust regression findings for Elected and the level of ethnic diversity are similar where both fail to detect a significant statistical relationship (β_{A1} = -0.048, p > 0.05; β_{B1} = -0.028, p > 0.05). Both models also fail to detect a significant statistical relationship amongst SEA and the level of ethnic diversity (β_{A2} = -0.045, p > 0.05; β_{B2} = 0.0007, p > 0.05). A similar insignificant statistical relationship is found amongst Employees and the level of ethnic diversity (β_{A3} = 0.0000002, p > 0.05; β_{B3} = 0.0000001, p > 0.05). In addition, both models indicate that unionization does not influence the level of ethnic diversity in NYC departments (β_{A6} = -0.057, p > 0.05; β_{B6} = -0.023, p > 0.05). However, the OLS and robust regression models differ with respect to the statistical significance of Mhcluster. While the findings of the OLS regression model show an insignificant statistical relationship amongst Mhcluster and the level of ethnic diversity (β_{A13} = -0.014, p > 0.05), the findings of the robust regression model show a significant negative relationship amongst the predictor and the level of ethnic diversity (β_{B13} = -0.016, p < 0.01). In contrast to the OLS regression model which fails to explain any of the variance, the robust regression model explains 14% (R^2 = 0.14) of the variance.

With respect to the statistical findings for the unbiased (S_{AN}) age diversity scores, the OLS and robust regression analyses differ with respect to the statistical relationships amongst some of the predictors and the level of age diversity in NYC departments (see Exhibit 8-4). The OLS and robust regression models detect a similar statistical positive relationship amongst Elected and the level of age diversity (β_{A1} = 0.012, p < 0.05; β_{B1} = 0.014, p < 0.05). However, the analyses differ with respect to the statistical relationship amongst Pctunion and the level of age diversity. For instance, the OLS regression model detects a positive statistical relationship amongst the variables (β_{A6} = 0.021, p < 0.05); robust regression does not (β_{B6} = 0.018, p > 0.05). The OLS regression model also reveals a negative statistical relationship amongst Mcluster and the level of age diversity (β_{A8} = -0.005, p < 0.05). By contrast, the robust regression model fails to detect a similar statistical relationship amongst Mcluster and the level of age diversity (β_{B8} = -0.004, p > 0.05). Both models also differ with respect to the statistical relationship amongst Mhcluster and the level of age diversity. While the OLS regression model finds a positive statistical relationship amongst the variables (β_{A13} = 0.003, p < 0.05), the robust regression model detects an insignificant statistical relationship amongst the variables (β_{B13} = 0.002, p >

0.05). The OLS regression model explains 30% ($R^2 = 0.30$) of the variance; the robust regression model explains 21% ($R^2 = 0.21$) of the variance.

The statistical findings generated by the robust regression model are suspect despite the downweighing of the atypical diversity scores and measures amongst the independent variables. While robust regression adjusts for atypical scores, the method does not correct for nonnormality, nonlinearity, multicollinearity, or truncation. As discussed in previous chapters, the distribution of each set of diversity scores violates the assumption of normality. The relationships amongst the diversity scores and some of the independent variables are nonlinear. With respect to truncation, the distributions of each diversity score range from 0 to a specific EMV value under 1. As stated in previous chapters, the distributions of the gender diversity scores range from 0 to 0.50; the distributions of the ethnic diversity scores range from 0 to 0.80 if ethnicity is categorized into 5 groups. Multiple levels of truncations exist for the distributions of the age diversity scores. With respect to collinearity amongst the predictors, the VIF scores show that multicollinearity is present and should be a concern (see Chapter 7).

Summary

This chapter illustrated the use of robust regression to downweigh the influence of atypical values on regression coefficients. While robust regression minimizes the influence of atypical measurements, the method does not address other statistical issues that plague the Simpson diversity scores calculated from the employment data reported by NYC departments for fiscal year 2019. Briefly, the diversity scores for age, gender, and age violate the assumption of normality, linearity, multicollinearity, and truncation. Consequently, the regression coefficients generated by the robust regression models are suspect due to the assumption violations.

The issue of measurement truncation is addressed in the next chapter. Each distribution of diversity scores has a specific EMV value that is based on the number of categories that are used to report the number or percent of employees in each group. The EMV value restricts the range of the distributions from 0 to the maximum value allowed. When distributions of scores are truncated to a very restricted range, OLS regression and robust regression generate biased regression coefficients. In Chapter 9, Tobit regression is used to illustrate how to address the issue of truncation. In the case of the distributions of unbiased (S_N) diversity scores with values that exceed the EMV, Tobit regression eliminates the high scores and makes appropriate statistical adjustments. However, Tobit regression does not address issues related to nonlinearity or multicollinearity (see Chapter 11).

Key words

Downweighing refers to the process of assigning weights to atypical values of variables to decrease their influence so that regression coefficients are reliable and stable.

Residuals refer to the difference obtained by subtracting a predicted value from the actual value. Small residual or error values indicate that the predicated value approximates the actual value; large error values indicate the predicated value varies greatly from the actual value.

Robust regression is a set of statistical procedures developed to assess the relationship amongst a quantitative continuous dependent variable and a set of independent variables that contain atypically small or large measurements so that the underlying assumptions of least squares regression are violated.

Tuning refers to the process of assigning a constant to downweigh outliers. Low tuning constants downweigh atypical values quickly but may produce unstable estimates; conversely, high tuning constants lessen the downweighing of atypical values.

References

Alma, Özlem Gürünlü. 2011. "Comparison of robust regression methods in linear regression". *International Journal of Contemporary Mathematical Sciences*, Vol. 6: 409 – 421.

Bingen, Franz, Siau, Carlos, and Rousseeuw, Peter. 1986. "Applying robust regression techniques to institutional data". *Research in Higher Education*, Vol. 25: 277 – 297.

Filzmoser, Peter, and Todorov, Valentin. 2011. "Review of robust multivariate statistical methods in high dimension". *Analytica Chimica Acta*, Vol. 705: 2 – 14.

Hamilton, Lawrence C. 1991. "How robust is robust regression?". *Stata Technical Bulletin*, STB-2: 21 – 26.

Preisser, John S., and Qaqish, Bahjat F. 1999. "Robust regression for clustered data with application to binary responses". *Biometrics*, Vol. 55: 574 – 579.

Szpiro, Adam A., Rice, Kenneth M., and Lumley, Thomas. 2010. "Model-robust regression and a Bayesian "sandwich" estimator". *The Annals of Applied Statistics*, Vol. 4: 2099 – 2113.

Verardi, Vincenzo, and Croux, Christophe. 2009. Robust regression in Stata. *The Stata Journal*, 9(3), 439 – 453.

Verardi, Vincenzo, and Dehon, Catherine. 2010. "Multivariate outlier detection in Stata". *The Stata Journal*, Vol. 10: 259 – 266.

Western, Bruce. 1995. "Concepts and suggestions for robust regression analysis". *American Journal of Political Science*, Vol. 39: 786-817.

Yaffee, Robert A. 2002. "Robust regression analysis: some popular statistical package options". *Statistics, Social Science, and Mapping Group Academic Computing Services Information Technology Services*, 1 – 12.

CHAPTER 9

ANALYSIS OF DIVERSITY WITH TOBIT REGRESSION

While some independent and dependent variables have distributions that are *censored*, the distributions of Simpson diversity coefficients are truncated by an EMV that is determined by the number of categories that are created for a demographic (or social) characteristic of interest such as age, ethnicity, and gender. Statistically speaking, Simpson diversity scores that are calculated for age, ethnic, gender, and organizational heterogeneity are limited dependent variables (LDVs) because their distributions have a predetermined minimum (0) and maximum value ($S_M = \frac{n-1}{n}$). As discussed in previous chapters, the distributions of Simpson diversity scores do not fall below 0, and they do not exceed a specific empirical maximum value (EMV) for the set of diversity coefficients unless measurement errors occur. Each demographic (or social) characteristic has its own EMV score that is calculated based on a specific number of categories used in the classification schema. Stated differently, an EMV score of each demographic (or social) characteristic differs based on the following formula: $EMV = \frac{n-1}{n}$, where n represents the number of categories. Because the distributions of Simpson diversity scores fail to satisfy several of the underlying assumptions required to perform OLS regression, a regression method capable of addressing censored or truncated measurements is more appropriate to use vis-à-vis OLS regression.

Although OLS regression is used extensively to assess the statistical relationships amongst a set of predictors and diversity scores for age, ethnic, gender, and other demographic- or social-based characteristics, the measurements of the predictors and dependent variables need to satisfy the underlying assumptions to obtain unbiased, reliable, and stable regression coefficients. This chapter illustrates the use of Tobit regression to analyze the statistical relationships amongst the predicators used in previous regression analyses and the biased (S_B) and unbiased (S_N) Simpson diversity scores for age, ethnicity, gender, and organizational heterogeneity calculated for NYC departments based on employment data for fiscal year 2019. A brief overview of Tobit regression is presented prior to undertaking the analyses. The same statistical models analyzed previously with OLS and robust regression are tested in this chapter. Comparisons of OLS and Tobit regression findings are undertaken to assess similarities or differences in the predictive power of the statistical methods.

Overview of Tobit regression

Tobin (1955 and 1958) developed Tobit regression to analyze the relationship amongst independent variables and quantitative continuous dependent variables with censored (or truncated) distributions. In developing Tobit regression, Tobin (1955 and 1958) noted that linear-based methods such as OLS regression do not adequately represent the relationship of a set of predictors and a dependent variable with a lower or upper limit in a straight line. Statistically, the concentration of values between a minimum and maximum value hinders the robustness of OLS regression to generate reliable regression coefficients. In addition, Tobin (1955 and 1958) recognized that the underlying assumptions of OLS regression are not satisfied when a distribution of scores is restricted by a minimum or maximum value. Tobin also recognized that many LDVs do not have values that fall below 0 so that negative values are not possible. In the case of Simpson diversity scores, the lowest possible value is 0, and the maximum possible value is determined by $\frac{n-1}{n}$, where n represents the number of categories. Further, Tobin (1955 and 1958) noted that methods such as *probit regression* that categorize LDVs dichotomously are inefficient because of the loss of quantitative information that occurs when the data are classified into 2 categories. Unlike probit regression, Tobit regression uses all of the quantitative information provided by the dependent variable when estimating a regression line (e.g., McDonald and Moffitt, 1980). As described by Tobin (1958), Tobit regression is a hybrid of probit and OLS regression.

McDonald and Moffitt (1980) summarize Tobit regression thusly:

$$y_t = X_t\beta + \mu_t \qquad \text{if } X_t\beta \ X_t\beta > 0$$

$$= 0 \qquad \text{if } X_t\beta \ X_t\beta \leq 0$$

$$t = 1, 2, 3, \ldots N,$$

where

y_t represents the dependent variable;

X_t represents the vector of independent variables;

β represents the vector of unknown coefficients;

μ_t represents an independently distributed error term that is assumed to be normal with a 0 mean and constant variance σ^2; and,

N represents the number of observations.

The expected value of y in the model is as follows (see McDonald and Moffitt, 1980):

$Ey = X\beta F(z) + \sigma f(z),$

where

z represents the product of $X\beta/\sigma$;
f(z) represents unit normal density; and,
F(z) represents the cumulative normal distribution function.

With respect to the expected values of y above the limit (y*), McDonald and Moffitt (1980) define the expected value of y* as $X\beta$ plus the expected value of the truncated normal error term. The expected value of y* is as follows (see McDonald and Moffitt, 1980):

$Ey^* = E(y \mid y > 0)$
$= E(y \mid u > -X\beta)$
$= X\beta + \sigma f(z)/F(z).$

Lastly, McDonald and Moffitt (1980, 1) note that the following formula expresses the "basic relationship between the expected value of all observations, Ey, the expected value conditional upon being above the limit, Ey*, and the probability of being above the limit, F(z):"

$Ey = F(z)Ey^*.$

Briefly, Tobit regression tests the relationship amongst a predictor and dependent variable with a *likelihood ratio*, which estimates the probability of a particular event occurring (see Tobit 1958). Before the relationships amongst predictors and a dependent variable are tested with the likelihood-ratio method, the maximum likelihood solution for the dependent and independent variables is obtained (see Tobin 1958). After obtaining the maximum likelihood solution, expected values of the dependent variable are calculated (e.g., McDonald and Moffitt, 1980; Tobin, 1958). The statistical output provides the regression coefficients and *marginal effects* estimates when requested. In Tobit regression, the regression coefficients estimate the unit change in the predicated value of the dependent variable per a unit change in the independent variable. For instance, a regression coefficient of 0.50 ($\beta = 0.50$, $p < 0.05$) is interpreted as follows: a unit change in X is associated with a 0.50 unit increase in the predicted value of Y. With respect to interpreting marginal effects, a marginal effect of 0.02 indicates that the level of Y increases by 2% per a unit increase in X. In this chapter, only Tobit regression coefficients are reported and interpreted.

Underlying assumptions of Tobit regression

Like OLS and robust regression, Tobit regression requires satisfying the underlying statistical assumptions with respect to the independent and dependent variables prior to undertaking the analysis. With the exception of data censoring (or truncation), the underlying assumptions of Tobit regression are the following:

1. The dependent variable is quantitative continuous but has either a minimum or maximum value;
2. The relationship between the dependent and independent variables is linear so that changes in the values of the independent variables are associated with the predicted values of the dependent variable;
3. The values of the dependent variable are normally distributed;
4. The values of the independent and dependent variables are not interconnected and are not calculated in part or in whole on the same data sources; and,
5. There are no significant high collinear statistical relationships amongst the set of independent variables.

Similar to OLS and robust regression, Tobit regression produces regression coefficients that are biased, unreliable, and unstable when statistical assumptions are not adequately satisfied.

Tobit regression models

Tobit regression analyses are undertaken for the biased (S_B) and unbiased (S_N) diversity scores for age, ethnicity, gender, and organizational heterogeneity. The same independent variables that were used to conduct the OLS and robust regression analyses are used to perform the Tobit regression analyses below. The generic theoretical statistical model guiding the Tobit regression analysis is the following:

$$\hat{S} = \alpha + \beta_1 \text{Elected} + \beta_2 \text{SEA} + \beta_3 \text{Employees} + \beta_4 \text{Myos} + \beta_5 \text{Mftsal} + \beta_6 \text{Pctunion} + \beta_7 \text{Wcluster} + \beta_8 \text{Mcluster} + \beta_9 \text{O40cluster} + \beta_{10} \text{Wscluster} + \beta_{11} \text{Mscluster} + \beta_{12} \text{Whcluster} + \beta_{13} \text{Mhcluster} + \varepsilon_{ij}.$$

The terms of the regression equation are the following:

$\hat{S}$ refers to the Simpson diversity scores calculated separately for age, ethnicity, gender, and organizational diversity for fiscal year 2019;

α refers to the y-axis intercept for the regression line;

B_n refers to the regression coefficient associated with each independent variable in the equation that is significant statistically at $p < 0.05$;

Elected refers to whether the department is an elected office (1) or another type of organization (0);

SEA refers to the percent of the adopted operating budget that is allocated to salary expenses in fiscal year 2019;

Employees refers to the total number of employees on the payroll in each department in fiscal year 2019;

Myos refers to the median number of years of service of each department's workforce in fiscal year 2019;

Mftsal refers to the median full-time salary of each department's workforce in fiscal year 2019;

Pctunion refers to the percent of workforce in each department that has membership in a collective bargaining unit in fiscal year 2019;

Wcluster refers to the relative clustering score obtained by dividing the percent of women employees by the percent of men employees in each department to assess the magnitude of women-dominated employment in fiscal year 2019;

Mcluster refers to the relative clustering score obtained by dividing the percent of minority employees by the percent of White employees in each department to assess the magnitude of minority-dominated employment in fiscal year 2019;

O40cluster refers to the relative clustering score obtained by dividing the percent of employees under the age of 40 by the percent of employees over the age of 40 in each department to assess the magnitude of employment of older persons in fiscal year 2019;

Wscluster refers to the relative clustering score obtained by dividing the percent of women employees that terminated their employment by the percent of men employees that terminated their employment in each department to assess the magnitude of women-dominated termination in fiscal year 2019;

Mscluster refers to the relative clustering score obtained by dividing the percent of minority employees that terminated their employment by the percent of White employees that terminated their employment in each department to assess the magnitude of minority-dominated termination in fiscal year 2019;

Whcluster refers to the relative clustering score obtained by dividing the percent of women hired by the percent of men hired in each department to assess the magnitude of women-dominated hiring in fiscal year 2019;

Mhcluster refers to the relative clustering score obtained by dividing the percent of minorities hired by the percent of men hired in each department to assess the magnitude of minority-dominated hiring in fiscal year 2019; and,

ε_{ij} refers to measurement error in the statistical model.

In Chapter 7, Exhibit 7-5 illustrates the hypothesized statistical relationships amongst the predicators and the diversity scores for age, ethnicity, gender, and organizational heterogeneity.

As in Chapter 7 and 8, each regression coefficient (β) is tested for statistical significance at $\alpha = 0.05$. For each Tobit regression analysis performed, the left censoring limit is set at 0 because the minimum value of the Simpson diversity index is 0. However, the right censoring limit for each statistical model differs because each set of diversity scores differs with respect to its EMV. For example, the right censoring limit for the gender diversity scores is set at 0.50 (EMV $= \frac{n-1}{n} = \frac{2-1}{2} = 0.50$). The right censoring limit for the ethnic diversity scores is set at 0.80 (EMV $= \frac{n-1}{n} = \frac{5-1}{5} = 0.80$). The issue of setting the right censoring limit for the age diversity scores is not straightforward because most of NYC departments have age group categories with missing data. As stated in Chapter 5, an EMV of 0.909 (EMV $= \frac{n-1}{n} = \frac{11-1}{11} = 0.909$) is attained by 3 departments with employee data in each of the 11 age group categories. For the departments with employee data in 10 of the 11 age group categories, the EMV is 0.90 (EMV $= \frac{n-1}{n} = \frac{10-1}{10} = 0.90$). The departments with employee data in 5 of the 11 age group categories have an EMV of 0.80 (EMV $= \frac{n-1}{n} = \frac{5-1}{5} = 0.80$). Setting the right censoring limit at 0.90 would exclude the 3 departments with employee data in each age group category, while setting the right censoring limit at 0.80 would eliminate 64 departments from the regression analysis. To retain each NYC department in the Tobit regression analysis for the age diversity scores, a right censoring limit of 0.91 is used.

Tobit regression analysis

Exhibit 9-1 summarizes the statistical findings of the Tobit regression analyses for the age, ethnic, gender, and organizational diversity scores for NYC departments for fiscal year 2019. The Tobin regression analysis of the biased (S_B) diversity scores for gender shows that a unit increase in Employees is associated with less than a 0.001 unit decrease in the predicted value of a S_{GB} score ($\beta1 = -0.0000005$, $p < 0.05$), indicating that smaller NYC departments have higher levels of gender diversity in comparison to larger departments (see Panel A). The level of gender diversity also declines as the percent of unionized employees increases. Specifically, a unit increase in Pctunion is associated with a 0.06 unit decrease in the predicted value of a S_{GB} score ($\beta6 = -0.063$, $p < 0.05$), indicating that departments with higher rates of unionization hire more men than women. The findings also show insignificant statistical relationships amongst the other predictors and the level of gender diversity in NYC departments. Although the Tobit model for gender diversity yields significant statistical results, the negative pseudo r squared value (Pseudo $R^2 = -0.11$) indicates that the statistical model has poor predictive power due to not following the trend of the data.

Analysis of Diversity with Tobit Regression

Exhibit 9-1 Tobit regression analysis for age, ethnic, gender, and organizational diversity for NYC departments for fiscal year 2019

A. Tobit regression for biased (S_B) diversity scores

Predictors	Gender Diversity (S_{GB})		Ethnic Diversity (S_{EB})		Age Diversity (S_{AB})		Organizational Diversity (S_{OOB})	
	β Coefficient	t-statistic	β Coefficient	t-statistic	β Coefficient	t-statistic	β Coefficient	t-statistic
Elected	0.0112221 (0.0107147)	1.05	-0.0346973 (0.0324908)	-1.07	0.0279632 (0.0068536) ***	4.08	0.001096 (0.0122864)	0.09
SEA	-0.0014382 (0.0234270)	-0.06	-0.0548222 (0.0312798)	-1.75	-0.0228484 (0.0102773) *	-2.22	-0.0259384 (0.0146840)	-1.77
Employees	-0.0000005 (0.0000002) *	-2.26	0.0000004 (0.0000003)	1.39	0.0000002 (0.0000001) ***	2.88	0.0000000 (0.0000001)	0.24
Myos	-0.0034428 (0.0028847)	-1.19	-0.0023674 (0.0022717)	-1.04	-0.0007287 (0.0008083)	-0.90	-0.0020965 (0.0013969)	-1.50
Mflsal	-0.0000006 (0.0000004)	-1.48	-0.0000011 (0.0000007)	-1.41	-0.0000003 (0.0000002) *	-2.10	-0.0000007 (0.0000003) *	-2.36
Petunion	-0.063178 (0.0281994) *	-2.24	-0.0380349 (0.0367024)	-1.04	0.042687 (0.0162382) *	2.59	-0.0192598 (0.0176888)	-1.09
Wcluster	-0.0101079 (0.0121165)	-0.83	-0.016799 (0.0194294)	-0.86	-0.0071759 (0.0046709)	-1.54	-0.0109213 (0.0082817)	-1.32
Mcluster	0.005718 (0.0048904)	1.17	0.0094895 (0.0115522)	0.82	-0.0081465 (0.0041144)	-1.98	0.0018557 (0.0040334)	0.46
O40cluster	0.0095105 (0.0075231)	1.26	0.0066266 (0.0103632)	0.64	0.0029221 (0.0022500)	1.30	0.0062165 (0.0051582)	1.21
Wscluster	0.0113072 (0.0085851)	1.32	-0.0101793 (0.0161960)	-0.63	-0.0033757 (0.0036789)	-0.92	-0.0004205 (0.0059477)	-0.07
Mscluster	0.0019989 (0.0040525)	0.49	0.0014905 (0.0081020)	0.18	0.0006032 (0.0026612)	0.23	0.0012938 (0.0032608)	0.40
Whcluster	-0.004965 (0.0027544)	-1.8	0.0011866 (0.0053722)	0.22	0.0010566 (0.0010974)	0.96	-0.0009891 (0.0019238)	-0.51
Mhcluster	-0.0008838 (0.0027330)	-0.32	-0.0121854 (0.0064391)	-1.89	0.0047118 (0.0019388) *	2.43	-0.0028417 (0.0023593)	-1.20
Intercept	0.5570962 (0.0441606) ***	12.62	0.8507759 (0.0752755) ***	11.30	0.877492 (0.0197187) ***	44.50	0.7614507 (0.0309821) ***	24.58
/Sigma	0.051086 (0.0102841)		0.0691281 (0.0095915)		0.0176838 (0.0018854)		0.0330086 (0.0044417)	
$F_{13,59}$	5.40 ***		2.49 **		4.20 ***		3.14 **	
Pseudo R²	-0.11		-0.08		-0.16		-0.05	
Uncensored N	71		72		72		72	

Chapter 9

B. Tobit regression for unbiased (S_N) diversity scores

Predictors	Gender Diversity (S_{GN})			Ethnic Diversity (S_{EN})			Age Diversity (S_{AN})			Organizational Diversity (S_{NOD})	
	β Coefficient	t-statistic		β Coefficient	t-statistic		β Coefficient	t-statistic		β Coefficient	t-statistic
Elected	-0.0073641 (0.0019470)	-3.78	***	-0.048213 (0.0326156)	-1.48		0.0125348 (0.0055777)	2.25	*	-0.0149228 (0.0111468)	-1.34
SEA	0.0066664 (0.0030664)	2.17	*	-0.0455908 (0.0327432)	-1.39		-0.0104432 (0.0075953)	-1.37		-0.0163159 (0.0116630)	-1.40
Employees	-0.0000001 (0.0000000)	-4.75	***	0.0000002 (0.0000003)	0.87		0.0000001 (0.0000001)	1.01		0.0000001 (0.0000001)	0.76
Myos	0.0001017 (0.0001846)	0.55		-0.0021419 (0.0023341)	-0.92		-0.0005328 (0.0007438)	-0.72		-0.0008515 (0.0008075)	-1.05
Mfisal	0.0000000 (0.0000000)	0.83		-0.0000010 (0.0000008)	-1.32		-0.0000003 (0.0000001)	-2.23	*	-0.0000004 (0.0000003)	-1.60
Pcturion	-0.0090207 (0.0044288)	-2.04		-0.0573847 (0.0393857)	-1.46		0.0207722 (0.0098883)	2.10	*	-0.0164661 (0.0146287)	-1.13
Wcluster	0.0048519 (0.0014269)	3.40	**	-0.0080546 (0.0203402)	-0.40		0.0030452 (0.0031660)	0.96		0.0003555 (0.0069158)	0.05
Mcluster	0.0005669 (0.0008667)	0.65		0.0125151 (0.0124830)	1.00		-0.0055869 (0.0021419)	-2.61	*	0.0029011 (0.0040934)	0.71
O40cluster	-0.0004253 (0.0007686)	-0.55		0.0054227 (0.0104335)	0.52		0.0019535 (0.0017843)	1.09		0.0022419 (0.0035373)	0.63
Wscluster	0.0004035 (0.0010564)	0.38		-0.0108045 (0.0167915)	-0.64		-0.0035016 (0.0034698)	-1.01		-0.0048505 (0.0058149)	-0.83
Mscluster	-0.0001281 (0.0005372)	-0.24		0.0005037 (0.0083661)	0.06		-0.0003891 (0.0020982)	-0.19		-0.0001904 (0.0029019)	-0.07
Whcluster	-0.0007245 (0.0002707)	-2.68	*	-0.0000665 (0.0057181)	-0.01		-0.0004047 (0.0008860)	-0.46		-0.0004417 (0.0018685)	-0.24
Mhcluster	-0.0006232 (0.0004622)	-1.35		-0.0140542 (0.0069294)	-2.03		0.0029747 (0.0011453)	2.60	*	-0.0040637 (0.0023538)	-1.73
Intercept	0.4797674 (0.0061570)	77.92	***	0.8625738 (0.0793638)	10.87	***	0.8894504 (0.0140071)	63.50	***	0.7449143 (0.0281764)	26.44	***
/Sigma	0.0046437 (0.0004960)			0.0701083 (0.0093955)			0.0138356 (0.0012063)			0.0237549 (0.0029806)	
$F_{13,59}$	4.68	***		1.80			2.04			1.73	
Pseudo R²	-0.11			-0.08			-0.07			-0.04	
Uncensored N	68			72			72			72	

Standard errors are in parentheses. * $p < 0.05$; ** $p < 0.01$; *** $p < 0.001$

Different statistical findings are obtained for the unbiased (S_{GN}) gender diversity scores which are partially due to the removal of cases with coefficients that exceed the EMV value of 0.50 (see Panel B). As Panel B shows, the change from a NYC department headed by a nonelected official to one headed by an elected official is associated with a 0.01 unit decrease in the predicted value of a S_{GN} score ($\beta_1 = -0.007$, $p < 0.001$), indicating that elected officials hire more men than women. In addition, a unit increase in Employees is associated with less than a 0.001 unit decrease in the predicated value of a S_{GN} score ($\beta_2 = -0.0000001$, $p < 0.001$), indicating that smaller departments have higher levels of gender diversity in comparison to larger departments. On the other hand, NYC departments composed predominately of women have higher levels of gender diversity. Statistically, a unit increase in Wcluster is associated with a 0.005 point increase in the predicated value of a S_{GN} score ($\beta_7 = 0.0048$, $p < 0.01$). However, the level of gender diversity decreases when the rate of women hired exceeds the rate of men hired. The findings show that a unit increase in Whcluster is associated with a less than a 0.001 unit decrease in the predicated value of a S_{GN} score ($\beta_{12} = -0.0007$, $p < 0.05$). Statistical insignificant findings are found for the other predicators in the model. Despite the significant statistical findings, the negative pseudo R^2 indicates that the model has poor predictive power due to not following the trend of the data.

The statistical findings for the biased (S_B) and unbiased (S_N) diversity scores for ethnicity are consistent (see Exhibit 9-1). Each predicator is unrelated statistically with differences in the level of ethnic diversity amongst NYC departments. In Panel A, an insignificant statistical finding is obtained for Elected ($\beta_{A1} = -0.035$, $p > 0.05$). Similarly, Panel B shows that Elected is unassociated with the S_{EN} scores ($\beta_{B1} = -0.048$, $p > 0.05$). These findings indicate that the level of ethnic diversity is similar amongst NYC departments that are headed by elected and nonelected officials. The same is true for the other predicators in the statistical model.

The statistical findings for the biased (S_B) and unbiased (S_N) diversity scores for age differ (see Exhibit 9-1). In Panel A, a unit increase in Elected is associated with a 0.03 unit increase in the predicated value of a S_{AB} score ($\beta_1 = 0.028$, $p < 0.001$), indicating that the change from a NYC department headed by a nonelected official to one headed by an elected official increases the level of age diversity. However, the level of age diversity decreases as budget allocations for salary expenses (SEA) increase. Statistically, a unit increase in SEA is associated with a 0.02 unit decrease in the predicated value of a S_{AB} score ($\beta_2 = -0.023$, $p < 0.05$). The findings also show that the level of age diversity increases as the size of the workforce increases. More specifically, a unit increase in Employees is associated with less than a 0.001

unit increase in the predicated value of a S_{AB} score ($\beta_3 = 0.0000002$, p < 0.001). However, a unit increase in Mftsal is associated with less than a 0.001 unit decrease in the predicted value of a S_{AB} score ($\beta_5 = -0.0000003$, p < 0.05), indicating that departments with workforces that have higher median full-time salaries have lower levels of age diversity in comparison to departments with workforces with lower median full-time salaries. On the other hand, unionization is associated with higher levels of age diversity. The findings reveal that a unit increase in Pctunion is associated with a 0.04 unit increase in the predicated value of a S_{AB} score ($\beta_6 = -0.042$, p < 0.05). When departments hire more persons of color in comparison to whites, the level of age diversity in the workforce increases. In fact, a unit increase in Mhcluster is associated with a 0.005 unit increase in the predicated value of a S_{AB} score ($\beta_{13} = 0.0047$, p < 0.05). As Panel A shows, the statistical associations of the other predicators with the S_{AB} scores are insignificant statistically at $\alpha = 0.05$. Again, the negative pseudo R^2 indicates that the model has poor predictive power.

The Tobin regression model for the unbiased (S_N) age diversity scores yields different statistical findings (see Panel B). A positive association exists amongst Elected and the S_{AN} scores where the change from a NYC department headed by a nonelected official to a department headed by an elected official is associated with a 0.01 unit increase in the predicated value of a S_{AN} score ($\beta_1 = 0.013$, p < 0.05). However, the level of age diversity decreases as the median full-time salary of the workforce increases. The findings show that a unit increase in Mftsal is associated with less than a 0.001 decrease in the predicted value of a S_{AN} score ($\beta_5 = -0.0000003$, p < 0.05). By contrast, the level of age diversity increases as the percent of unionized employees increases in NYC departments. The findings reveal that a unit increase in Pctunion is associated with a 0.02 unit increase in the predicated value of a S_{AN} score ($\beta_6 = 0.021$, p < 0.05). With respect to the statistical relationship amongst Mcluster and age diversity, the findings show that a unit increase in Mcluster is associated with a 0.01 unit decrease in the predicated value of a S_{AN} score ($\beta_8 = -0.005$, p < 0.05), indicating that NYC departments composed predominately of persons of color hire fewer young applicants in comparison to departments composed primarily of Whites. On the other hand, NYC departments that hire more persons of color than White applicants increase their level of age diversity. The findings show that a unit increase in Mhcluster is associated with a 0.003 unit increase in the predicated value of a S_{AN} score ($\beta_{13} = 0.0029$, p < 0.05). Despite the significant findings, the negative pseudo R^2 indicates that the model has poor predictive power.

The differences in the statistical findings are due partially to measurement errors associated with using the formula to calculate unbiased (S_N) diversity scores for age, ethnicity, and gender. As discussed in previous chapters, S_N scores are statistically higher than the S_B scores where some S_N scores exceed the EMV score. When the S_B and S_N gender diversity scores are analyzed, several cases with high S_{GN} scores were eliminated from the Tobit analysis which reduced sample size to 68 from 72 and found more predictors that are related statistically with the S_{GN} scores. A review of the negative pseudo R^2 values shows that the level of explained variance is similar for the biased and unbiased gender diversity scores although the findings differ with respect to the number of predicators that are significant statistically; however, the models have poor predictive power. In regard to the range and spread of diversity scores, S_N scores are centered more closely around the mean and the distributions have less variation in comparison to the S_B scores, which affects the findings of the unbiased (S_{AN}) age diversity scores. The regression coefficients for the S_{AN} model also have higher levels of estimation bias due to high scores resulting from overcorrecting for workforce size and due to overestimating the level of age diversity in departments where a limited number of age group categories contain employment data. A review of the negative pseudo R^2 values shows that the model for the biased (S_{AB}) age diversity scores explains a greater percent of the variance in comparison to the model for the unbiased (S_{AN}) age diversity scores. As a caveat, the negative pseudo R^2 indicates that the statistical model does not follow the trend of the age diversity data.

Comparison of OLS and Tobit regression

Exhibit 9-2 highlights the OLS and Tobit regression findings for the biased (S_B) diversity scores for age, ethnicity, gender, and organizational heterogeneity. In terms of the statistical findings for gender diversity, the findings of the OLS regression analysis show that none of the predictors are related statistically with the S_{GB} scores (see Panel A). In Panel B, the findings of the Tobit regression analysis reveal that Employees is related inversely with gender diversity (β_{B3} = -0.0000005, p < 0.05). The Tobit analysis also shows a significant inverse statistical relationship amongst Pctunion and the S_{GB} scores (β_{B6} = -0.063, p < 0.05). Because Tobit regression is designed to analyze distributions with truncation vis-à-vis OLS regression, the Tobit model seems to produce a more reliable assessment of the statistical relationships amongst the predictors and the S_{GB} scores. The negative pseudo R^2 values obtained by the statistical models may also provide a more accurate assessment of the relationships amongst the diversity scores and the independent variables.

Exhibit 9-2 Comparison of OLS and Tobit regression findings for biased (S_B) scores for age, ethnic, gender, and organizational diversity for NYC departments for fiscal year 2019

A. OLS regression for biased (S_B) diversity scores

Predictors	Gender Diversity (S_GB)		Ethnic Diversity (S_EB)		Age Diversity (S_AB)		Organizational Diversity (S_BOD)		VIF
	β Coefficient	t-statistic	β Coefficient	t-statistic	β Coefficient	t-statistic	β Coefficient	t-statistic	
Elected	0.0100222 (0.0211684)	0.47	-0.0346973 (0.0288702)	-1.20	0.02796320 (0.0073853)	3.79 ***	0.0010960 (0.0137855)	0.08	1.67
SEA	-0.0001446 (0.0311158)	0.00	-0.0548222 (0.0424367)	-1.29	-0.02284840 (0.0108558)	-2.10 *	-0.0259384 (0.0202635)	-1.28	1.58
Employees	-0.0000005 (0.0000004)	-1.37	0.0000004 (0.0000005)	0.76	0.00000021 (0.0000001)	1.67	0.0000000 (0.0000002)	0.13	1.37
Myos	-0.0031933 (0.0023399)	-1.36	-0.0023674 (0.0031912)	-0.74	-0.00072870 (0.0008163)	-0.89	-0.0020965 (0.0015238)	-1.38	2.44
Mfisal	-0.0000006 (0.0000006)	-0.90	-0.0000011 (0.0000008)	-1.25	-0.0000033 (0.0000002)	-1.53	-0.0000007 (0.0000004)	-1.61	2.03
Pctunion	-0.0618134 (0.0351700)	-1.76	-0.0380349 (0.0479660)	-0.79	0.04206870 (0.0122703)	3.43 **	-0.0192598 (0.029037)	-0.84	2.11
Wcluster	-0.0087890 (0.0152766)	-0.58	-0.0167990 (0.0208348)	-0.81	-0.00717590 (0.0053298)	-1.35	-0.0109213 (0.0099486)	-1.10	2.34
Mcluster	0.0042241 (0.0081005)	0.52	0.0094895 (0.0110477)	0.86	-0.00814650 (0.0028261)	-2.88 **	0.0018557 (0.0052753)	0.35	4.63
O40cluster	0.0091009 (0.0076699)	1.19	0.0066266 (0.0104604)	0.63	0.00292210 (0.0026759)	1.09	0.0062165 (0.0049948)	1.24	2.49
Wscluster	0.0112934 (0.0139977)	0.88	-0.0101793 (0.0190906)	-0.53	-0.00337570 (0.0048836)	-0.69	-0.0004205 (0.0091157)	-0.05	2.21
Mscluster	0.0017878 (0.0070739)	0.25	0.0014905 (0.0096476)	0.15	0.00060320 (0.0024680)	0.24	0.0012938 (0.0046067)	0.28	2.53
Whcluster	-0.0052104 (0.0053404)	-0.98	0.0011866 (0.0072834)	0.16	0.00105660 (0.0018632)	0.57	-0.0009891 (0.0034778)	-0.28	1.65
Mhcluster	-0.0010515 (0.0050718)	-0.21	-0.0121854 (0.0069171)	-1.76	0.00471180 (0.0017695)	2.66 *	-0.0028417 (0.0033029)	-0.86	4.09
Intercept	0.5560840 (0.0633018)	8.78 ***	0.8507759 (0.0863331)	9.85 ***	0.87749200 (0.0220850)	39.73 ***	0.7614507 (0.0412239)	18.47 ***	
$F_{13,58}$	1.56		0.89		4.76		0.96		2.40
R^2	0.26		0.17		0.52		0.18		
Adjusted R^2	0.09		-0.02		0.41		-0.01		
N	72		72		72		72		

Analysis of Diversity with Tobit Regression

B. Tobit regression for biased (S_B) diversity scores

Predictors	Gender Diversity (S_{GB})		Ethnic Diversity (S_{EB})		Age Diversity (S_{AB})		Organizational Diversity (S_{OB})	
	β Coefficient	t-statistic	β Coefficient	t-statistic	β Coefficient	t-statistic	β Coefficient	t-statistic
Elected	0.0112221 (0.0107147)	1.05	-0.0346973 (0.0324908)	-1.07	0.0279632 (0.0068536)	4.08 ***	0.001096 (0.0122864)	0.09
SEA	-0.0014382 (0.0234270)	-0.06	-0.0548222 (0.0312798)	-1.75	-0.0228484 (0.0102773)	-2.22 *	-0.0259384 (0.0146840)	-1.77
Employees	-0.0000005 (0.0000002)	-2.26 *	0.0000004 (0.0000003)	1.39	0.0000002 (0.0000001)	2.88 ***	0.0000000 (0.0000001)	0.24
Myos	-0.0034428 (0.0028847)	-1.19	-0.0023674 (0.0022717)	-1.04	-0.0007287 (0.0008083)	-0.90	-0.0020965 (0.0013969)	-1.50
Mfisal	-0.0000006 (0.0000004)	-1.48	-0.0000011 (0.0000007)	-1.41	-0.0000003 (0.0000002)	-2.10 *	-0.0000007 (0.0000003)	-2.36 *
Petunion	-0.063178 (0.0281994)	-2.24 *	-0.0380349 (0.0367024)	-1.04	0.420687 (0.0162382)	2.59 *	-0.0192598 (0.0176888)	-1.09
Wcluster	-0.0101079 (0.0121165)	-0.83	-0.016799 (0.0194294)	-0.86	-0.0071759 (0.0046709)	-1.54	-0.0109213 (0.0082817)	-1.32
Mcluster	0.005718 (0.0048904)	1.17	0.0094895 (0.0115322)	0.82	-0.0081465 (0.0041144)	-1.98	0.0018557 (0.0040334)	0.46
O40cluster	0.0095105 (0.0075231)	1.26	0.0066266 (0.0103632)	0.64	0.029221 (0.0022500)	1.30	0.0062165 (0.0051582)	1.21
Wscluster	0.0113072 (0.0085851)	1.32	-0.0101793 (0.0161960)	-0.63	-0.0033757 (0.0036789)	-0.92	-0.0004205 (0.0059477)	-0.07
Mscluster	0.0019989 (0.0040525)	0.49	0.014905 (0.0081020)	0.18	0.006032 (0.0026612)	0.23	0.012938 (0.0032608)	0.40
Whcluster	-0.004965 (0.0027544)	-1.8	0.0011866 (0.0053722)	0.22	0.0010566 (0.0019974)	0.96	-0.0009891 (0.0019238)	-0.51
Mhcluster	-0.0008838 (0.0027330)	-0.32	-0.0121854 (0.0064391)	-1.89	0.0047118 (0.0019388)	2.43 *	-0.0028417 (0.0023593)	-1.20
Intercept	0.5570962 (0.0441606)	12.62 ***	0.8507759 (0.0752755)	11.30 ***	0.877492 (0.0197187)	44.50 ***	0.7614507 (0.0309821)	24.58
Sigma	0.051086 (0.0102841)		0.0691281 (0.0095915)		0.0176838 (0.0018854)		0.030086 (0.044417)	
$F_{13,59}$	5.40 ***		2.49 **		4.20 ***		3.14 **	
Pseudo R^2	-0.11		-0.08		-0.16		-0.05	
Uncensored N	71		72		72		72	

Standard errors are in parentheses. * p < 0.05; ** p < 0.01; *** p < 0.001

The OLS and Tobit models show that none of the predicators are related statistically with the biased (S_{EB}) ethnic diversity scores. These insignificant statistical findings are explained partially by the existence of negligible differences in S_{EB} scores amongst NYC departments. The Simpson diversity index may lack the discriminatory power necessary to detect subtle differences in the level of ethnic diversity amongst NYC departments. The insignificant statistical findings also are due to the nonlinearity of the distribution of scores. OLS and Tobit regression models do not adjust for nonlinearity in the data. They also do not address assumption violations related to multicollinearity and nonnormality.

When comparing the OLS and Tobit regression findings for the biased (S_{AB}) age diversity scores, similar results are obtained (see Exhibit 9-2). In Panel A, the OLS regression model obtains a positive statistical relationship amongst Elected and the S_{AB} scores (β_{A1} = 0.023, p < 0.001). The Tobit regression model obtains a similar relationship amongst the variables (β_{B1} = 0.023, p < 0.001; see Panel B). The findings for SEA also are similar for the OLS and Tobit models where an inverse relationship exists amongst SEA and the S_{AB} scores (β_{A2} = -0.023, p < 0.05; β_{B2} = -0.023, p < 0.05). However, the models differ with respect to the findings for Employees. In Panel A, the OLS model shows that Employees is unrelated statistically with age diversity (β_{A3} = -0.0000002, p > 0.05); by contrast, the Tobit model detects a positive relationship amongst Employees and age diversity (β_{B3} = 0.0000002, p < 0.001). The models also differ with respect to the statistical relationship amongst Mftsal and the S_{AB} scores. Panel A reveals an insignificant statistical finding for Mftsal and age diversity (β_{A5} = -0.0000003, p > 0.05); Panel B shows a significant inverse relationship amongst the variables (β_{B5} = -0.0000003, p < 0.05). With respect to the relationship amongst Pctunion and age diversity, both models detect a positive statistical association amongst the variables scores (β_{A6} = 0.042, p < 0.05; β_{B6} = 0.042, p < 0.05). Different findings are obtained for Mcluster and age diversity. While the OLS model finds a significant inverse relationship amongst Mcluster and the S_{AB} scores (β_{A8} = -0.008, p < 0.05); the Tobit model fails to detect a similar relationship amongst the variables (β_{B8} = -0.008, p > 0.05; see Panel B). Lastly, the OLS and Tobit models obtain a similar positive relationship amongst Mhcluster and age diversity (β_{A13} = 0.005, p < 0.05; β_{B13} = 0.005, p < 0.05).

The comparative analysis for the OLS and Tobit regression findings for the unbiased (S_N) diversity scores for age, ethnicity, gender, and organizational heterogeneity is presented in Exhibit 9-3. In Panel A, the OLS model shows a negative statistical relationship amongst Elected and gender diversity (β_{A1}

= -0.009, p < 0.01). The Tobit model finds a similar negative relationship amongst the variables (β_{B2} = -0.007, p < 0.001; see Panel B). For the predictor SEA, the OLS model fails to detect a significant statistical relationship amongst the predictor and gender diversity (β_{A2} = 0.007, p > 0.05; see Panel A); the Tobit models shows a positive relationship amongst SEA and gender diversity (β_{B2} = 0.007, p < 0.05; see Panel B). For Employees, the OLS model fails to detect a significant statistical relationship amongst the predictor and gender diversity (β_{A3} = -0.0000001, p > 0.05); by contrast, the Tobit model shows a significant inverse relationship amongst the predictor and gender diversity (β_{B3} = -0.0000001, p < 0.001). The models also differ with respect to the relationship amongst Pctunion and gender diversity. An inverse relationship amongst Pctunion and gender diversity is detected by the OLS model (β_{A6} = -0.013, p < 0.01), but an insignificant statistical relationship is detected by the Tobit model in regard to the predictor and gender diversity (β_{B6} = -0.009, p > 0.05; see Panel B), In regard to Wcluster, the OLS model reveals a significant inverse relationship amongst the predictor and gender diversity (β_{A7} = -0.006, p < 0.01; see Panel A). The Tobit model shows a similar inverse relationship amongst the predictor and gender diversity (β_{B7} = -0.005, p < 0.01; see Panel B). However, the models differ with respect to the statistical relationship amongst Whcluster and gender diversity. The OLS model fails to detect a significant relationship amongst Whcluster and gender diversity (β_{A12} = 0.005, p > 0.05; see Panel A). A significant negative relationship amongst the variables is detected by the Tobit model (β_{B12} = -0.0007, p < 0.05; see Panel B). By eliminating the cases with S_{EN} scores that exceeded the EMV value of 0.50, the Tobit regression model was able to find more significant statistical relationships amongst the predictors and the level of gender diversity in comparison to the OLS regression model.

Exhibit 9-3 Comparison of OLS and Tobit regression findings for unbiased (S_N) scores for age, ethnic, gender, and organizational diversity for NYC departments for fiscal year 2019

A. OLS regression for unbiased (S_N) diversity scores

Predictors	Gender Diversity (S_{GN})		Ethnic Diversity (S_{EN})		Age Diversity (S_{AN})		Organizational Diversity (S_{ON})		VIF
	β Coefficient	t-statistic	β Coefficient	t-statistic	β Coefficient	t-statistic	β Coefficient	t-statistic	
Elected	-0.0090903 (0.0026007)	-3.50 **	-0.0482130 (0.0292796)	-1.65	0.0125348 (0.0057782)	2.17 *	-0.0149228 (0.0099208)	-1.50	1.67
SEA	0.0070863 (0.0038229)	1.85	-0.0455908 (0.0430385)	-1.06	-0.0104432 (0.0084934)	-1.23	-0.0163159 (0.0145828)	-1.12	1.58
Employees	-0.0000001 (0.0000000)	-2.02	0.0000002 (0.0000005)	0.49	0.0000001 (0.0000001)	0.56	0.0000001 (0.0000002)	0.41	1.37
Myos	0.0001202 (0.0002875)	0.42	-0.0021419 (0.0032365)	-0.66	-0.0005328 (0.0006387)	-0.83	-0.0008515 (0.0010966)	-0.78	2.44
Mftsal	0.0000000 (0.0000001)	0.55	-0.0000010 (0.0000009)	-1.17	-0.0000003 (0.0000002)	-1.57	-0.0000004 (0.0000003)	-1.41	2.03
Pctunion	-0.0127857 (0.0043210)	-2.96 **	-0.0573847 (0.0486462)	-1.18	0.0207722 (0.0096001)	2.16 *	-0.0164661 (0.0164828)	-1.00	2.11
Wcluster	0.0060758 (0.0018769)	3.24 **	-0.0080546 (0.0211302)	-0.38	0.0030452 (0.0041700)	0.73	0.0003555 (0.0071596)	0.05	2.34
Mcluster	0.0017751 (0.0009952)	1.78	0.0125151 (0.0112044)	1.12	-0.0055869 (0.0022111)	-2.53 *	0.0029011 (0.0037964)	0.76	4.63
O40cluster	-0.0006505 (0.0009423)	-0.69	0.0054227 (0.0106087)	0.51	0.0019535 (0.0020936)	0.93	0.0022419 (0.0035946)	0.62	2.49
Wscluster	-0.0002454 (0.0017198)	-0.14	-0.0108045 (0.0193613)	-0.56	-0.0035016 (0.0038209)	-0.92	-0.0048505 (0.0065602)	-0.74	2.21
Mscluster	-0.0006858 (0.0008691)	-0.79	0.0005037 (0.0097844)	0.05	-0.0003891 (0.0019309)	-0.20	-0.0001904 (0.0033153)	-0.06	2.53
Whcluster	-0.0008539 (0.0006561)	-1.30	-0.0000665 (0.0073867)	-0.01	-0.0004047 (0.0014577)	-0.28	-0.0004417 (0.0025028)	-0.18	1.65
Mhcluster	-0.0011117 (0.0006231)	-1.78	-0.0140542 (0.0070152)	-2.00	0.0029747 (0.0013844)	2.15 *	-0.0040637 (0.0023770)	-1.71	4.09
Intercept	0.4827186 (0.0077772)	62.07 ***	0.8625738 (0.0875573)	9.85 ***	0.8894504 (0.0172790)	51.48 ***	0.7449143 (0.0296671)	25.11 ***	
$F_{13,58}$		4.54 ***		0.92		1.91 *		0.87	
R^2		0.50		0.17		0.30		0.16	
Adjusted R^2		0.39		-0.02		0.14		-0.02	
N		72		72		72		72	2.40

Analysis of Diversity with Tobit Regression

B. Tobigt regression for unbiased (S_N) diversity scores

Predictors	Gender Diversity (S_{GN})			Ethnic Diversity (S_{EN})			Age Diversity (S_{AN})			Organizational Diversity (S_{OON})		
	β Coefficient	t-statistic		β Coefficient	t-statistic		β Coefficient	t-statistic		β Coefficient	t-statistic	
Elected	-0.0073641 (0.0019470)	-3.78	***	-0.048213 (0.0326156)	-1.48		0.0125348 (0.0055777)	2.25	*	-0.0149228 (0.0111468)	-1.34	
SEA	0.0066664 (0.0030664)	2.17	*	-0.0455908 (0.0327432)	-1.39		-0.0104432 (0.0075953)	-1.37		-0.0163159 (0.0116630)	-1.40	
Employees	-0.0000001 (0.0000000)	-4.75	***	0.0000002 (0.0000003)	0.87		0.0000001 (0.0000001)	1.01		0.0000001 (0.0000001)	0.76	
Myos	0.0001017 (0.0001846)	0.55		-0.0021419 (0.0023341)	-0.92		-0.0005328 (0.0007438)	-0.72		-0.0008515 (0.0008075)	-1.05	
Mftsal	0.0000000 (0.0000000)	0.83		-0.0000010 (0.0000008)	-1.32		-0.0000003 (0.0000001)	-2.23	*	-0.0000004 (0.0000003)	-1.60	
Petunion	-0.0090207 (0.0044288)	-2.04		-0.0573847 (0.0393857)	-1.46		0.0207722 (0.0098883)	2.10	*	-0.0164661 (0.0146287)	-1.13	
Wcluster	0.0048519 (0.0014269)	3.40	**	-0.0080546 (0.0203402)	-0.40		0.0030452 (0.0031660)	0.96		0.0003555 (0.0069158)	0.05	
Mcluster	0.0005669 (0.0008667)	0.65		0.0125151 (0.0124830)	1.00		-0.0055869 (0.0021419)	-2.61	*	0.0029011 (0.0040934)	0.71	
O4Ocluster	-0.0004253 (0.0007686)	-0.55		0.0054227 (0.0104335)	0.52		0.0019535 (0.0017843)	1.09		0.022419 (0.035373)	0.63	
Wscluster	0.0004035 (0.0010564)	0.38		-0.0108045 (0.0167915)	-0.64		-0.0035016 (0.0034698)	-1.01		-0.0048505 (0.0058149)	-0.83	
Mscluster	-0.0001281 (0.0005372)	-0.24		0.0005037 (0.0083661)	0.06		-0.0003891 (0.0020982)	-0.19		-0.0001904 (0.0029019)	-0.07	
Whcluster	-0.0007245 (0.0002707)	-2.68	*	-0.0000665 (0.0057181)	-0.01		-0.0004047 (0.0008860)	-0.46		-0.0004417 (0.0018685)	-0.24	
Mhcluster	-0.0006232 (0.0004622)	-1.35		-0.0140542 (0.0069294)	-2.03		0.0029747 (0.0011453)	2.60	*	-0.0040637 (0.0023558)	-1.73	
Intercept	0.4797674 (0.0061570)	77.92	***	0.8625738 (0.0793638)	10.87	***	0.8894504 (0.0140071)	63.50	***	0.7449143 (0.0281764)	26.44	***
/Sigma	0.0046437 (0.0004960)			0.0701083 (0.0093955)			0.0138356 (0.0012063)			0.0237549 (0.0029806)		
$F_{13,59}$	4.68		***	1.80			2.04			1.73		
Pseudo R²	-0.11			-0.08			-0.07			-0.04		
Uncensored N	68			72			72			72		

Standard errors are in parentheses. * $p < 0.05$; ** $p < 0.01$; *** $p < 0.001$

The OLS and Tobit regression models produce inconsistent statistical findings for the unbiased (S_N) scores for age diversity (see Exhibit 9-3). For Elected, the OLS and Tobit models show a similar positive relationship amongst the predictor and the S_{AN} scores ($\beta_{A1} = 0.012$, $p < 0.05$; $\beta_{B1} = 0.012$, $p < 0.05$). However, the models differ with respect to the relationship amongst Mftsal and age diversity. The OLS model fails to detect a significant statistical relationship amongst the predicator and age diversity ($\beta_{A5} = -0.0000003$, $p > 0.05$; see Panel A), but the Tobit model detects a significant inverse relationship amongst the predictor and age diversity ($\beta_{B5} = -0.0000003$, $p < 0.05$; see Panel B). The models are similar with respect to the relationship amongst Pctunion and age diversity. Specifically, the OLS model reveals a significant positive relationship amongst the predictor and age diversity ($\beta_{A6} = 0.021$, $p < 0.05$), and the Tobit model finds a similar relationship amongst the two variables ($\beta_{B6} = 0.021$, $p < 0.05$). With respect to the relationship amongst Mcluster and age diversity, the models produce similar findings. The OLS model shows a significant inverse relationship amongst Mcluster and age diversity ($\beta_{A8} = -0.005$, $p < 0.05$). A similar finding is obtained by the Tobit model ($\beta_{B8} = -0.005$, $p < 0.05$). With respect to Mhcluster, the OLS and Tobit models detect a similar positive relationship amongst the predictor and age diversity ($\beta_{A13} = 0.003$, $p < 0.05$; $\beta_{B13} = 0.003$, $p < 0.05$). Although the OLS and Tobit regression models show significant statistical relationships amongst the predictors and the S_{AN} scores, the OLS and Tobit regression findings are suspect because the S_N scores for the departments are incompatible, because the formula for calculating the unbiased (S_N) scores overcorrects for the size of the workforce, and because the predictors have moderate levels of multicollinearity.

Summary

This chapter applied Tobit regression to the age, ethnic, and gender diversity scores calculated for NYC departments based on employment data reported for fiscal year 2019. As discussed at the beginning of the chapter and throughout the book, each distribution of diversity scores is a LDV where the maximum score (i.e., EMV $= \frac{n-1}{n}$) is determined by the number of categories that are created to classify employees. When a demographic characteristic has two categories, the EMV value of the dependent variable is 0.50. When 11 categories are used, the EMV of the distribution of scores is 0.909. When the distribution of the dependent variable is truncated from 0 to 1, Tobit regression is recommended. As is the case with all regression methods, the extent to which the Tobit regression coefficients are reliable, stable, and valid depends on satisfying the underlying assumptions of the statistical method. The negative pseudo R^2 values obtained by the Tobit analyses indicated that the statistical models have poor predictive power due to not following the trend of the diversity scores.

Because the distributions of the diversity scores are skewed and nonnormal, the next chapter presents an alternative statistical method to OLS, robust, and Tobit regression. Quantile regression methods may produce stable estimates when the distribution of a measure is nonnormal and skewed. They also address the issue of atypical values more efficiently in comparison to OLS and robust regression when the assumption of normality is violated. Unlike Tobit regression models, quantile regression does not make an assumption in regard to whether the data are censored or truncated. As will be discussed in the next chapter, quantile regression focuses on the median and on the conditional distribution of the diversity scores.

Key words

Censored (data) refers to a distribution of scores where some measurements are unobserved or not validated so that the range of scores has a lower or upper cutoff or the range of scores is set between a minimum or maximum value due to not being able to collect data on all subjects. By contrast, truncated data refers to distributions of scores where measurements are confined or restricted so that values do not fall below a minimum value or exceed a maximum value.

Likelihood ratio is a statistic that estimates the probability that a particular outcome will occur.

Marginal effects refer to statistics that estimate the change in the magnitude of the dependent variable generated by a unit change in the independent variable.

Probit regression is a statistical method that regresses a set of predictors on a binary dependent variable to estimate the probability that a case with a set of particular characteristics will fall into one of the categories.

References

McDonald, John F., and Moffitt, Robert A. 1980. "The uses of Tobit analysis". *The Review of Economics and Statistics*, Vol. 62: 318 – 321.
Tobin, James. 1955. *Estimation of relationships for limited dependent variables*. New Haven, CT: Cowles Foundation, Yale University.

Tobin, James. 1958. "Estimation of relationships for limited dependent variables". *Econometrica*, Vol. 26: 24 – 36.

CHAPTER 10

ANALYSIS OF DIVERSITY WITH QUANTILE REGRESSION

Quantile regression is used primarily in economics due to its econometric foundation and origin (e.g., Buhai, 2005; Hao and Naiman, 2007; Koenker and Bassett Jr, 1978; Meligkotsidou, Vrontos, and Vrontos, 2009). Since its development by Koenker and Basset (1978), the use of quantile regression has expanded to many disciplines outside of economic. In recent years, quantile regression has been applied to the study of ethnic and gender diversity in public organizations (e.g., Guajardo, 2016). The appeal and increased use of quantile regression has been fostered by advances in the method and by its statistical advantages over OLS regression when assumptions underlying OLS are not satisfied.

This chapter applies quantile regression to the Simpson diversity scores for age, ethnicity, gender, and organizational heterogeneity that are calculated based on employment data reported by NYC departments for fiscal year 2019. A brief overview of quantile regression is provided. The quantile statistical model guiding the analyses is discussed prior to performing the analyses. A comparative analysis of the OLS and quantile regression findings is undertaken to examine similarities and differences between the models. The chapter concludes with a brief summary.

In this chapter, the quantile regression analyses are restricted to the 50th percentile. *Assessing Organizational Diversity with Quantile Regression* discusses the application of quantile regression to the analysis of demographic diversity in organizations more thoroughly. In *Assessing Organizational Diversity with Quantile Regression*, quantile regression analyses are performed for diversity scores for age, ethnicity, and gender at the 25th, 50th, 75th, and 90th percentiles.

Overview of Quantile Regression

Quantile regression is median-centered while OLS and other linear regression methods (LRMs) are focused on the mean of a distribution of scores (e.g., Davino, Furno, and Vistocco, 2014; Davino, Romano, and Naes, 2015; Hao and Naiman, 2007; Koenker, 2005; Koenker and Bassett Jr, 1978; Koenker and Hallock, 2001). In contrast to LRMs that assess how a set of predictors effect the conditional mean, quantile regression models assess how a set of predictors effect the conditional median and the values of the dependent variable at various quantiles (τ, where $0 < \tau < 1$; e.g., Davino, Furno, and Vistocco, 2014; Hao and Naiman, 2007; Koenker, 2005; Talbert and Cade, 2013; Yu, Lu, and Sandler, 2003). Second, while LRMs use least squares estimation, quantile regression models use least absolute distance (or value) estimation (e.g., Davino, Furno, and Vistocco, 2014; Hao and Naiman, 2007; Koenker, 2005; Talbert and Cade, 2013; Yu, Lu, and Sandler, 2003). Hao and Naiman (2007) define the absolute distance as the following: $|Y - m|$, where Y represents the values of the dependent variable and m represents the median. In addition, Hao and Naiman (2007, p. 17) note that one can "measure how far Y is from m by the absolute distance $|Y - m|$ and measure the average distance in [a] population by the mean absolute distance $E|Y - m|$." For a particular percentile, the following formula is used to minimize the mean absolute distance (e.g., Hao and Naiman, 2007): $Y:E[qy(Y,q)]$. With respect to obtaining the regression coefficients that minimize the sum of absolute residuals, the following formula is used (e.g., Hao and Naiman, 2007): $E_i|y_i - \beta 0 - \beta 1 x_i|$.

Quantile regression analysis yields intercept and regression coefficients that are interpreted in a manner similar to those produced by LRMs (e.g., Brit, 2011; Dade and Noon, 2003; Davino, Romano, and Naes, 2015; Hao and Naiman, 2007). As Brit (2011, 357) states, "The quantile regression coefficients represent the effect of a one-unit change in the independent variable on the dependent variable at the τ quantile" (e.g., 5th, 25th, or 90th quantile). When a predictor is coded dichotomously (e.g., 0,1), the regression coefficient is interpreted as the change in the conditional quantile brought about by changing from one group to another (e.g., Hao and Naiman, 2007). With respect to interpreting the intercepts, the intercepts represent the estimated conditional quantile function of the distribution of the response (or dependent) variable and its covariates at each quantile specified in the study (e.g., Koenker and Hallock, 2001).

Underlying assumptions of Quantile regression

Like OLS, robust, and Tobit regression, quantile regression requires satisfying a number of underlying statistical assumptions in regard to the independent and dependent variables prior to undertaking the analysis. The underlying assumptions of quantile regression are the following:

1. The dependent variable is quantitative continuous;
2. The relationship between the dependent and independent variables is linear so that changes in the values of the independent variables are associated with the *conditional distribution* of the predicted values of the dependent variable at various percentiles;
3. The values of the independent and dependent variables are not interconnected and are not calculated in part or in whole on the same data sources; and,
4. There are no significant high collinear statistical relationships amongst the set of independent variables.

Similar to other regression methods, quantile regression produces regression coefficients that are biased, unreliable, and unstable when statistical assumptions are not adequately satisfied.

Quantile regression models

Quantile regression analyses are undertaken for the biased (S_B) and unbiased (S_N) diversity scores for age, ethnicity, gender, and organizational heterogeneity. The same independent variables that were used to conduct the OLS, robust, and Tobit regression analyses are used to perform the quantile regression analyses below. The generic theoretical statistical model guiding the quantile regression analysis is the following:

$\hat{S}(\Theta) = \alpha(\Theta) + \beta_1 Elected(\Theta) + \beta_2 SEA(\Theta) + \beta_3 Employees(\Theta) + \beta_4 Myos(\Theta) + \beta_5 Mftsal(\Theta) + \beta_6 Pctunion(\Theta) + \beta_7 Wcluster(\Theta) + \beta_8 Mcluster(\Theta) + \beta_9 O40cluster(\Theta) + \beta_{10} Wscluster(\Theta) + \beta_{11} Mscluster(\Theta) + \beta_{12} Whcluster(\Theta) + \beta_{13} Mhcluster(\Theta) + \varepsilon_{ij}(\Theta)$.

The terms of the regression equation are the following:

$\hat{S}$ refers to the Simpson diversity scores calculated separately for age, ethnicity, gender, and organizational diversity for fiscal year 2019;

Θ represents the conditional distribution of a Simpson diversity score at a particular percentile;

α refers to the y-axis intercept for the regression line;

B_n refers to the regression coefficient associated with each independent variable in the equation that is significant statistically at $p < 0.05$;

Elected refers to whether the department is an elected office (1) or another type of organization (0);

SEA refers to the percent of the adopted operating budget that is allocated to salary expenses in fiscal year 2019;

Employees refers to the total number of employees on the payroll in each department in fiscal year 2019;

Myos refers to the median number of years of service of each department's workforce in fiscal year 2019;

Mftsal refers to the median full-time salary of each department's workforce in fiscal year 2019;

Pctunion refers to the percent of the workforce in each department that has membership in a collective bargaining unit in fiscal year 2019;

Wcluster refers to the relative clustering score obtained by dividing the percent of women employees by the percent of men employees in each department to assess the magnitude of women-dominated employment in fiscal year 2019;

Mcluster refers to the relative clustering score obtained by dividing the percent of minority employees by the percent of White employees in each department to assess the magnitude of minority-dominated employment in fiscal year 2019;

O40cluster refers to the relative clustering score obtained by dividing the percent of employees under the age of 40 by the percent of employees over the age of 40 in each department to assess the magnitude of employment of older persons in fiscal year 2019;

Wscluster refers to the relative clustering score obtained by dividing the percent of women employees that terminated their employment by the percent of men employees that terminated their employment in each department to assess the magnitude of women-dominated termination in fiscal year 2019;

Mscluster refers to the relative clustering score obtained by dividing the percent of minority employees that terminated their employment by the percent of White employees that terminated their employment in each department to assess the magnitude of minority-dominated termination in fiscal year 2019;

Whcluster refers to the relative clustering score obtained by dividing the percent of women hired by the percent of men hired in each department to assess the magnitude of women-dominated hiring in fiscal year 2019;

Mhcluster refers to the relative clustering score obtained by dividing the percent of minorities hired by the percent of men hired in each department to assess the magnitude of minority-dominated hiring in fiscal year 2019; and,

ε_{ij} refers to measurement error in the statistical model.

As in previous chapters, each regression coefficient (β) is tested for statistical significance at $\alpha = 0.05$. In this chapter, the analyses are restricted to the 50th percentile although relationships amongst the predictors and the various sets of diversity scores may be analyzed at various percentiles such as the 5th, 25th, 75th, or 90th percentile. *Assessing Organizational Diversity with Quantile Regression* provides a more thorough discussion and presentation of the use of quantile regression to assess the relationships amongst the predictors and different sets of diversity scores for age, ethnicity, and gender. As stated throughout the book, Exhibit 7-5 illustrates the hypothesized statistical relationships amongst the predicators and the diversity scores for age, ethnicity, gender, and organizational heterogeneity.

Quantile regression analysis

Exhibit 10-1 summarizes the statistical findings of the quantile analyses for the biased (S_B) and unbiased (S_N) diversity scores calculated for NYC departments based on their employment data for fiscal year 2019. In Panel A, the findings show a significant inverse relationship amongst Wcluster and gender diversity where the level of gender heterogeneity decreases as the number of women in the workforce increases ($\beta_7 = -0.033$, $p < 0.001$). More specifically, a unit increase in Wcluster is associated with a 0.03 unit decrease in the conditional distribution of gender diversity at the 50th percentile. The findings show insignificant statistical relationships amongst the other predictors and gender diversity. For instance, NYC departments headed by elected officials have similar levels of diversity as departments headed by nonelected officials (β_1 = 0.009, p > 0.05). An insignificant statistical relationship exists amongst SEA and the level of gender diversity where the percent of an operating budget allocated for salary expenses does not influence gender diversity (β_2 = -0.008, p > 0.05). The findings also show an insignificant statistical relationship amongst Employees and gender diversity where NYC departments have similar levels of gender diversity regardless of the size of the workforce (β_3 = -0.0000004, p > 0.05). At the 50th percentile, the model explains 29% (pseudo R^2 = 0.29) of the variance.

The quantile analysis shows insignificant statistical findings for each predictor in terms to their relationship with the unbiased (S_N) gender diversity scores (see Panel B). NYC departments headed by elected and nonelected officials have similar levels of gender diversity at the 50th percentile (β_1 = -0.005, p > 0.05). Regardless of the size of the workforce (Employees), the level of gender diversity is similar amongst the departments (β_3 = 0.0000, p > 0.05). In addition, workforces with low and high levels of unionization have similar levels of gender diversity (β_6 = -0.01, p > 0.05). As Panel B summarizes, insignificant statistical relationships exist for the other predictors in the model at the 50th percentile.

Exhibit 10-1 Quantile regression analysis for age, ethnic, gender, and organizational diversity for NYC departments for fiscal year 2019

A. Quantile regression for biased (S_B) diversity scores

Predictors	Gender Diversity (S_{GB})		Ethnic Diversity (S_{EB})		Age Diversity (S_{AB})		Organizational Diversity (S_{BOD})	
	β Coefficient	t-statistic	β Coefficient	t-statistic	β Coefficient	t-statistic	β Coefficient	t-statistic
Elected	0.0095435 (0.0065794)	1.45	-0.0169477 (0.0228909)	-0.74	0.0263662 (0.0077143)	3.42 **	0.0130972 (0.0096593)	1.36
SEA	-0.0081683 (0.0134915)	-0.61	-0.0195947 (0.0361404)	-0.54	-0.0132320 (0.0147463)	-0.90	-0.0276283 (0.0169621)	-1.63
Employees	-0.0000004 (0.0000014)	-0.26	0.0000004 (0.0000038)	0.11	0.0000001 (0.0000008)	0.17	0.0000001 (0.0000010)	0.06
Myos	0.0003857 (0.0012471)	0.31	-0.0032070 (0.0031529)	-1.02	-0.0005659 (0.0010932)	-0.52	-0.0010243 (0.0013827)	-0.74
Mflsal	-0.0000001 (0.0000004)	-0.41	-0.0000008 (0.0000006)	-1.47	-0.0000002 (0.0000002)	-1.11	-0.0000006 (0.0000003)	-2.12 *
Petunion	0.0005360 (0.0185088)	0.03	-0.0310569 (0.0296550)	-1.05	0.0428845 (0.0267512)	1.60	0.0076087 (0.0156114)	0.49
Wcluster	-0.0329842 (0.0071815)	-4.59 ***	-0.0195268 (0.0371152)	-0.53	-0.0006026 (0.0130244)	-0.05	-0.0183521 (0.0126659)	-1.43
Mcluster	-0.0022291 (0.0046673)	-0.48	0.0108832 (0.0185522)	0.59	-0.0041093 (0.0052471)	-0.78	-0.0041811 (0.0053301)	-0.78
O40cluster	-0.0047221 (0.0040130)	-1.18	0.0109298 (0.0075074)	1.46	0.0013487 (0.0039880)	0.34	0.003607 (0.0034257)	1.05
Wscluster	0.0027258 (0.0044565)	0.61	-0.0098466 (0.0200557)	-0.49	-0.0053318 (0.0097010)	-0.55	-0.0022723 (0.0051232)	-0.44
Mscluster	0.0013311 (0.0042314)	0.31	-0.0020092 (0.0082032)	-0.24	-0.0001180 (0.0026063)	-0.05	0.0010203 (0.0024995)	0.41
Whcluster	-0.0025138 (0.0033749)	-0.74	0.0047772 (0.0517627)	0.09	0.0000261 (0.0157812)	0.00	0.0001821 (0.0107255)	0.02
Mhcluster	-0.0017136 (0.0024006)	-0.71	-0.0027869 (0.0089971)	-0.31	0.0026700 (0.0029156)	0.92	-0.0007977 (0.0033446)	-0.24
Intercept	0.5062108 (0.0313857)	16.13 ***	0.8143940 (0.0541657)	15.04 ***	0.8671696 (0.0350441)	24.75 ***	0.7454742 (0.0271242)	27.48 ***
Raw sum of deviations	1.235		1.820		0.584		0.926	
Min sum of deviations	0.872		1.592		0.427		0.730	
Pseudo R²	0.29		0.13		0.27		0.21	
N	72		72		72		72	

B. Quantile regression for unbiased (S_N) diversity scores

Predictors	Gender Diversity (S_{GN})		Ethnic Diversity (S_{EN})		Age Diversity (S_{AN})		Organizational Diversity (S_{NOD})	
	β Coefficient	t-statistic	β Coefficient	t-statistic	β Coefficient	t-statistic	β Coefficient	t-statistic
Elected	-0.0047704 (0.0028216)	-1.69	-0.0323222 (0.0205194)	-1.58	0.0163321 (0.0072712)	2.25 *	-0.0128774 (0.0057497)	-2.24 *
SEA	0.0040277 (0.0028556)	1.41	-0.0023565 (0.0391128)	-0.06	-0.0148491 (0.0113238)	-1.31	0.0007072 (0.0114558)	0.06
Employees	0.0000000 (0.0000001)	-0.60	0.0000002 (0.0000040)	0.05	0.0000001 (0.0000006)	0.08	0.0000001 (0.0000012)	0.07
Myos	0.0003627 (0.0002585)	1.40	-0.0014971 (0.0032307)	-0.46	-0.0008717 (0.0010468)	-0.83	-0.0012885 (0.0006746)	-1.91
Mftsal	0.0000000 (0.0000000)	-0.50	-0.0000003 (0.0000007)	-0.51	-0.0000004 (0.0000002)	-2.45 *	-0.0000004 (0.0000002)	-1.75
Pctunion	-0.010149 (0.0082155)	-1.24	-0.0188662 (0.0394500)	-0.48	0.0141552 (0.0138710)	1.02	-0.0094359 (0.0097183)	-0.97
Wcluster	0.0011474 (0.0036753)	0.31	-0.0114244 (0.0308816)	-0.38	0.0067986 (0.0076578)	0.89	-0.0001856 (0.0069883)	-0.03
Mcluster	-0.0003088 (0.0008349)	-0.37	0.0230197 (0.0181896)	1.27	-0.003599 (0.0032666)	-1.10	0.0045787 (0.0047057)	0.97
O40cluster	-0.0004831 (0.0010076)	-0.48	0.0018082 (0.0127828)	0.14	0.0029294 (0.0025157)	1.16	0.0020622 (0.0019846)	1.04
Wscluster	0.001809 (0.0021535)	0.84	-0.0092775 (0.0133147)	-0.70	-0.0044199 (0.0084237)	-0.52	-0.0071921 (0.0053192)	-1.35
Mscluster	0.0004686 (0.0010154)	0.46	0.0006814 (0.005495)	0.13	-0.0006863 (0.0020814)	-0.33	-0.0021179 (0.0017577)	-1.20
Whcluster	-0.0004102 (0.0048812)	-0.08	0.004441 (0.0184342)	0.24	-0.0016051 (0.0106765)	-0.15	0.0018781 (0.0038010)	0.49
Mhcluster	-0.0000891 (0.0003903)	-0.23	-0.0082208 (0.0097651)	-0.84	0.0018426 (0.0025545)	0.72	-0.0043534 (0.0032176)	-1.35
Intercept	0.4834346 (0.0088943)	54.35 ***	0.7597285 (0.0769203)	9.88 ***	0.9100567 (0.0198685)	45.80 ***	0.7333728 (0.0201226)	36.45 ***
Raw sum of deviations	0.164		1.825		0.459		0.640	
Min sum of deviations	0.136		1.583		0.362		0.540	
Pseudo R²	0.17		0.13		0.21		0.16	
N	72		72		72		72	

Standard errors are in parentheses. * $p < 0.05$; ** $p < 0.01$; *** $p < 0.001$

The quantile models for the ethnic diversity scores also yield insignificant statistical findings. In Panel A, the quantile analysis shows that none of the predictors are associated statistically with a change in the conditional distribution of the ethnic diversity scores (see Exhibit 10-1). For example, the levels of ethnic diversity are statistically the same for departments headed by elected officials and those headed by nonelected officials (β_1 = -0.017, $p > 0.05$). The findings also show that the level of budgeted salary expenses (SEA) does not influence the level ethnic diversity in NYC departments (β_2 = -0.019, $p > 0.05$). In addition, regardless of the size of the workforce (Employees), NYC department have similar levels of ethnic diversity (β_3 = 0.0000004, $p > 0.05$). Despite differences in the percent of unionization (Pctunion), the level of ethnic diversity is similar amongst NYC departments (β_6 = -0.031, $p > 0.05$). Briefly, Panel B shows similar insignificant statistical findings for the predictors and the unbiased (S_N) diversity scores for ethnicity.

In terms of the findings of the age diversity scores, the quantile analysis for the biased (S_B) scores reveals that one predictor is associated statistically with the level of age diversity (see Exhibit 10-1). The findings reveal a significant positive relationship amongst Elected and the level of age diversity (β_1 = 0.026, $p < 0.01$; see Panel A) where departments headed by elected officials have higher levels of age diversity in comparison to those headed by nonelected officials. More specifically, the move from a department headed by an elected official to a department headed by a nonelected official is associated with a 0.02 unit increase in the conditional distribution of age diversity at the 50th percentile. As Panel A summarizes, insignificant statistical findings exist amongst the other predicators and the level of age diversity calculated for NYC departments.

Slightly different statistical findings are obtained for the unbiased (S_N) diversity scores for age (see Panel B). A positive statistical relationship is found for Elected and the level of age diversity. The findings show that the move from a department headed by a nonelected official to one headed by an elected official is associated with a 0.02 unit increase in the conditional distribution of age diversity at the 50th percentile (β_1 = 0.016, $p < 0.05$). However, a significant inverse relationship exists amongst Mftsal and the level of age diversity. The findings show that a unit increase in Mftsal is associated with less than a 0.0001 unit decrease in the conditional distribution of age diversity at the 50th percentile (β_5 = -0.0000004, $p < 0.05$). Insignificant statistical findings exist amongst the other predictors and the level of age diversity.

Comparison of OLS and quantile regression

Exhibit 10-2 highlights the OLS and quantile regression findings for the biased (S_B) diversity scores for age, ethnic, gender, and organizational heterogeneity. In Panel A, the OLS regression findings indicate that none of the predictors are associated statistically with the level of gender diversity (S_{GB}) calculated for NYC departments. However, the quantile regression model shows a significant inverse relationship amongst Wcluster and the level of gender diversity at the 50th percentile (β_{B7} = -0.033, p < 0.001), where a unit increase in Wcluster is associated with a 0.03 unit decrease in the conditional distribution of gender diversity (S_{GB}; see Panel B). Similar to the OLS regression findings, none of the remaining predictors are associated statistically with the level of gender diversity.

In regard to the statistical findings for ethnic diversity, the OLS and quantile regression findings are consistent where none of the predicators are associated statistically with changes in the level of ethnic diversity. For instance, the OLS analysis reveals an insignificant statistical finding for Elected (β_{A1} = -0.033, p > 0.05; see Panel A). A similar insignificant statistical finding for Elected is obtained by the quantile analysis (β_{B1} = -0.017, p > 0.05; see Panel B).

Exhibit 10-2 Comparison of OLS and quantile regression findings for biased (S$_B$) scores for age, ethnic, gender, and organizational diversity for NYC departments for fiscal year 2019

A. OLS regression for biased (S$_B$) diversity scores

Predictors	Gender Diversity (S$_{GB}$)		Ethnic Diversity (S$_{EB}$)		Age Diversity (S$_{AB}$)		Organizational Diversity (S$_{BOD}$)		
	β Coefficient	t-statistic	β Coefficient	t-statistic	β Coefficient	t-statistic	β Coefficient	t-statistic	VIF
Elected	0.0100222 (0.0211684)	0.47	-0.0346973 (0.0288702)	-1.20	0.02796320 (0.0073853)	3.79 ***	0.0010960 (0.0137855)	0.08	1.67
SEA	-0.0001446 (0.0311158)	0.00	-0.0548222 (0.0424367)	-1.29	-0.02284840 (0.0108558)	-2.10 *	-0.0259384 (0.0202635)	-1.28	1.58
Employees	-0.0000005 (0.0000004)	-1.37	0.0000004 (0.0000005)	0.76	0.00000021 (0.0000001)	1.67	0.0000000 (0.0000002)	0.13	1.37
Myos	-0.0031933 (0.0023399)	-1.36	-0.0023674 (0.0031912)	-0.74	-0.00072870 (0.0008163)	-0.89	-0.0020965 (0.0015238)	-1.38	2.44
Mfhsal	-0.0000006 (0.0000006)	-0.90	-0.0000011 (0.0000008)	-1.25	-0.00000033 (0.0000002)	-1.53	-0.0000007 (0.0000004)	-1.61	2.03
Petunion	-0.0618134 (0.0351700)	-1.76	-0.0380349 (0.0479660)	-0.79	0.04206870 (0.0122703)	3.43 **	-0.0192598 (0.0229037)	-0.84	2.11
Wcluster	-0.0087890 (0.0152766)	-0.58	-0.0167890 (0.0208348)	-0.81	-0.00711590 (0.0053298)	-1.35	-0.0109213 (0.0099486)	-1.10	2.34
Mcluster	0.0042241 (0.0081005)	0.52	0.0094895 (0.0110477)	0.86	-0.00814650 (0.0028261)	-2.88 **	0.0018557 (0.0052753)	0.35	4.63
O40cluster	0.0091009 (0.0076699)	1.19	0.0066266 (0.0104604)	0.63	0.0029210 (0.0026759)	1.09	0.0062165 (0.0049948)	1.24	2.49
Wscluster	0.0122934 (0.0139977)	0.88	-0.0101793 (0.0190906)	-0.53	-0.00337570 (0.0048836)	-0.69	-0.0004205 (0.0091157)	-0.05	2.21
Mscluster	0.0017878 (0.0070739)	0.25	0.0014905 (0.0096476)	0.15	0.00060320 (0.0024680)	0.24	0.0012938 (0.0046067)	0.28	2.53
Whcluster	-0.0052104 (0.0053404)	-0.98	0.0011866 (0.0072834)	0.16	0.00105660 (0.0018632)	0.57	-0.0009891 (0.0034778)	-0.28	1.65
Mhcluster	-0.0010515 (0.0050718)	-0.21	-0.0121854 (0.0069171)	-1.76	0.00471180 (0.0017695)	2.66 *	-0.0028417 (0.0033029)	-0.86	4.09
Intercept	0.5560840 (0.0633018)	8.78 ***	0.8507759 (0.0863331)	9.85 ***	0.87749200 (0.0220850)	39.73 ***	0.7614507 (0.0412239)	18.47 ***	
$F_{13,58}$		1.56		0.89		4.76		0.96	
R²		0.26		0.17		0.52		0.18	
Adjusted R²		0.09		-0.02		0.41		-0.01	
N		72		72		72		72	2.40

B. Quantile regression for biased (S$_B$) diversity scores

Predictors	Gender Diversity (S$_{GB}$)		Ethnic Diversity (S$_{EB}$)		Age Diversity (S$_{AB}$)		Organizational Diversity (S$_{OOB}$)	
	β Coefficient	t-statistic	β Coefficient	t-statistic	β Coefficient	t-statistic	β Coefficient	t-statistic
Elected	0.0095435 (0.0065794)	1.45	-0.0016477 (0.0228909)	-0.74	0.0263662 (0.0077143)	3.42 **	0.0130972 (0.0096593)	1.36
SEA	-0.0081683 (0.0134915)	-0.61	-0.0195947 (0.0361404)	-0.54	-0.0132320 (0.0147463)	-0.90	-0.0276283 (0.0169621)	-1.63
Employees	-0.0000004 (0.0000014)	-0.26	0.0000004 (0.0000038)	0.11	0.0000001 (0.0000008)	0.17	0.0000001 (0.0000010)	0.06
Myos	0.0003857 (0.0012471)	0.31	-0.0032070 (0.0031529)	-1.02	-0.0005659 (0.0010932)	-0.52	-0.0010243 (0.0013827)	-0.74
Mfisal	-0.0000001 (0.0000004)	-0.41	-0.0000008 (0.0000006)	-1.47	-0.0000002 (0.0000002)	-1.11	-0.0000006 (0.0000003)	-2.12 *
Pctunion	0.0005360 (0.0185088)	0.03	-0.0310569 (0.0296550)	-1.05	0.0428845 (0.0267512)	1.60	0.0076087 (0.0156114)	0.49
Wcluster	-0.0329842 (0.0071815)	-4.59 ***	-0.0195268 (0.0371152)	-0.53	-0.0006026 (0.0130244)	-0.05	-0.0183521 (0.0128659)	-1.43
Mcluster	-0.0022291 (0.0046673)	-0.48	0.0108832 (0.0185522)	0.59	-0.0041093 (0.0052471)	-0.78	-0.0041811 (0.0053301)	-0.78
O40cluster	-0.0047221 (0.0040130)	-1.18	0.0109298 (0.0075074)	1.46	0.0013487 (0.0039880)	0.34	0.003607 (0.0034257)	1.05
Wscluster	0.0027258 (0.0044565)	0.61	-0.0098466 (0.0200557)	-0.49	-0.0053318 (0.0097010)	-0.55	-0.0022723 (0.0051232)	-0.44
Mscluster	0.0013311 (0.0042314)	0.31	-0.0020092 (0.0082032)	-0.24	-0.0001180 (0.0026063)	-0.05	0.0010203 (0.0024995)	0.41
Whcluster	-0.0025138 (0.0033749)	-0.74	0.0047772 (0.0517627)	0.09	0.0000261 (0.0157812)	0.00	0.001821 (0.0107255)	0.02
Mhcluster	-0.0017136 (0.0024006)	-0.71	-0.0027869 (0.0089971)	-0.31	0.0026700 (0.0029156)	0.92	-0.0007997 (0.0033446)	-0.24
Intercept	0.5062108 (0.0313857)	16.13 ***	0.8143940 (0.0541657)	15.04 ***	0.8671696 (0.0350441)	24.75 ***	0.7454742 (0.0271242)	27.48 ***
Raw sum of deviations	1.235		1.820		0.584		0.926	
Min sum of deviations	0.872		1.592		0.427		0.730	
Pseudo R²	0.29		0.13		0.27		0.21	
N	72		72		72		72	

Standard errors are in parentheses. * $p < 0.05$; ** $p < 0.01$; *** $p < 0.001$

The statistical findings for the OLS and quantile regression models differ with respect to the relationships amongst the predictors and the level of age diversity in NYC departments for fiscal year 2019 (see Exhibit 10-2). In Panel A, the OLS regression findings show a significant positive relationship amongst Elected and the level of age diversity (β_{A1} = 0.028, p < 0.001), where the move from a department headed by a nonelected official to one headed by an elected official increases the level of age diversity by 0.03 points. In Panel B, the quantile regression findings reveal a similar significant positive relationship amongst Elected and the level of age diversity (β_{B1} = 0.026, p < 0.01), where the move from a department headed by a nonelected official to one headed by an elected official is associated with a 0.03 unit increase in the conditional distribution of age diversity. In the case of SEA, the OLS regression findings show a significant inverse relationship amongst the predicator and the level of age diversity (β_{A2} = -0.023, p < 0.05), where a unit increase in SEA decreases the level of age diversity by 0.02 points at the 50th percentile. The quantile regression findings show an insignificant statistical relationship amongst SEA and the conditional distribution of age diversity at the 50th percentile (β_{B2} = -0.013, p > 0.05). The OLS and quantile regression findings also differ with respect to the statistical relationship amongst Pctunion and the level of age diversity. While the OLS regression findings show a significant positive relationship amongst Pctunion and the level of age diversity (β_{A6} = 0.042, p < 0.01), the quantile regression model reveals the absence of a significant relationship amongst the predictor and the level of age diversity at the 50th percentile (β_{B6} = 0.043, p > 0.05). In terms of the relationship amongst Mcluster and age diversity, the OLS regression model detects a significant inverse relationship amongst the predictor and the level of age diversity (β_{A8} = -0.008, p < 0.01); the quantile regression model finds an insignificant statistical relationship amongst Mcluster and the level of age diversity at the 50th percentile (β_{B8} = 0.043, p > 0.05). The OLS regression model also reveals a significant positive relationship amongst Mhcluster and the level of age diversity (β_{A13} = 0.005, p < 0.05); however, the quantile regression model shows the absence of a significant relationship amongst Mhcluster and the level of age diversity at the 50th percentile (β_{B13} = 0.003, p > 0.05). Lastly, the OLS regression model explains 52% (R^2 = 0.52) of the variance, and the quantile model explains approximately 27% (pseudo R^2 = 0.27) of the variance.

Exhibit 10-3 summarizes the statistical findings of the OLS and quantile regression models for the unbiased (S_N) diversity scores for age, ethnicity, gender, and organizational heterogeneity for NYC departments for fiscal year 2019. In Panel A, the OLS regression findings show that 3 predictors are related statistically with gender diversity; in Panel B, the quantile regression findings reveal insignificant statistical findings for each predictor at the 50th percentile. With respect to Elected, the OLS regression findings reveal a significant inverse relationship amongst the predictor and the level of gender diversity (β_{A1} = -0.009, p < 0.01); the quantile regression findings show the absence of a significant statistical relationship amongst the predictor and the level of gender diversity at the 50th percentile (β_{B1} = -0.005, p > 0.05). The OLS regression model also indicates that Pctunion and the level of gender diversity are related inversely (β_{A6} = -0.013, p < 0.01). At the 50th percentile, the quantile regression model fails to detect a significant statistical relationship amongst the predictor and gender diversity (β_{B6} = -0.01, p > 0.05). In contrast to the OLS regression model which shows a significant positive relationship amongst Wcluster and the level of gender diversity (β_{A7} = 0.006, p < 0.01), the quantile regression model fails to detect a significant statistical relationship amongst the predicator and the level of gender diversity at the 50th percentile (β_{B7} = 0.001, p > 0.05). With respect to the other predictors in the model, the OLS and quantile regression models are consistent in so far as producing insignificant statistical findings for gender diversity.

Briefly, the OLS and quantile regression models are consistent in terms of yielding insignificant statistical findings for the unbiased (S_{GN}) ethnic diversity scores (see Exhibit 10-3). For example, both models indicate the absence of a significant statistical relationship amongst Elected and the level of ethnic diversity in NYC departments for fiscal year 2019 (β_{A1} = -0.048, p > 0.05; β_{B1} = -0.032, p > 0.05). Similarly, the models reveal an insignificant statistical relationship amongst SEA and the level of ethnic diversity (β_{A2} = -0.045, p > 0.05; β_{B2} = -0.002, p > 0.05). In addition, the models are consistent with respect to the lack of a significant relationship amongst Employees and the level of ethnic diversity (β_{A3} = 0.0000002, p > 0.05; β_{B3} = 0.0000002, p > 0.05). These findings also are consistent with those summarized in Exhibit 10-2.

Exhibit 10-3 Comparison of OLS and quantile regression findings for unbiased (S_N) scores for age, ethnic, gender, and organizational diversity for NYC departments for fiscal year 2019

A. OLS regression for unbiased (S_N) diversity scores

Predictors	Gender Diversity (S_{GN})		Ethnic Diversity (S_{EN})		Age Diversity (S_{AN})		Organizational Diversity (S_{NOBJ})		
	β Coefficient	t-statistic	β Coefficient	t-statistic	β Coefficient	t-statistic	β Coefficient	t-statistic	VIF
Elected	-0.0090903 (0.0026607)	-3.50 **	-0.0482130 (0.0292796)	-1.65	0.0125348 (0.0057782)	2.17 *	-0.0149228 (0.0099208)	-1.50	1.67
SEA	0.0070863 (0.0038229)	1.85	-0.0455908 (0.0430385)	-1.06	-0.0104432 (0.0084934)	-1.23	-0.0163159 (0.0145828)	-1.12	1.58
Employees	-0.0000001 (0.0000000)	-2.02	0.0000002 (0.0000005)	0.49	0.0000001 (0.0000001)	0.56	0.0000001 (0.0000002)	0.41	1.37
Myos	0.0001202 (0.0002875)	0.42	-0.0021419 (0.0032365)	-0.66	-0.0005328 (0.0006387)	-0.83	-0.0008515 (0.0010966)	-0.78	2.44
Mftsal	0.0000000 (0.0000001)	0.55	-0.0000010 (0.0000009)	-1.17	-0.0000003 (0.0000002)	-1.57	-0.0000004 (0.0000003)	-1.41	2.03
Pctunion	-0.0127857 (0.0043210)	-2.96 **	-0.0573847 (0.0486462)	-1.18	0.0207722 (0.0096001)	2.16 *	-0.0164661 (0.0164828)	-1.00	2.11
Wcluster	0.0060758 (0.0018769)	3.24 **	-0.0080546 (0.0211302)	-0.38	0.0030452 (0.0041700)	0.73	0.0003555 (0.0071596)	0.05	2.34
Mcluster	0.0017751 (0.0009952)	1.78	0.0125151 (0.0112044)	1.12	-0.0055869 (0.0022111)	-2.53 *	0.0029011 (0.0037964)	0.76	4.63
O4Ocluster	-0.0006505 (0.0009423)	-0.69	0.0054227 (0.0106087)	0.51	0.0019535 (0.0020936)	0.93	0.0022419 (0.0035946)	0.62	2.49
Wscluster	-0.0002454 (0.0017198)	-0.14	-0.0108045 (0.0193613)	-0.56	-0.0035016 (0.0038209)	-0.92	-0.0048505 (0.0065602)	-0.74	2.21
Mscluster	-0.0006858 (0.0008691)	-0.79	0.0005037 (0.0097844)	0.05	-0.0003891 (0.0019309)	-0.20	-0.0001904 (0.0033153)	-0.06	2.53
Whcluster	-0.0008539 (0.0006561)	-1.30	-0.0000665 (0.0073867)	-0.01	-0.0004047 (0.0014577)	-0.28	-0.0004417 (0.0025028)	-0.18	1.65
Mhcluster	-0.0011117 (0.0006231)	-1.78	-0.0140542 (0.0070152)	-2.00	0.0029747 (0.0013844)	2.15 *	-0.0040637 (0.0023770)	-1.71	4.09
Intercept	0.4827186 (0.0077772)	62.07 ***	0.8625738 (0.0875573)	9.85 ***	0.8894504 (0.0172790)	51.48 ***	0.7449143 (0.0296671)	25.11 ***	
$F_{13,58}$	4.54 ***		0.92		1.91		0.87		
R^2	0.50		0.17		0.30		0.16		
Adjusted R^2	0.39		-0.02		0.14		-0.02		
N	72		72		72		72		2.40

B. Quantile regression for unbiased (S_N) diversity scores

Predictors	Gender Diversity (S_{GN})		Ethnic Diversity (S_{EN})		Age Diversity (S_{AN})		Organizational Diversity (S_{ON})	
	β Coefficient	t-statistic	β Coefficient	t-statistic	β Coefficient	t-statistic	β Coefficient	t-statistic
Elected	-0.0047704 (0.0028216)	-1.69	-0.0323222 (0.0205194)	-1.58	0.0163321 (0.0072712)	2.25 *	-0.0128774 (0.0057497)	-2.24 *
SEA	0.0040277 (0.0028556)	1.41	-0.0023565 (0.0391128)	-0.06	-0.0148491 (0.0113238)	-1.31	0.0007072 (0.0114558)	0.06
Employees	0.0000000 (0.0000001)	-0.60	0.0000002 (0.0000040)	0.05	0.0000001 (0.0000006)	0.08	0.0000001 (0.0000012)	0.07
Myos	0.0003627 (0.002585)	1.40	-0.0014971 (0.0032307)	-0.46	-0.0008717 (0.0010468)	-0.83	-0.0012885 (0.0006746)	-1.91
Mfitsal	0.0000000 (0.0000000)	-0.50	-0.0000003 (0.0000007)	-0.51	-0.0000004 (0.0000002)	-2.45 *	-0.0000004 (0.0000002)	-1.75
Pctunion	-0.010149 (0.0082155)	-1.24	-0.0188662 (0.0394500)	-0.48	0.0141552 (0.0138710)	1.02	-0.0094359 (0.0097183)	-0.97
Wcluster	0.0011474 (0.0036753)	0.31	-0.0114244 (0.0300816)	-0.38	0.0067986 (0.0076578)	0.89	-0.0001856 (0.0069883)	-0.03
Mcluster	-0.0003088 (0.0008349)	-0.37	0.0230197 (0.0181896)	1.27	-0.003599 (0.0032666)	-1.10	0.0045787 (0.0047057)	0.97
O40cluster	-0.0004831 (0.0010076)	-0.48	0.0018082 (0.0127828)	0.14	0.0029294 (0.0025157)	1.16	0.0020622 (0.0019846)	1.04
Wscluster	0.001809 (0.0021535)	0.84	-0.0092775 (0.0133147)	-0.70	-0.0044199 (0.0084237)	-0.52	-0.0071921 (0.0053192)	-1.35
Mscluster	0.0004686 (0.0010154)	0.46	0.0006814 (0.0054495)	0.13	-0.0006863 (0.0020814)	-0.33	-0.0021179 (0.0017577)	-1.20
Whcluster	-0.0004102 (0.0048812)	-0.08	0.004441 (0.0184342)	0.24	-0.0016051 (0.0106765)	-0.15	0.0018781 (0.0038010)	0.49
Mhcluster	-0.0000891 (0.0003903)	-0.23	-0.0082208 (0.0097651)	-0.84	0.0018426 (0.0025545)	0.72	-0.0043534 (0.0032176)	-1.35
Intercept	0.4834346 (0.0088943)	54.35 ***	0.7597285 (0.0769203)	9.88 ***	0.9100567 (0.0198685)	45.80 ***	0.7333728 (0.0201226)	36.45 ***
Raw sum of deviations	0.164		1.825		0.459		0.640	
Min sum of deviations	0.136		1.583		0.362		0.540	
Pseudo R²	0.17		0.13		0.21		0.16	
N	72		72		72		72	

Standard errors are in parentheses. * p < 0.05; ** p < 0.01; *** p < 0.001

In terms of the findings for the unbiased (S_{AN}) age diversity scores, the OLS and quantile regression models differ with respect to the statistical relationships of some of the predictors (see Exhibit 10-3, Panel A and B). Although both models show a significant positive relationship amongst Elected and the level of age diversity ($\beta_{A1} = 0.012$, $p < 0.05$; $\beta_{B1} = 0.016$, $p < 0.05$), they differ with respect to the relationship amongst Mftsal and age diversity. The OLS model fails to detect a significant statistical finding for Mftsal ($\beta_{A5} = -0.0000003$, $p > 0.05$; see Panel A); by contrast, the quantile model shows a significant inverse relationship amongst the predictor and the level of age diversity ($\beta_{B5} = -0.0000004$, $p < 0.05$). Inconsistent findings also are obtained for Pctunion. Specifically, the OLS model detects a significant positive relationship ($\beta_{A6} = 0.021$, $p < 0.05$), and the quantile model fails to detect a similar relationship at the 50th percentile ($\beta_{B6} = 0.014$, $p > 0.05$). In addition, the regression models produce inconsistent findings for Mcluster. The OLS model reveals a significant negative relationship amongst Mcluster and the level of age diversity ($\beta_{A8} = -0.005$, $p < 0.05$); the quantile model fails to detect a significant statistical finding for the predictor and age diversity ($\beta_{B8} = -0.001$, $p > 0.05$). Similar inconsistent findings are obtained for Mhcluster. For the remainder of the predictors, the OLS and quantile regression models yield consistent findings.

Generally speaking, measurement error contributes partially to the inconsistent findings obtained by the OLS and quantile regression models. For instance, the OLS regression model yields significant statistical findings for gender diversity; however, atypical scores produce biased regression coefficients. The quantile model adjusts for the atypical scores by using the median instead of the mean. Stated differently, atypical values bias the regression coefficients obtained by OLS regression more so in comparison to the regression coefficients obtained by quantile regression.

With respect to the OLS and quantile regression findings obtained for ethnic diversity, the consistency of the findings may be due to measurement and statistical factors. First, the distributions of the ethnic diversity scores are nonmoral, negatively skewed, and moderately clustered. As such, the level of ethnic diversity may be very similar in NYC departments due to measurement clustering which limit the OLS and quantile regression models to detect significant relationships. The nonlinearity of the predictors and of the ethnic diversity scores also hinder the statistical models from detecting significant statistical relationships. In the case of the unbiased (S_{EN}) ethnic diversity scores, the distribution is more compact where the scores are moderately clustered. In terms of the measurement of ethnic diversity with the Simpson index, the index may lack sufficient discriminatory power to detect subtle differences in the level of ethnic diversity.

Measurement error in the calculation of the diversity scores for age most likely account for the differences in the OLS and quantile regression findings. The distribution of the biased (S_{AB}) diversity scores for age has high coefficients for departments with smaller workforces and with missing data for multiple age group categories. This issue of measurement error becomes more pronounced when the formula for calculating unbiased (S_{AN}) diversity scores is applied to the data. Specifically, the formula for obtaining unbiased diversity scores overcorrects for the size of the workforce and further increases the value of the high diversity scores of departments with small workforces. The atypical diversity scores for age contribute to the significant statistical findings obtained by the OLS regression model. By using the median and by using the conditional distribution of the diversity scores for age, quantile regression adjusts for the atypical scores and produces less biased estimates.

Summary

This chapter applied quantile regression to the age, ethnic, gender, and organizational diversity scores for NYC departments for fiscal year 2019. The statistical findings show that few of the predictors are related significantly with age and gender diversity. Similar to the OLS, robust, and Tobit regression models, the quantile regression analyses failed to detect significant statistical relationships amongst the predictors and ethnic diversity. For age diversity, the findings obtained by the quantile regression model are fairly consistent with those obtained by the robust and Tobit regression models. Because the quantile regression model focused exclusively on the conditional distribution of the age diversity scores at the 50th percentile, it is unclear whether the predictors have significant statistical relationships at the 5th, 25th, 75th, or other percentiles. Although the diversity scores for age are incompatible and are inflated for several departments, the findings obtained by the quantile regression model are consistent with the findings obtained by the robust and Tobit regression models; however, the findings are suspect because of the moderate level of multicollinearity amongst the predictors.

As stated previously, quantile regression does not address the issue of collinearity amongst the predictors. Similar to the statistical findings produced by the OLS, robust, and Tobit regression models, the findings obtained with the use of quantile regression are suspect due to the low and moderate levels of collinearity amongst the predictors. The next chapter applies ridge regression to address the issue multicollinearity amongst the independent variables. In undertaking the ridge regression analyses, it is important to keep in mind that the issues of nonlinearity, nonnormality, outliers, and truncation are not addressed by the statistical method.

Key words

Conditional distribution refers to the continuum of values of the dependent variable that may be analyzed with quantile regression. Unlike OLS regression which focuses on the distribution of values around the mean of a dependent variable, quantile regression focuses on the entire distribution of values and performs a regression analysis at different percentiles along the continuum of values to assess the relationships amongst the predictors and the dependent variable at different locations.

Quantile regression is a median-based statistical method that assesses the relationships amongst a set of predictors and a dependent variable across the conditional distribution of the dependent variable at specified percentiles such the 25th, 50th, 75th, and 90th percentiles.

References

Britt, Chester L. 2009. "Modeling the distribution of sentence length decisions under a guidelines system: An application of quantile regression models". *Journal of Quantitative Criminology*, Vol. 25: 341 – 370.

Buhai, I. Sebastian. 2005. "Quantile regression: overview and selected applications". *Ad Astra*, Vol. 4: 1 – 17.

Cade, Brian S., and Noon, Barry R. 2013. "A gentle introduction to quantile regression for ecologists". *Frontiers in Ecology and the Environment*, Vol. 1: 412 – 420.

Davino Cristina, Furno, Marilena, and Vistocco, Domenico. 2014. *Quantile Regression: Theory and applications*. New York: John Wiley and Sons, Ltd.

Davino, Cristina, Romano, Rosaria, and Naes, Tormod. 2015. "The use of quantile regression in consumer studies". *Food Quality and Preference*, Vol. 40: 230 – 239.

DeLisi, Matt, Beaver, Kevin M., Wright, Kevin A., Wright, John Paul, Vaughn, Michael G., Trulson, Chad R. 2011. "Criminal specialization revisited: A simultaneous quantile regression approach". *American Journal of Criminal Justice*, Vol. 36: 73 – 92.

Guajardo, Salomón A. 2016. "Ethnic diversity in policing: An application of quantile regression to the New York City Police Department". *Journal of Ethnicity in Criminal Justice*, Vol. 14: 254 – 289.

Hao, Lingxin, and Naiman, Daniel Q. 2007. *Quantile regression*. Thousand Oaks, CA: Sage Publications Inc.

Koenker, Roger, and Bassett Jr, Gilbert. 1978. Regression quantiles. *Econometrica*, Vol. 46: 33 – 50.

Koenker, Roger, and Hallock, Kevin F. 2001. "Quantile regression". *Journal of Economic Perspectives*, Vol. 15: 143 – 156.

Koenker, Roger. 2005. *Quantile regression*. New York: Cambridge University Press.

Meligkotsidou, Loukia, Vrontos, Ioannis D., and Vrontos, Spyridon D. 2009. "Quantile regression analysis of hedge fund strategies". *Journal of Empirical Finance*, Vol. 16: 264 – 279.

Talbert, Marian K., and Cade, Brian S. 2013. *User manual for Blossom statistical package for R*. Reston, VA: U.S. Geological Survey.

Yu, Keming, Lu, Zud, and Sandler, Julian. 2003. "Quantile regression: Applications and current research areas". *The Statistician*, Vol. 52: 331 – 350.

CHAPTER 11

ANALYSIS OF DIVERSITY WITH RIDGE REGRESSION

In previous chapters, the discussion about satisfying the underlying statistical assumptions of the regression models centered on whether each set of biased (S_B) and unbiased (S_N) Simpson diversity scores where independent of each other, normally distributed, and related linearly with the predictors. The discussion also addressed whether the distributions of the diversity scores were truncated or contained atypical coefficients. In discussing whether the diversity scores satisfied the underlying statistical assumptions of each regression model used thus far, insufficient attention was given to the associations amongst the set of predictors. As discussed in previous chapters, the predictors used in the OLS, robust, Tobit, and quantile regression models are collinear and violate the underlying assumption that the predictors should not be related statistically with each other. In Chapter 7, the VIF coefficients obtained for the OLS regression model indicate the presence of moderate levels of collinearity amongst some of the predictors. Because multiple underlying statistical assumptions are violated, the findings produced by the OLS, robust, Tobit, and quantile regression models are biased to some extent and should be viewed with skepticism.

This chapter focuses on the application of ridge regression to reduce the level of collinearity amongst the predictors to obtain more reliable and stable regression coefficients. Specifically, ridge regression is applied to the biased (S_B) and unbiased (S_N) Simpson diversity scores for age, ethnicity, gender, and organizational heterogeneity that were calculated based on employment data reported by NYC departments for fiscal year 2019. For consistency with previous chapters, this chapter presents a brief overview of ridge regression. The ridge regression model guiding the analyses is discussed prior to performing the statistical analyses. Similar to previous chapters, the statistical findings obtained by the ridge regression analyses are compared to those obtained by the OLS regression model. By comparing the statistical findings of the OLS and ridge regression models concurrently, it is possible to identify similarities and differences amongst the models. A brief summary of the key points is provided at the end of the chapter.

Overview of ridge regression

Hoel (1962) is credited with introducing *ridge analysis* to assess the statistical issues that arise from the inclusion of *nonorthogonal predictors* in OLS regression. The use of ridge analysis led to the creation and further development of ridge regression. In developing ridge regression, Hoel and Kennard (1970a and 1970b) created the statistical method to resolve the issue of collinearity amongst nonorthogonal independent variables. Stated simply, ridge regression consists of the *ridge trace* and the application of a tuning (or shrinkage) parameter ($k \geq 0$) which reduces the OLS regression sums of squares to stabilize the regression coefficients which are inflated by the collinearity amongst a set of predictors (Hoel and Kennard, 1970a). The purpose of ridge regression is to obtain reliable and stable regression coefficients by reducing the level of collinearity amongst predictors that are related statistically.

Exhibit 11-1 illustrates the steps necessary to undertake a ridge regression analysis. In discussing Exhibit 11-1, each step of the process is used in this chapter. The first step is to conduct an OLS regression analysis of the relationships amongst the predictors and each set of Simpson diversity scores for age, ethnicity, gender, and the overall level of organizational heterogeneity. Before undertaking an OLS regression analysis, the data are assessed in terms of meeting the underlying statistical assumptions (see Chapter 7). To assess whether collinearity exists amongst the predictors, a correlation matrix is reviewed to assess if any of the predictors are related statistically with each other. If there are significant associations amongst the variables, ridge regression should be considered or performed jointly or subsequent to performing the OLS regression analysis.

Exhibit 11-1 Ridge regression process

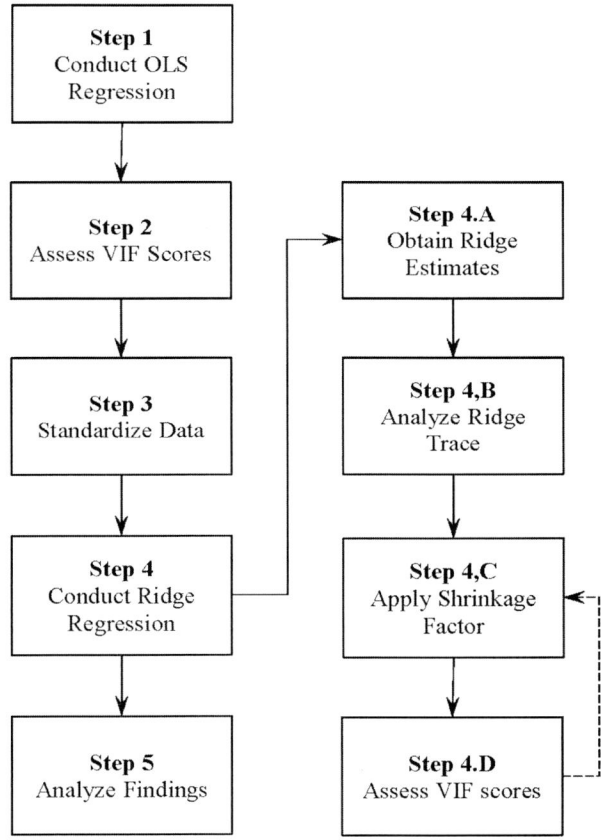

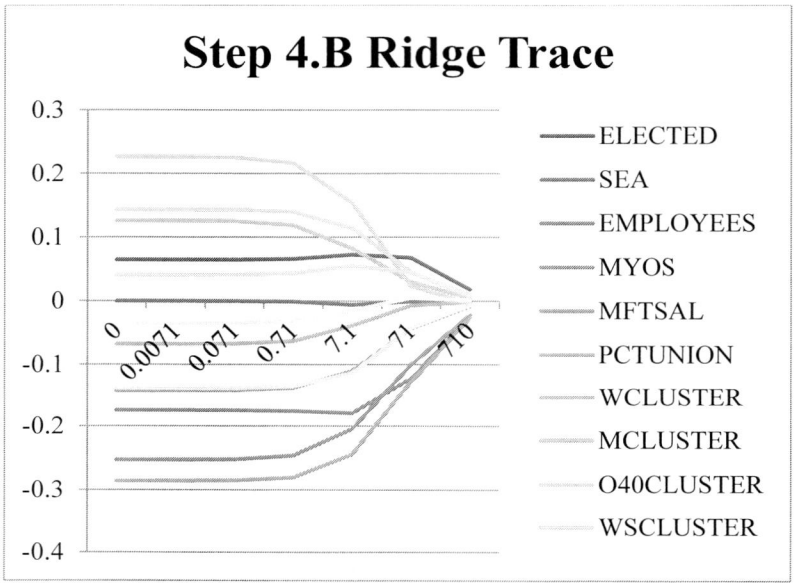

After conducting the OLS regression analysis, the VIF scores are reviewed to determine whether any of the variables contribute to collinearity or to inflating the regression coefficients (see Exhibit 11-1). In Chapter 7, the OLS VIF scores for the predictors range from 1.37 to 4.63 and indicate the presence of moderate degrees of collinearity amongst the predictors. As discussed in Chapter 7, the findings of the OLS regression analysis are suspect because of multiple assumption violations related to the lack of linearity, the lack of normality, and the presence of atypical diversity coefficients. The presence of moderate degrees of multicollinearity amongst the predictors also contributes to the instability and unreliability of the regression coefficients.

In Step 3, each predictor and each set of Simpson diversity scores is standardized to undertake the ridge regression analysis (see Exhibit 11-1). The standardized values of the predictors and diversity scores are then used to perform the ridge regression analysis in Step 4. For this chapter, standardized values are obtained for each predictor and each set of diversity scores.

As illustrated in Step 4, the process of performing a ridge regression analysis is four-fold and entails the following:

1. Obtain ridge estimates;
2. Assess the ridge trace to determine the point where the estimates for most of the predictors are stabilized;
3. Apply a shrinkage factor to the estimates to reduce the collinearity amongst the predictors; and,
4. Obtain VIF scores to assess whether the shrinkage factor should be increased to reduce the collinearity further.

To obtain ridge estimates for the standardized predictors, the following formula is used: $\hat{\beta}* = (X'X + \lambda 1_p)^{-1}X'Y$, where $\lambda 1_p$ represents the ridge (or value) that is added to the main diagonal of X'X. More specifically, λ is the constant (i.e., biasing estimator) and 1 is the p x p identity matrix. The formula is applied to the standardized values of each predictor and diversity score obtained in Step 3. After obtaining the ridge estimates, the ridge trace is used to determine the value of λ that would reduce the variance and produce stable regression coefficients (see Exhibit 11-1). After reviewing the ridge trace plot, a shrinkage factor of 7 is applied in Step 4.C to the standardized predictors used to assess the diversity scores for age, ethnicity, gender, and organizational heterogeneity. In Step 4.D, the ridge regression (RR) VIF scores for the standardized predictors are obtained by applying the following formula: $VIF = (n-1) (X'X + \lambda 1_p)^{-1}X'X(X'X + \lambda 1_p)^{-1}$. This formula is applied to the standardized predictors used in the ridge regression model discussed below. When the VIF scores are obtained for the standardized predictors, the coefficients range from 0.97 to 1.7, indicating that the levels of collinearity amongst the predictors is negligible (see Exhibit 11-2).

In Step 5, the ridge regression findings are discussed. The discussion also includes comparing the statistical findings of the ridge regression to those obtained by the OLS regression model. The discussion of the findings is presented below after presenting the generic statistical model.

Underlying Assumptions of Ridge Regression

Similar to OLS, robust, Tobit regression, and quantile regression, ridge regression requires that a number of underlying assumptions be met in regard to the independent and dependent variables prior to undertaking the analysis. The underlying statistical assumptions of ridge regression are the following:

1. The dependent variable is quantitative continuous;

2. The errors of the dependent and independent variables are normally distributed;
3. The relationship between the dependent and independent variables is linear so that changes in the values of the independent variables are associated with changes in the values of the dependent variable; and,
4. The values of the independent and dependent variables are not interconnected and are not calculated in part or in whole on the same data sources.

Like the regression methods discussed in previous chapters, ridge regression produces regression coefficients that are biased, unreliable, and unstable when statistical assumptions are not adequately satisfied.

Ridge regression model

Ridge regression analyses are undertaken for the biased (S_B) and unbiased (S_N) diversity scores for age, ethnicity, gender, and organizational heterogeneity. The same independent variables that were used for the OLS, robust, Tobit, and quantile regression analyses are used to perform ridge regression analyses below. Although the ridge regression model may be presented in matrix form, the following generic theoretical statistical model is used to be consistent with the presentation in previous chapters:

$$\hat{S} = \beta_1 \text{Elected} + \beta_2 \text{SEA} + \beta_3 \text{Employees} + \beta_4 \text{Myos} + \beta_5 \text{Mftsal} + \beta_6 \text{Pctunion} + \beta_7 \text{Wcluster} + \beta_8 \text{Mcluster} + \beta_9 \text{ O40cluster} + \beta_{10} \text{Wscluster} + \beta_{11} \text{Mscluster} + \beta_{12} \text{Whcluster} + \beta_{13} \text{Mhcluster} + \varepsilon_{ij}.$$

The terms of the regression equation are the following:

$\hat{S}$ refers to the Simpson diversity scores calculated separately for age, ethnicity, gender, and organizational diversity for fiscal year 2019;

B_n refers to the regression coefficient associated with each independent variable in the equation that is significant statistically at $p < 0.05$;

Elected refers to whether the department is an elected office (1) or other type of organization (0);

SEA refers to the percent of the adopted operating budget that is allocated to salary expenses in fiscal year 2019;

Employees refers to the total number of employees on the payroll in each department in fiscal year 2019;

Myos refers to the median number of years of service of each department's workforce in fiscal year 2019;

Mftsal refers to the median full-time salary of each department's workforce in fiscal year 2019;

Pctunion refers to the percent of the workforce in each department that has membership in a collective bargaining unit in fiscal year 2019;

Wcluster refers to the relative clustering score obtained by dividing the percent of women employees by the percent of men employees in each department to assess the magnitude of women-dominated employment in fiscal year 2019;

Mcluster refers to the relative clustering score obtained by dividing the percent of minority employees by the percent of White employees in each department to assess the magnitude of minority-dominated employment in fiscal year 2019;

O40cluster refers to the relative clustering score obtained by dividing the percent of employees under the age of 40 by the percent of employees over the age of 40 in each department to assess the magnitude of employment of older persons in fiscal year 2019;

Wscluster refers to the relative clustering score obtained by dividing the percent of women employees that terminated their employment by the percent of men employees that terminated their employment in each department to assess the magnitude of women-dominated termination in fiscal year 2019;

Mscluster refers to the relative clustering score obtained by dividing the percent of minority employees that terminated their employment by the percent of White employees that terminated their employment in each department to assess the magnitude of minority-dominated termination in fiscal year 2019;

Whcluster refers to the relative clustering score obtained by dividing the percent of women hired by the percent of men hired in each department to assess the magnitude of women-dominated hiring in fiscal year 2019;

Mhcluster refers to the relative clustering score obtained by dividing the percent of minorities hired by the percent of men hired in each department to assess the magnitude of minority-dominated hiring in fiscal year 2019; and,

ε_{ij} refers to measurement error in the statistical model.

As in previous chapters, each regression coefficient (β) is tested for statistical significance at $\alpha = 0.05$. Exhibit 7.5 illustrates the hypothesized statistical relationships amongst the predicators and the diversity scores for age, ethnicity, gender, and organizational heterogeneity.

Ridge regression analysis

The statistical findings of the ridge regression analyses for the standardized biased (S_B) and unbiased (S_N) diversity scores calculated for NYC departments based on employment data for fiscal year 2019 are summarized in Exhibit 11-2. In Panel A, the findings of the standardized biased (S_{BG}) diversity scores for gender show that the ridge regression model is insignificant statistically and lacks explanatory power ($F_{13,59} = 1.38$, $p > 0.05$). Accordingly, the association amongst each predictor and the standardized S_{BG} scores is insignificant statistically. For instance, the relationship amongst Pctunion and the S_{BG} scores is insignificant at $\alpha = 0.05$ ($\beta_{A2} = -0.001$, $p > 0.05$). In addition, Employees is unrelated statistically with the standardized S_{BG} scores ($\beta_{A3} = 0.000$, $p > 0.05$). The findings also show that the level of gender diversity is statistically equal amongst NYC departments headed by an elected and nonelected official ($\beta_{A1} = 0.011$, $p > 0.05$).

In Panel B, the statistical findings for the standardized unbiased (S_{GN}) gender diversity scores are consistent with the findings of the S_{GB} scores (see Exhibit 11-2). Specifically, the ridge regression model for the standardized S_{GN} scores is statistically insignificant and lacks explanatory power ($F_{13,59} = 0.13$, $p > 0.05$). As such, each relationship amongst the predictors and the S_{GN} scores is insignificant. For instance, SEA is unrelated statistically with the S_{GN} scores ($\beta_{B2} = 0.005$, $p > 0.05$). Employees also is unrelated statistically with the S_{GN} scores ($\beta_{B3} = 0.000$, $p > 0.05$). The findings also indicate that the level of gender diversity is statistically equal amongst NYC departments headed by elected and nonelected officials ($\beta_{B1} = 0.004$, $p > 0.05$).

Exhibit 11-2 Ridge regression analysis for age, ethnic, gender, and organizational diversity for NYC departments for fiscal year 2019

A. Ridge regression for biased (S_B) diversity scores

Predictors	Gender Diversity (S_{GB}) β Coefficient	t-statistic	Ethnic Diversity (S_{EB}) β Coefficient	t-statistic	Age Diversity (S_{AB}) β Coefficient	t-statistic	Organizational Diversity (S_{BOD}) β Coefficient	t-statistic	RR VIF
Elected	0.011282592 (0.0173964)	0.65	-0.0298145 (0.0237597)	-1.25	0.0226643 (0.0064653)	3.51 **	0.001377455 (0.0113169)	0.12	1.11
SEA	-0.00130779 (0.0262374)	-0.05	-0.0481989 (0.0358345)	-1.35	-0.0210116 (0.0097511)	-2.15 *	-0.023506107 (0.0170682)	-1.38	1.10
Employees	-0.0000005 (0.0000003)	-1.65	0.0000003 (0.0000004)	0.63	0.0000002 (0.0000001)	1.59	0.0000000 (0.0000002)	-0.10	0.97
Myos	-0.00261898 (0.0017342)	-1.51	-0.0020497 (0.0023685)	-0.87	-0.0003190 (0.0006445)	-0.50	-0.001662579 (0.0011281)	-1.47	1.32
Mftsal	-0.0000004 (0.0000005)	-0.90	-0.0000009 (0.0000007)	-1.29	-0.0000003 (0.0000002)	-1.78	-0.0000005 (0.0000003)	-1.70	1.22
Pctunion	-0.05279181 (0.0272893)	-1.93	-0.0243050 (0.0372711)	-0.65	0.0346892 (0.0101420)	3.42 **	-0.01435872 (0.0177525)	-0.80	1.25
Wcluster	-0.00576895 (0.0116238)	-0.50	-0.0122774 (0.0158756)	-0.77	-0.0073729 (0.0043200)	-1.71	-0.008474739 (0.0075616)	-1.12	1.33
Mcluster	0.00270647 (0.0049544)	0.55	0.0039674 (0.0067666)	0.59	-0.0048844 (0.0018413)	-2.65 *	0.000595892 (0.0032230)	0.18	1.70
O40cluster	0.006147975 (0.0056567)	1.09	0.0046078 (0.0077258)	0.60	0.0019106 (0.0021023)	0.91	0.004222106 (0.0036798)	1.15	1.33
Wscluster	0.009588653 (0.0109267)	0.88	-0.0092437 (0.0149234)	-0.62	-0.0022753 (0.0040609)	-0.56	-0.00064343 (0.0071081)	-0.09	1.33
Mscluster	0.00297362 (0.0053558)	0.43	0.0018092 (0.0073148)	0.25	0.0005409 (0.0019905)	0.27	0.001549153 (0.0034841)	0.44	1.43
Whcluster	-0.00431068 (0.0044749)	-0.96	0.0009197 (0.0061117)	0.15	0.0008766 (0.0016631)	0.53	-0.000838124 (0.0029110)	-0.29	1.14
Mhcluster	-0.00050806 (0.0032181)	-0.16	-0.0082072 (0.0043952)	-1.87	0.0026946 (0.0011960)	2.25 *	-0.002006897 (0.0020934)	-0.96	1.62
$F_{13,59}$	1.38		0.71		3.46 **		0.65		1.30
R^2	0.48		0.14		0.43		0.15		
Adjusted R^2	0.23		-0.06		0.31		-0.04		
N	72		72		72		72		

B. Ridge regression for unbiased (S_N) diversity scores

Predictors	Gender Diversity (S_{GN})		Ethnic Diversity (S_{EN})		Age Diversity (S_{AN})		Organizational Diversity (S_{ON})		RR VIF
	β Coefficient	t-statistic	β Coefficient	t-statistic	β Coefficient	t-statistic	β Coefficient	t-statistic	
Elected	0.00414733 (0.0174310)	0.24	-0.0409436 (0.0241700)	-1.69	0.01001384 (0.0048765)	2.05 *	-0.01201389 (0.0081657)	-1.57	1.11
SEA	0.004797688 (0.0262895)	0.18	-0.0394486 (0.0364534)	-1.08	-0.00957863 (0.0073547)	-1.30	-0.014145035 (0.0123155)	-1.15	1.10
Employees	-0.0000006 (0.0000003)	-1.87	0.0000002 (0.0000004)	0.37	0.0000000 (0.0000001)	0.58	0.0000000 (0.0000001)	0.31	0.97
Myos	-0.00256274 (0.0173376)	-1.47	-0.0019799 (0.0024094)	-0.82	-0.00027088 (0.0004861)	-0.56	-0.00740582 (0.0008140)	-0.91	1.32
Mfisal	-0.0000004 (0.0000005)	-0.81	-0.0000008 (0.0000007)	-1.18	-0.0000002 (0.0000001)	-1.75	-0.0000003 (0.0000002)	-1.43	1.22
Pctunion	-0.06348764 (0.0273435)	-2.32	-0.0404827 (0.0379149)	-1.07	0.016701816 (0.0076496)	2.18 *	-0.011520621 (0.0128092)	-0.90	1.25
Wcluster	-0.00118622 (0.0116469)	-0.10	-0.0047055 (0.0161498)	-0.29	0.0014249 (0.003583)	0.44	0.000654135 (0.0054561)	0.12	1.33
Mcluster	0.003702472 (0.0049642)	0.75	0.00580045 (0.0068834)	0.84	-0.00333802 (0.0013888)	-2.40 *	0.00118025 (0.0023255)	0.51	1.70
O40cluster	0.005731849 (0.0056679)	1.01	0.00384018 (0.0078592)	0.49	0.001348479 (0.0015857)	0.85	0.001597726 (0.0026552)	0.60	1.33
Wscluster	0.009663418 (0.0109484)	0.88	-0.0096281 (0.0151812)	-0.63	-0.00221627 (0.0036029)	-0.72	-0.00398324 (0.0051288)	-0.78	1.33
Mscluster	0.00180502 (0.0053664)	0.34	0.00101617 (0.0074411)	0.14	-0.00030775 (0.0015013)	-0.20	0.0000469 (0.0025139)	0.02	1.43
Whcluster	-0.0049761 (0.0044838)	-1.10	-0.0000709 (0.0062173)	-0.01	-0.00026576 (0.0012544)	-0.21	-0.00035606 (0.0021005)	-0.16	1.14
Mhcluster	-0.00117091 (0.0032245)	-0.36	-0.0093286 (0.0044711)	-2.09	0.001615143 (0.0009021)	1.79	-0.00279654 (0.0015105)	-1.85	1.62
$F_{13,59}$	0.13		0.75		1.41		0.69		1.30
R^2	0.51		0.13		0.24		0.13		
Adjusted R^2	0.26		-0.06		0.07		-0.06		
N	72		72		72		72		

Standard errors are in parentheses. * $p < 0.05$; ** $p < 0.01$

Insignificant statistical findings are obtained for the standardized biased (S_{EB}) and unbiased (S_{EN}) diversity scores for ethnicity (see Exhibit 11-2). In Panel A, the findings show that the ridge regression model for the standardized S_{EB} scores is insignificant statistically and lacks explanatory power ($F_{13,59} = 0.71$, $p > 0.05$). Each predictor is unrelated statistically with the S_{EB} scores. For example, the relationship amongst SEA and the S_{EB} scores is insignificant statistically at $\alpha = 0.01$ ($\beta_{A2} = -0.048$, $p > 0.05$). A similar insignificant statistical relationship exists for Employees ($\beta_{A3} = 0.000$, $p > 0.05$). The level of ethnic diversity amongst NYC departments is similar regardless of whether they are headed by an elected or nonelected official ($\beta_{A1} = -0.029$, $p > 0.05$).

As stated above, the ridge regression model yields insignificant statistical findings for each the predictor and the S_{EN} scores ($F_{13,59} = 0.75$, $p > 0.05$; see Panel B). Again, the level of ethnic diversity is statistically equal amongst NYC departments regardless of whether they are headed by an elected or nonelected official ($\beta_{B1} = -0.041$, $p > 0.05$). SEA is unrelated statistically with the S_{EN} scores ($\beta_{B2} = -0.039$, $p > 0.05$). Employees also is unrelated statistically with the S_{EN} scores ($\beta_{B3} = 0.000$, $p > 0.05$).

With respect to age diversity, the ridge regression model for the standardized biased (S_{AB}) scores is significant statistically ($F_{13,59} = 3.46$, $p < 0.01$) and explains 43% ($R^2 = 0.43$) of the variance (see Panel A). Elected is related positively with the S_{AB} scores, where the move from a NYC department headed by a nonelected official to one headed by an elected official is associated with a 0.02 point increase in the level of age diversity ($\beta_{A1} = 0.023$, $p < 0.01$). Pctunion also is related positively with the S_{AB} scores, where a unit increase in the percent of unionization is associated with a 0.04 point increase in the level of age diversity ($\beta_{A6} = 0.035$, $p < 0.01$). In addition, a unit increase in Mhcluster is associated with a 0.003 point increase in the level of age diversity ($\beta_{A13} = 0.003$, $p < 0.05$). However, SEA and Mcluster are related negatively with the S_{AB} scores. For instance, a unit increase in SEA is associated with a 0.021 point decrease in the S_{AB} scores ($\beta_{A2} = -0.021$, $p < 0.05$). A unit increase in Mcluster is associated with a 0.005 point decrease in the S_{AB} scores ($\beta_{A8} = -0.005$, $p < 0.05$). The remainder of the predictors have insignificant statistical relationships with the S_{AB} scores at $\alpha = 0.05$.

Different statistical findings are produced by the ridge regression model for the standardized unbiased (S_{AN}) diversity scores for age (see Panel B). Specifically, the ridge regression model is insignificant statistically and lacks explanatory power at $\alpha = 0.05$ ($F_{13,59} = 1.41$, $p > 0.05$). Because the regression model lacks statistical significance, each predictor is unrelated statistically with the standardized S_{AN} scores. With respect to the positive relationship amongst Pctunion and the S_{AN} scores ($\beta_{A6} = 0.017$, $p < 0.05$), the finding is meaningless due to the model's lack of statistical significance. The same holds true for the relationships amongst Employees and Mcluster and the S_{AN} scores.

The statistical findings for the standardized S_{AB} and S_{AN} diversity scores for age are suspect because the unstandardized (or raw) S_{AB} and S_{AN} scores are incompatible. As discussed in Chapter 5, the age diversity scores are based on different numbers of age group categories with employment data so that the coefficients reflect different workforce structures in terms of age. Similarly, the standardized S_{AB} and S_{AN} scores are incompatible. As such, the findings obtained by the ridge regression models are suspect, although the level of multicollinearity amongst the predictors is addressed adequately. The findings also are suspect because the standardized scores are nonlinear and violated the assumption of normality. As discussed in previous chapters, the distributions of the raw biased (S_{AB}) and unbiased (S_{AN}) diversity scores for age are negatively skewed and heavy tailed. Ridge regression addresses the issue of multicollinearity amongst the predictors. However, the statistical method does not address the issue of violating the assumption of normality and or the issue of nonlinearity. The issue of normality and nonlinearity is addressed with the use of a diversity index that produces a distribution of diversity scores that are normally distributed.

In regard to the overall level of organizational diversity, the ridge regression models for the standardized biased (S_{BOD}) and unbiased (S_{NOD}) scores for organizational heterogeneity yield insignificant statistical findings. In Panel A. the regression model for the standardized S_{BOD} scores is insignificant statistically and lacks explanatory power at $\alpha = 0.05$ ($F_{13,59} = 0.65$, $p > 0.05$). Consequently, each predictor has an insignificant statistical relationship with the standardized S_{BOD} scores. The findings for the standardized S_{NOD} scores are similar (see Panel B). The regression model is insignificant statistically and lacks explanatory power at $\alpha = 0.05$ ($F_{13,59} = 0.69$, $p > 0.05$). Subsequently, the relationships amongst the predictors and the standardized S_{NOD} scores are insignificant statistically.

Comparison of OLS and ridge regression

Exhibit 11-3 summarizes the OLS and ridge regression findings for the biased (S_B) diversity scores for age, ethnic, gender, and organizational heterogeneity. In regard to the biased diversity scores for gender (S_{GB}), the

Exhibit 11-3 Comparison of OLS and ridge regression findings for biased (S_B) scores for age, ethnic, gender, and organizational diversity for NYC departments for fiscal year 2019

A. OLS regression for biased (S_B) diversity scores

Predictors	Gender Diversity (S_{GB})		Ethnic Diversity (S_{EB})		Age Diversity (S_{AB})		Organizational Diversity (S_{OOB})		OLS VIF
	β Coefficient	t-statistic	β Coefficient	t-statistic	β Coefficient	t-statistic	β Coefficient	t-statistic	
Elected	0.0100222 (0.0211684)	0.47	-0.0346973 (0.0288702)	-1.20	0.02796320 (0.0073853)	3.79 ***	0.0010960 (0.0137855)	0.08	1.67
SEA	-0.0001446 (0.0311158)	0.00	-0.0548222 (0.0424367)	-1.29	-0.02284840 (0.0108558)	-2.10 *	-0.0259384 (0.0202635)	-1.28	1.58
Employees	-0.0000005 (0.0000004)	-1.37	0.0000004 (0.0000005)	0.76	0.0000021 (0.0000001)	1.67	0.0000000 (0.0000002)	0.13	1.37
Myos	-0.0031933 (0.0023399)	-1.36	-0.0023674 (0.0031912)	-0.74	-0.00072870 (0.0008163)	-0.89	-0.0020965 (0.0015238)	-1.38	2.44
Mtfsal	-0.0000006 (0.0000006)	-0.90	-0.0000011 (0.0000008)	-1.25	-0.00000033 (0.0000002)	-1.53	-0.0000007 (0.0000004)	-1.61	2.03
Pctunion	-0.0618134 (0.0351700)	-1.76	-0.0380349 (0.0479660)	-0.79	0.04206870 (0.0122703)	3.43 **	-0.0192598 (0.0229037)	-0.84	2.11
Wcluster	-0.0087890 (0.0152766)	-0.58	-0.0167990 (0.0208348)	-0.81	-0.00711590 (0.0053298)	-1.35	-0.0109213 (0.0099486)	-1.10	2.34
Mcluster	0.0042241 (0.0081005)	0.52	0.0094895 (0.0110477)	0.86	-0.00814650 (0.0028261)	-2.88 **	0.0018557 (0.0052753)	0.35	4.63
O40cluster	0.0091009 (0.0076699)	1.19	0.0066266 (0.0104604)	0.63	0.00292210 (0.0026759)	1.09	0.0062165 (0.0049948)	1.24	2.49
Wscluster	0.0122934 (0.0139977)	0.88	-0.0101793 (0.0190906)	-0.53	-0.00337570 (0.0048836)	-0.69	-0.0004205 (0.0091157)	-0.05	2.21
Mscluster	0.0017878 (0.0070739)	0.25	0.0014905 (0.0096476)	0.15	0.00060320 (0.0024680)	0.24	0.0012938 (0.0046067)	0.28	2.53
Whcluster	-0.0052104 (0.0053404)	-0.98	0.0011866 (0.0072834)	0.16	0.00105660 (0.0018632)	0.57	-0.0009891 (0.0034778)	-0.28	1.65
Mhcluster	-0.0010515 (0.0050718)	-0.21	-0.0121854 (0.0069171)	-1.76	0.00471180 (0.0017695)	2.66 *	-0.0028417 (0.0033029)	-0.86	4.09
Intercept	0.5560840 (0.0653018)	8.78 ***	0.8507759 (0.0863331)	9.85 ***	0.87749200 (0.0220850)	39.73 ***	0.7614507 (0.0412239)	18.47 ***	
$F_{13,58}$	1.56		0.89		4.76		0.96		2.40
R^2	0.26		0.17		0.52		0.18		
Adjusted R^2	0.09		-0.02		0.41		-0.01		
N	72		72		72		72		

Chapter 11

B. Ridge regression for biased (S_B) diversity scores

Predictors	Gender Diversity (S_GB)		Ethnic Diversity (S_EB)		Age Diversity (S_AB)		Organizational Diversity (S_OB)		RR VIF
	β Coefficient	t-statistic	β Coefficient	t-statistic	β Coefficient	t-statistic	β Coefficient	t-statistic	
Elected	0.011282592 (0.0173964)	0.65	-0.0298145 (0.0237597)	-1.25	0.0226643 (0.0064653)	3.51 **	0.001377455 (0.0113169)	0.12	1.11
SEA	-0.001307793 (0.0262374)	-0.05	-0.0481989 (0.0358345)	-1.35	-0.0210116 (0.0097511)	-2.15 *	-0.023506107 (0.0170682)	-1.38	1.10
Employees	-0.0000005 (0.0000003)	-1.65	0.0000003 (0.0000004)	0.63	0.0000002 (0.0000001)	1.59	0.0000000 (0.0000002)	-0.10	0.97
Myos	-0.002618977 (0.0017342)	-1.51	-0.0020497 (0.0023685)	-0.87	-0.0003190 (0.0006445)	-0.50	-0.001662579 (0.0011281)	-1.47	1.32
Mfisal	-0.0000004 (0.0000005)	-0.90	-0.0000009 (0.0000007)	-1.29	-0.0000003 (0.0000002)	-1.78	-0.0000005 (0.0000003)	-1.70	1.22
Pctunion	-0.052791808 (0.0272893)	-1.93	-0.0243050 (0.0372711)	-0.65	0.0346892 (0.0101420)	3.42 **	-0.014135872 (0.0177525)	-0.80	1.25
Wcluster	-0.005768952 (0.0116238)	-0.50	-0.0122774 (0.0158756)	-0.77	-0.0073779 (0.0043200)	-1.71	-0.008474739 (0.0075616)	-1.12	1.33
Mcluster	0.002704647 (0.0049544)	0.55	0.0039674 (0.0067666)	0.59	-0.0048844 (0.0018413)	-2.65 *	0.000595892 (0.0032230)	0.18	1.70
O40cluster	0.006147975 (0.0056567)	1.09	0.0046078 (0.0077258)	0.60	0.0019106 (0.0021023)	0.91	0.004222106 (0.0036798)	1.15	1.33
Wscluster	0.009588653 (0.0109267)	0.88	-0.0092243 (0.0149234)	-0.62	-0.0022753 (0.0040609)	-0.56	-0.0064343 (0.0071081)	-0.09	1.33
Mscluster	0.002297362 (0.0053558)	0.43	0.0018092 (0.0073148)	0.25	0.0005409 (0.0019905)	0.27	0.001549153 (0.0034841)	0.44	1.43
Whcluster	-0.004310675 (0.0044749)	-0.96	0.0009197 (0.0061117)	0.15	0.0008766 (0.0016631)	0.53	-0.000838124 (0.0029110)	-0.29	1.14
Mhcluster	-0.000508056 (0.0032181)	-0.16	-0.0082072 (0.0043952)	-1.87	0.0026946 (0.0011960)	2.25 *	-0.002006897 (0.0020934)	-0.96	1.62
$F_{13,59}$	1.38		0.71		3.46 **		0.65		1.30
R^2	0.48		0.14		0.43		0.15		
Adjusted R^2	0.23		-0.06		0.31		-0.04		
N	72		72		72		72		

Standard errors are in parentheses. * $p < 0.05$; ** $p < 0.01$; *** $p < 0.001$

OLS and ridge regression findings are consistent. In Panel A, the OLS regression model is insignificant statistically and lacks explanatory power at $\alpha = 0.05$ ($F_{13,58} = 1.56$, p > 0.05) where each predictor has an insignificant relationship with the S_{GB} scores. In Panel B, the ridge regression model yields similar findings. The ridge regression model is insignificant statistically and lacks explanatory power at $\alpha = 0.05$ ($F_{13,59} = 1.38$, p > 0.05). Each predictor also has an insignificant statistical relationship with the standardized S_{GB} scores.

The OLS and ridge regression models are consistent in terms of the statistical findings for the biased (S_{EB}) scores for ethnic diversity. As Panel A summarizes, the OLS regression model is insignificant statistically and lacks explanatory power at $\alpha = 0.05$ ($F_{13,58} = 0.89$, p > 0.05). Again, each predictor has an insignificant association with the S_{EB} scores. In Panel B, the ridge regression model also is insignificant statistically and lacks explanatory power at $\alpha = 0.05$ ($F_{13,59} = 0.71$, p > 0.05). As such, the predictors are unrelated statistically with the standardized S_{EB} scores.

As highlighted in Exhibit 11-3, the OLS and ridge regression findings are consistent in regard to the biased (S_{AB}) diversity scores for age. In Panel A, the OLS regression model is significant statistically ($F_{13,58} = 4.76$, p < 0.001) and explains 52% ($R^2 = 0.52$) of the variance. Elected is related positively with the S_{AB} scores ($\beta_{A1} = 0.028$, p < 0.001) where moving from a NYC department headed by a nonelected official to one headed by an elected official increases the level of age diversity by about 0.03 points. Pctunion also is related positively with the S_{AB} scores ($\beta_{A6} = 0.042$, p < 0.01) where a unit increase in unionization increases the level of age diversity by 0.04 points. A positive relationship exists amongst Mhcluser and the S_{AB} scores where a unit increase in the relative clustering of minority hires increases the level of age diversity by 0.005 points ($\beta_{A13} = 0.005$, p < 0.05). SEA, however, is related negatively with the S_{AB} scores ($\beta_{A2} = -0.023$, p < 0.05) where a unit increase the predictor decreases the level of age diversity by 0.023 points. Mcluster, also is related negatively with the S_{AB} scores ($\beta_{A8} = -0.008$, p < 0.01) where a unit increase in relative clustering of minority employees decreases the level of age diversity by 0.008 points. The remaining predictors are unrelated statistically with the S_{AB} scores.

The statistical findings of the ridge regression model are consistent with those obtained by the OLS regression model; however, they differ slightly (see Panel B). The ridge regression model is significant statistically ($F_{13,59}$ = 3.46, $p < 0.01$) and explains 43% ($R^2 = 0.43$) of the variance. For instance, Elected is related positively with the S_{AB} scores ($\beta_{A1} = 0.023$, $p < 0.01$) where moving from a NYC department headed by a nonelected official to one headed by an elected official increases the level of age diversity by 0.023 points. Pctunion also is related positively with the S_{AB} scores ($\beta_{A6} = 0.035$, $p < 0.01$) where a unit increase in unionization increases the level of age diversity by about 0.04 points. A positive relationship exists amongst Mhcluser and the S_{AB} scores where a unit increase in the relative clustering of minority hires increases the level of age diversity by 0.003 points ($\beta_{A13} = 0.003$, $p < 0.05$). On the other hand, SEA is related negatively with the S_{AB} scores ($\beta_{A2} = -0.021$, $p < 0.05$) where a unit increase in the salary expense allocation decreases the level of age diversity by about 0.02 points. Mcluster also is related negatively with the S_{AB} scores ($\beta_{A8} = -0.005$, $p < 0.05$) where a unit increase in the relative clustering of minority employees decreases the level of age diversity by 0.005 points. The remaining predictors are unrelated statistically with the S_{AB} scores.

Because of the issue of collinearity amongst the predictors, the regression coefficients obtained by the OLS regression model differ from those obtained by the ridge regression model. In Panel A, Elected has an OLS VIF coefficient of 1.67; in Panel B, the predictor has a ridge regression (RR) VIF coefficient of 1.11. Because the ridge regression model reduces the level of collinearity of the predictor in relation to the other predictors, the regression coefficient decreases from 0.028 ($\beta_{A1} = 0.028$, $p < 0.001$) to 0.023 ($\beta_{B1} = 0.023$, $p < 0.01$). In regard to Pctunion, the predictor has an OLS VIF coefficient of 2.11 and a RR VIF coefficient of 1.25. The regression coefficient decreases from 0.042 ($\beta_{A6} = 0.042$, $p < 0.01$) to 0.035 ($\beta_{B6} = 0.035$, $p < 0.01$) due to the decrease in the level of collinearity. The negative regression coefficient for Mcluster decreases with a decline in the level of collinearity. When the VIF coefficient for Mcluster decreases from 4.63 (OLS VIF = 4.63) to 1.70 (RR VIF = 1.70), the regression coefficient increases from -0.008 ($\beta_{A8} = -0.008$, $p < 0.01$) to -0.005 ($\beta_{B8} = -0.005$, $p < 0.05$). Although the S_{AB} scores violate the assumptions of linearity and normality, the findings of the ridge regression model indicate the reduction of multicollinearity amongst the predictors produces more stable regression coefficients.

In terms of the statistical findings for the overall level of organizational diversity, the findings of the OLS and ridge regression models are consistent (see Exhibit 11-3). As Panel A shows, the OLS regression model for the S_{BOD} scores is insignificant statistically and lacks explanatory power ($F_{13,58} = 0.96$, $p > 0.05$). Similarly, the ridge regression model for the S_{BOD} scores is insignificant statistically and lacks explanatory power ($F_{13,59} = 0.65$, $p > 0.05$; see Panel B). In each regression model, the predictors are unrelated statistically with the S_{BOD} scores.

Exhibit 11-4 presents the statistical findings of the OLS and ridge regression models for the unbiased (S_N) diversity scores for age, ethnicity, gender, and organizational heterogeneity for NYC departments for fiscal year 2019. The findings for the unbiased (S_{GN}) diversity scores for gender are inconsistent for the OLS and ridge regression models. In Panel A, the OLS regression model is significant statistically ($F_{13,58} = 4.54$, $p < 0.001$) and explains 50% ($R^2 = 0.50$) of the variance. Elected is related negatively with the S_{GN} scores ($\beta_{A1} = -0.009$, $p < 0.01$) where moving from a NYC department headed by a nonelected official to one headed by an elected official decreases the level of gender diversity by 0.009 points. Pctunion also is related negatively with the S_{GN} scores ($\beta_{A6} = -0.013$, $p < 0.01$) where a unit increase in unionization decreases the level of gender diversity by 0.013 points. However, a unit increase in Wcluster increases the level of gender diversity by 0.006 points ($\beta_{A7} = 0.006$, $p < 0.01$). On the other hand, the ridge regression model is insignificant statistically and lacks explanatory power ($F_{13,59} = 0.13$, $p > 0.05$; see Panel B). As summarized in Panel B, each predictor is statistically unrelated with the S_{GN} scores at $\alpha = 0.05$.

The differences in the OLS and ridge regression findings are due to measurement error and to the level of collinearity amongst the predictors. As discussed in previous chapters, the formula for obtaining unbiased diversity scores overcorrects for the size of NYC departments where smaller workforces have higher heterogeneity measurements for gender. In addition, the unstandardized diversity scores for gender violate the assumption of linearity, normality, and outliers. As indicated by the OLS VIF coefficients, the unstandardized predictors violate the assumption of multicollinearity. When the unbiased S_{GN} scores and the predictors are standardized and ridge estimators are obtained, insignificant statistical regression coefficients are obtained by the ridge regression model due to reducing the collinearity amongst the predictors.

Exhibit 11-4 Comparison of OLS and ridge regression findings for unbiased (S_N) scores for age, ethnic, gender, and organizational diversity for NYC departments for fiscal year 2019

A. OLS regression for unbiased (S_N) diversity scores

Predictors	Gender Diversity (S_{GS})		Ethnic Diversity (S_{EN})		Age Diversity (S_{AN})		Organizational Diversity (S_{OOD})		OLS VIF
	β Coefficient	t-statistic	β Coefficient	t-statistic	β Coefficient	t-statistic	β Coefficient	t-statistic	
Elected	-0.0090903	-3.50 **	-0.0482130	-1.65	0.0125348	2.17 *	-0.0149228	-1.50	1.67
	(0.0026007)		(0.0292796)		(0.0057782)		(0.0099208)		
SEA	0.0070863	1.85	-0.0455908	-1.06	-0.0104432	-1.23	-0.0163159	-1.12	1.58
	(0.0038229)		(0.0430385)		(0.0084934)		(0.0145828)		
Employees	-0.0000001	-2.02	0.0000002	0.49	0.0000001	0.56	0.0000001	0.41	1.37
	(0.0000000)		(0.0000005)		(0.0000001)		(0.0000002)		
Myos	0.0001202	0.42	-0.0021419	-0.66	-0.0005328	-0.83	-0.0008515	-0.78	2.44
	(0.0002875)		(0.0032365)		(0.0006387)		(0.0010966)		
Mfisal	0.0000000	0.55	-0.0000010	-1.17	-0.0000003	-1.57	-0.0000004	-1.41	2.03
	(0.0000001)		(0.0000009)		(0.0000002)		(0.0000003)		
Pctunion	-0.0127857	-2.96 **	-0.0573847	-1.18	0.0207722	2.16 *	-0.0164661	-1.00	2.11
	(0.0043210)		(0.0486462)		(0.0096001)		(0.0164828)		
Wcluster	0.0060758	3.24 **	-0.0080546	-0.38	0.0030452	0.73	0.0003555	0.05	2.34
	(0.0018769)		(0.0211302)		(0.0041700)		(0.0071596)		
Mcluster	0.0017751	1.78	0.0125151	1.12	-0.0055869	-2.53 *	0.0029011	0.76	4.63
	(0.0009952)		(0.0112044)		(0.0022111)		(0.0037964)		
O40cluster	-0.0006505	-0.69	0.0054227	0.51	0.0019535	0.93	0.0022419	0.62	2.49
	(0.0009423)		(0.0106087)		(0.0020936)		(0.0035946)		
Wscluster	-0.0002454	-0.14	-0.0108045	-0.56	-0.0035016	-0.92	-0.0048505	-0.74	2.21
	(0.0017198)		(0.0193613)		(0.0038209)		(0.0065602)		
Mscluster	-0.0006858	-0.79	0.0005037	0.05	-0.0003891	-0.20	-0.0001904	-0.06	2.53
	(0.0008691)		(0.0097844)		(0.0019309)		(0.0033153)		
Whcluster	-0.0008539	-1.30	-0.0000665	-0.01	-0.0004047	-0.28	-0.0004417	-0.18	1.65
	(0.0006561)		(0.0073867)		(0.0014577)		(0.0025028)		
Mhcluster	-0.0011117	-1.78	-0.0140542	-2.00	0.0029747	2.15 *	-0.0040637	-1.71	4.09
	(0.0006231)		(0.0070152)		(0.0013844)		(0.0023770)		
Intercept	0.4827186	62.07 ***	0.8625738	9.85 ***	0.8894504	51.48 ***	0.7449143	25.11 ***	
	(0.0077772)		(0.0875573)		(0.0172790)		(0.0296671)		
$F_{13,58}$	4.54		0.92		1.91		0.87		2.40
R^2	0.50		0.17		0.30		0.16		
Adjusted R^2	0.39		-0.02		0.14		-0.02		
N	72		72		72		72		

Analysis of Diversity with Ridge Regression

B. Ridge regression for unbiased (S_U) diversity scores

Predictors	Gender Diversity (S_{GN}) β Coefficient	t-statistic	Ethnic Diversity (S_{EN}) β Coefficient	t-statistic	Age Diversity (S_{AN}) β Coefficient	t-statistic	Organizational Diversity (S_{NOD}) β Coefficient	t-statistic	RR VIF
Elected	0.004141733 (0.0174310)	0.24	-0.040943592 (0.0241700)	-1.69	0.010017384 (0.0048765)	2.05 *	-0.012801389 (0.0081657)	-1.57	1.11
SEA	0.004797688 (0.0262895)	0.18	-0.039448591 (0.0364534)	-1.08	-0.009578633 (0.0073547)	-1.30	-0.014145035 (0.0123155)	-1.15	1.10
Employees	-0.0000006 (0.0000003)	-1.87	0.0000002 (0.0000004)	0.37	0.0000000 (0.0000001)	0.58	0.0000000 (0.0000001)	0.31	0.97
Myos	-0.002562739 (0.0017376)	-1.47	-0.001979862 (0.0024094)	-0.82	-0.000270884 (0.0004861)	-0.56	-0.000740582 (0.0008140)	-0.91	1.32
Mfisal	-0.0000004 (0.0000005)	-0.81	-0.0000008 (0.0000007)	-1.18	-0.0000002 (0.0000001)	-1.75	-0.0000003 (0.0000002)	-1.43	1.22
Petunion	-0.063487639 (0.0273435)	-2.32	-0.04048266 (0.0379149)	-1.07	0.016701816 (0.0076496)	2.18 *	-0.011520621 (0.0128092)	-0.90	1.25
Wcluster	-0.001186221 (0.0116469)	-0.10	-0.004705466 (0.0161498)	-0.29	0.0014249 (0.0032583)	0.44	0.000654135 (0.0054561)	0.12	1.33
Mcluster	0.003702472 (0.0049642)	0.75	0.005800445 (0.0068834)	0.84	-0.003338019 (0.0013888)	-2.40 *	0.00118025 (0.0023255)	0.51	1.70
O40cluster	0.005731849 (0.0056679)	1.01	0.00384018 (0.0078592)	0.49	0.001348479 (0.0015857)	0.85	0.001597726 (0.0026552)	0.60	1.33
Wscluster	0.009663418 (0.0109484)	0.88	-0.009628082 (0.0151812)	-0.63	-0.002216273 (0.0030629)	-0.72	-0.003982324 (0.0051288)	-0.78	1.33
Mscluster	0.00180502 (0.0053664)	0.34	0.00101617 (0.0074411)	0.14	-0.000307749 (0.0015013)	-0.20	0.0000469 (0.0025139)	0.02	1.43
Whcluster	-0.004937611 (0.0044838)	-1.10	-0.0000709 (0.0062173)	-0.01	-0.000265759 (0.0012544)	-0.21	-0.000335606 (0.0021005)	-0.16	1.14
Mhcluster	-0.001170912 (0.0032245)	-0.36	-0.009328619 (0.0044711)	-2.09	0.001615143 (0.0009021)	1.79	-0.002796554 (0.0015105)	-1.85	1.62
$F_{13,59}$	0.13		0.75		1.41		0.69		1.30
R^2	0.51		0.13		0.24		0.13		
Adjusted R^2	0.26		-0.06		0.07		-0.06		
N	72		72		72		72		

Standard errors are in parentheses. * $p < 0.05$; ** $p < 0.01$; *** $p < 0.001$

With respect to the statistical findings for the unbiased (S_{EN}) diversity scores for ethnicity, the findings of the OLS and ridge regression models are consistent. The OLS regression model is insignificant statistically and lacks explanatory power ($F_{13,58} = 0.92$, $p > 0.05$; see Panel A). As shown in Panel A, each predictor is unrelated statistically with the S_{EN} scores. The ridge regression model also is insignificant statistically and lacks explanatory power ($F_{13,59} = 0.75$, $p > 0.05$; see Panel B). The relationships amongst the predictors and the S_{EN} scores are insignificant statistically at $\alpha = 0.05$. The same holds true for the OLS and ridge regression findings for the S_{NOD} scores which assess the overall level of organizational diversity.

The OLS and ridge regression findings for the unbiased (S_{AN}) diversity scores for age are inconsistent (see Exhibit 11-4). In Panel A, the OLS regression model is significant statistically ($F_{13,58} = 1.91$, $p < 0.05$) and explains 30% ($R^2 = 0.30$) of the variance. Elected is related positively with the S_{AN} scores ($\beta_{A1} = 0.013$, $p < 0.05$), indicating that moving from a NYC department headed by a nonelected official to one headed by an elected official increases the level of age diversity by 0.013 points. Pctunion also is related positively with the S_{AN} scores ($\beta_{A6} = 0.021$, $p < 0.05$), indicating that a unit increase in unionization increases the level of age diversity by 0.013 points. In addition, the level of age diversity increases by 0.003 points with a unit increase in Mhcluster ($\beta_{A13} = 0.003$, $p < 0.05$). However, the level of age diversity decreases by 0.005 points with a unit increase in Mcluster ($\beta_{A8} = -0.005$, $p < 0.05$). The remaining predictors are unrelated statistically with the S_{AN} scores. In Panel B, the ridge regression model for the S_{AN} scores is insignificant statistically and lacks explanatory power at $\alpha = 0.05$ ($F_{13,59} = 1.41$, $p > 0.05$). Accordingly, each predictor in the ridge model is unrelated statistically with the S_{AN} scores.

Without repeating the points made above about the differences in the OLS and ridge regression findings for the unbiased S_{GN} scores, the differences in the OLS and ridge regression coefficients for the S_{AN} scores are attributable to the reduction in the levels of the collinearity amongst the predictors. As a result of reducing the level of collinearity amongst the independent variables, the ridge regression model yields smaller regression coefficients in comparison to the OLS predictors with significant statistical relationships.

Summary

This chapter applied ridge regression to the age, ethnic, gender, and organizational diversity scores for NYC departments for fiscal year 2019. In regard to the biased (S_{AB}) diversity scores for age, the statistical findings show that few predictors are related statistically with age diversity. Similar to the OLS, robust, and quantile regression models, the ridge regression analysis obtained insignificant findings for the biased (S_{EB}) diversity scores for ethnicity. Because the ridge regression models focused exclusively on the reduction of collinearity amongst the predictors, the extent to which the nonlinearity and nonnormality of the diversity scores impact the regression coefficients is unclear. Although the biased diversity scores for age (S_{AB}) are incompatible and are inflated for several departments, the findings obtained by the ridge regression model are consistent with the findings of the OLS, robust, and Tobit regression models; however, the findings of the OLS, robust, and Tobit regression models are suspect because of the moderate levels of collinearity amongst the predictors.

In the following chapter, the regression models for the diversity scores are compared simultaneously. The comparative analysis begins with reviewing the statistical findings of the regression models for the biased (S_B) scores. Similarities and differences amongst the statistical findings of the regression models are discussed as well.

Key words

Nonorthogonal predictors refers to independent variables that are correlated statistically so their values vary jointly.

Ridge analysis refers to the process of assessing and reducing the collinearity amongst a set of predictors with statistical techniques such as ridge regression.

Ridge estimates refer to the estimators obtained from applying a shrinkage factor to reduce the levels of collinearity amongst a set of independent variables that are correlated statistically.

Ridge trace refers to a two-dimensional plot that displays the coefficient estimates for the predictors as the shrinkage parameter (k or lambda (λ)) increases to infinity (∞). Generally, the selection of λ is based on the point where most of the estimates for the predictors begin to stabilize.

References

Hoerl, Arthur E. 1962. "Application of ridge analysis to regression problems". *Chemical Engineering Progress*, Vol. 58: 54 – 59.

Hoerl, Arthur E., and Kennard, Robert W. 1970a. "Ridge regression: Applications to nonorthogonal problems". *Technometrics*, Vol. 12: 69 – 82.

Hoerl, Arthur E., and Kennard, Robert W. 1970b. "Ridge regression: Biased estimation for nonorthogonal problems". *Technometrics*, Vol. 12: 55 – 67.

CHAPTER 12

COMPARISON OF STATISTICAL METHODS

The calculation of biased (S_B) and unbiased (S_N) Simpson diversity scores for age, ethnicity, and gender for NYC departments permit the coefficients to be analyzed with different regression methods. In turn, the analysis of the diversity scores with different regression methods allow for identifying the predictors that are related statistically with each set of diversity coefficients. Because most of the research on age, ethnic, and gender diversity use OLS regression to analyze the relationships amongst a set of predictors and heterogeneity, the statistical analyses of the diversity scores began with OLS regression knowing that the distributions of the scores violated several of the underlying assumptions of the method such linearity, normality, truncation, and multicollinearity. The violation of several of the underlying assumptions of OLS regression provided the basis for undertaking robust, Tobit, quantile, and ridge regression. The statistical findings allow for assessing the performance of OLS regression in relation to the other models in light of the assumption violations.

In this chapter, *horizontal* and *vertical comparisons* of the statistical findings are undertaken. The horizontal comparisons discuss whether the models yield consistent findings with respect to the statistical relationships amongst the predictors and the biased (S_B) and unbiased (S_N) diversity scores for age, ethnicity, and gender. By contrast, the vertical comparisons discuss how the findings of the unbiased (S_N) diversity scores differ to those pertaining to the biased (S_B) coefficients. The discussion begins with the horizontal and vertical comparisons of the findings for age diversity.

Comparison of regression analyses for age diversity

Exhibit 12-1 summarizes the statistical findings of the regression analyses performed to assess the relationships amongst a set of predictors and the biased (S_B) and unbiased (S_N) Simpson diversity scores for age. In Panel A, the findings of the analyses are consistent with respect to the positive statistical relationship amongst Elected and age diversity where NYC departments headed by an elected official have higher levels of age diversity in comparison to departments headed by a nonelected official. With the exception of the insignificant statistical finding obtained by the quantile regression model for SEA, the other regression models yield a significant negative statistical relationship amongst SEA and age diversity, where an increase in the budget allocation for salary expenses is associated with a decrease in the level of age diversity. With respect to Employees, the Tobit regression model yields a significant negative statistical relationship amongst the predictor and age diversity while the other models find an insignificant statistical relationship amongst the predictor and the level of age diversity. Each model shows an insignificant statistical relationship amongst Myos and age diversity where the median years of service within the departments does not increase or decrease the level of age diversity. However, the models yield inconsistent findings for the statistical relationship amongst Mftsal and age diversity. For instance, the OLS, quantile, and ridge regression models yield an insignificant statistical relationship amongst the predictor and age diversity where the median full-time salary does not increase or decrease age diversity. By contrast, the robust and Tobit models find a significant negative statistical relationship amongst Mftsal and age diversity. In regard to Pctunion, the OLS, robust, Tobit, and ridge regression models yield a significant positive statistical relationship amongst the predictor and age diversity. Of the 5 models, the OLS and ridge models find a significant negative statistical relationship amongst Mcluster and age diversity where an increase in the number of persons of color in the workforce is associated with a decrease in the level of age diversity. The models, however, produce inconsistent findings for Mhcluster. For instance, the OLS, Tobit, and ridge models reveal a significant positive statistical relationship amongst the predictor and age diversity, but the robust and quantile models yield an insignificant statistical relationship amongst the predictor and age diversity. With respect to the remaining predictors, the models produce insignificant statistical findings.

The statistical models yield fairly consistent findings for the unbiased (S_N) diversity scores for age (see Exhibit 12-1, Panel B). Each model yields a significant positive statistical relationship amongst Elected and age diversity where the move from a NYC department headed by a nonelected official to one headed by an elected official is associated with an increase in the level of age diversity. The models differ with respect to the statistical relationship amongst Mftsal and age diversity. While the OLS, robust, and ridge models produce an insignificant statistical finding for the predictor and age diversity, the Tobit and quantile models reveal a significant negative statistical relationship amongst the predictor and age diversity where age heterogeneity decreases as Mftsal increases. The models also

Exhibit 12-1 Comparative analysis of findings for age diversity for NYC departments for fiscal year 2019

A. Regression findings for biased (S_{aj}) diversity scores for age

Predictors	OLS Regression β Coefficient	t-statistic		Robust Regression β Coefficient	t-statistic		Tobit Regression β Coefficient	t-statistic		Quantile Regression β Coefficient	t-statistic		Ridge Regression β Coefficient	t-statistic		OLS VIF	RR VIF
Elected	0.0296320 (0.0073853)	3.79	***	0.0267727 (0.00565020)	4.74	***	0.0296632 (0.0068856)	4.08	***	0.0263662 (0.0077143)	3.42	**	0.0226643 (0.0064653)	3.51	**	1.67	1.11
SEA	-0.0238484 (0.0108558)	-2.10	*	-0.0195238 (0.0084027o)	-2.32	**	-0.0238484 (0.0102773)	-2.22	*	-0.0123320 (0.0147463)	-0.90		-0.0210116 (0.0097511)	-2.15	*	1.58	1.10
Employees	0.0000021 (0.0000001)	1.67		0.0000001 (0.0000010)	1.48		0.0000002 (0.0000001)	2.88	***	0.0000001 (0.0000008)	0.17		0.0000002 (0.0000001)	1.59		1.37	0.97
Myos	-0.0007270 (0.0008163)	-0.89		-0.0005524 (0.00063450)	-0.87		-0.0007287 (0.0008083)	-0.90		-0.0005659 (0.0010932)	-0.52		-0.0003190 (0.0006445)	-0.50		2.44	1.32
Mfktal	-0.0000033 (0.0000002)	-1.53		-0.0000004 (0.0000017)	-2.34	*	-0.0000003 (0.0000002)	-2.10	*	-0.0000002 (0.0000002)	-1.11		-0.0000003 (0.0000002)	-1.78		2.03	1.22
Pctunion	0.0420687 (0.0122703)	3.43	**	0.0336151 (0.00944210)	3.56	**	0.0420687 (0.0162382)	2.59	*	0.0428845 (0.0267512)	1.60		0.0346892 (0.0104420)	3.42	**	2.11	1.25
Wcluster	-0.00717590 (0.0053298)	-1.35		-0.0022155 (0.00419980)	-0.50		-0.0071759 (0.0046709)	-1.54		-0.0006026 (0.0130244)	-0.05		-0.0073779 (0.0043200)	-1.71		2.34	1.33
Mcluster	-0.00814650 (0.0028261)	-2.88	**	-0.0024224 (0.0023810)	-1.11		-0.0081465 (0.0041144)	-1.98	*	-0.0041093 (0.0052471)	-0.78		-0.0048844 (0.0018413)	-2.65	*	4.63	1.70
O4Icluster	0.0292210 (0.0026759)	1.09		0.0003157 (0.02047780)	0.15		0.0029221 (0.0022500)	1.30		0.0013487 (0.0039880)	0.34		0.0019106 (0.0021023)	0.91		2.49	1.33
Wscluster	-0.00337570 (0.0048836)	-0.69		-0.0072143 (0.00394540)	-1.83		-0.0033757 (0.0036789)	-0.92		-0.0053318 (0.0097010)	-0.55		-0.0022753 (0.0040609)	-0.56		2.21	1.33
Mscluster	0.0060320 (0.0024680)	0.24		0.0004856 (0.00189810)	0.26		0.0006032 (0.0026612)	0.23		-0.0001180 (0.0090201)	-0.05		0.0005409 (0.0019905)	0.27		2.53	1.43
Whcluster	0.00105660 (0.0018652)	0.57		0.0041461 (0.03306010)	1.09		0.0010566 (0.0010974)	0.96		0.0000261 (0.0157812)	0.00		0.0008766 (0.0016611)	0.53		1.65	1.14
Mhcluster	0.00471180 (0.0017695)	2.66	*	0.0014934 (0.0136690)	1.09		0.0047118 (0.0019388)	2.43	*	0.0026700 (0.0029156)	0.92		0.0026946 (0.0011960)	2.25	*	4.09	1.62
Intercept	0.87740200 (0.0220850)	39.73	***	0.8868285 (0.01695250)	52.31	***	0.877492 (0.0197187)	44.50	***	0.8671696 (0.0359441)	24.75	***				2.40	1.30
$F_{1,50}$	4.76		***	5.91		***	4.20		***	0.27			3.46		**		
R^2	0.52			0.19			-0.16						0.43				
Adjusted R^2	0.41												0.31				
N	72			72			72			72			72				

Chapter 12

B. Regression findings for unbiased (S₀) diversity scores for age

Predictors	OLS Regression β Coefficient	t-statistic		Robust Regression β Coefficient	t-statistic		Tobit Regression β Coefficient	t-statistic		Quantile Regression β Coefficient	t-statistic		Ridge Regression β Coefficient	t-statistic		OLS VIF	RR VIF
Elected	0.0125348 (0.0057782)	2.17	*	0.0141544 (0.0056955)	2.49	*	0.0125348 (0.0055777)	2.25	*	0.0163321 (0.0072712)	2.25	*	0.010017384 (0.0048765)	2.05	*	1.67	1.11
SEA	-0.0104432 (0.0084934)	-1.23		-0.0035481 (0.0083719)	-0.42		-0.0104432 (0.0075953)	-1.37		-0.0148491 (0.0113238)	-1.31		-0.0095863 (0.0073547)	-1.30		1.58	1.10
Employees	0.0000001 (0.0000001)	0.56		0.0000000 (0.0000001)	0.49		0.0000001 (0.0000001)	1.01		0.0000000 (0.0000006)	0.08		0.0000000 (0.0000001)	0.58		1.37	0.97
Myos	-0.0005328 (0.0006387)	-0.83		-0.0007293 (0.0006296)	-1.16		-0.0005328 (0.0007438)	-0.72		-0.0008717 (0.0010468)	-0.83		-0.00027088 (0.004861)	-0.56		2.44	1.32
Mfinal	-0.0000003 (0.0000002)	-1.57		-0.0000003 (0.0000002)	-1.95		-0.0000003 (0.0000001)	-2.23	*	-0.0000004 (0.0000002)	-2.45	*	-0.0000002 (0.0000001)	-1.75		2.03	1.22
Petunion	0.0207722 (0.0096001)	2.16	*	0.0180636 (0.0094628)	1.91		0.0207722 (0.0088883)	2.10	*	0.0141552 (0.0138710)	1.02		0.01670816 (0.0076496)	2.18	*	2.11	1.25
Wcluster	0.0030452 (0.0041700)	0.73		0.0045524 (0.0041103)	1.11		0.0030452 (0.0031660)	0.96		0.0067986 (0.0076578)	0.89		0.0014249 (0.0032583)	0.44		2.34	1.33
Mcluster	-0.0055869 (0.0022111)	-2.53	*	-0.0041274 (0.0021795)	-1.89		-0.0055869 (0.0021419)	-2.61	*	-0.003599 (0.0032666)	-1.10		-0.00333802 (0.0013888)	-2.40	*	4.63	1.70
OMcluster	0.0019535 (0.0020936)	0.93		0.0018670 (0.0020636)	0.90		0.0019535 (0.0017843)	1.09		0.0029294 (0.0025157)	1.16		0.00148479 (0.0015857)	0.85		2.49	1.33
Wixcluster	-0.0035016 (0.0038209)	-0.92		-0.0040953 (0.0037662)	-1.09		-0.0035016 (0.0034698)	-1.01		-0.0044199 (0.0084237)	-0.52		-0.00221627 (0.0036629)	-0.72		2.21	1.33
Mixcluster	-0.0003891 (0.0019309)	-0.20		0.0004643 (0.0019033)	0.24		-0.0003891 (0.0020982)	-0.19		-0.0006863 (0.0020814)	-0.33		-0.00030775 (0.0015013)	-0.20		2.53	1.43
Whcluster	-0.0004047 (0.0014577)	-0.28		-0.0004949 (0.0014369)	-0.34		-0.0004047 (0.0008860)	-0.46		-0.0016051 (0.0106765)	-0.15		-0.00026576 (0.0012544)	-0.21		1.65	1.14
Mhcluster	0.0029747 (0.0013844)	2.15	*	0.0020906 (0.0013646)	1.53		0.0029747 (0.0011453)	2.60	*	0.0018426 (0.0025545)	0.72		0.001615143 (0.0009021)	1.79		4.09	1.62
Intercept	0.8894504 (0.0172790)	51.48	***	0.8927956 (0.0170318)	52.42	***	0.8894504 (0.0140071)	63.50	***	0.9100567 (0.0198685)	45.80	***					
$F_{1,58}$	1.91		*	1.93		*	2.04						1.41			$F_{1,58}$	
R^2	0.30			0.21			-0.07			0.21			0.24			2.40	1.30
Adjusted R^2	0.14												0.07				
N	72			72			72			72			72				

Standard errors are in parentheses. * $p < 0.05$; ** $p < 0.01$; *** $p < 0.001$

differ with respect to the statistical relationship amongst Pctunion and age diversity. For example, the OLS, Tobit, and ridge models yield a significant positive statistical relationship amongst the predictor and age diversity, while the robust and quantile models produce an insignificant statistical relationship amongst the predictor and age diversity. In addition, inconsistent findings are found for Mcluster. On the one hand, the OLS, Tobit, and ridge models produce a significant negative statistical relationship amongst the predictor and age diversity; on the other hand, the robust and quantile models reveal the existence of an insignificant statistical relationship amongst the predictor and the age diversity. The models also produce inconsistent findings for Mhcluster. While the OLS and Tobit models yield a significant positive statistical relationship amongst the predictor and age diversity, the robust, quantile, and ridge models yield an insignificant statistical relationship amongst the predictor and age diversity. Each model produces insignificant statistical findings for the other predictors in the equation.

When the findings are compared vertically for the same regression method, the models produce drastically different results for the biased (S_{AB}) and unbiased (S_{AN}) diversity scores for age. In Panel A, the OLS regression model shows that 5 predictors are related statistically with the level of age diversity when the formula ($S = 1 - \sum p^2$) for calculating biased (S_B) scores is used. When the formula for calculating unbiased (S_N) diversity scores is used, the OLS model produces significant statistical results for 4 of the predictors (see Panel B). In addition, drastically different findings are obtained by the robust regression model for the biased (S_{AB}) and unbiased (S_{AN}) diversity scores for age. For the S_{AB} diversity scores, the robust model yields significant statistical findings for 4 of the predictors (see Panel A). However, the model yields a significant statistical finding for 1 predictor when the analysis is applied to the S_{AN} diversity scores. When comparing the findings produced by the Tobit models, the findings are fairly consistent for each predictor. Similarly, the findings produced by the quantile models are fairly consistent. In regard to the findings obtained by the ridge regression model, the findings differ for the S_{AB} and S_{AN} diversity scores for age. In Panel A, the ridge model yields significant statistical findings for 5 of the predictors; in Panel B, the model produces significant statistical findings for 3 of the predictors.

As stated in previous chapters, the findings produced by each of the statistical methods should be viewed with skepticism because of measurement error and because of moderate levels of multicollinearity amongst the predictors. Measurement error accounts for the differences in the findings between the biased (S_B) and unbiased (S_N) diversity scores. While the S_{AB} scores are incompatible and contain atypical values, the S_{AN} scores overcorrect for the size of the workforce where smaller NYC departments receive higher diversity scores. Furthermore, the S_{AN} scores are increased further for the smaller departments that do not have employment data in each of the 11 age group categories. The measurement error is compounded further due to the clustering of diversity scores where the scores of smaller departments are similar to the scores of larger departments that have employment data for most of the age group categories. The net effect of calculating unbiased (S_N) diversity scores for NYC departments is that the distribution of scores becomes more compact and reduces the variation amongst the scores.

Comparison of regression analyses for ethnic diversity

The regression models produce consistent findings for the level of ethnic diversity that existed in NYC departments in fiscal year 2019 (see Exhibit 12-2) For instance, each regression model found insignificant statistical relationships amongst the predictors and the biased (S_{EB}) diversity scores for ethnicity (see Panel A). Similar statistical findings are obtained for the unbiased (S_{EN}) diversity scores for ethnicity (see Panel B). When the findings are viewed vertically, the finding are consistent for each regression model.

The lack of statistical significance for ethnic diversity may be due to several factors. First, the Simpson diversity index may lack sufficient discriminatory power to detect subtle differences in the level of ethnic diversity in NYC departments. Second, the moderate level of multicollinearity amongst the predictors may obfuscate the existence of a statistical relationship of some of the predictors due to information redundancy in the models. Third, the level of ethnic diversity is indeed the same in each NYC department so that insignificant statistical findings would be obtained not matter which diversity index is used to measure ethnic heterogeneity. Because subsequent companion books apply different diversity indices to the same data, the issues discussed above are addressed more thoroughly.

Exhibit 12-2 Comparative analysis of findings for ethnicity diversity for NYC departments for fiscal year 2019

A. Regression findings for biased (%a) diversity scores for ethnicity

Predictors	OLS Regression β Coefficient	OLS t-statistic	Robust Regression β Coefficient	Robust t-statistic	Tobit Regression β Coefficient	Tobit t-statistic	Quantile Regression β Coefficient	Quantile t-statistic	Ridge Regression β Coefficient	Ridge t-statistic	OLS VIF	RR VIF
Elected	-0.0346973 (0.0288702)	-1.20	-0.0094976 (0.01965210)	-0.48	-0.0346973 (0.0324908)	-1.07	-0.0169477 (0.0228909)	-0.74	-0.0298145 (0.0237597)	-1.25	1.67	1.11
SEA	-0.0548222 (0.0424367)	-1.29	-0.0189735 (0.02922560)	-0.65	-0.0548222 (0.0312798)	-1.75	-0.0195947 (0.0361404)	-0.54	-0.0481989 (0.0358345)	-1.35	1.58	1.10
Employees	0.0000004 (0.0000005)	0.76	0.0000002 (0.00000033)	0.70	0.0000004 (0.0000003)	1.39	0.0000004 (0.0000038)	0.11	0.0000003 (0.0000004)	0.63	1.37	0.97
Myos	-0.0023674 (0.0031912)	-0.74	-0.0041546 (0.00226070)	-1.88	-0.0023674 (0.0022717)	-1.04	-0.0032070 (0.0031529)	-1.02	-0.0020497 (0.0023685)	-0.87	2.44	1.32
Mftsal	-0.0000011 (0.0000008)	-1.25	-0.0000011 (0.00000058)	-1.84	-0.0000011 (0.0000007)	-1.41	-0.0000008 (0.0000006)	-1.47	-0.0000009 (0.0000007)	-1.29	2.03	1.22
Pctunion	-0.0380349 (0.0479660)	-0.79	-0.0057253 (0.03284050)	-0.17	-0.0380349 (0.0367024)	-1.04	-0.0310569 (0.0296550)	-1.05	-0.0243050 (0.0372711)	-0.65	2.11	1.25
Wcluster	-0.0167900 (0.0208348)	-0.81	-0.0123534 (0.01537250)	-0.80	-0.016790 (0.0194294)	-0.86	-0.0195268 (0.0371152)	-0.53	-0.0122774 (0.0158756)	-0.77	2.34	1.33
Mcluster	0.0094895 (0.0110477)	0.86	0.0007930 (0.00758600)	0.10	0.0094895 (0.0115322)	0.82	0.0108832 (0.0185522)	0.59	0.0039674 (0.0067660)	0.59	4.63	1.70
O4Mcluster	0.0066266 (0.0104604)	0.63	0.0098268 (0.00712250)	1.38	0.0066266 (0.0103632)	0.64	0.0109298 (0.0075074)	1.46	0.0046078 (0.0077258)	0.60	2.49	1.33
Wscluster	-0.0101793 (0.0190906)	-0.53	-0.0087620 (0.01372240)	-0.64	-0.0101793 (0.0161960)	-0.63	-0.0098466 (0.0200557)	-0.49	-0.0092437 (0.0149234)	-0.62	2.21	1.33
Mscluster	0.0014905 (0.0096476)	0.15	-0.0035680 (0.00660160)	-0.54	0.0014905 (0.0081020)	0.18	-0.0020092 (0.0082032)	-0.24	0.0018902 (0.0073148)	0.25	2.53	1.43
Whcluster	0.0011866 (0.0072834)	0.16	0.0034325 (0.01328010)	0.26	0.0011866 (0.0053722)	0.22	0.004772 (0.0517627)	0.09	0.0009197 (0.0066117)	0.15	1.65	1.14
Mhcluster	-0.0121854 (0.0069171)	-1.76	-0.0090088 (0.00475420)	-1.89	-0.0121854 (0.0064391)	-1.89	-0.0027869 (0.0089971)	-0.31	-0.0082072 (0.0043952)	-1.87	4.09	1.62
Intercept	0.8507759 (0.0863331)	9.85 ***	0.8379511 (0.05896250)	14.21 ***	0.8507759 (0.0752755)	11.30 ***	0.8143940 (0.0541657)	15.04 ***			2.40	1.30
$F_{(3,58)}$	0.89		1.91		2.49	**	0.13		0.71			
R^2	0.17		0.16						0.14			
Adjusted R^2	-0.02				-0.08				-0.06			
N	72		72		72		72		72			

Chapter 12

B. Regression findings for unbiased (S_u) diversity scores for ethnicity

Predictors	OLS Regression β Coefficient	OLS t-statistic	Robust Regression β Coefficient	Robust t-statistic	Tobit Regression β Coefficient	Tobit t-statistic	Quantile Regression β Coefficient	Quantile t-statistic	Ridge Regression β Coefficient	Ridge t-statistic	OLS VIF	RR VIF
Elected	-0.0482130 (0.0292796)	-1.65	-0.0281521 (0.0190953)	-1.47	-0.048213 (0.0326156)	-1.48	-0.0323222 (0.0205194)	-1.58	-0.04094359 (0.0241700)	-1.69	1.67	1.11
SEA	-0.0455908 (0.0430385)	-1.06	0.0007349 (0.0283975)	0.03	-0.0455908 (0.0327432)	-1.39	-0.0023565 (0.0391128)	-0.06	-0.03944859 (0.0364534)	-1.08	1.58	1.10
Employees	0.0000002 (0.0000005)	0.49	0.0000001 (0.0000003)	0.29	0.0000002 (0.0000003)	0.87	0.0000002 (0.0000040)	0.05	0.0000002 (0.0000004)	0.37	1.37	0.97
Myos	-0.0021419 (0.0032365)	-0.66	-0.0033892 (0.0021442)	-1.58	-0.0021419 (0.0023341)	-0.92	-0.0014971 (0.0032307)	-0.46	-0.00197986 (0.0024094)	-0.82	2.44	1.32
Mfltal	-0.0000010 (0.0000009)	-1.17	-0.0000010 (0.0000006)	-1.81	-0.0000010 (0.0000008)	-1.32	-0.0000003 (0.0000007)	-0.51	-0.0000008 (0.0000007)	-1.18	2.03	1.22
Petunion	-0.0573847 (0.0486462)	-1.18	-0.0247552 (0.0319100)	-0.78	-0.0573847 (0.0393887)	-1.46	-0.0188662 (0.0394500)	-0.48	-0.04048266 (0.0379149)	-1.07	2.11	1.25
Wcluster	-0.0080546 (0.0211302)	-0.38	-0.0055382 (0.0149369)	-0.36	-0.0080546 (0.0203402)	-0.40	-0.0114244 (0.0300816)	-0.38	-0.00470547 (0.0161498)	-0.29	2.34	1.33
Mcluster	0.0125151 (0.0112044)	1.12	0.0082375 (0.0073710)	1.12	0.0125151 (0.0124830)	1.00	0.0230197 (0.0181896)	1.27	0.00580445 (0.0068834)	0.84	4.63	1.70
Ofcluster	0.0054227 (0.0106087)	0.51	0.0075631 (0.0069207)	1.09	0.0054227 (0.0104353)	0.52	0.0018082 (0.0127828)	0.14	0.00384018 (0.0078592)	0.49	2.49	1.33
Wscluster	-0.0108045 (0.0193613)	-0.56	-0.0068724 (0.013336)	-0.52	-0.0108045 (0.016915)	-0.64	-0.0092775 (0.0131471)	-0.70	-0.00962808 (0.0151812)	-0.63	2.21	1.33
Mscluster	0.0005037 (0.0097844)	0.05	-0.0045363 (0.0064146)	-0.71	0.0005037 (0.0083661)	0.06	0.0006814 (0.0054495)	0.13	0.0010617 (0.0074411)	0.14	2.53	1.43
Whcluster	-0.0000665 (0.0073867)	-0.01	0.0012684 (0.0012630)	0.10	-0.0000665 (0.0057181)	-0.01	0.004441 (0.0184942)	0.24	-0.0000709 (0.0062173)	-0.01	1.65	1.14
Mhcluster	-0.0140542 (0.0070152)	-2.00	-0.0106518 (0.0046195)	-3.47 **	-0.0140542 (0.0060294)	-2.03	-0.0082208 (0.0097651)	-0.84	-0.00932862 (0.0044711)	-2.09	4.09	1.62
Intercept	0.8625738 (0.0875573)	9.85 ***	0.8419254 (0.0572919)	14.70 ***	0.8625738 (0.0798638)	10.87 ***	0.759728 (0.0769203)	9.88 ***				
$F_{(1,58)}$	0.92		3.10		1.80						2.40	1.30
R^2	0.17		0.14		-0.08		0.13		0.75			
Adjusted R^2	-0.02								0.13			
N	72		72		72		72		-0.06			
									72			

Standard errors are in parentheses. * $p < 0.05$; ** $p < 0.01$; *** $p < 0.001$

Comparison of regression analyses for gender diversity

The horizontal analysis shows that the regression models yield different findings for gender diversity (see Exhibit 12-3). For the biased diversity scores for gender (S_{GB}), the OLS, Tobit, quantile, and ridge models fail to detect a significant statistical relationship amongst Elected and gender diversity for NYC departments (see Panel A). The robust model, however, shows a significant positive statistical relationship amongst the predictor and gender diversity. With respect to Employees, the OLS, robust, quantile, and ridge models find an insignificant statistical relationship amongst the predictor and gender diversity. By contrast, the Tobit model reveals the existence of a significant inverse statistical relationship amongst the predictor and gender diversity. The models also differ with respect to the statistical relationship amongst Pctunion and gender diversity. Of the 5 regression models, the Tobit models yields a significant inverse statistical relationship amongst Pctunion and gender diversity; the others do not. The findings for Wcluster also differ across the regression models. For instance, a significant inverse statistical relationship is detected by the robust and quantile models, while the OLS, Tobit, and ridge models detect an insignificant statistical relationship amongst the predictor and gender diversity. Each model produces insignificant statistical findings for the other predictors in the equation.

Panel B of Exhibit 12-3 shows that the regression models differ with respect to the statistical findings of the unbiased gender diversity scores (S_{GN}). The OLS and Tobit models yield a significant inverse statistical relationship amongst Elected and gender diversity, while the robust, quantile, and ridge models fail to detect a similar statistical relationship. With respect to the statistical relationship amongst SEA and gender diversity, the Tobi model reveals a significant positive statistical relationship; the other models do not. In addition, the robust and Tobit models reveal a significant inverse statistical relationship amongst Employees and gender diversity, while the OLS, quantile, and ridge models yield insignificant statistical findings. The OLS model finds a significant inverse statistical relationship amongst Pctunion and gender diversity, while the other models do not find a similar statistical relationship. With respect to Wcluster, the OLS and Tobit models show a significant positive statistical relationship amongst the predictor and gender diversity, while the robust, quantile, and ridge models yield insignificant statistical findings for the predictor. The robust model shows a significant positive statistical relationship amongst Mscluster and gender diversity; the other models detect an insignificant statistical relationship

Exhibit 12-3 Comparative analysis of findings for gender diversity for NYC departments for fiscal year 2019

A. Regression findings for biased (b_i) diversity scores for gender

Predictors	OLS Regression β Coefficient	t-statistic	Robust Regression β Coefficient	t-statistic	Tobit Regression β Coefficient	t-statistic	Quantile Regression β Coefficient	t-statistic	Ridge Regression β Coefficient	t-statistic	OLS VIF	RR VIF
Elected	0.0100222 (0.0211684)	0.47	0.0059029 (0.00286070)	2.06 *	0.0112221 (0.0107147)	1.05	0.0095435 (0.0065794)	1.45	0.01282592 (0.01173964)	0.65	1.67	1.11
SEA	-0.0001446 (0.0311158)	0.00	-0.0027584 (0.0420490)	-0.66	-0.0014382 (0.0234270)	-0.06	-0.0081683 (0.0134915)	-0.61	-0.0013079 (0.0262374)	-0.05	1.58	1.10
Employees	-0.0000005 (0.0000004)	-1.37	-0.0000001 (0.0000005)	-1.19	-0.0000006 (0.0000002)	-2.26 *	-0.0000004 (0.0000014)	-0.26	-0.0000005 (0.0000003)	-1.65	1.37	0.97
Myos	-0.0031933 (0.0023399)	-1.36	-0.0003185 (0.00031620)	-1.01	-0.0034428 (0.0028847)	-1.19	0.0003857 (0.0012471)	0.31	-0.00261898 (0.0017342)	-1.51	2.44	1.32
Mftsal	-0.0000006 (0.0000006)	-0.90	-0.0000001 (0.00000008)	-1.21	-0.0000006 (0.0000004)	-1.48	-0.0000001 (0.0000004)	-0.41	-0.0000004 (0.0000005)	-0.90	2.03	1.22
Pctsuman	-0.0618134 (0.0351700)	-1.76	0.0004566 (0.00475280)	0.10	-0.063178 (0.0281994)	-2.24 *	0.0005560 (0.0185088)	0.03	-0.0529181 (0.0272893)	-1.93	2.11	1.25
Wcluster	-0.0087890 (0.0152766)	-0.58	-0.0565638 (0.0206450)	-27.4 ***	-0.0101079 (0.0121165)	-0.83	-0.0329842 (0.0071815)	-4.59 ***	-0.00576895 (0.0116238)	-0.50	2.34	1.33
Mcluster	0.0642241 (0.0081005)	0.52	-0.0008274 (0.00109470)	-0.76	0.005718 (0.0048904)	1.17	-0.0022291 (0.0046673)	-0.48	0.002704647 (0.0049544)	0.55	4.63	1.70
OAcluster	0.091009 (0.0076699)	1.19	0.0012566 (0.0010365)	1.22	0.0095105 (0.0075231)	1.26	-0.0047221 (0.0040130)	-1.18	0.006147975 (0.0056567)	1.09	2.49	1.33
Wscluster	0.012934 (0.019977)	0.88	-0.0021786 (0.00189160)	-1.15	0.013072 (0.0085851)	1.32	0.0027258 (0.0044565)	0.61	0.009588653 (0.0109267)	0.88	2.21	1.33
Mscluster	0.0017878 (0.0070739)	0.25	-0.0001767 (0.00095600)	-0.18	0.0019989 (0.0040525)	0.49	0.0013311 (0.0042314)	0.31	0.002297362 (0.0053558)	0.43	2.53	1.43
Whcluster	-0.0052104 (0.0053404)	-0.98	-0.0008221 (0.00072170)	-1.14	-0.004965 (0.0027544)	-1.8	-0.0025138 (0.0033749)	-0.74	-0.00431068 (0.0044749)	-0.96	1.65	1.14
Mhcluster	-0.0010515 (0.0050718)	-0.21	0.0001115 (0.0006840)	0.16	-0.0008838 (0.0027330)	-0.32	-0.0017136 (0.0024006)	-0.71	-0.00050806 (0.0032181)	-0.16	4.09	1.62
Intercept	0.5560840 (0.0633018)	8.78 ***	0.5130728 (0.0085450)	59.98 ***	0.5579062 (0.0441606)	12.62 ***	0.5062108 (0.0313857)	16.13 ***			2.40	1.30
$F_{(13,58)}$	1.56		149.81		5.40 ***				1.38			
R^2	0.26		0.62		-0.11		0.29		0.48			
Adjusted R^2	0.09								0.23			
N	72		72		71		72		72			

Comparison of Statistical Methods

B. Regression findings for unbiased (S_u) diversity scores for ethnicity

Predictors	OLS Regression β Coefficient	t-statistic		Robust Regression β Coefficient	t-statistic		Tobit Regression β Coefficient	t-statistic		Quantile Regression β Coefficient	t-statistic		Ridge Regression β Coefficient	t-statistic	OLS VIF	RR VIF
Elected	-0.0090903 (0.0026607)	-3.50	**	-0.0017363 (0.0010450)	-1.66		-0.0073641 (0.0019470)	-3.78	***	-0.0047704 (0.0028216)	-1.69		0.004141733 (0.0174310)	0.24	1.67	1.11
SEA	0.0070863 (0.0038229)	1.85		0.0019828 (0.0015361)	1.29		0.0066664 (0.0030664)	2.17	*	0.0040277 (0.0028556)	1.41		0.004797688 (0.0262895)	0.18	1.58	1.10
Employees	-0.0000001 (0.0000000)	-2.02	*	0.0000000 (0.0000000)	-2.06	*	-0.0000000 (0.0000000)	-4.75	***	0.0000000 (0.0000001)	-0.60		-0.0000006 (0.0000003)	-1.87	1.37	0.97
Myos	0.0001202 (0.0002875)	0.42		0.0002270 (0.0001155)	1.96		0.0001017 (0.0001846)	0.55		0.0003627 (0.0002585)	1.40		-0.00256274 (0.0017376)	-1.47	2.44	1.32
Mbtsai	0.0000000 (0.0000001)	0.55		0.0000000 (0.0000000)	-0.82		0.0000000 (0.0000000)	0.83		0.0000000 (0.0000000)	-0.50		-0.0000004 (0.0000005)	-0.81	2.03	1.22
Pctunion	-0.0127857 (0.0043210)	-2.96	**	-0.0029348 (0.0017363)	-1.69		-0.0090207 (0.0044288)	-2.04	*	-0.010149 (0.0082155)	-1.24		-0.06348764 (0.0273435)	-2.32	2.11	1.25
Wcluster	0.0060758 (0.0018769)	3.24	**	0.0006207 (0.0007542)	0.82		0.0048519 (0.0014269)	3.40	**	0.0011474 (0.0036753)	0.31		-0.00118622 (0.0116469)	-0.10	2.34	1.33
Mcluster	0.0017751 (0.0009952)	1.78		-0.0007481 (0.0003999)	-1.87		0.0005669 (0.0008667)	0.65		-0.0003088 (0.0008349)	-0.37		0.003702472 (0.0049642)	0.75	4.63	1.70
O&hcluster	-0.0006505 (0.0009423)	-0.69		-0.0000789 (0.0003786)	-0.21		-0.0004253 (0.0007686)	-0.55		-0.0004831 (0.0010076)	-0.48		0.005731849 (0.0056679)	1.01	2.49	1.33
Wscluster	-0.0002454 (0.0017198)	-0.14		0.0011797 (0.0006910)	1.71		0.0004035 (0.0010564)	0.38		0.001809 (0.0021535)	0.84		0.009663418 (0.0109484)	0.88	2.21	1.33
Mscluster	-0.0006858 (0.0008691)	-0.79		0.0010303 (0.0003492)	2.95	**	-0.0001281 (0.0005372)	-0.24		0.0004686 (0.0010154)	0.46		0.00180502 (0.0055664)	0.34	2.53	1.43
Whcluster	-0.0008539 (0.0006561)	-1.30		-0.0003292 (0.0002636)	-1.25		-0.0007245 (0.0002707)	-2.68	*	-0.0004102 (0.0004812)	-0.08		-0.00493761 (0.0044838)	-1.10	1.65	1.14
Mhcluster	-0.0011117 (0.0006231)	-1.78		-0.0002446 (0.0002594)	-0.98		-0.0006232 (0.0004622)	-1.35		-0.0000891 (0.0003903)	-0.23		-0.00117091 (0.0032245)	-0.36	4.09	1.62
Intercept	0.4827186 (0.0077772)	62.07	***	0.4793348 (0.0031251)	153.38	***	0.4797674 (0.0061570)	77.92	***	0.4834346 (0.0088943)	54.35	***				
$F_{1,58}$	4.54		***	2.58			4.68		***	0.17			$F_{1,58}$	0.13	2.40	1.30
R^2	0.50			0.20			-0.11							0.51		
Adjusted R^2	0.39													0.26		
N	72			72			68			72				72		

Standard errors are in parentheses. * p < 0.05, ** p < 0.01, *** p < 0.001

amongst the predictor and gender diversity. With respect to the statistical significance of Whcluster, the Tobit model finds a significant negative statistical relationship amongst the predictor and gender diversity, while the other models detect an insignificant statistical relationship. As Panel B summarizes, the models produce similar findings for the other predictors.

The vertical analysis for gender diversity indicates that each regression model produces inconsistent statistical findings for several of the variables. When the OLS regression findings for the biased (S_B) and unbiased (S_N) diversity scores for gender are compared, the analysis of the S_{GN} scores produces significant statistical findings for Elected, PCTunion, and Wcluster (see Panel B). The OLS model for the S_{GB} scores yields insignificant statistical findings for each predictor (see Panel A). Panel B also shows that the robust regression analysis produces inconsistent findings for the S_{GB} and S_{GN} scores. Specifically, the robust model finds a significant positive statistical relationship amongst Elected and the S_{GB} scores and a significant inverse statistical relationship amongst Wcluster and the S_{GB} scores. When the robust regression model is performed for the S_{GN} scores, the findings reveal a significant negative statistical relationship amongst SEA and gender diversity and a significant positive statistical relationship amongst Mscluster and gender diversity. In addition, the Tobit regression analysis produces inconsistent findings for the S_{GB} and S_{GN} scores. For example, the Tobit model detects a significant inverse statistical relationship amongst Employees and Pctunion and the S_{GB} scores. When the same Tobit analysis is performed on the S_{GN} scores, the findings show significant statistical relationships amongst Elected, SEA, Employees, Wcluster, and Whcluster and the S_{GN} scores. With the exception of the significant finding for Wcluster, the quantile model produces insignificant statistical findings for each predictor. Lastly, the ridge regression model produces consistent findings for the S_{GB} and S_{GN} scores.

Measurement error accounts for the differences in the statistical findings. The biased (S_B) diversity scores for gender are statistically lower and contain less variation in comparison to the unbiased (S_N) scores. In addition, there are fewer atypical scores in the distribution of the S_{GB} scores in comparison to distribution of S_{GN} scores. The robust and Tobit regression models adjusted for the atypical S_{GN} scores and detected more significant statistical relationships amongst the predictors and gender diversity. The quantile regression model fails to detect any significant statistical relationships amongst the predictors and the S_{GB} and S_{GN} scores due its focus on the median and due to being influence less by atypical values. Because the quantile analysis is restricted to the 50th percentile, it is unknown whether significant statistical relationships exist at other percentiles along the distributions of the S_{GB} and S_{GN} scores. *Assessing Organizational Diversity with Quantile Analysis* focuses exclusively on the application of quantile regression and addresses the issue more thoroughly.

Summary

The comparative analysis of the regression findings reveals several important methodological and statistical issues in regard to the measurement and analysis of age, ethnic, and gender diversity. Methodologically, the selection of the analytical method to analyze diversity scores should be based on the statistical properties of the diversity scores. In the case of the Simpson diversity scores calculated for age, ethnicity, and gender for NYC departments, the distributions of the scores are truncated due to the number of categories used to classify employees based on their demographic and social characteristics. The truncation of the diversity scores from 0 to $\frac{n-1}{n}$ require that regression methods for truncated data be used to analyze the statistical relationships amongst predictors and the diversity scores obtained with the application of the Simpson diversity index. Statistically, OLS regression analysis should be avoided when the distribution of diversity scores is negatively skewed and nonnormal. When the distribution of diversity scores is truncated, skewed, and nonnormal, the regression coefficients obtained with OLS regression are suspect. In addition, the clustering of values along the continuum of the distribution of diversity scores leads to a lack of linearity. The use of the formula to calculate unbiased (S_N) diversity scores reduces the variability in the distributions of the diversity scores and contributes further to a lack of linearity amongst the predictors and the measures of heterogeneity.

The statistical properties of the Simpson diversity scores should be considered when using OLS regression to construct a causal model for age, ethnic, or gender diversity. As will be discussed in the next chapter, the underlying assumptions of OLS regression should be satisfied to develop a reliable and valid causal statistical model. Based on the comparative analysis of the statistical findings undertaking in this chapter, OLS and robust regression will be used to develop a causal model for age and ethnic diversity. Although Tobit regression is the most appropriate method to use based on the truncation of the distributions of the diversity scores, several of the mediating variables that are used to construct the causal model are quantitative continuous variables that have no minimum or maximum limits.

Key words

Horizontal comparison (analysis) refers to the comparison of findings produced by different types of methods.

Vertical comparison (analysis) refers to the comparison of findings produced by the same method for different or similar measures.

CHAPTER 13

PATH ANALYSIS OF ORGANIZATIONAL DIVERSITY

During the past 15 or so years, *causal modeling* methods have been applied to the study of organizational diversity (e.g., Boehm, Kunze, and Bruch, 2014; Buse, Bernstein, and Bilimoria, 2016; Ellwart, Bündgens, and Rack, 2013; Guajardo, 2014; Gazley, Chang, and Bingham, 2010; Kearney, Gebert, and Voelpel, 2009; Li, Gong, Burmeister, Wang, Alterman, Alonso, and Robinson, 2021; Pitts, 2006). In some studies, demographic diversity serves as an *exogenous variable* that influences an organizational outcome (e.g., Boehm, Kunze, and Bruch, 2014; Ellwart, Bündgens, and Rack, 2013; Gazley, Chang, and Bingham, 2010; Kearney, Gebert, and Voelpel, 2009; Li, Gong, Burmeister, Wang, Alterman, Alonso, and Robinson, 2021; Moon and Christensen, 2020; Pitts, 2005). Several studies treat demographic diversity as a *mediating variable* of an organizational outcome (e.g., Guajardo, 2014; Pitts, 2006). In most of the studies, demographic diversity serves as an *endogenous variable* that is influenced by exogenous and mediating variables. The position taken in this book is that demographic (or social) diversity is an intervening (or mediating) variable that influences organizational performance. For purposes of this chapter, however, age and gender diversity are treated as endogenous variables. *Assessing Organizational Diversity with Structural Equation Modeling* treats age, ethnic, and gender diversity as intervening variables of organizational performance.

This chapter applies *path analysis* to develop a causal model for age and gender diversity for NYC departments based on the employment data that they reported for fiscal year 2019. In developing the causal models, diversity scores for age and gender serve as endogenous variables. OLS and robust regression are used to perform the statistical analyses. After performing the statistical analyses, the findings are used to diagram the direct and indirect relationships of the significant statistical exogenous and mediating variables with age and gender diversity. Throughout the chapter, the differences between the OLS and robust regression findings are discussed and compared.

Prior to undertaking the statistical analyses, an overview of the talent acquisition process (TAP) used by most nonprofit, private, and public organizations is presented. The TAP framework is used to construct a theoretical causal model of the direct and indirect effects of the exogenous and mediating variables. After discussing the causal model, path analysis is discussed. To undertake the path analysis, a Pearson pairwise correlation analysis is performed to identify the exogenous variables that are related statistically with the endogenous variables. The correlation matrix also serves to identify the exogenous variables that are related statistically with the mediating variables. OLS and robust regression analyses performed in previous chapters are used to identify the exogenous variables as well.

Overview of talent acquisition

Exhibit 13-1 diagrams how position vacancies and the number of new hires impact the level of demographic (or social) diversity in the workforce of nonprofit, private, and public organizations. As Exhibit 13-1 shows, an organization's workforce has a preexisting level of diversity in terms of age, ethnicity, gender, and other demographic characteristics. The preexisting level of demographic diversity changes as employees leave the workforce and as employees are added the workforce to fill position vacancies (e.g., Abzug, 2017; Akingbola, 2015; Guajardo, 2015; Pitts, 2006; Pynes, 2013). For instance, when employees retire or resign from an organization, the level of demographic diversity changes in terms of age, ethnicity, and gender simultaneously as positions become vacant. Because an organization's workforce is always changing, the level of demographic diversity changes continuously.

During times of organizational growth, new positions are added to the workforce. The new positions allow an organization to change the level of diversity. When organizations face an economic downturn or a financial hardship, they often furlough employees to lessen the fiscal impact on the organization. In turn, employee layoffs (or terminations) change an organization's level of diversity in regard to age, ethnicity, gender, or other demographic characteristics. In short, employee separations and the acquisition of new employees have *direct* and *indirect effects* on an organization's level of demographic diversity.

Exhibit 13-1 Talent acquisition and organizational diversity

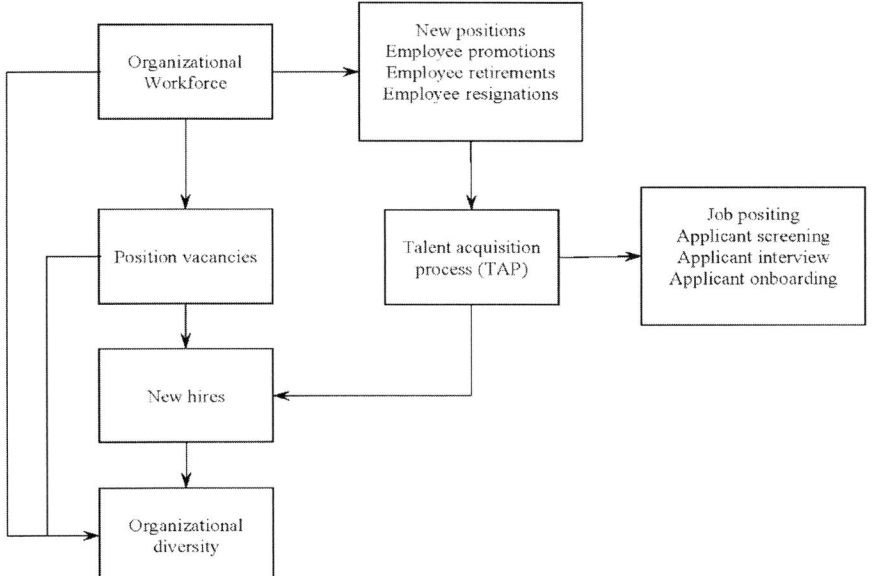

An organization's talent acquisition process (TAP) is triggered by the creation of new positions or by position vacancies due to employee separations. First, the units with position vacancies obtain approval to fill the vacancies from either the finance or talent acquisition department (TAD). Upon obtaining approval, the unit and TAD staffs work collaboratively to create advertisements for the vacant positions. After the job advertisements are created, TAD posts the job advertisements for the new and vacant positions. Once the job postings are closed, TAD and unit staff review the pool of applicants with respect to work experience and employment suitability. In so doing, they identify applicants that meet the job requirements. After the screening phase is completed, initial (or screening) interviews are scheduled and held with the applicants that were identified during the screening phase. In selecting specific applicants for an initial (or screening) interview, the pool of qualified applicants is reduced further. At the end of the applicant screening process, TAD and unit staffs have identified the applicants that will be invited for in-person or online interviews. At the conclusion of the interviewing phase, the applicants that are selected for employment are extended a job offer. The applicants that accept the job offer are then hired and onboarded into the workforce.

As stated above, the number of new hires has a direct effect on the level of diversity of an organization's workforce. When men or women are hired at different rates, the level of gender diversity changes negatively or positively. The age composition of the new hires also has a direct effect on the level of age diversity that exists in the workforce. In addition, when persons of color or Whites are hired at different rates, the level of ethnic diversity changes negatively or positively. The same is true for other forms and types of demographic and social diversity.

In Exhibit 13-1, an organization's workforce has several dimensions that serve as exogenous variables. For instance, organizational factors such as the type of organization and the size of the workforce have direct and indirect effects on the level of diversity. Financial factors such as the size of the operating budget and employment compensation also have direct and indirect effects on the level of diversity. Lastly, human capital factors such as the demographic composition of the workforce, the years of service of employees, and the percent of the workforce that is unionized have direct and indirect effects on the level of diversity.

Employee turnover and the number of new hires also have direct and indirect effects on the level of diversity. With respect to the indirect effects of the exogenous organizational variables, employment separation serves as a mediating variable which either increases or decreases the level of diversity. Similarly, the number of new hires is a mediating variable in terms of indirect effects of the organizational factors. The number of new hires also mediates the indirect effects of workforce turnover in so far as increasing or decreasing the level of diversity.

In Exhibit 13-1, the various types of diversity such as age, ethnicity, and gender serve as endogenous variables. In organizations, diversity is a function and product of the demographic and social composition of employees in the workforce. Stated simply, the levels of the different forms and types of diversity in an organization fluctuate concomitantly with demographic and social changes that occur in the workforce.

Theoretical causal model of age, ethnic, and gender diversity

Based on Exhibit 13-1 and on prior research (e.g., Abzug, 2017; Akingbola, 2015; Guajardo, 2015; Pitts, 2006; Pynes, 2013), Exhibit 13-2 provides a theoretical causal model that is based on the employee data reported by NYC departments for fiscal year 2019. Organizational factors should have a positive direct effect on organizational turnover, on the number of new hires, and on organizational diversity. For instance, departments headed by elected officials should have higher rates of employee turnover in comparison to departments headed by nonelected officials. The reason is that elected officials in NYC serve a 4-year term, offer little long-term job security to employees, and have greater levels of turnover due to employees transferring to other departments or obtaining more secure jobs in the private sector. With respect to the direct effect on the number of new hires, departments headed by elected officials generally have positions where employees are appointed to job positions or where they serve as at-will employees so that their employment is subject to termination at any time. In addition, the departments headed by elected officials generally have more positions that are exempt from civil service requirements and that are not subject to collective bargaining which facilitates hiring new employees at a faster rate in comparison to departments headed by nonelected officials. With respect to the direct effect on organizational diversity, elected officials generally hire individuals within their districts that possess the demographic and social characteristics that are important to them. By contrast, nonelected officials heading NYC departments generally have less discretion in hiring applicants that possess demographic characteristics that they view as important for employment.

Financial factors should have a negative direct effect on turnover and on the number of new hires but should have a positive effect on organizational diversity (see Exhibit 13-2). NYC departments with larger budget allocations for salary expenses should have less turnover in comparison to departments with fewer financial resources for salary expenses. The reason is that departments with larger allocations dedicated to salary expenses have greater financial resources to offer merit increases and to offer greater economic security to employees. In terms of the negative direct effect on the number of new hires, NYC departments with larger allocations for salary expenses should have fewer new employees due to having less workforce turnover in comparison to departments with smaller budget allocations for salary expenses. With respect to the positive direct effect on diversity, departments with larger allocations for salary expenses have more stable workforces so that their preexisting level of diversity increases in comparison to departments with fewer financial resources allocated to salary expenses.

Exhibit 13-2 Theoretical causal model for age, ethnic, and gender diversity for the NYC departments

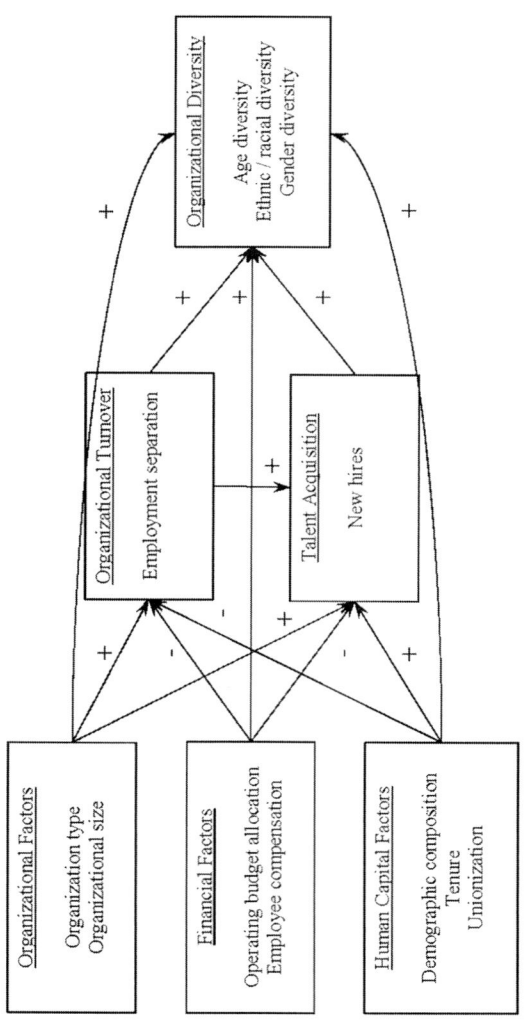

Employee compensation should have a negative direct effect on turnover and on the number of new hires but should have a positive direct effect on organizational diversity (see Exhibit 13-2). Because NYC departments with higher median full-time salaries have workforces with greater economic security in comparison to departments with lower median full-time salaries, they have lower rates of employee turnover. In turn, the lower rate of employee turnover in these departments reduces the number of new hires entering the workforces. With respect to the positive effect on organizational diversity, NYC departments with higher median full-time salaries have gains in the level of organizational diversity in comparison to departments with lower levels of compensation due to having the ability to keep and attract employees with different demographic characteristics.

Human capital factors should have a negative direct effect on employee turnover but should have a positive effect on the number of new hires and on organizational diversity (see Exhibit 13-2). For NYC departments, the preexisting demographic composition of the workforee should provide an healthy work environment where there are few retirements and resignations. Specifically, NYC departments with more demographically heterogenous workforces should have lower rates of employee turnover in comparison to departments with less demographically heterogenous workforces. The reason is that more demographically heterogenous departments should have workplace environments where employees with different demographic characteristics are productive and have a sense of belonging. Conversely, the demographic composition of NYC departments should have a positive direct effect on the number of new hires. NYC departments with more heterogenous workforces are more likely to hire employees with different demographic characteristics in comparison to departments with more demographically homogenous workforces. The demographic composition of NYC departments also increases the level of demographic diversity. For instance, an increase in the number of employees under the age of 40 should increase the level of age diversity in NYC departments. Similarly, an increase of employees from multiple ethnic groups should increase the level of ethnic diversity.

Employee tenure should have a negative direct effect on turnover and should have a positive effect on the number of new hires and on organizational diversity (see Exhibit 13-2). NYC departments with workforces where employees have more years of service should have lower rates of retirements and resignations in comparison to departments where employees have fewer years of service. The reason is that employees with greater years of service are less likely to terminate their employment prematurely because they are vested in the department, have an established career, and have an established social network within and without the department. By contrast, employees with fewer years of service are more apt to resign because they do not have a vested interest or a defined career path in the department. With respect to the positive direct effect on the number of new hires, NYC departments with employees with greater years of service should have an increase in the number of new hires. The reason for this is that departments with employees with greater tenure hire applicants that aspire to establish a career with the department. In terms of the positive direct effect on organizational diversity, departments with employees with greater years of service may increase the level of diversity in the workforce. They do so in terms of age, ethnic, gender, and other forms of diversity.

The level of unionization in NYC departments should have a negative direct effect on turnover but should have a positive direct effect on the number of new hires and on the level of organizational diversity (see Exhibit 13-2). Departments with a greater percent of employees belonging to a collective bargaining unit should have lower rates of employee turnover. Because unions offer job security to their members, employees with collective bargaining representation are less likely to retire prematurely and are less likely to resign in comparison to employees holding nonunion jobs. As such, departments with workforces with more unionized employees should have lower employee turnover. Conversely, employee turnover would be greater in the departments with fewer unionized employees due to a lack of adequate job security. In addition, unionization should have a positive effect on the number of new hires because union representatives have a vested interest in expanding union membership and in expanding political power. Concomitant with increasing union membership, unionization should increase the level of organizational diversity due to increasing the demographic composition of the workforce.

As illustrated in Exhibit 13-2, employee turnover should have a positive direct effect on the number of new hires and on the level of organizational diversity. Turnover provides organizations with opportunities to hire new employees with different demographic (or social) characteristics. When they do so, they change the level of age, ethnic, gender, and other forms of diversity that exist in the workforce simultaneously. For instance, when NYC departments fill position vacancies with employees under or over the age of 40, they change the level of age diversity. As NYC departments fill vacancies with employees from different ethnic groups, they also change the level of ethnic diversity. In terms of the positive effect of the number of new hires, NYC departments with higher rates of turnover have more positions to fill. As such, they need to hire numerous new employees to fill the job vacancies. If they do not do so, they face the possibility of not filling some of the vacant positions within the fiscal year.

As a mediating variable, employee turnover affects the indirect relationships of exogenous variables on the level of organizational diversity (see Exhibit 13-2). Briefly, turnover adds to the positive effect that organizational factors should have on workforce diversity. More precisely, organizational type and size should have a positive indirect effect on workforce diversity. Turnover also would add to the positive effect that organizational factors should have on the number of new hires. As such, organizational type and size would have a positive indirect effect on the number of new hires. On the one hand, turnover would increase the negative effect that financial and human capital factors should have on the level of organizational diversity. In the case of the financial factors, employee compensation and the percent of the operating budget allocated to salary expenses would have a negative indirect effect on the level of organizational diversity. With respect to the human capital factors, the demographic composition of the workforce, the degree of employee tenure, and the percent of the workforce that is unionized would have negative indirect effects on the level of organizational diversity.

The number of new hires should have a positive direct effect on the level of organizational diversity (see Exhibit 13-2). As organizations hire new employees with different demographic and social characteristics, the level of organizational diversity increases. In the case of NYC departments, the level of organizational diversity should increase as new hires replace those that retired or resigned from their full-time positions. For instance, the level of age diversity should increase as individuals under the age of 40 enter the workforce. Ethnic diversity should also increase as more applicants from different racial backgrounds are hired. Departments with workforces composed predominantly of men (or women) should experience an increase in the level of gender diversity.

As a mediating variable, the number of new hires mediates the indirect relationship of employee turnover and of the exogenous variables (see Exhibit 13-2). First, the number of new hires adds to the positive effect that turnover has on the level of organizational diversity by providing for a positive indirect effect amongst the endogenous variables and organizational diversity. In addition, the number of new hires provides for a positive indirect effect amongst organizational factors and workforce diversity. For example, the number of new hires adds to the positive effect that organization type and size should have on the level of organizational diversity. The variable also adds to the positive effect that human capital factors should have on the level of organizational diversity. As Exhibit 13-2 shows, the number of new hires provides for positive indirect effects amongst the level of demographic composition, years of service (tenure), and the percent of the workforce that is unionized on the level of organizational diversity. Lastly, the variable adds to the negative effect that financial factors should have on the level of organizational diversity by providing for negative indirect effects amongst employee compensation and the percent of the operating budget allocated to salary expenses.

Constructing a testable causal model for NYC departments

Although the theoretical causal model presented in Exhibit 13-2 illustrates the direct and indirect effects of the exogenous and mediating variables on the level of organizational diversity, many of the hypothesized direct and indirect effects discussed above are insignificant statistically. The Pearson pairwise correlation analysis presented in Chapter 7 reveals that several of the exogenous variables have insignificant statistical relationships with the mediating variables, which suggests that those variables should have an insignificant statistical indirect effect on the level of diversity. In addition, the OLS, robust, Tobit, quantile, and ridge regression analyses presented in previous chapters found insignificant statistical relationships amongst several of the exogenous variables and the diversity scores for age, ethnicity, and gender, which indicates that those variables have insignificant statistical direct effects on the level of demographic diversity. The findings of the statistical analyses undertaken in previous chapters help to construct causal models with exogenous and mediating variables that are likely to have significant statistical direct and indirect effects on organizational diversity.

Exhibit 13-3 summarizes the Pearson pairwise correlation analysis undertaken for the exogenous and mediating variables discussed above. Elected is related positively with the biased diversity score for gender (S_{GB}), suggesting that the exogenous variable has a positive direct effect on the level of gender diversity. However, Employees is related negatively with S_{GB}, suggesting that the exogenous variable has a negative direct effect on the level of gender diversity. Similarly, Myos is related negatively with S_{GB}. Pctunion also is related negatively with S_{GB}. The other exogenous variables have insignificant statistical relationships with S_{GB}.

Exhibit 13-3 Pearson correlation matrix for independent variables and diversity scores

	Elected	SEA	Employees	Myos	Mfisal	Petunion	Wcluster	Mcluster	O40cluster	Wscluster	Mscluster	Wbcluster	Mbcluster	H_AB	H_AU	H_EB	H_EU	H_BB	H_BU	H_SCB	H_QCU
Elected	1.00																				
SEA	0.391 ***	1.00																			
Employees	-0.119	-0.021	1.00																		
Myos	-0.200	-0.118	0.144	1.00																	
Mfisal	-0.068	0.196	-0.029	0.168	1.00																
Petunion	-0.449 ***	-0.316 **	0.250 *	0.281 *	-0.398 ***	1.00															
Wcluster	0.024	-0.069	0.287 *	0.077	-0.172	-0.029	1.00														
Mcluster	-0.226	-0.381 **	0.019	0.085	-0.363 **	0.346 **	0.209	1.00													
O40cluster	-0.228	-0.239 *	-0.054	0.703 ***	0.205	0.143	0.147	0.036	1.00												
Wscluster	0.155	-0.104	0.217	-0.131	-0.295 *	0.005	0.650 ***	0.142	-0.053	1.00											
Mscluster	-0.044	-0.318 **	-0.013	0.022	-0.493 ***	0.266 *	0.118	0.710 ***	0.012	0.102	1.00										
Wbcluster	-0.007	-0.199	0.078	0.075	-0.152	0.063	0.519 ***	0.047	0.200	0.513 ***	0.017	1.00									
Mbcluster	-0.243	-0.433 ***	0.006	0.146	-0.270 *	0.331 **	0.118	0.850 ***	0.072	0.084	0.653 ***	0.005	1.00								
H_AB	0.168	-0.209	0.131	0.016	-0.374 **	0.391 ***	-0.171	0.023	-0.049	-0.014	0.216	0.022	0.184	1.00							
H_AU	0.175	-0.176	0.115	-0.001	-0.378 **	0.359 **	-0.126	-0.006	-0.060	0.001	0.198	0.023	0.161	0.987 ***	1.00						
H_EB	-0.128	-0.162	0.001	-0.168	-0.142	0.029	-0.105	-0.038	-0.061	-0.084	0.020	0.028	-0.115	0.044	0.020	1.00					
H_EU	-0.147	-0.118	-0.023	-0.183	-0.098	-0.039	-0.055	-0.047	-0.068	-0.076	-0.015	0.023	-0.147	-0.101	-0.109	0.985 ***	1.00				
H_BB	0.222	0.044	-0.296 *	-0.264 *	-0.090	-0.304 **	-0.023	0.045	-0.070	0.081	0.102	-0.079	0.007	0.040	0.062	0.278 *	0.282 *	1.00			
H_BU	0.199	0.089	-0.314 **	-0.273	-0.042	-0.368 **	0.026	0.029	-0.073	0.087	0.061	-0.081	-0.029	-0.107	-0.068	0.255 *	0.289 *	0.984 ***	1.00		
H_SCB	0.089	-0.217	-0.004	-0.170	-0.347 **	0.1736	-0.1775	0.004	-0.0883	-0.037	0.176	0.008	0.045	0.662 ***	0.645 ***	0.725 ***	0.627 ***	0.485 ***	0.374 *	1.00	
H_QCU	0.067	-0.159	-0.054	-0.224	-0.310 **	0.062	-0.106	-0.027	-0.109	-0.024	0.128	0.002	-0.019	0.480 ***	0.495 ***	0.802 ***	0.747 ***	0.572 ***	0.505 ***	0.959 ***	1.00

Exogenous Variables: Elected, SEA, Employees, Myos, Mfisal, Petunion, Wcluster, Mcluster, O40cluster
Mediating Variables: Wscluster, Mscluster, Wbcluster, Mbcluster
Dependent Variables: H_AB, H_AU, H_EB, H_EU, H_BB, H_BU, H_SCB, H_QCU

* p < 0.05; p < 0.01; p < 0.001

With respect to the statistical relationships amongst the exogenous variables and the biased diversity scores for age (S_{AB}), Exhibit 13-3 shows several significant statistical findings. First, a negative statistical relationship exists amongst SEA and S_{AB}, where SEA should have a negative direct effect on S_{AB}. Second, Mftsal is related negatively with S_{AB} and should have a negative direct effect on the level of age diversity. Third, Pctunion is related positively with S_{AB} and should have a positive direct effect on the level of age diversity. Lastly, insignificant statistical findings are obtained for the other exogenous variables.

The Pearson pairwise correlation analysis also shows insignificant statistical findings for the mediating variables (see Exhibit 13-3). For instance, Wscluster has an insignificant statistical relationship with the biased diversity scores for age (S_{AB}) and gender (S_{GB}), indicating the absence of direct effects on the level of age and gender diversity. Whcluster also has an insignificant statistical relationship with S_{AB} and S_{GB}. Similar insignificant statistical findings exist for the other mediating variables.

Several of the exogenous variables are related statistically with the mediating variables (see Exhibit 13-3). For example, SEA is related negatively with Mscluster and Mhcluster. However, it is unclear whether SEA has an indict effect on the level of age and gender diversity because the Pearson pairwise correlation analysis examines the association amongst two variables at a time. Mftsal is related negatively with Mscluster and Mhcluster, but it is unclear whether Mftsal has an indirect effect on age and gender diversity. In addition, Pctunion is related positively with Mscluster and Mhcluster. However, it is unclear whether Pctunion has indirect effects on age and gender diversity. The correlation analysis also shows a positive relationship amongst Wscluster and Whcluster and amongst Mscluster and Mhcluster, suggesting that positive direct effects amongst the pairs of mediating variables.

Exhibit 13-4 presents the OLS regression findings for age and gender diversity. The findings indicate that Elected is related positively with age diversity (S_{AB}). Pctunion also is related positively with S_{AB}. In Exhibit 13-4, Mhcluster is an exogenous variable rather than a mediating variable and is related positively with S_{AB}. SEA is related negatively with age diversity. Mcluster is related negatively with S_{AB} as well. With respect to the findings for gender diversity, Exhibit 13-4 shows insignificant statistical relationships amongst the predictors and S_{AB}.

Path Analysis of Organizational Diversity

Exhibit 13-4 OLS regression findings for age and gender diversity for NYC departments for fiscal year 2019

Predictors	Age Diversity (S_{AB})		Gender Diversity (S_{GB})		VIF
	β Coefficient	t-statistic	β Coefficient	t-statistic	
Elected	0.02796320 (0.0073853)	3.79 ***	0.0100222 (0.0211684)	0.47	1.67
SEA	-0.02284840 (0.0108558)	-2.10 *	-0.0001446 (0.0311158)	0.00	1.58
Employees	0.00000021 (0.00000001)	1.67	-0.0000005 (0.0000004)	-1.37	1.37
Myos	-0.00072870 (0.0008163)	-0.89	-0.0031933 (0.0023399)	-1.36	2.44
Mftsal	-0.00000033 (0.0000002)	-1.53	-0.0000006 (0.0000006)	-0.90	2.03
Pctunion	0.04206870 (0.0122703)	3.43 **	-0.0618134 (0.0351700)	-1.76	2.11
Wcluster	-0.00717590 (0.0053298)	-1.35	-0.0087890 (0.0152766)	-0.58	2.34
Mcluster	-0.00814650 (0.0028261)	-2.88 **	0.0042241 (0.0081005)	0.52	4.63
O40cluster	0.00292210 (0.0026759)	1.09	0.0091009 (0.0076699)	1.19	2.49
Wscluster	-0.00337570 (0.0048836)	-0.69	0.0122934 (0.0139977)	0.88	2.21
Mscluster	0.00060320 (0.0024680)	0.24	0.0017878 (0.0070739)	0.25	2.53

Chapter 13

Whcluster	0.00105660	0.57	-0.0052104	-0.98	1.65
	(0.0018632)		(0.0053404)		
Mhcluster	0.00471180	2.66 *	-0.0010515	-0.21	4.09
	(0.0017695)		(0.0050718)		
Intercept	0.87749200	39.73 ***	0.5560840	8.78 ***	
	(0.0220850)		(0.0633018)		
$F_{13,58}$	4.76 ***		1.56		2.40
R^2	0.52		0.26		
Adjusted R^2	0.41		0.09		
N	72		72		

Standard errors are in parentheses. * $p < 0.05$; ** $p < 0.01$; *** $p < 0.001$

Because robust regression adjusts for atypical low and high scores, slightly different statistical findings are obtained for the exogenous variables (see Exhibit 13-5). Elected is related positively with S_{AB}. Pctunion also is related positively with S_{AB}. Both SEA and Mftsal are related negatively with S_{AB}. However, Mcluster has an insignificant statistical relationship with S_{AB}. The findings also show that Elected is related positively with gender diversity (S_{GB}). By contrast, Wcluster is related negatively with S_{GB}.

Based on the Pearson pairwise correlation and regression analyses discussed above, the causal model for age diversity consists of 5 exogenous variables and 2 mediating variable (see Exhibit 13-6). Elected is hypothesized to have a positive direct effect on age diversity (S_{AB}) and have no indirect effects on S_{AB}. SEA and Mftsal are hypothesized to have positive or negative direct effects on S_{AB} and negative indirect effects on S_{AB} mediated by Mscluster and Mhcluster. In addition, SEA and Mftsal are hypothesized to have negative direct effects on Mscluster and Mhcluster. Mcluster and Pctunion are hypothesized to have positive direct effects on S_{AB}. These exogenous variables are hypothesized to have positive direct effects on Mscluster and Mhcluster. When Mhcluster serves as a mediating variable, Mcluster and Pctunion should have positive indirect effects on S_{AB}. Mcluster is hypothesized to have a positive effect on S_{AB}.

The causal model for gender diversity consists of 7 exogenous variables and 2 mediating variables (see Exhibit 13-7). Elected and Employees are hypothesized to have positive direct effects on gender diversity (S_{GB}) and have no indirect effects on S_{GB}. SEA and Mftsal are hypothesized to have positive or negative direct effects on S_{GB} and no indirect effects on S_{GB}. These exogenous variables also are hypothesized to have negative direct effects on the mediating variables (Wscluster and Whcluster). In addition, SEA and Mftsal are hypothesized to have an indirect effect on Whcluster when Wscluster serves as a mediating variable. Wcluster, Myos, and Pctunion are hypothesized to have positive effects on S_{GB}. They are also hypothesized to have either positive or negative direct effects on Wscluster and positive effects on Whcluster. Because the mediating variables are hypothesized to have insignificant statistical direct effects on S_{GB}, Wcluster, Myos, and Pctunion should have insignificant statistical indirect effects on S_{GB}. However, the variables should have positive or negative indirect effects on Whcluster.

Exhibit 13-5 Robust regression findings for age and gender diversity for NYC departments for fiscal year 2019

Predictors	Age Diversity (S_{AB})		Gender Diversity (S_{GB})	
	β Coefficient	t-statistic	β Coefficient	t-statistic
Elected	0.0267727 (0.00565020)	4.74 ***	0.0059029 (0.00286070)	2.06 *
SEA	-0.0195238 (0.00840270)	-2.32 **	-0.0027584 (0.00420490)	-0.66
Employees	0.0000001 (0.00000010)	1.48	-0.0000001 (0.00000005)	-1.19
Myos	-0.0005524 (0.00063450)	-0.87	-0.0003185 (0.00031620)	-1.01
Mftsal	-0.0000004 (0.00000017)	-2.34 *	-0.0000001 (0.00000008)	-1.21
Pctunion	0.0336151 (0.00944210)	3.56 **	0.0004566 (0.00475280)	0.10
Wcluster	-0.0022155 (0.00441980)	-0.50	-0.0565638 (0.00206450)	-27.4 ***
Mcluster	-0.0024224 (0.00218110)	-1.11	-0.0008274 (0.00109470)	-0.76
O40cluster	0.0003157 (0.00204780)	0.15	0.0012646 (0.00103650)	1.22
Wscluster	-0.0072143 (0.00394540)	-1.83	-0.0021786 (0.00189160)	-1.15
Mscluster	0.0004856 (0.00189810)	0.26	-0.0001767 (0.00095600)	-0.18

Path Analysis of Organizational Diversity

Whcluster	0.0041461 (0.00380610)	1.09	-0.0008221 (0.00072170)	-1.14
Mhcluster	0.0014934 (0.00136690)	1.09	0.0001115 (0.00068540)	0.16
Intercept	0.8868285 (0.01695250)	52.31	0.5130728 (0.00855450)	59.98 ***
$F_{13,58}$		5.91 ***		149.81 ***
R^2		0.19		0.62
AICR		133.93		155.15
BICR		168.89		200.12
Deviance		0.01		0.01
N		72		72

Standard errors are in parentheses. * $p < 0.05$; ** $p < 0.01$; *** $p < 0.001$

Exhibit 13-6 Hypothesized causal model for age diversity for the NYC departments

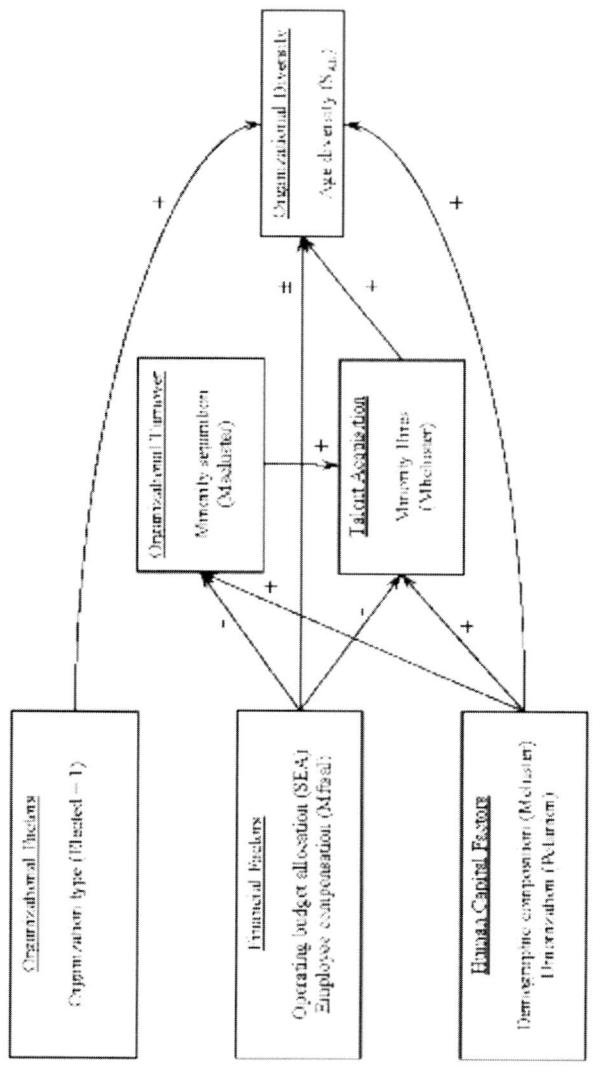

Exhibit 13-7 Hypothesized causal model for gender diversity for the NYC departments

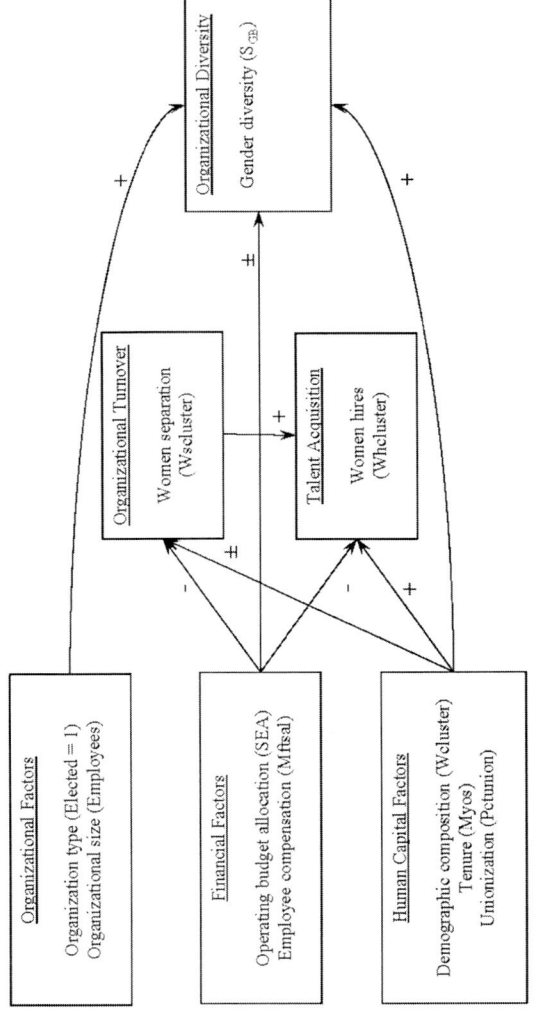

Overview of path analysis

Path analysis has existed since the 1920s (e.g., Lleras, 2005; Wright, 1921 and 1934). Statistically, path analysis is an extension of regression analysis where direct effects of exogenous variables on an endogenous variable are examined quantitatively and where indirect effects of exogenous variables on an endogenous variable are examined through direct effects of mediating variables on an endogenous variable (e.g., Akintunde, 2012; Baron and Kenny, 1986; Lleras, 2005; Norman and Streiner, 2003). Stated simply, path analysis models the causal relationships amongst exogenous, mediating, and endogenous variables and provides estimates of the total effect of exogenous and mediating variables on an endogenous variable.

The steps necessary for undertaking a path analysis of organizational diversity are the following:

1. Develop a theoretical causal model of the relationships amongst the exogenous and mediating variables on organizational diversity. Exhibit 13-2 provides a theoretical causal model of organizational diversity for NYC departments.
2. Develop statistical models that examine the direct effects of exogenous and mediating variables on organizational diversity;
3. Perform the appropriate regression analysis to obtain unstandardized (or standardized) regression coefficients for the path analysis; and,
4. Construct the path diagram for the significant statistical direct and indirect effects of the exogenous and mediating variables on organizational diversity.

In this chapter, the path diagrams for age and gender diversity are based solely on the significant statistical findings.

Assumptions of path analysis

Because path analysis is an extension of OLS regression, the assumptions underlying path analysis are similar to those of OLS regression (e.g., Baron and Kenny, 1986; Lleras, 2005; Norman and Streiner, 2003). They are the following:

- Causation – the causal relationships amongst exogenous, mediating, and endogenous flow in one direction so that the endogenous variables do not "cause" the mediating variables;

- Independence – the residuals amongst exogenous or mediating variables are not correlated statistically;
- Linearity – the relationships amongst exogenous, mediating, and endogenous variables are linear;
- Measurement error – there is an absence in measurement error in the mediating variables;
- Multicollinearity – the level of collinearity amongst exogenous or mediating variables is low; and,
- Normality – endogenous variables are normally distributed.

Violating the assumptions underlying path analysis will produce unreliable and unstable path coefficients of direct or indirect effects attributable to the exogenous and mediating variables.

In order for a variable to function as a mediator, the following criteria should be satisfied (e.g., Baron and Kenny, 1986):

1. Variations in the levels of an exogenous variable account for significant variations in the presumed mediator;
2. Variations in the mediator account for significant variations in the endogenous variable, and,
3. When paths of exogenous variables are controlled, a previously significant relationships amongst exogenous and endogenous variables are no longer significant statistically.

When a direct effect of a mediating variable on an endogenous variable is insignificant statistically, indirect effects of exogenous variables on an endogenous variable are statistically meaningless.

In this chapter, OLS and robust regression are used to examine the direct and indirect effects of the exogenous and mediating variables on age and gender diversity. Tobit regression is inappropriate to use because the mediating variables have negative and positive values although the distributions of the age and gender diversity scores are truncated from 0 to $\frac{n-1}{n}$, where n represents the number of categories for each of the demographic characteristics. As a reminder, the underlying assumptions of OLS regression are the following:

1. The dependent (endogenous) variable is quantitative continuous;
2. The relationships between the dependent (exogenous) and independent (endogenous) variables are linear so that changes in the

values of the exogenous variables produce a change in the values of the endogenous variable;

3. The values of the endogenous variable are normally distributed;
4. The values of the exogenous and endogenous variables are not interconnected and are not calculated in part or in whole on the same data sources;
5. There are no outliers so that the exogenous and endogenous variables do not have extreme low or high values;
6. There are no significant high collinear statistical relationships amongst the set of exogenous variables; and,
7. There is truncation so that the values of the exogenous and endogenous variables do not have a minimum or maximum limit.

As stated throughout the book, regression coefficients are biased, unreliable, and invalid despite the robustness of OLS regression when assumptions are violated.

Statistical models for path analysis

Exhibit 13-6 and 13-7 show that 3 statistical models are necessary to test the direct and indirect effects of the exogenous variables on the level of age and gender diversity. The statistical models for the path analysis for age diversity are the following:

$\widehat{Mscluster} = \alpha = \beta_1 \text{Elected} + \beta_2 \text{SEA} + \beta_3 \text{Mftsal} + \beta_4 \text{Mcluster} + \beta_5 \text{Pctunion} + \varepsilon_{ij}$,

$\widehat{Mhcluster} = \alpha = \beta_1 \text{Elected} + \beta_2 \text{SEA} + \beta_3 \text{Mftsal} + \beta_4 \text{Mcluster} + \beta_5 \text{Pctunion} + \beta_6 \text{Mscluster} + \varepsilon_{ij}$,

$\widehat{SAB} = \alpha = \beta_1 \text{Elected} + \beta_2 \text{SEA} + \beta_3 \text{Mftsal} + \beta_4 \text{Mcluster} + \beta_5 \text{Pctunion} + \beta_6 \text{Mscluster} + \beta_7 \text{Mhcluster} + \varepsilon_{ij}$,

where

$\widehat{Mscluster}$ represents the predicted relative clustering score of the number of persons of color that terminated their employment in each NYC department in fiscal year 2019;

$\widehat{Mhcluster}$ represents the predicted relative clustering score of the number of persons of color that were hired by each NYC department in fiscal year 2019;

$\widehat{SAB}$ represents the predicted biased Simpson diversity score for age for each NYC department in fiscal year 2019;

α represents the value at the y-intercept;

βn represents the regression coefficient of each exogenous and mediating variable in the equation;

Elected refers to NYC departments headed by an elected official (1);

SEA presents the percent of the operating budget allocated to salary expenses in fiscal year 2019;

Mftsal represents the median full-time salary in each NYC department in fiscal year 2019;

Mcluster represents the relative clustering score for the number persons of color in each department's workforce in fiscal year 2019;

Pctunion represents the percent of employees in each NYC department that is a member of a collective bargaining unit in fiscal year 2019;

Mscluster is a mediating variable that represents the relative clustering of the number of persons of color that terminated their employment in each NYC department in fiscal year 2019;

Mhcluster is a mediating variable that represents the relative clustering of the number of persons of color that were hired in each NYC department in fiscal year 2019; and,

ε_{ij} represents measurement error.

The statistical models for the path analysis for gender diversity are the following:

$\widehat{Wscluster} = \alpha = \beta_1 \text{Elected} + \beta_2 \text{Employees} + \beta_3 \text{SEA} + \beta_4 \text{Mftsal} + \beta_5 \text{Wcluster} + \beta_6 \text{Myos} + \beta_7 \text{Pctunion} + \varepsilon_{ij},$

$\widehat{Whcluster} \; \alpha = \beta_1 \text{Elected} + \beta_2 \text{Employees} + \beta_3 \text{SEA} + \beta_4 \text{Mftsal} + \beta_5 \text{Wcluster} + \beta_6 \text{Myos} + \beta_7 \text{Pctunion} + \beta_8 \text{Wscluster} + \varepsilon_{ij},$

$\widehat{SGB} = \alpha = \beta_1 \text{Elected} + \beta_2 \text{Employees} + \beta_3 \text{SEA} + \beta_4 \text{Mftsal} + \beta_5 \text{Wcluster} + \beta_6 \text{Myos} + \beta_7 \text{Pctunion} + \beta_8 \text{Wscluster} + \beta_9 \text{Whcluster} + \varepsilon_{ij},$

where

$\overline{Wscluster}$ represents the predicted relative clustering score of the number of women that terminated their employment in each NYC department in fiscal year 2019;

$\overline{Whcluster}$ represents the predicted relative clustering score of the number of women that were hired by each NYC department in fiscal year 2019;

$\overline{SGB}$ represents the predicted biased Simpson diversity score for gender for each NYC department in fiscal year 2019;

α represents the value at the y-intercept;

βn represents the regression coefficient of each exogenous and mediating variable in the equation;

Elected refers to NYC departments headed by an elected official (1);

Employees represents the total number of employees in each NYC department in fiscal year 2019;

SEA presents the percent of the operating budget allocated to salary expenses in fiscal year 2019;

Mftsal represents the median full-time salary in each NYC department in fiscal year 2019;

Wcluster represents the relative clustering score of the number of women in each department's workforce in fiscal year 2019;

Myos represents the median years of service of the employees in each NYC department in fiscal year 2019;

Pctunion represents the percent of employees in each NYC department that is a member of a collective bargaining unit in fiscal year 2019;

Wscluster is a mediating variable that represents the relative clustering of the number of women that terminated their employment in each NYC department in fiscal year 2019;

Whcluster is a mediating variable that represents the relative clustering of the number of women that were hired in each NYC department in fiscal year 2019; and,

ε_{ij} represents measurement error.

In each of the first models, the direct effects of the exogenous variables on the first mediating variable are tested. The second model includes the exogenous variables and the first mediating variable in the equation to test for direct effects on the second mediating variable and to identify whether the exogenous variables have any indirect effects on the second mediating variable. The third model includes the exogenous and mediating variables in the equation to test for direct and indirect effects on age and gender diversity. Each regression coefficient is tested for statistical significance at $\alpha = 0.05$, and the significant statistical findings are used to diagram the direct and indirect effects.

Path analysis findings

The OLS regression findings for age diversity are summarized in Exhibit 13-8. First, the findings show that Mftsal is related negatively with Mscluster ($\beta_{3A} = -0.00003$, p < 0.01), where a unit increase in Mftsal decreases the number of persons of color that terminate their employment with NYC departments. The other exogenous variables have insignificant statistical relationships with Mscluster. Second, the findings show that Mcluster is related positively with Mhcluster ($\beta_{5B} = 1.097211$, p < 0.001), where a unit increase in the relative clustering of the number of persons of color increases the number of persons of color that are hired by NYC departments. Insignificant statistical findings exist for the other exogenous variables as well as for Mscluster. In the third equation, 4 exogenous variables have direct effects on the level of age diversity. For instance, Elected has a positive direct effect on age diversity ($\beta_{1C} = 0.026$, p < 0.001), where changing from a department headed by a nonelected official to one headed by an elected official increases the level of age diversity. Pctunion also has a positive effect on age diversity ($\beta_{4C} = 0.049$, p < 0.001). However, SEA has a negative effect on age diversity ($\beta_{2C} = -0.025$, p < 0.05). Mcluster also has a negative direct effect on age diversity ($\beta_{5C} = -0.009$, p < 0.01). As a mediating variable, Mhcluster has a positive direct effect on age diversity ($\beta_{7C} = 0.004$, p < 0.01).

Exhibit 13-8 OLS regression analysis for age diversity with mediating variables for NYC departments for fiscal year 2019

Predictors	Mediating Variables				Dependent Variable (S_{AB})	
	Mscluster		Mhcluster		Age Diversity (S_{AB})	
	β Coefficient	t-statistic	β Coefficient	t-statistic	β Coefficient	t-statistic
Elected	0.3431074 (0.3678435)	0.93	0.0143766 (0.5120193)	0.03	0.0264293 (0.0071732)	3.68 ***
SEA	-0.4372422 (0.5163082)	-0.85	-1.169944 (0.7178527)	-1.63	-0.024667 (0.0102602)	-2.40 *
Mftsal	-0.0000255 (0.0000094)	-2.71 **	0.0000179 (0.0000137)	1.30	-0.0000002 (0.0000002)	-1.05
Pctunion	-0.1906875 (0.5587762)	-0.34	0.453383 (0.7733929)	0.59	0.0490079 (0.0108634)	4.51 ***
Mcluster	0.5247049 (0.0784333)		1.097211 (0.1405035)	7.81 ***	-0.0093324 (0.0027404)	-3.41 **
Mscluster	-		0.2381652 (0.1702188)	1.4	0.0013349 (0.0024203)	0.55
Mhcluster	-		-		0.0045897 (0.0017377)	2.64 *
Intercept	2.518714 (1.0021090)	2.51 *	-0.8539061 (1.4505860)	-0.59	0.861204 (0.0203761)	42.27 ***

Path Analysis of Organizational Diversity

Predictors	VIF	Tolerance		VIF	Tolerance		VIF	Tolerance	
Elected	1.56	0.641		1.58	0.633		1.58	0.633	
SEA	1.35	0.741		1.36	0.735		1.42	0.704	
Mftsal	1.45	0.690		1.62	0.617		1.66	0.602	
Pctunion	1.65	0.606		1.66	0.602		1.67	0.599	
Mcluster	1.35	0.741		2.26	0.442		4.38	0.228	
Mscluster	-	-		2.38	0.420		2.45	0.408	
Mhcluster	-	-		-	-		3.96	0.253	
Average VIF	1.47			1.81			2.44		
$F_{5,66}$	18.20		***	$F_{6,65}$	32.11	***	$F_{7,64}$	8.09	***
R^2	0.58			R^2	0.75		R^2	0.47	
Adjusted R^2	0.55			Adjusted R^2	0.72		Adjusted R^2	0.41	
N	72			N	72		N	72	

Standard errors are in parentheses. * $p < 0.05$; ** $p < 0.01$; *** $p < 0.001$

The statistical findings also show that relatively low levels of multicollinearity exist amongst the exogenous and mediating variables (see Exhibit 13-8). In the first equation, the VIF scores are below 2.0, indicating a low level of collinearity amongst the variables. The levels of collinearity amongst the variables also are low in the second equation. However, the statistical relationship amongst Mcluster and Mscluster should be of concern. In the third equation, the VIF scores for Mcluster and Mhcluster show a moderate degree of collinearity amongst the variables.

Exhibit 13-9 provides the path analysis of the exogenous and mediating variables with significant statistical direct and indirect effects on age diversity. As Exhibit 13-9 shows, Elected has a positive direct effect on age diversity of 0.026. Pctunion has a positive direct effect on age diversity of 0.049. Both SEA and Mcluster have negative direct effects on age diversity. Mhcluster has a negative direct effect on age diversity of 0.005. However, Mcluster has a positive direct effect on Mhcluster of 1.097. When the statistical relationship amongst Mcluster and Mhcluster is taken together, Mcluster has a negative indirect effect on age diversity of .005 (-0.005 = -0.005 x 1.097).

When the same path analysis is performed with robust regression, drastically different statistical findings are obtained (see Exhibit 13-10). For instance, the findings show that Mcluster is related positively with Mscluster ($\beta_{5A} = 0.569$, $p < 0.001$), indicating a positive effect where a unit increase in Mcluster increases the level of age diversity in NYC departments. Insignificant statistical findings are obtained for the other exogenous variables. The findings for Mhcluster show that Mftsal is related positively with the endogenous variable ($\beta_{3B} = 0.00002$, $p < 0.05$), indicating a positive effect where the number of persons of color that are hired increases with a unit increase in the median full-time salary. Mcluster also is related positively with Mhcluster ($\beta_{5B} = 1.327$, $p < 0.001$). The findings for the other exogenous variables are insignificant statistically. In regard to the findings for age diversity, Elected is related positively with age diversity ($\beta_{1C} = 0.021$, $p < 0.001$), where the change from a department headed by a nonelected official to one headed by an elected official increases the level of age diversity. On the other hand, Mftsal is related negatively with age diversity ($\beta_{3C} = -0.0000003$, $p < 0.05$), indicating that Mftsal has a negative direct effect on age diversity. The other exogenous variables have insignificant statistical findings.

Exhibit 13-9 OLS regression causal model for age diversity for the NYC departments

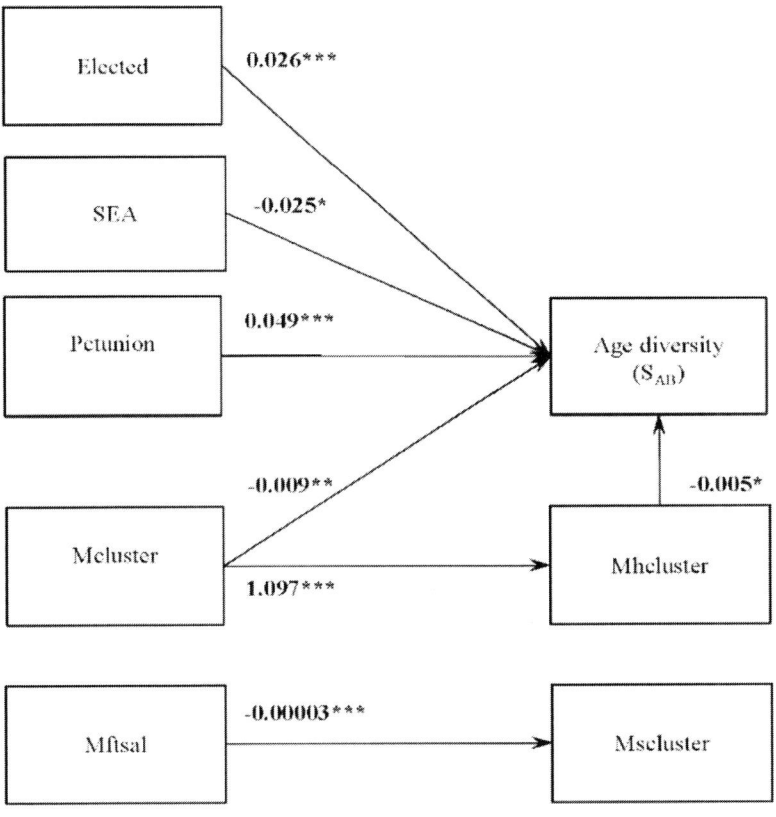

* p < 0.05; ** p < 0.01; *** p < 0.001

Exhibit 13-10 Robust regression analysis for age diversity with mediating variables for NYC departments for fiscal year 2019

	Mediating Variables				Dependent Variable	
	Mscluster		Mhcluster		Age Diversity (S_{AB})	
Predictors	β Coefficient	t-statistic	β Coefficient	t-statistic	β Coefficient	t-statistic
Elected	0.2920107	1.18	-0.2368983	-0.65	0.0215176	4.11 ***
	(0.2465492)		(0.3645343)		(0.0052405)	
SEA	-0.4220022	-1.22	0.3957003	0.77	-0.0136504	-1.82
	(0.3460584)		(0.5110782)		(0.0074958)	
Mftsal	-0.00001	-1.59	0.0000203	2.07 *	-0.0000003	-2.37 *
	(0.0000063)		(0.0000098)		(0.0000001)	
Pctunion	0.5538051	1.48	0.3394722	0.62	0.0378727	4.77
	(0.3745228)		(0.5506203)		(0.0079365)	
Mcluster	0.5688429	10.82 ***	1.327063	13.27 ***	-0.0026795	-1.34
	(0.0525704)		(0.1000321)		(0.0020020)	
Mscluster	-		0.0153182	0.13	-0.0008637	-0.49
			(0.1211880)		(0.0017682)	
Mhcluster	-		-		0.0017086	1.35
					(0.0012695)	
Intercept	0.7085862	1.05	-1.877971	-1.82	0.8746031	58.75 **
	(0.6716690)		(1.0327500)		(0.0148862)	
$F_{5,66}$	41.99 ***		$F_{6,65}$	62.85 ***	$F_{7,64}$	9.22 ***
R^2	0.51		R^2	0.20	R^2	0.14
AICR	86.161		AICR	114.669	AICR	124.886
BICR	103.588		BICR	133.147	BICR	144.929
Deviance	32.900		Deviance	66.293	Deviance	0.013
N	72		N	72	N	72

Standard errors are in parentheses. * p < 0.05; ** p < 0.01; *** p < 0.001

Exhibit 13-11 summarizes the significant statistical findings obtained by the robust regression analysis. The path analysis shows that 2 exogenous variables have direct effects on age diversity. Elected has a positive direct effect on age diversity, and Mftsal has a negative direct effect on age diversity. Both exogenous variables fail to have significant statistical indirect effects on age diversity. Similarly, Mhcluster and Mscluster fail to have significant statistical direct or indirect effects on age diversity.

Exhibit 13-11 Robust regression causal model for age diversity for the NYC departments

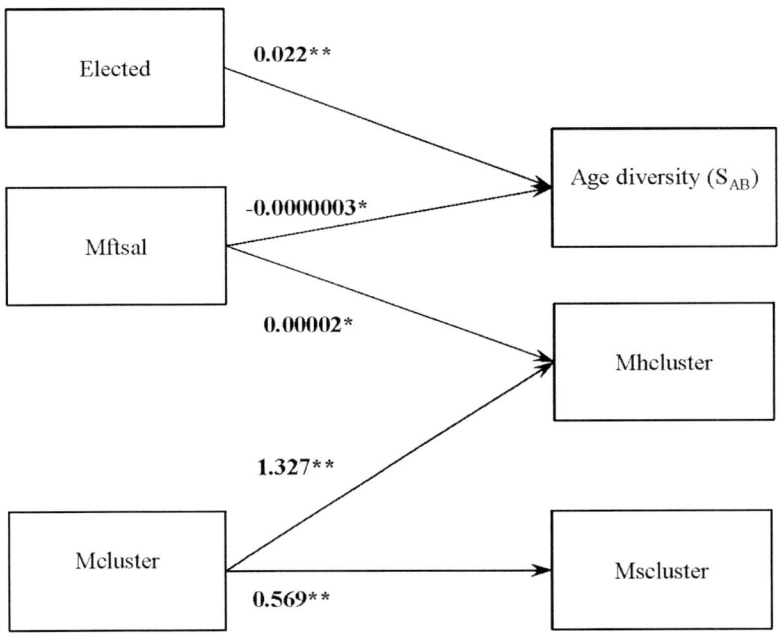

$* \; p < 0.05; \; ** \; p < 0.001$

The differences in the OLS and robust regression findings are explained by how the statistical methods address atypical scores. For the OLS findings, low and high scores in the exogenous and the endogenous variables influence the calculation of the regression coefficients. They also influence the percent of the variation that is explained by the predictors. By contrast, robust regression decreases the influence of the atypical values and provides less biased regression coefficients and R^2 values. In fact, the R^2 values obtained by robust regression are lower than those obtained by OLS regression.

The OLS findings for gender diversity summarized in Exhibit 13-12 are consistent with those in Exhibit 13-4. Insignificant statistical relationships exist amongst the exogenous variables and gender diversity. However, some of the exogenous variables have positive direct effects on Wscluster and Whcluster. First, Wcluster has a positive effect on Wscluster, where a unit increase in the exogenous variable increases the number of women that terminate their employment ($\beta_{7A} = 0.654$, $p < 0.05$). Wcluster also has a positive effect on Whcluster, where a unit increase in the exogenous variable increases the number of women that are hired by NYC departments ($\beta_{7B} = 0.799$, $p < 0.05$). Wscluster has a positive effect on Whcluster, where a unit increase in the number of women that terminate their employment increases the number of women that are hired by NYC departments ($\beta_{8B} = 0.7358595$, $p < 0.05$).

The VIF scores for each OLS regression model show that multicollinearity is not an issue. In the first regression model, each exogenous variable has a VIF score under 2, indicating very low levels of collinearity amongst the predictors. The levels of multicollinearity amongst the predictors are low in the second model as well. Similar findings are obtained by the third model.

Exhibit 13-12 OLS regression analysis for gender diversity with mediating variables for NYC departments for fiscal year 2019

Predictors	Mediating Variables				Dependent Variable	
	Wscluster		Whcluster		Gender Diversity (S$_{GB}$)	
	β Coefficient	t-statistic	β Coefficient	t-statistic	β Coefficient	t-statistic
Elected	0.3084553 (0.1907525)	1.62	0.056868 (0.5054412)	0.11	0.0075572 (0.0205451)	0.37
SEA	-0.3025646 (0.2615709)	-1.16	-0.7642689 (0.6864158)	-1.11	-0.0126643 (0.0281717)	-0.45
Employees	0.0000022 (0.0000032)	0.69	-0.0000084 (0.0000082)	-1.02	-0.0000006 (0.0000003)	-1.89
Myos	-0.0266667 (0.0156448)	-1.70	0.0257194 (0.0415447)	0.62	-0.0013112 (0.0016937)	-0.77
Mftsal	-0.0000048 (0.0000052)	-0.92	0.0000037 (0.0000135)	0.27	-0.0000006 (0.0000006)	-1.12
Pctunion	0.1414115 (0.3226769)	0.44	0.3446793 (0.8393122)	0.41	-0.058633 (0.0341584)	-1.72
Wcluster	0.6537663 (0.1023196)	6.39 **	0.7991709 (0.3400998)	2.35 *	-0.0032214 (0.0144160)	-0.22
Wscluster	-		0.7358595 (0.3246497)	2.27 *	0.0113687 (0.0137225)	0.83
Whcluster	-		-		-0.0051815 (0.0051206)	-1.01
Intercept	0.607414 (0.5281323)	1.15	-0.2492366 (1.3857660)	-0.18	0.5636554 (0.0563372)	10.01 **

Chapter 13

Predictors	VIF	Tolerance	VIF	Tolerance	VIF	Tolerance
Elected	1.56	0.6410	1.620	0.6173	1.62	0.6173
SEA	1.28	0.7813	1.310	0.7634	1.33	0.7519
Employees	1.21	0.8264	1.220	0.8197	1.24	0.8065
Myos	1.25	0.8000	1.310	0.7634	1.32	0.7576
Mftsal	1.62	0.6173	1.640	0.6098	1.64	0.6098
Pctunion	2.04	0.4902	2.050	0.4878	2.05	0.4878
Wcluster	1.21	0.8264	1.980	0.5051	2.15	0.4651
Wscluster	-	-	2.030	0.4926	2.19	0.4566
Whcluster	-	-	-	-	1.56	0.6410
Average VIF	1.45		1.64		1.68	
	$F_{7,64}$	9.39 ***	$F_{8,63}$	4.43 ***	$F_{9,62}$	2.07
	R^2	0.51	R^2	0.36	R^2	0.23
	Adjusted R^2	0.45	Adjusted R^2	0.28	Adjusted R^2	0.12
	N	72	N	72	N	72

Standard errors are in parentheses. * $p < 0.05$; ** $p < 0.001$

The OLS regression path analysis for gender diversity is summarized in Exhibit 13-13 First, none of the exogenous variables have significant statistical direct or indirect effects with gender diversity. However, Wcluster has a positive direct effect on Wscluster and Whcluster. The findings also show that Wcluster has a positive significant indirect effect on Whcluster of 0.481 (0.481 = 0.654 x 0.736). Wscluster has a positive direct effect on Whcluster of 0.736.

Exhibit 13-13 OLS regression causal model for gender diversity for the NYC departments

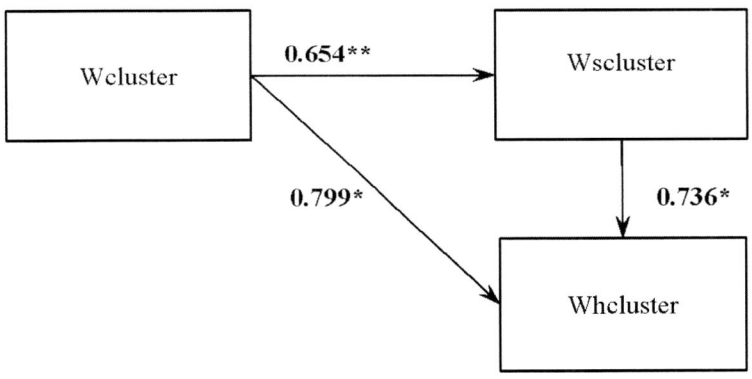

* p < 0.05; ** p < 0.001

When the statistical models for the mediating and endogenous variables are tested with robust regression, different findings are obtained (see Exhibit 13-14). First, SEA has a negative direct effect on Wscluster (β_{2A} = -0.448, p < 0.05). Insignificant statistical findings are obtained for the other exogenous variables. In the second model, Wcluster has a positive direct effect on Whcluster of 0.25 (β_{7B} = 0.250, p < 0.01). In addition, Wscluster has a positive effect on Whcluster of 0.76 (β_{8B} = 0.761, p < 0.01). Similar to the findings in the first model, insignificant statistical findings are obtained for the other exogenous variables. In the third model, Employees has a negative direct effect on gender diversity less than -0.001 (β_{3C} = -0.0000003, p < 0.05). The findings also show that Wscluster has a negative direct effect on gender diversity of about 0.04 (β_{7C} = -0.038, p < 0.001). Insignificant statistical findings are obtained for the other exogenous variables and for the mediating variables.

Chapter 13

Exhibit 13-4 Robust regression analysis for gender diversity with mediating variables for NYC departments for fiscal year 2019

| | Mediating Variables | | | | Dependent Variable | |
| | Wscluster | | Whcluster | | Gender Diversity (S_{GB}) | |
Predictors	β Coefficient	t-statistic	β Coefficient	t-statistic	β Coefficient	t-statistic
Elected	0.2501276 (0.1514890)	1.65	0.077071 (0.1265063)	0.61	0.0106039 (0.0072349)	1.47
SEA	-0.4482198 (0.2077306)	-2.16 *	0.1256545 (0.1751934)	0.72	0.0001661 (0.0099206)	0.02
Employees	0.0000022 (0.0000025)	0.88	-0.0000003 (0.0000021)	-0.13	-0.0000003 (0.0000001)	-2.42 *
Myos	-0.0194021 (0.0124246)	-1.56	-0.0128504 (0.0105440)	-1.22	0.000108 (0.0005964)	0.18
Mftsal	-0.0000014 (0.0000041)	-0.35	-0.0000015 (0.0000034)	-0.44	-0.0000003 (0.0000002)	-1.46
Pctunion	0.0599312 (0.2562589)	0.23	0.2389771 (-0.2100454)	1.14	-0.0124139 (0.0120288)	-1.03
Wcluster	0.7187578 (0.0812587)	8.85	0.2502348 (0.0857634)	2.92 **	-0.0382597 (0.0050765)	-7.54 ***
Wscluster	-		0.7611888 (0.0819103)	9.29 **	0.0018939 (0.0048323)	0.39
Whcluster	-		-		-0.0021472 (0.0018032)	-1.19
Intercept	0.3870461 (0.4194245)	0.92	-0.0604185 (0.3469389)	-0.17	0.5136113 (0.0198389)	25.89 ***

Path Analysis of Organizational Diversity

$F_{7,64}$	16.18	***	$F_{8,62}$	33.50	***	$F_{9,62}$	17.78	***
R^2	0.48		R^2	0.55		R^2	0.48	
AICR	96.573		AICR	116.829		AICR	92.189	
BICR	119.173		BICR	141.592		BICR	122.354	
Deviance	11.492		Deviance	8.005		Deviance	0.028	
N	72		N	72		N	72	

Standard errors are in parentheses. * p < 0.05; ** p < 0.01; *** p < 0.001

Exhibit 13-15 summarizes the statistical findings of the path analysis obtained by the robust regression models. As Exhibit 13-15 illustrates, SEA has a negative direct effect on Wscluster of 0.45 and a negative indirect effect on Whcluster of 0.33 (-0.327 = -0.448 x 0.761). Wscluster has a positive direct effect on Whcluster of 0.76, and Wcluster has a positive direct effect on Whcluster of 0.25. With respect to direct effects of the exogenous variables on gender diversity, Wcluster has a positive direct effect on the endogenous variable of 0.04. Employees has a positive direct effect on gender diversity of less than 0.001.

Exhibit 13-15 Robust regression causal model for gender diversity for the NYC departments

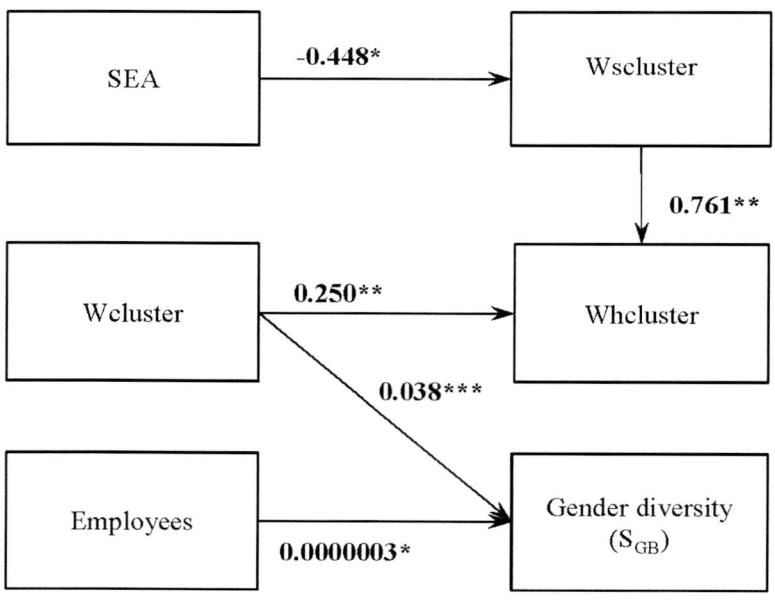

$* \ p < 0.05; ** \ p < 0.01; *** \ p < 0.001$

The differences in the findings produced by the OLS and robust regression models are due to how the statistical methods handle atypical values. In comparison to the OLS regression models, the robust regression models adjusted for atypical values amongst the exogenous and mediating variables and detected significant statistical direct and indirect effects. After adjusting for the atypical values, the robust regression models also obtained higher R^2 values in comparison to the OLS regression models

Summary

This chapter applied path analysis to age and gender diversity scores calculated for NYC departments based on employment data for fiscal year 2019. In so doing, this chapter demonstrated the usefulness of path analysis in analyzing direct and indirect effects of exogenous and mediating variables on age and gender diversity. OLS and robust regression models were used to obtain path coefficients for the exogenous and mediating variables. The findings indicated that the robust regression models yielded different results in comparison the OLS models. The reason for the differences in the findings is that the robust regression models adjusted for atypical values amongst the exogenous and mediating variables and amongst the age and gender diversity scores. The OLS models failed to do so. *Assessing Organizational Diversity with Structural Equation Modeling* presents a more thorough discussion of causal modeling and analysis with respect to organizational diversity.

The insignificant statistical findings amongst several of the exogenous and mediating variables are likely due to the clustering of the diversity scores around the mean, to the nonlinearity of the distribution of the diversity scores, and to the limited discriminatory power of the Simpson diversity index. *Assessing Organizational Diversity with the Shannon Index* applies the Shannon diversity index to the same data and replicates the statistical analyses. Differences in the statistical findings are attributed to the ability of the Shannon index to detect subtle differences in organizational diversity.

The next chapter summarizes the key points of the book. Special attention is given to the measurement and analysis of the diversity scores for age, ethnicity, and gender. Special attention also is given to the regression analyses presented in the book.

Key words

Causal modeling refers to the process of constructing the statistical relationships amongst two or more exogenous or mediating variables and one or more endogenous variables.

Direct effect refers to the influence that an exogenous variable has on an endogenous variable in the absence of a mediating variable.

Endogenous variable refers to a set of measurements or values that change due to changes in the values of a set of exogenous or mediating variables.

Exogenous variable refers to a set of measurements or values that are related statistically to an endogenous variable where the changes in the values of the endogenous are due to changes in the values of the exogenous variable.

Indirect effect refers to the changes that an exogenous variable has on an endogenous variable due to the statistical relationship amongst the exogenous, mediating, and endogenous variables.

Mediating variable refers to a set of measurements that help to explain the statistical relationships amongst two or more exogenous variables and an endogenous variable.

Path analysis refers to a statistical technique that examines and tests the causal relationships among a set of exogenous, mediating, and endogenous variables.

References

Abzug, Rikki. 2017. "Recruitment and selection for nonprofit organizations". In *The nonprofit human resource management handbook: From theory to practice*, edited by Jessica K. A. Word and Jessica E. Sowa, 87-100. New York, NY: Routledge.

Akingbola, Kunle. 2015. *Managing human resources for nonprofits*. New York, NY: Routledge.

Akintunde, Akinnola N. 2012. "Path analysis step by step using excel". *Journal of Technical Science and Technologies*, Vol. 1: 09 – 15.

Baron, Reuben M. and Kenny, David A. 1986. "The moderator–mediator variable distinction in social psychological research: Conceptual, strategic, and statistical considerations". *Journal of Personality and Social Psychology*, Vol. 51: 1173 – 1182.

Boehm, Stephan A., Kunze, Florian, and Bruch, Heike. 2014. "Spotlight on age-diversity climate: The impact of age-inclusive HR practices on firm-level outcomes". *Personnel Psychology*, Vol. 67: 667 – 704.

Buse, Kathleen, Bernstein, Ruth Sessler, and Bilimoria, Diana. 2016. "The influence of board diversity, board diversity policies and practices, and board inclusion behaviors on nonprofit governance practices". *Journal of Business Ethics*, Vol. 133: 179 – 191.

Ellwart, Thomas, Bündgens, Silke, and Rack, Oliver. 2013. "Managing knowledge exchange and identification in age diverse teams". *Journal of Managerial Psychology*, Vol. 28: 950 – 972.

Gazley, Beth, Chang, Won Kyung, and Bingham, Lisa Blomgren. 2010. "Board diversity, stakeholder representation, and collaborative performance in community mediation centers". *Public Administration Review*, Vol. 70: 610 – 620.

Guajardo, Salomón A. 2014. "Workforce diversity: Assessing the impact of minority integration on intra-group interaction". *International Journal of Police Science and Management*, Vol. 16: 205 – 220.

Guajardo, Salomón A. 2015. "Assessing organizational efficiency and workforce diversity: An application of data envelopment analysis to New York City agencies". *Public Personnel Management*, Vol. 44: 239 – 265.

Kearney, Eric, Gebert, Diether, and Voelpel, Sven C. 2009. "When and how diversity benefits teams: The importance of team members' need for cognition". *Academy of Management Journal*, Vol. 52: 581 – 598.

Li, Yixuan, Gong, Yaping, Burmeister, Anne, Wang, Mo, Alterman, Valeria, Alonso, Alexander, and Robinson, Samuel. 2021. "Leveraging age diversity for organizational performance: An intellectual capital perspective". *Journal of Applied Psychology*, Vol. 106: 71 – 91.

Lleras, Christy. 2005. "Path analysis". *Encyclopedia of Social Measurement*, Vol. 3: 25 – 30.

Moon, Kuk-Kyoung, and Christensen, Robert K. 2020. "Realizing the performance benefits of workforce diversity in the US federal government: The moderating role of diversity climate". *Public Personnel Management*, Vol. 49: 141 – 165.

Norman, Geoffrey R. and Streiner, David L. 2003. *PDQ statistics*. Hamilton, Ontario: BC Decker Inc.

Pitts, David W. 2005. "Diversity, representation, and performance: Evidence about race and ethnicity in public organizations". *Journal of Public Administration Research and Theory*, Vol 15: 615 – 631.

Pitts, David W. 2006. "Modeling the impact of diversity management". *Review of Public Personnel Administration*, Vol. 26: 245 – 268.

Pynes, Joan E. 2013. *Human resources management for public and nonprofit organizations: A strategic approach*. New York, NY: John Wiley and Sons.

Wright, Sewall. 1921. "Correlation and Causation". *Journal of Agricultural Research*, Vol. 20: 555 – 585.

Wright, Sewall. 1934. "The method of path coefficients". *The Annals of Mathematical Statistics*, Vol. 5: 161 – 215.

CHAPTER 14

SUMMARY

This book discussed the application of the Simpson diversity index ($S = 1 - \sum p^2$) to demographic employment data reported by NYC departments for fiscal year 2019. In applying the Simpson index to the employment data, diversity scores for age, ethnic, gender, and organizational heterogeneity were calculated. Unbiased diversity scores also were calculated to adjust for the size of each department's workforce. The biased (S_B) and unbiased (S_N) diversity scores for age, ethnic, and gender were compared individually for equality. The findings revealed that the S_N scores were significantly larger in comparison to the S_B scores and that the distributions of the S_N scores had scores above the EMV (EMV $= \frac{n-1}{n}$) value.

After completing the descriptive statistical analyses of the diversity scores, several multivariate regression analyses were performed to identify the organizational and workforce factors related statistically with age, ethnic, and gender diversity. The OLS regression analyses yielded different findings for the 3 sets of diversity scores. Robust regression analyses were undertaken to adjust for atypical scores and yielded different statistical findings in comparison to those obtained by the OLS regression models. Because the distribution of each set of diversity scores are truncated from 0 to $\frac{n-1}{n}$, Tobit regression was performed and yielded different findings in comparison to those obtained by the OLS regression models. Once the regression analyses were completed, Path analyses were performed to assess whether the predictors (i.e., exogenous variables) had direct or indict effects on age and gender diversity. The path analyses conducted with OLS and robust regression yielded different statistical findings.

This chapter highlights the important measurement and analytical issues that should be considered when the Simpson index is used to calculate diversity scores for age, ethnicity, gender, and other forms of demographic (or social) heterogeneity. This chapter also stresses the importance of assessing the distributions of diversity scores for normality, multicollinearity, and truncation so that an appropriate statistical method is selected to perform the multivariate analyses.

Measurement issues

The application of the Simpson index to demographic employment data reported by NYC departments for fiscal year 2019 underscores the importance of understanding how the reliability and validity of diversity scores are affected by measurement issues. First, the categorization of demographic (or social) characteristics into different groups impacts the reliability and validity of Simpson diversity scores. As illustrated in Chapter 4, the categorization of ethnicity as White or minority yields diversity scores that are statistically lower in comparison to when ethnicity is categorized into 5 distinct ethnic groups. The reliability and validity of diversity scores for demographic (or social) characteristics become suspect when the Simpson diversity index is applied to employment data that are reported in multiple formats.

The issue of measurement reliability and validity becomes more paramount when the formula for calculating unbiased Simpson diversity scores is applied to employment data. For instance, as discussed in Chapter 4, the reliability and validity of the diversity scores for ethnicity is questionable because the formula for obtaining unbiased scores overcorrects for the size of the workforce so that NYC departments with small workforces have larger coefficients in comparison to departments with larger workforces. In addition, the unbiased diversity scores for ethnicity are statistically higher in comparison to the biased scores for ethnicity. The same holds true for the biased and unbiased diversity scores for age and gender. Moreover, the application of the formula for obtaining unbiased Simpson diversity scores produces coefficients that exceed the EMV associated with the number of categories created to report the employment data associated with age, ethnicity, and gender. For instance, several of the unbiased diversity scores for gender exceeded the EMV of 0.50 (EMV $= \frac{n-1}{n} = \frac{2-1}{2} = 0.50$). The use of the Simpson diversity index formula for obtaining unbiased scores should be applied with caution because coefficients larger than the EMV are likely to occur.

The compatibility of Simpson diversity scores is compromised when a number of the categories for a demographic (or social) characteristic have missing data. As discussed in Chapter 5, numerous NYC departments had missing employment data for a number of the age group categories so that the diversity scores were incompatible. For instance, NYC departments with similar diversity scores for age had workforces that differed greatly in terms of the number and distribution of employees across the various age group categories. In addition, the age group categories with missing data also contributed to having multiple EMV values within the same distribution of scores. Specifically, the EMV for NYC departments with employment data in each of the 11 age group categories was 0.91 (EMV $= \frac{n-1}{n} = \frac{11-1}{11} =$ 0.909), while departments with employment data for 10 of the age group categories had an EMV of 0.90. NYC departments with employment data for 5 of the age group categories had an EMV of 0.80. The degree of compatibility of diversity scores for a particular demographic (or social) characteristic depends on whether each category constructed for the demographic characteristic of interest contains employment data.

The discriminatory power of the Simpson index is compromised when the formula for obtaining unbiased diversity scores is used. As discussed above and in previous chapters, unbiased diversity scores are statistically higher in comparison to biased coefficients because the formula overcorrects for the size of the workforce. From a measurement perspective, the increase in the value of the diversity score is a function of the formula and not a function of an increase in demographic (or social) heterogeneity within the workforce. In regard to compromising the discriminatory power of the Simpson index, the distribution of the unbiased diversity scores is more compact and centers around the mean in comparison to the distribution of the biased diversity scores. By overcorrecting for the size of the workforce and by producing statistically higher scores where smaller workforces have higher scores than larger workforces, the variability in the distribution of unbiased diversity scores is smaller in comparison to the variability in the distribution of biased diversity scores, indicating a loss of discriminatory power to detect subtle differences in heterogeneity. This book takes the position that the formula for obtaining unbiased Simpson diversity scores should be used sparingly.

Analytical issues

When deciding to undertake multivariate analyses, the properties of the distribution of a set of diversity scores should be assessed thoroughly to ensure that the underlying assumptions of the statistical method that is selected are satisfied. Statistically, when data violate underlying statistical assumptions, biased, unreliable, and unstable estimates are produced. As discussed in previous chapters, the distributions of the diversity scores for age, ethnicity, and gender are negatively skewed, heavy tailed, and violate the assumption of normality. Under these conditions, the use of OLS regression to conduct multivariate analysis is suspect at best.

The statistical nature and properties of the distribution of a diversity score should drive the selection of the analytical method that will be used to perform the analysis. As discussed in previous chapters and as will be discussed in the companion books that follow, diversity indices produce scores that range theoretically from 0 to 1. In the case of the Simpson index, the range of the distribution of a particular diversity score is from 0 to $\frac{n-1}{n}$. Similar to other diversity indices, the Simpson index produces a limited dependent variable where the range of the scores is truncated. When data are truncated (or censured), regression methods for censured data are optimal to use because they are designed specifically to address data with minimum or maximum scores.

Statistically unrelated independent variables should be used in multivariate analyses to minimize issues of multicollinearity and to obtain unbiased, reliable, and stable estimates. In prior studies, percent Black or Hispanic, percent minority, percent women, and other similarly interrelated and interconnected predictors have been used in multivariate analysis of ethnic and gender diversity. These types of predictors have total number of employees as the denominator, and they have data that overlap with each other. For instance, when percent Black and percent women are used concomitantly as predictors in OLS regression, the number of Black women is accounted for in the variable percent women. When percent minority and percent women are used as predictors in the same analysis, Asian, Black, Hispanic, or Native American women are accounted for in the variable percent women. This book purposefully avoided using these types of interrelated and interconnected variables as predictors so that the level of multicollinearity would be minimized. In this book, a measure of relative clustering for women was created and used instead of "percent women." Similarly, a measure of relative clustering for minorities was created and used to replace "percent minority." The Pearson pairwise correlation analysis indicated that these variables are uncorrelated statistically. In addition, the VIF scores revealed a lack of collinearity amongst these variables. When undertaking a multivariate regression analysis of diversity, the selection of the independent variables is crucial to avoid issues of multicollinearity and so that unbiased, reliable, and stable estimates are obtained.

Some studies treat age, ethnic, or gender diversity as exogenous variables when conducting multivariate regression analyses of organizational performance. In reality, diversity in terms of age, ethnicity, or gender is an endogenous variable that is determined by the demographic and social factors that exist in an organization's workforce. Stated differently, demographic (or social) diversity within an organization is an endogenous variable that is influenced by fluctuations in the demographic (or social) composition of the workforce. This book takes the position that age, ethnic, gender, or other forms of demographic or social diversity cannot exist in an organization without the workforce undergoing constant demographic (or social) change. In regard to the use of age, ethnic, gender, or other forms of diversity to assess organizational performance, this book takes the position that organizational diversity is an intervening (or mediating) variable that helps to explain the direct or indirect statistical relationships of exogenous variables and organizational performance. As will be discussed in *Assessing Organizational Diversity with Structural Equation Modeling*, demographic diversity is an endogenous variable that serves as an intervening (or mediating) variable when organizational performance serves as the dependent (or endogenous) variable.

Concluding remarks

Although the Simpson diversity index is invariant to ordering sequences and possesses high measurement efficiency, the index has limitations in regard to simultaneously taking into account the size of the workforce and the number of categories used in the categorization of a demographic (or social) characteristic. When the size of the workforce is taken into account, Simpson diversity scores for some organizations are significantly higher and exceed the empirical maximum value. The discriminatory power of the index becomes compromised when the formula to calculate unbiased diversity scores is applied to the same employment data. Despite its frequent use in the study of organizational diversity, the temptation to use the Simpson index exclusively to calculate diversity scores for organizations should be resisted. As a prolog to *Assessing Organizational Diversity with the Shannon Index*, the Shannon index may be better suited for measuring and analyzing demographic (or social) diversity in your organization.

References

Abzug, Rikki. 2017. "Recruitment and selection for nonprofit organizations". In *The nonprofit human resource management handbook: From theory to practice*, edited by Jessica K. A. Word and Jessica E. Sowa, 87-100. New York, NY: Routledge.

Akingbola, Kunle. 2015. *Managing human resources for nonprofits*. New York, NY: Routledge.

Akintunde, Akinnola N. 2012. "Path analysis step by step using excel". *Journal of Technical Science and Technologies*, Vol. 1: 09 – 15.

Akram, Farheen, Abrar ul Haq, Muhammad, Natarajan, Vinodh K., and Chellakan, R. Stephen. 2020. "Board heterogeneity and corporate performance: An insight beyond agency issues". *Cogent Business and Management*, Vol. 7: 1809299.

Alexander, Jeffrey, Nuchols, Beverly, Bloom, Joan, and Lee, Shoou-Yih. 1995. "Organizational demography and turnover: An examination of multiform and nonlinear heterogeneity". *Human Relations*, Vol. 48: 1455 – 1480.

Alma, Özlem Gürünlü. 2011. "Comparison of robust regression methods in linear regression". *International Journal of Contemporary Mathematical Sciences*, Vol. 6: 409 – 421.

Baron, Reuben M. and Kenny, David A. 1986. "The moderator–mediator variable distinction in social psychological research: Conceptual, strategic, and statistical considerations". *Journal of Personality and Social Psychology*, Vol. 51: 1173 – 1182.

Biemann, Torsten. and Kearney. Eric. 2010. "Size does matter: How varying group sizes in a sample affect the most common measures of group diversity". *Organizational Research Methods*, Vol. 13: 582 – 599.

Bingen, Franz, Siau, Carlos, and Rousseeuw, Peter. 1986. "Applying robust regression techniques to institutional data". *Research in Higher Education*, Vol. 25: 277 – 297.

Blau, Peter Michael. 1977. *Inequality and heterogeneity*. New York, NY: Free Press.

Boehm, Stephan A., Kunze, Florian, and Bruch, Heike. 2014. "Spotlight on age-diversity climate: The impact of age-inclusive HR practices on firm-level outcomes". *Personnel Psychology*, Vol. 67: 667 – 704.

Britt, Chester L. 2009. "Modeling the distribution of sentence length decisions under a guidelines system: An application of quantile regression models". *Journal of Quantitative Criminology*, Vol. 25: 341 – 370.

Buhai, I. Sebastian. 2005. "Quantile regression: overview and selected applications". *Ad Astra*, Vol. 4: 1 – 17.

Buse, Kathleen, Bernstein, Ruth Sessler, and Bilimoria, Diana. 2016. "The influence of board diversity, board diversity policies and practices, and board inclusion behaviors on nonprofit governance practices". *Journal of Business Ethics*, Vol. 133: 179 – 191.

Cade, Brian S., and Noon, Barry R. 2013. "A gentle introduction to quantile regression for ecologists". *Frontiers in Ecology and the Environment*, Vol. 1: 412 – 420.

Campbell, Kevin, and Mínguez-Vera, Antonio. 2008. "Gender diversity in the boardroom and firm financial performance". *Journal of Business Ethics*, Vol. 83: 435 – 451.

Chatman, Jennifer. A., and Flynn, Francis J. 2001. "The influence of demographic heterogeneity on the emergence and consequences of cooperative norms in work teams". *Academy of Management Journal*, Vol. 44: 956 – 974.

Cheong, Calvin W. H., and Sinnakkannu, Jothee. 2014. "Ethnic diversity and firm financial performance: Evidence from Malaysia". *Journal of Asia-Pacific Business*, Vol. 15: 73 – 100.

Chikoto, Grace L., Ling, Qianhua, and Neely, Daniel G. 2016. "The adoption and use of the Hirschman–Herfindahl Index in nonprofit research: Does revenue diversification measurement matter?". *Voluntas: International Journal of Voluntary and Nonprofit Organizations*, Vol. 27: 1425 – 1447.

Choi, Sungjoo, and Rainey, Hal G. 2010. "Managing diversity in US federal agencies: Effects of diversity and diversity management on employee perceptions of organizational performance". *Public Administration Review*, Vol. 70: 109 – 121.

Choi, Sungjoo. 2010. "Diversity in the US federal government: Antecedents and correlates of diversity in federal agencies". *Review of Public Personnel Administration*, Vol. 30: 301 – 321

Cornwell, Christopher, and Kellough, J. Edward. 1994. "Women and minorities in federal government agencies: Examining new evidence from panel data". *Public Administration Review*, Vol. 54: 265 – 270.

Daoud, Jamal I. (2017). "Multicollinearity and regression analysis". *Journal of Physics: Conference Series*, Vol. 949: 012009.

Davino Cristina, Furno, Marilena, and Vistocco, Domenico. 2014. *Quantile Regression: Theory and applications*. New York: John Wiley and Sons, Ltd.

Davino, Cristina, Romano, Rosaria, and Naes, Tormod. 2015. "The use of quantile regression in consumer studies". *Food Quality and Preference*, Vol. 40: 230 – 239.

De Meulenaere, Kim, Boone, Christophe, and Buyl, Tine. 2016. "Unraveling the impact of workforce age diversity on labor productivity: The moderating role of firm size and job security". *Journal of Organizational Behavior*, Vol. 37: 193 – 212.

DeLisi, Matt, Beaver, Kevin M., Wright, Kevin A., Wright, John Paul, Vaughn, Michael G., Trulson, Chad R. 2011. "Criminal specialization revisited: A simultaneous quantile regression approach". *American Journal of Criminal Justice*, Vol. 36: 73 – 92.

Ellwart, Thomas, Bündgens, Silke, and Rack, Oliver. 2013. "Managing knowledge exchange and identification in age diverse teams". *Journal of Managerial Psychology*, Vol. 28: 950 – 972.

Ferrero-Ferrero, Idoya, Fernández-Izquierdo, M. Ángeles, and Muñoz-Torres, M. Jesús. 2015. "Age diversity: An empirical study in the board of directors". *Cybernetics and Systems*, Vol. 46: 249 – 270.

Filzmoser, Peter, and Todorov, Valentin. 2011. "Review of robust multivariate statistical methods in high dimension". *Analytica Chimica Acta*, Vol. 705: 2 – 14.

Gazley, Beth, Chang, Won Kyung, and Bingham, Lisa Blomgren. 2010. "Board diversity, stakeholder representation, and collaborative performance in community mediation centers". *Public Administration Review*, Vol. 70: 610 – 620.

Grabosky, Peter N., and Rosenbloom, David H. 1975. "Racial and ethnic integration in the federal service". *Social Science Quarterly*, Vol. 56: 71 – 84.

Guajardo, Salomón A. 1996. "Representative bureaucracy: An estimation of the reliability and validity of the Nachmias-Rosenbloom MV Index". *Public Administration Review*, Vol. 56: 467-477.

Guajardo, Salomón A. 2013. "Workforce diversity: An application of diversity and integration indices to small agencies". *Public Personnel Management*, Vol. 41: 27 – 40.

Guajardo, Salomón A. 2014. "Workforce diversity: Assessing the impact of minority integration on intra-group interaction". *International Journal of Police Science and Management*, Vol. 16: 205 – 220.

Guajardo, Salomón A. 2014. "Workforce diversity: Ethnicity and gender diversity and disparity in the New York City Police Department". *Journal of Ethnicity in Criminal justice*, Vol. 12: 93 – 115.

Guajardo, Salomón A. 2015. "Assessing organizational efficiency and workforce diversity: An application of data envelopment analysis to

New York City agencies". *Public Personnel Management*, Vol. 44: 239 – 265.

Guajardo, Salomón A. 2015. "Measuring diversity in police agencies". *Journal of Ethnicity in Criminal Justice,* Vol. 13: 1 – 15.

Guajardo, Salomón A. 2016. "Ethnic diversity in policing: An application of quantile regression to the New York City Police Department". *Journal of Ethnicity in Criminal Justice*, Vol. 14: 254 – 289.

Hamilton, Lawrence C. 1991. "How robust is robust regression?". *Stata Technical Bulletin*, STB-2: 21 – 26.

Hao, Lingxin, and Naiman, Daniel Q. 2007. *Quantile regression.* Thousand Oaks, CA: Sage Publications Inc.

Harrison, David A., and Klein, Katherine J. 2007. "What's the difference? Diversity constructs as separation, variety, or disparity in organizations". *Academy of Management Review*, Vol. 32: 1199 – 1228.

Hendrick, Rebecca. 2002. "Revenue diversification: Fiscal illusion or flexible financial management". *Public Budgeting and Finance*, Vol. 22: 52 – 72.

Hoerl, Arthur E. 1962. "Application of ridge analysis to regression problems". *Chemical Engineering Progress*, Vol. 58: 54 – 59.

Hoerl, Arthur E., and Kennard, Robert W. 1970a. "Ridge regression: Applications to nonorthogonal problems". *Technometrics*, Vol. 12: 69 – 82.

Hoerl, Arthur E., and Kennard, Robert W. 1970b. "Ridge regression: Biased estimation for nonorthogonal problems". *Technometrics*, Vol. 12: 55 – 67.

Jordan, Meagan M., and Wagner, Gary A. 2008. "Revenue diversification in Arkansas cities: The budgetary and tax effort impacts". *Public Budgeting and Finance*, Vol: 28: 68 – 82.

Kearney, Eric, Gebert, Diether, and Voelpel, Sven C. 2009. "When and how diversity benefits teams: The importance of team members' need for cognition". *Academy of Management Journal*, Vol. 52: 581 – 598.

Kellough, J. Edward, and Elliott, Euel. 1992. "Demographic and organizational influences on racial/ethnic and gender integration in federal agencies". *Social Science Quarterly,* Vol. 73: 1 – 11.

Kellough, J. Edward. 1990. "Integration in the public workplace: Determinants of minority and female employment in federal agencies". *Public Administration Review*, Vol. 50: 557 – 566.

Khan, Imran, Khan, Ismail, and Senturk, Ismail. 2019. "Board diversity and quality of CSR disclosure: Evidence from Pakistan". *Corporate Governance: The International Journal of Business in Society*, Vol. 19: 1187 – 1203.

Kim, Pan Suk. 1993. "Racial integration in the American federal government: With special reference to Asian-Americans". *Review of Public Personnel Administration*, Vol. 13: 52 – 66.

Klein, Katherine. J., Conn, Amy Buhl, Smith, D. Brent, and Sorra, Joann Speer. 2001. "Is everyone in agreement? An exploration of within-group agreement in employee perceptions of the work environment". *Journal of Applied Psychology*, Vol. 86: 3 – 16.

Koenker, Roger, and Bassett Jr, Gilbert. 1978. Regression quantiles. *Econometrica*, Vol. 46: 33 – 50.

Koenker, Roger, and Hallock, Kevin F. 2001. "Quantile regression". *Journal of Economic Perspectives*, Vol. 15: 143 – 156.

Koenker, Roger. 2005. *Quantile regression*. New York: Cambridge University Press.

Kolo, Philipp. 2012. *Measuring a new aspect of ethnicity: The appropriate diversity index* (No. 221). Göttingen, Lower Saxony, Germany: Ibero-America Institute for Economic Research (IAI), University of Göttingen.

Lee-Kuen, Irean Yap, Sok-Gee, Chan, and Zainudin, Rozaimah. 2017. "Gender diversity and firms' financial performance in Malaysia". *Asian Academy of Management Journal of Accounting and Finance*, Vol. 13: 41 – 62.

Leslie, Lisa M. 2017. "A status-based multilevel model of ethnic diversity and work unit performance". *Journal of Management*, Vol. 43: 426 – 454.

Lewis, Gregory B. 1991. "Turnover and the quiet crisis in the federal civil service". *Public Administration Review*, Vol. 51: 145 – 155.

Li, Yixuan, Gong, Yaping, Burmeister, Anne, Wang, Mo, Alterman, Valeria, Alonso, Alexander, and Robinson, Samuel. 2021. "Leveraging age diversity for organizational performance: An intellectual capital perspective". *Journal of Applied Psychology*, Vol. 106: 71 – 91.

Lieberson, Stanley. 1969. "Measuring population diversity". *American Sociological Review*, Vol. 34: 850 – 862.

Lind, Douglas A., Marchal, William G., and Wathen, Samuel A. 2017. *Statistical techniques in business and economics.* Seventeenth edition. New York, NY: McGraw-Hill Education.

Lleras, Christy. 2005. "Path analysis". *Encyclopedia of social measurement*, Vol. 3: 25 – 30.

Massey, Douglas S., and Denton, Nancy A. 1988. "The dimensions of residential segregation". *Social Forces*, Vol. 67: 281 – 315.

McDonald, Daniel. G., and Dimmick, John. 2003. "The conceptualization and measurement of diversity". *Communication Research*, Vol. 30: 60 – 79.

McDonald, John F., and Moffitt, Robert A. 1980. "The uses of Tobit analysis". *The Review of Economics and Statistics*, Vol. 62: 318 – 321.

McIntosh, Robert P. 1967. "An index of diversity and the relation of certain concepts to diversity." *Ecology*, Vol. 48: 392 – 404.

Meligkotsidou, Loukia, Vrontos, Ioannis D., and Vrontos, Spyridon D. 2009. "Quantile regression analysis of hedge fund strategies". *Journal of Empirical Finance*, Vol. 16: 264 – 279.

Michie, Jonathan, and Oughton, Christine. 2013. *Measuring diversity in financial services markets: A diversity index.* London, England: Centre for Financial and Management Studies, University of London.

Moon, Kuk-Kyoung, and Christensen, Robert K. 2020. "Realizing the performance benefits of workforce diversity in the US federal government: The moderating role of diversity climate". *Public Personnel Management*, Vol. 49: 141 – 165.

Mueller, John H., Schuessler, Karl F., and Costner, Herbert L. 1970. *Statistical reasoning in sociology.* Second edition. New York, NY: Houghton Mufflin Company.

Nachmias, David, and Rosenbloom, David H. 1973. "Measuring Bureaucratic Representation and Integration". *Public Administration Review*, Vol. 33: 590 – 597.

Norman, Geoffrey R. and Streiner, David L. 2003. *PDQ statistics.* Hamilton, Ontario: BC Decker Inc.

Oba, Victor Chiedu, and Fodio, Musa Inuwa. 2013. "Boards' gender mix as a predictor of financial performance in Nigeria: An empirical study". *International Journal of Economics and Finance*, Vol. 5: 170 – 178.

Pett, Marjorie A., Lackey, Nancy R., and Sullivan, John J. 2003. *Making sense of factor analysis: The use of factor analysis for instrument development in health care research.* Thousand Oaks, California: Sage Publications Inc.

Pitts, David W. 2005. "Diversity, representation, and performance: Evidence about race and ethnicity in public organizations". *Journal of Public Administration Research and Theory*, Vol 15: 615 – 631.

Pitts, David W. 2006. "Modeling the impact of diversity management". *Review of Public Personnel Administration*, Vol. 26: 245 – 268.

Poulos, Tammy Meredith, and Doerner, William G. 1996. "Women in law enforcement: The distribution of females in Florida policing agencies". *Women and Criminal Justice*, Vol. 8: 19 – 3.

Preisser, John S., and Qaqish, Bahjat F. 1999. "Robust regression for clustered data with application to binary responses". *Biometrics*, Vol. 55: 574 – 579.

Pynes, Joan E. 2013. *Human resources management for public and nonprofit organizations: A strategic approach*. New York, NY: John Wiley and Sons.

Randel, Amy E., and Jaussi, Kimberly S. 2003. "Functional background identity, diversity, and individual performance in cross-functional teams". *Academy of Management Journal*, Vol. 46: 763 – 774.

Riccucci, Norma M. 1986. "Female and minority employment in city government: The role of unions". *Policy Studies Journal*, Vol. 15: 3 – 15.

Rousseeuw, Peter J, Van Aelst, Stefan., Van Driessen, Katrien., and Agulló, Jose. 2004. "Robust multivariate regression". *Technometrics*, Vol. 46: 293 – 305.

Shannon, Claude Elwood. 1948. "A mathematical theory of communication". *The Bell System Technical Journal*, Vol. 27: 379 – 423.

Shrestha, Noora. 2020. "Detecting multicollinearity in regression analysis". *American Journal of Applied Mathematics and Statistics*, Vol. 8: 39 – 42.

Simpson, Edward Hugh. 1949. "Measurement of diversity". *Nature*, Vol. 163: 688.

Starks, Glenn. L. 2009. "Minority representation in senior positions in U.S. federal agencies: A paradox of underrepresentation". *Public Personnel Management*, Vol. 38: 79 – 90.

Szpiro, Adam A., Rice, Kenneth M., and Lumley, Thomas. 2010. "Model-robust regression and a Bayesian "sandwich" estimator". *The Annals of Applied Statistics*, Vol. 4: 2099 – 2113.

Talbert, Marian K., and Cade, Brian S. 2013. *User manual for Blossom statistical package for R*. Reston, VA: U.S. Geological Survey.

Timmerman, Thomas A. 2000. "Racial diversity, age diversity, interdependence, and team performance". *Small Group Research*, Vol. 31: 592 – 606.

Tobin, James. 1955. *Estimation of relationships for limited dependent variables*. New Haven, CT: Cowles Foundation, Yale University.

Tobin, James. 1958. "Estimation of relationships for limited dependent variables". *Econometrica*, Vol. 26: 24 – 36.

Verardi, V. and Croux, Christophe. 2009. Robust regression in Stata. *The Stata Journal*, 9(3), 439 – 453.

Verardi, Vincenzo, and Dehon, Catherine. 2010. "Multivariate outlier detection in Stata". *The Stata Journal*, Vol. 10: 259 – 266.

Western, Bruce. 1995. "Concepts and suggestions for robust regression analysis". *American Journal of Political Science*, Vol. 39: 786-817.

Wilcox, Allen R. (1967). *Indices of qualitative variation*. Oak Ridge, TN: Oak Ridge National Laboratory, U.S. Atomic Energy Commission.

Williams, Brett, Onsman, Andrys, and Brown, Ted. 2010, "Exploratory factor analysis: A five-step guide for novices". *Journal of Emergency Primary Health Care (JEPHC)*, Vol. 8: 1 – 13.

Wright, Sewall. 1921. "Correlation and Causation". *Journal of Agricultural Research*, Vol. 20: 555 – 585.

Wright, Sewall. 1934. "The method of path coefficients". *The Annals of Mathematical Statistics*, Vol. 5: 161 – 215.

Yaffee, Robert A. 2002. "Robust regression analysis: some popular statistical package options". *Statistics, Social Science, and Mapping Group Academic Computing Services Information Technology Services*, 1 – 12.

Yong, An Gie, and Pearce, Sean. 2013. "A beginner's guide to factor analysis: Focusing on exploratory factor analysis". *Tutorials in Quantitative Methods for Psychology*, Vol. 9: 79 – 94.

Yoo, Wonsuk, Mayberry, Robert, Bae, Sejong, Singh, Karan, He, Qinghua Peter, and Lillard Jr, James W. 2014. "A study of effects of multicollinearity in the multivariable analysis". *International Journal of Applied Science and Technology*, Vol. 4: 9 –19.

Yu, Keming, Lu, Zud, and Sandler, Julian. 2003. "Quantile regression: Applications and current research areas". *The Statistician*, Vol. 52: 331 – 350.

GLOSSARY

Age diversity refers to how well an organization's workforce is heterogeneous in terms of the employment of men and women of different ages.

Biased measurements refer to coefficients or scores that are either high or low due to the formula that is used to obtain the value.

Causal modeling refers to the process of constructing the statistical relationships amongst two or more exogenous or mediating variables and one or more endogenous variables.

Censored (data) refers to a distribution of scores where some measurements are unobserved or not validated so that the range of scores has a lower or upper cutoff or the range of scores is set between a minimum or maximum value due to not being able to collect data on all subjects. By contrast, truncated data refers to distributions of scores where measurements are confined or restricted so that values do not fall below a minimum value or exceed a maximum value.

Clustering refers to the level of concentration of members of a particular demographic groups in an organization's workforce.

Coefficient of determination is a statistic which indicates the amount of variance this is explained by a set of predictors. In simultaneous OLS regression, adjusted R^2 and R^2 summarize the amount of variance that is explained by the model.

Coefficient of variation (CV) refers to the measure obtained by dividing the standard deviation (σ) of a set of data by the mean ($\bar{x}$) to get an estimate of the dispersion of data points around the mean. Symbolically, the formula is as follows: $\mathrm{CV} = \dfrac{\sigma}{\mu}$

Composite diversity index refers to a summary score that is calculated by combining age, ethnic, gender, or other demographic- or social-based diversity measures.

Conditional distribution refers to the continuum of values of the dependent variable that may be analyzed with quantile regression. Unlike OLS regression which focuses on the distribution of values around the mean of a dependent variable, quantile regression focuses on the entire distribution of values and performs a regression analysis at different percentiles along the continuum of values to assess the relationships amongst the predictors and the dependent variable at different locations.

Confidence interval refers to a range of estimated values with a lower and upper limit that indicates where an average score is likely to fall when multiple samples are obtained.

Convergent validity refers to whether two or more sets of scores that measure the same construct are correlated statistically with each other.

Correlational analysis refers to the statistical technique of matching the values of two or more sets of measures to assess how closely their values are similar to each other.

Cross-sectional studies refer to research projects that collect and analyze data on subjects for one specific time period. By contrast, longitudinal studies collect and analyze data on subjects for multiple time periods such as days, weeks, months, and years.

Dependent variables refer to a set or sets of measures that have values that are influenced positively or negatively as the values of other sets of measures increase or decrease.

Descriptive statistics refer to measures that summarize the distribution, central tendency, and variability in a set of data.

Direct effect refers to the influence that an exogenous variable has on an endogenous variable in the absence of a mediating variable.

Discriminatory power refers to the extent to which a diversity index can detect subtle differences in heterogeneity when compared to another index.

Diversity refers to the probability that individuals chosen randomly from a particular population will have the same (or different) demographic or social characteristics.

Downweighing refers to the process of assigning weights to atypical values of variables to decrease their influence so that regression coefficients are reliable and stable.

Eigenvalue refers to the factor by which an eigenvector is scaled or stretched.

Empirical maximum value (EMV) refers to the actual highest diversity coefficient that is attainable by an index based on the number of distinct categories within a particular population.

Endogenous variable refers to set of measurements or values that change due to changes in the values of a set of exogenous or mediating variables.

Ethnic diversity refers to how well an organization's workforce is heterogeneous in terms of the employment of men and women from different ethnic and racial groups.

Exogenous variable refers to a set of measurements or values that are related statistically to an endogenous variable where the changes in the values of the endogenous are due to changes in the values of the exogenous variable.

Factor analysis refers to the statistical technique used to assess whether a set of correlated measures are structurally similar in that they provided redundant numerical information in regards to what they are purportedly measuring.

Gender diversity refers to how well an organization's workforce is heterogeneous in terms of the employment of men and women.

Horizontal comparison (analysis) refers to the comparison of findings produced by different types of methods.

Independent variables refer to a set of measures that are hypothesized to influence either positively or negatively the values of a dependent variable.

Indirect effect refers to the changes that an exogenous variable has on an endogenous variable due to the statistical relationship amongst the exogenous, mediating, and endogenous variables.

Integration refers to the hiring of minorities and women into an organization's workforce.

Intercept refers to the point where the regression line passes through the y-axis.

Intervening variable refers to a measure that is influenced by a set of factors where that measure then influences a particular outcome.

Involuntary terminations refer to separations where employees are fired or where employees are removed from positions due to actions that are beyond their control to end their employment with the organization such as suffering a fatality while on duty.

Kurtosis refers to the thickness of the tails of a distribution of scores in a set of data.

Likelihood ratio is a statistic that estimates the probability that a particular outcome will occur.

Limited dependent variable (LDV) refers to the quantitative distribution of scores of a variable that is restricted to a particular range so that values are not numerically continuous.

Marginal effects refer to statistics that estimate the change in the magnitude of the dependent variable generated by a unit change of an independent variable.

Mean refers to the average score of a set of data. Mathematically, the average is calculated by adding all of the numbers (x) and then dividing the sum by the number of observations (n). The formula for calculating the average is as follows: $\bar{x} = \frac{\Sigma x}{n}$

Measurement compatibility refers to whether two or more scores obtained in the same manner have the same meaning or interpretation when the scores are calculated on the data with different characteristics.

Measurement efficiency refers to the number of mathematical operations that are needed to obtain a diversity coefficient. Indices that require fewer mathematical operations are more efficient in the use of the data in comparison to those that require numerous sets of calculations to obtain a diversity score.

Measurement invariance refers to the ability of an index to produce the same numerical value regardless of the order in which the data are arranged for analysis.

Measurement reliability refers to whether a method used to calculate a set of scores produces consistent results over multiple applications of the method.

Measurement validity refers to whether similar inferences can be made on a set of scores that are calculated from data with different characteristics.

Measures of central tendency refer to measures that summarize the typical scores in a set of data.

Measures of distribution refer to measures that summarize the frequency or occurrence of scores in a set a data.

Measures of variability refer to measures that summarize the spread of scores in a set of data.

Median refers to the value that splits a set of data at the 50% point.

Mediating variable refers to a set of measurements that help to explain the statistical relationships amongst two or more exogenous variables and an endogenous variable.

Multicollinearity refers to the extent to which independent variables are associated statistically with each other so that their relationships provide redundant information into the regression equation and produce statistically biased and unreliable results.

Multivariate analysis refers to the statistical assessment of how a set of two or more measures influence the values of one or more dependent variables.

Nonorthogonal predictors refers to independent variables that are correlated statistically so their values vary jointly.

Normality refers to whether the scores in a set of data are symmetrically distributed so that they fit under a bell-shaped curve.

Oblimin oblique rotation refers to the statistical technique for performing oblique rotations to transform vectors in a factor or principal component analysis into a simpler structure so that measures that assess the same construct are grouped together.

Occupational diversity refers to how well an organization's workforce is heterogenous in terms of the number of employees in different classes and types of job classifications and titles.

Organizational diversity refers to how well an organization's workforce is heterogeneous in terms of the employment of men and women of different demographic, economic, and social backgrounds.

Outliners refers to scores that are 3 standard deviations below or above the mean of a set of data.

Pairwise correlation analysis refers to the statistical technique of matching the values of two sets of measures at a time to determine how closely the values are similar to each other.

Path analysis refers to a statistical technique that examines and tests the causal relationships among a set of exogenous, mediating, and endogenous variables.

Pearson correlation analysis refers to the statistical technique of matching the values of two or more sets of scores that are measured quantitatively.

Planned pairwise comparisons refer to statistical tests that compare two sets of scores for statistical significance prior to undertaking the analysis.

Predictors refer to independent variables used to estimate value changes in the dependent variable.

Probability refers to the chance or likelihood that an event will occur.

Probit regression is a statistical method that regresses a set of predictors on a binary dependent variable to estimate the probability that a case with a set of particular characteristics will fall into one of the categories.

Quantile regression is a median-based statistical method that assesses the relationships amongst a set of predictors and a dependent variable across the conditional distribution of the dependent variable at specified percentiles such the 25th, 50th, 75th, and 90th percentiles.

Reciprocal value refers to the measure obtained by dividing a number into 1: $RV = \frac{1}{x}$.

Regression coefficients refer to the unit of change that occurs in the dependent variable with each unit change that occurs in the independent variable. Each independent variable has a regression coefficient associated with it.

Residuals refer to the difference obtained by subtracting a predicted value from the actual value. Small residual or error values indicate that the predicated value approximates the actual value; large error values indicate the predicated value varies greatly from the actual value.

Ridge analysis refers to the process of assessing and reducing the collinearity amongst a set of predictors with statistical techniques such as ridge regression.

Ridge estimates refer to the estimators obtained from applying a shrinkage factor to reduce the levels of collinearity amongst a set of independent variables that are correlated statistically.

Ridge trace refers to a two-dimensional plot that displays the coefficient estimates for the predictors as the shrinkage parameter (k or lambda (λ)) increases to infinity (∞). Generally, the selection of λ is based on the point where most of the estimates for the predictors begin to stabilize.

Robust regression is a set of statistical procedures developed to assess the relationship amongst a quantitative continuous dependent variable and a set of independent variables that contain atypical small or large measurements so that the underlying assumptions of least squares regression are violated.

Simultaneous OLS regression refers to entering each of the independent variables specified in the statistical model concurrently so that the relationships of the predictors on the dependent variable are summarized in 1 equation. By contrast, forward selection OLS regression enters each independent variable individually into the analysis and at each step the equation summarizes the independent variables with significant statistical relationships with the dependent variable. At the end of the analysis, a summary equation is produced which contains only the independent variables with significant statistical regression coefficients.

Skewness refers to whether a distribution of scores leans to the right (positive) or to the left (negative) of the median. In a positively skewed distribution, the mean ($\bar{x}$) is larger than the median (M). Conversely, the mean ($\bar{x}$) is smaller than the median (M) in a negatively skewed distribution.

Standard deviation refers to a measure that indicates the average amount of variability in a set of data. A small standard deviation indicates that the data are centered around the mean, and a large standard deviation indicates that the data are dispersed further away from the mean. Values that are 3 standard deviations below or above the mean are generally treated as outliers.

Theoretical maximum value (TMV) refers to the purported highest coefficient that is attainable by an index based on the number of distinct categories within a particular population.

Truncation refers to measurement distributions that have either a minimum or maximum value so that a continuous variable can only have scores within a particular range of scores

Tuning refers to the process of assigning a constant to downweigh outliers. Low tuning constants downweigh atypical values quickly but may produce unstable estimates; conversely, high tuning constants lessen the downweighing of atypical values.

Variance inflation factor (VIF) is a statistic that assesses the level of collinearity amongst two or more independent variables in the regression equation. VIF scores are calculated by using the following formula: $\text{VIF} = \frac{1}{1 - R^2}$.

Vertical comparison (analysis) refers to the comparison of findings produced by the same method for different or similar measures.

Voluntary terminations refer to separations where employees end their employment with an organization by retiring or by resigning to vacate a position.

INDEX

Causal modeling xxii, 265, 303, 309
censored 188 – 189, 207, 319
clustering 147 – 148, 150 – 154,
    162, 172, 192 – 193, 212 – 213,
    225, 235 – 236, 243 – 249, 256,
    263, 286 – 289, 303, 309, 319
coefficient of determination (R^2)
    156, 162, 319
coefficient of variation (CV) 21, 37,
    319
collinearity 7 – 8, 138, 156, 159,
    161 – 162, 185, 226 – 227, 229
    – 230, 232, 233, 244 – 245, 248,
    - 249, 285, 292, 296, 309
comparisons:
    horizontal 251, 259, 264, 321
    pairwise 62, 69, 76, 98, 119, 324
    vertical 251, 262, 264, 326
conditional distribution 207, 211 –
    213, 218, 221, 226, 227, 319
confidence interval (CI) 26, 38, 320
convergent validity 105, 127, 320
correlation:
    analysis 7 – 8, 41, 72 – 73, 76,
        124 – 125, 276, 324
    Pearson pairwise 7 – 8, 41, 72 –
        73, 76, 124 – 125, 161, 274,
        276, 324
cross-sectional studies 4, 9, 320
descriptive statistics 26, 31, 38, 43,
    320
discriminatory power 35, 37 – 38,
    41, 75, 202, 303, 308, 310, 320
diversity:
    age 7, 78 – 103, 106 – 107, 109,
        116, 131, 133, 142 – 146,
        160 – 162, 176 – 177, 180,
        184 – 185, 193 – 194, 197 –
        199, 202 – 206, 217, 221,
        225 – 225, 239 – 240, 243 –
        144, 248 – 249, 251 – 252,
        255, 268, 271 – 273, 276,
        279, 289, 292, 295, 319
    definition 3, 13, 17, 320
    demographic 4, 143 – 145, 151,
        153 – 155, 265 – 266, 271,
        274
    ethnic 40 – 76, 109, 116, 124 –
        125, 131, 142 – 152, 159 –
        162, 176, 180, 184 – 185,
        193, 197, 102, 217 – 218,
        222, 225 – 226, 239, 243,
        256, 268, 271 – 273, 321
    gender 7 – 8, 15, 20 – 38, 40,
        106 – 107, 109, 116, 127,
        130 – 132, 133, 140, 142 –
        146, 149, 156, 159, 162,
        169, 177, 181, 193 – 194,
        197, 199, 202 – 203, 206,
        213 – 214, 218 – 222, 226,
        236, 245, 251, 259, 262 –
        263, 265, 268, 273 – 274,
        276, 279, 284 – 287, 296,
        299, 302 – 303, 306, 309 –
        310, 321
    occupational 105, 127, 324
    organizational (workforce) 7,
        12, 18, 20, 105 – 127, 133,
        142 – 143, 145, 147 – 148,
        156, 171, 192, 196, 211,
        226, 234, 240, 248 – 249,
        265, 269, 271, 274, 284,
        303, 310, 324
    social xx, xxii, 1, 3 – 5, 8 – 9,
        13, 140, 268, 310
diversity index
    biased xxi, 6, 8, 16 – 17, 20 –
        21, 26, 31, 35, 37, 40 – 41,

43, 52, 62, 70, 72, 74 – 75,
   78 – 79, 89, 93 – 94, 98, 102
   – 103, 105 – 107, 109, 116,
   119, 124 – 125, 129 – 131,
   133, 155 – 1565, 169, 171,
   173, 176 – 177, 180, 185,
   188, 191, 194, 197, 199,
   202, 211, 213, 217 – 218,
   226, 229, 234, 236, 239 –
   240, 243, 249, 251, 255 –
   256, 259, 262, 274, 276, 287
   – 288, 306 – 308, 319
composite 7, 105 – 107, 125, -
   127, 155, 319
Index of qualitative variation
   (IQV) 1
McIntosh xxi – xxii, 1 – 3
Shannon xxi, 1 – 5, 305, 310
Simpson xx – xxii, 1 – 3, 5 – 9,
   12 – 17, 20, 26, 31, 35, 37,
   40 – 41, 43, 62, 69, 72 – 75,
   78, 82. 102 – 103, 129 –
   131, 144, 147 – 148, 150 –
   151, 155, 160, 171, 185, 188
   – 189, 192, 194, 202, 209,
   211 = 212, 226, 229 – 203,
   232, 234, 251, 256, 263, 287
   – 288, 303, 306 - 310
   standardized 3, 6, 16 – 17, 26,
   31, 37, 43, 52, 59, 62, 69 –
   70, 74, 78 – 79, 82, 89, 93 –
   94, 98, 102 – 103, 105 –
   107, 109, 116, 119, 124 -
   125, 127, 232 – 233, 236,
   239 – 240, 243, 245
downweighing 168, 185 – 186, 320
Effect
   direct 226 – 305, 320
   marginal 191, 207, 322
eigenvalue 74, 76, 126, 321
Factor analysis xxii, 41, 73, 76, 106,
   321
   principal components 73, 125
   rotation 73 – 74, 106, 125 - 126
Heterogeneity xx – xxiii, 1 – 3, 5,
   12 – 13, 40, 127, 140, 142, 144

   – 145, 151, 155, 159 – 160, 162,
   167, 171, 173, 176 – 178, 180 –
   181, 188, 191, 193, 199, 202,
   209, 211, 213, 218, 221, 229 –
   230, 233 – 234, 236, 240, 245,
   251 – 252, 256, 263, 306, 308
   demographic xxi, 12
   ethnic 159, 176, 180, 256
   gender 1, 140, 146, 173, 213
   occupational xx, xxiii, 105, 127,
      324
   organizational 173, 177, 188,
      193, 209, 213, 221, 229,
      233, 236, 240, 245, 306
   social xxiii, 1, 3, 5, 12, 127
Independence 285
integration 1, 9, 321
intercept 129, 133, 147, 162, 171,
   192, 210, 212, 287 – 288, 321
Kurtosis 38, 43, 52, 59, 62, 94, 116,
   127, 322
Likelihood ratio 190, 207, 322
linearity 133, 169, 172, 185, 263,
   285, 307
Marginal effects 191, 207, 322
maximum value
   empirical (EMV) 13, 18, 188,
      310, 321
   theoretical (TMA) 13, 18, 326
measurement
   bias xx, xxii, 16 – 17, 69 – 70,
      75, 102
   compatibility xxii, 5 – 6, 82, 93,
      102 – 103, 307 – 308, 322
   efficiency 16, 18, 41, 82, 310,
      322
   error 35, 148, 168, 172, 188,
      193, 198, 213, 225 – 226,
      236, 245, 255 – 256, 262,
      285, 287, 289
   invariance 18, 310, 322
   reliability 5 – 6, 93, 102 – 103,
      307, 323
   validity 5, 82, 89, 93, 102 – 103,
      105, 127, 307, 320, 323
measures of

central tendency 20, 38, 323
variability (dispersion) 26, 38,
59, 263, 323
mean 26, 31, 35, 37 – 40, 43, 52, 59,
62, 69 – 70, 74 – 75, 94, 98,
116, 119, 169, 190, 199, 210,
225, 227, 303, 308, 327
median 8, 26, 31, 38, 43, 52, 59, 62,
94, 116, 138, 147, 150 – 151,
169, 172, 176, 192, 198, 207,
210, 212, 225 – 226, 235, 252,
262, 271, 287 – 288, 292, 323
multicollinearity 7, 129, 138, 156,
161 – 162, 170, 185 – 186, 202,
206, 226 – 227, 232, 240, 244 –
245, 251, 255 – 256, 285, 292,
296, 307, 309, 323
multivariate analysis (analyses) 127,
309, 323
Nonorthogonal predictors 230, 249,
323
normality 5 – 8, 20, 26, 31, 38, 40,
43, 52, 62, 174, 94, 106, 116,
127, 129, 131, 169 – 170, 185,
207, 232, 240, 244 – 245, 251,
285, 306, 309, 323
Oblimin oblique rotation 73 – 74,
76, 106, 125 – 126, 323
outliers 129 – 130, 159, 161 – 162,
169, 227, 245, 286, 324
Path analysis 8, 265 – 266, 284 –
287, 292, 295, 299, 302, 303 –
304, 324
predictors 7 -8, 129, 140, 156, 159 –
163, 173, 176 – 177, 181, 184 –
185, 188 – 190, 194, 197, 199,
203, 206, 210, 213 – 214, 217 –
218, 221 – 222, 225 – 227, 229
– 230, 232 – 233, 234, 239 –
240, 243 – 245, 248 – 249, 251
– 252, 255 – 256, 259, 262 –
263, 276, 296, 302, 309, 324
probability 3, 9, 13, 190, 324
probit regression 189, 207, 324
Reciprocal value 131, 163, 324

regression assumptions 4 – 5, 7, 129
– 130, 161, 169 – 171, 188 –
189, 191, 206, 209, 211, 229 –
230, 244, 251, 263, 284 – 286,
308
ordinary least squares (OLS)
130
path analysis 284 - 286
quantile 211
ridge 233 - 234
robust 170 - 171
Tobit 191
regression coefficient(s) 129, 133,
147, 156, 163, 167, 169, 171,
173, 185, 189, 191 – 193, 199,
208, 210, 212 – 213, 225, 229 –
230, 232 – 234, 236, 244 – 245,
248, 284, 286 – 298, 296, 324
residuals 168 – 170, 186, 210, 285,
325
ridge analysis 230, 249, 325
ridge estimates 233, 249, 325
ridge trace 230, 233, 249, 325
Skewness 5 – 7, 38, 43, 52, 59, 62,
94, 116, 127, 325
standard deviation 5 – 7, 38, 43, 52,
59, 62, 94, 116, 127, 325
Termination148, 150, 154, 163 –
164, 172, 193, 213, 235, 266,
269, 322, 326
involuntary 150, 163, 322
voluntary 150, 164, 326
truncation 129 – 130, 162 – 163,
171, 185, 191, 199, 227, 251,
263, 286, 307, 326
tuning 169, 186, 230, 326
Variable
dependent 1, 13, 127, 129 – 130,
155 – 156, 160, 167, 169 –
170, 186 – 189, 191, 206,
210 – 211, 227, 233 – 234,
287, 309 – 310, 320
endogenous 265 – 266, 268,
273, 284 – 285, 292, 296,
299, 302, 304, 310, 321

exogenous 265 – 266, 268, 273
– 274, 276, 279, 284 – 289,
292, 295 – 296, 299, 302 –
304, 306, 310, 321
independent 1, 129 – 130, 133,
138, 140, 142, 147 – 148,
159 – 160, 162, 167, 169 –
171, 173, 177, 185, 188 –
192, 210 – 212, 227, 230,
233 – 234, 239, 287, 309,
321

intervening xxii, 1, 9, 265, 310,
322
limited dependent variable 13,
18, 188, 322
mediating xxii, 8, 263, 265 –
266, 268, 273 – 276, 279,
284 – 285, 287 – 289, 292,
299, 302 – 304, 310, 323
Variance inflation factor (VIF) 156,
159, 161, 163, 185, 231, 232 –
233, 244 – 245, 292, 296, 309,
326